SCULPTURE

SCULPTURE

Tools,
Materials,
and
Techniques

WILBERT VERHELST

MEADOWS SCHOOL OF THE ARTS
SOUTHERN METHODIST UNIVERSITY

PRENTICE-HALL, INC., ENGLEWOOD CLIFFS, NEW JERSEY

Library of Congress Cataloging in Publication Data

Verhelst, Wilbert
  Sculpture: tools, materials, and techniques.

  Bibliography
  1. Sculpture. I. Title.
NB1140.V47   731.4   72–10335
ISBN 0–13–796615–6

PRINTED IN THE UNITED STATES OF AMERICA

10   9   8   7   6

PRENTICE-HALL INTERNATIONAL, INC., LONDON
PRENTICE-HALL OF AUSTRALIA, PTY. LTD., SYDNEY
PRENTICE-HALL OF CANADA, LTD., TORONTO
PRENTICE-HALL OF INDIA PRIVATE LIMITED, NEW DELHI
PRENTICE-HALL OF JAPAN, INC., TOKYO

Contents

Preface

This book is intended primarily as an introduction to tools, materials, and techniques. Although directed at sculptural design, it should prove equally useful in other three-dimensional areas. As well as traditional processes, I was particularly interested in providing basic information on recent industrial materials, tools, and processes that have become applicable to the field of sculpture and dimensional designing.

Often the beginning sculpture student is not overly familiar with the newer tools and materials. The language that is normally associated with industry or with the wood, metal, or plastic fabricator has also become the language of the sculptor. In many cases, rather than relying on the sculpture supply house, the sculptor has turned to the hardware store, lumber yard or industrial supplier. He is no longer so concerned with mallets, chisels, clay, or modeling tools but rather he is interested in nails, nuts, bolts, resins, and other kinds of industrial material and equipment. It has become as essential to know how to handle power saws and welding equipment as it is to know how to manipulate clay tools and chisels. The sculptor today

should be as much at home in a woodworking or metal shop as he is in a modeling studio.

As a result of this need to know more about the more recent developments in sculpture, I have placed emphasis on information and photographs of tools, materials, equipment, and sculpture in process. I have tried to present simple tools and techniques suitable for the beginner as well as more advanced information for the advanced student and for the practicing sculptor.

The abundance of twentieth-century technology applicable to sculpture has produced limitless resources for creative development for the sculptor or designer. To present precise detail for all processes used in sculpture today or industrial processes with potential are beyond the scope of an introductory book of this kind. This area has become so vast that it would require numerous volumes. At best, I would hope that this book might serve as a reference and guide to more extensive research in specific areas.

Acknowledgement is due the many individuals, industrial firms and suppliers that have helped to make this book possible. My indebtedness to students, sculptors, and other specialists cannot be overlooked. Learning about tools, materials, and techniques has oftentimes been a mutual experience that took place in the classroom, studio, fabrication shop, or during a rap session over a cold drink. Many of the industrial suppliers listed in the supply section of this book have generously contributed product and technical information. The bibliography lists numerous sources that proved helpful in developing concepts about tools, materials, and processes.

WILBERT VERHELST

Introduction

The past two decades have undoubtedly produced new visual attitudes, or if not new, at least highly dissimilar to prior ideas about sculpture. These attitudes have had distinct bearing on our acceptance of new technology and approaches to the solving of sculptural problems.

As well as an interest in new materials and devices, a new spatial concern for sculpture working beyond the limits of the pedestal has developed a new interest in large-scale works. Concepts encompassing exterior space or the interior environment of galleries, rooms, and buildings have further developed the artist's vision.

These concepts, along with an interest in technological advances and their application to sculpture, have produced a new form of sculpture as well as a new kind of sculptor. In many instances the sculptor no longer works as a lone individual but must rely on technical assistance from industry. The complexity of form or of presentation often demands that the execution or production of his concept must be carried out by other individuals; the work becomes a team effort rather than the product of one individual. Environmental art, the happening, and multi-media with increased specta-

tor involvement become new art forms alien to the traditional concept of sculpture.

This new interest in technology has consequently placed new demands on the artist and sculptor. The use of devices such as computers, lasers, electronic devices, and circuitry has placed the artist in a position to use knowledge and techniques not ordinarily associated with sculpture or the arts.

Until recently, much sculptural expression was the result of concepts of materials which had historical precedence. A proper approach to form was to think in terms of wood, cast bronze, or stone. The creative concept was bound to a notion of permanence. Self-expression was not closely linked to twentieth-century technology. Many of us educated twenty or thirty years ago remember only too well the rigidity of our education, the disdain for plastic or new materials, the dogma of purity of form and material. A concept of prior knowledge of art as the most essential criteria for creative development denied the logical evolution of tools and materials. The semantic and scientific rationale of experimentation and investigation as a means to discovery (the backbone of technology) was often denied the art student. His creative spirit was inhibited by aesthetic criteria for both form and material. In these surroundings the student's product too often simply mirrored a prior work of art. He was bound to his past by carefully packaged curricula and avenues of recognition.

Permanence of material, although undoubtedly desirable for some sculpture, should not be the determining factor in judging aesthetic merit. The sculptor who accepts impermanence as a condition in achieving self-expression certainly holds an acceptable and valid position. The choice of form and material should rest with the sculptor.

Traditional materials as well as the new continue to serve the sculptor as avenues to self-expression. Prejudice against the traditional processes can be as limiting as prejudice against the new. Misplaced concepts of aesthetic worth and significance are frequently attributed to both.

The discovery of a material or a visual property in a material or the restatement of a quality in a traditional material does not in itself constitute a work of significance. Ultimately, it is the sculptor's ability to transform the material into his statement that gives the work import.

Formal notions about design and form, although effective as a means to conceptualization of a work, also serve as obstacles to creative development. Exploration of unknown visual qualities, the willingness to experiment and depart from established concepts allow growth and subsequent new visual forms and experiences.

Materials are not easily shaped into the form the sculptor desires. The finished form may result in only an approximation of what he expected, and he is compelled to continue his search. He must learn to live with the insecurity of the unknown qualities that accompany experimentation. Attempting to reveal a personal feeling about form is not a comfortable or easy task. Developing the necessary skills with tools and material is essential to achieving this kind of personal ability. Results cannot always be expected to come from the first efforts. There is no substitute for the accumulation of experience of working with a material. Through experience, each sculptor develops many personal variations to material and technique in order to achieve his own form and style and technique.

Failure of first attempts should not be interpreted as a lack of ability; it should be recognized as a natural condition in attempting to master the complexity of three-dimensional expression. It is many times a case of re-educating the senses and acquiring those skills which make self-expression possible.

SCULPTURE

Modeling
and
Pattern-making

ONE

Modeling or patternmaking involves temporary or impermanent materials—the basic objective being to arrive at a sculptural form that will serve as a pattern or model to be reproduced in a more permanent material. Patterns can be of wood, wax, clay, urethane or polystyrene foam, plastic, plaster, metal, cardboard, or any other suitable material. The degree of permanence of the pattern often depends on the number of times it is to be used. Generally, the sculptor is satisfied with a pattern material resulting in a single reproduction, whereas industry demands permanent patterns for mass production.

In a sense, the casting technique, material, and form of the final reproduction determines the pattern material. Complex forms with textural surfaces usually merit modeling in clay or wax. Simple plane forms can be built more rapidly out of wood, cardboard, or other rigid materials. Proper selection of patternmaking material can save time and improve the quality of the final sculpture.

CLAY

Traditionally, modeling was done with earth clays, which are available from sculpture and ceramic-material suppliers as prepared modeling clays or dry powders to be mixed with water. The prepared modeling clays are most convenient for the sculptor and should be kept moist while in storage and during the modeling process. If allowed to dry out, earth clays can be reconditioned by breaking into small pieces and soaking in water; excess water is removed from the reconditioned clay mass by placing layers about two inches thick on dry plaster slabs, allowing the clay to dry until the desired working consistency is achieved. An unpainted concrete floor will work as effectively as plaster bats.

Synthetic clays with oil bases are also available. Since they do not dry out, they are preferred by some sculptors. Oil-based clay can be made by mixing dry powdered clay with wax, oil, and grease. A typical formula would be:

    5 qts. no. 30 motor oil,
    5 lbs. medium weight grease,
    20 lbs. microcrystaline wax,
    50 lbs. fine powered clay.

The oil, grease, and wax are first heated in a metal container. After the wax has melted, the powdered clay is mixed into the hot solution. A heavy-duty, one-half inch electric drill with a mixing blade is used to blend the mixture. If the clay is too hard, the mixture can be reheated and more oil can be added. If a harder mixture is desired, more clay is added. The clay solution can be poured into small greased cardboard boxes to cool to a putty-like consistency. In many cases, the earth clays are preferred because of their textural possibilities, ease of handling, tooling, and plasticity in finishing.

In simple massive forms, clay can be built up to the desired form without internal supports. However, in many cases an armature will be needed. The armature, like the steel framework of a building, serves to support the material. Simple armatures for heads and figures are sold by sculpture suppliers and are useful in small figurative work. In most cases today, however, the form the sculptor visualizes does not adapt itself in scale or configuration to this kind of armature.

An armature can be any material that will provide the needed form and support for the clay. In fact, careful consideration should be given to the armature material in relation to the sculptural design problem to be solved. A well-constructed armature of the right material will save time and frustration, since a faulty armature often means loss of the pattern or rebuilding the work.

When the only needed support is a center shaft or core, it can be wood, a polystyrene foam block, or a piece of galvanized pipe. Complex armatures can also be wood, galvanized pipe, or concrete reinforcing rod and wire mesh. Wood and pipe armatures are usually wrapped with wire to hold

Figure 1-1

Wood supports for clay
called butterflies on a pipe armature.

Figure 1-2

Wire armature for a small figure.

the clay to the armature. Clay is held in place on the underneath surfaces of the form by the use of wood cross members called "butterflies." (Figures 1-1 and 1-2)

Wood armatures can be assembled with nails or, for maximum strength, with wood screws. Fir or yellow pine is usually an adequate material. The wood armature should be shellacked with two coats of shellac to partially waterproof the material. When needed, one-eighth or one-fourth inch mesh hardware cloth can be stapled or tacked to the wood to hold the clay. (Figures 1-3, 1-4, 1-5, and 1-6) Although a wood armature is sometimes the best support for a clay structure, in many cases, a metal armature is far superior.

If you own oxyacetylene or arc-welding equipment, a welded armature constructed out of three-eighths-inch reinforcing rod is by far the best approach for large linear or complex armatures. The rod can be cut readily to appropriate lengths

Figure 1-3
Wood armature with wire hardware cloth covering.

Figure 1-4
Armature covered with clay, mold constructed on the right half by author, 1968.

Figure 1-5
Armature constructed with masonite strips.
Photograph by Marshall Brooks.

Figure 1-6
Armature covered with clay to form rough unfinished pattern by author, 1958. *Photograph by Marshall Brooks.*

Figure 1-7

Welded steel and hardware
cloth armature.

with the cutting torch. By heating the rod to a
bright red, it can be bent into any desired configuration. It can be assembled by fusion welding
or brazing. Building a steel armature is like building a bridge: diagonal supports are welded to transfer stresses and give the armature stability. To
prevent rust, the armature can be primed with a
rust-inhibiting primer, although this is not necessary. (Figure 1-7)

If welding equipment is not available, excellent metal armatures can be constructed out of
half-inch, or larger, galvanized steel pipe. (Figure
1-8) Flanges are screwed or bolted to the wood
base. Ninety-degree and 40-degree elbows and tees
are used to change directions. Piping can be purchased in various lengths, prethreaded to facilitate
assembly.

After the armature is constructed, the clay is
packed around it. The core of clay on the inside
should be reasonably firm and drier than the outer
layer. This can be accomplished by allowing the
core to dry slightly and firm up before applying
successive layers. Small blocks of styrofoam might
be included in the inner core to provide some of
the bulk. Excessively moist clay on the inner layer
will result in a greater degree of shrinkage, producing surface cracks as the work develops and
nears completion. As the clay is being applied, it
can be packed with a wood mallet or large, flat
stick.

Application of the final layer of clay will
depend on the surface texture desired. Some sculptors achieve complex surface variations, maintaining the plastic quality of the clay as an ultimate
aesthetic. Tooling and clay applied with fingers,
both producing varied textural results, are typical
of this approach. (Figure 1-9) In another approach,
the sculptor is unconcerned with the texture of the
clay; he uses the material merely as a patternmaking device. The clay is modeled to a smooth
surface, and the sculptor is concerned with the texture and qualities of the material in the final casting.

Figure 1-8

Fittings used to construct steel pipe armatures.
(A) 90° elbow; (B) steel pipe; (C) coupling;
(D) reducing coupling; (E) 45° elbow; (F) reducing
elbow; (G) tee; (H) reducing bushing; (I) nipple;
(J) flange.

4

Figure 1-9

Clay textures. (A) Clay roughly applied with fingers; (B) roughly applied clay with toothed tool texture; (C) clay roughly applied, flattened, and smoothed with flat wood tools; and (D) clay finished with flat wood tools. Final smooth finish is achieved with steel scrapers.

To give a clay model a smooth finish, the surface of the clay must be allowed to become firm. If the clay is too moist and soft, it tends to shift and the finishing tools dig into the surface. This is why earth clay is usually preferred: the sculptor can allow moisture to evaporate until the surface achieves the desired firmness for finishing. Applying water to clay and attempting to smooth it with

the fingers is a poor way to achieve a smooth surface; it softens the surface and encourages irregularities.

Another important concern in achieving good surfaces and contours is the direction the clay is tooled. Whenever possible, work across the contours. Figure 1-10 illustrates how irregularities are removed by working across the contour with the

Figure 1-10
Proper finishing technique, working across the contour of a clay pattern.

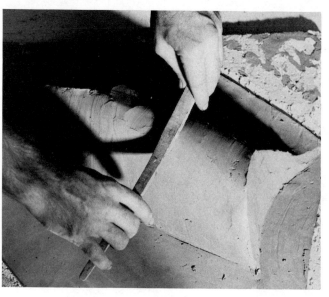

Figure 1-11
Improper finishing technique, working in the direction of the contour.

Figure 1-12
Flexible steel scrapers.

Figure 1-13
Clay finishing tools.

Figure 1-14
Studio-built clay finishing tools. A, B, N, K tools fashioned from pieces of old bandsaw blades. C and M, wire cutting and scraping tools. D through J, wood tools. L, paddle for packing clay.

straight edge of a tool. Figure 1-11 illustrates the improper method, working in the direction of the contour.

Clay-modeling tools can be obtained in a wide variety of shapes. There are flexible steel scrapers and rubber shapes ideal for smooth finishing; wooden shapes for contouring and for finishing in curved or inaccessible areas; and wire clay-cutters for cutting off excess material, texturing, and roughing out the form. (Figures 1-12 and 1-13)

The sculptor usually discovers the tools that most satisfactorily meet his needs. He can also fashion his own tools to solve particular modeling problems. Wire clay-cutters are simple to construct; thin sheet metal (about 26-gauge) can be cut to any desired shape for scrapers; wood shapes can be cut on a band saw or carved and sanded to any desired form. (Figure 1-14) I have always preferred to fashion most of my tools from strips of wood or sheet metal, which allows me to design a tool to a particular need, to reach inaccessible areas, to fit a particular contour, or to produce textural effects. For example, a rough-cut tool, slightly sanded or unsanded, will apply clay differently from a smoothly sanded tool. A tool design I have found extremely useful is the long-curved shape in Figure 1-14H. It can be made with wide, flat ends, round ends, or points. The principal advantage of the curve over the more conventional, straight tool is that it keeps the knuckles of the hand away from the surface and adapts to a greater variety of surfaces.

FOAM PATTERNS

Foam patterns are relatively new to the sculptor. Undoubtedly, their use will increase as more sculptors become aware of their potential. The light weight and ease of forming foam make it an exceptionally good material for large-scale patterns.

Polystyrene (styrofoam®) and urethane foam, readily available in sheets and blocks, can be carved, rasped, and easily fabricated into large shapes. An electric cutting wire can be used to cut the foam easily. (Figure 1-16) Proper ventilation should be provided, since inhaling the fumes from the burning foam may be irritating or toxic. A simple cutting tool can be fashioned, as in Figure 1-15. A length of band-saw blade wrapped with masking tape on one end or a key hole saw can also be used for sawing holes and for shaping the foam. Pieces can be cemented together with plaster of Paris mixed to a paste-like consistency or with adhesives. The blocks or pieces can be temporarily pinned with nails until the plaster sets. Patching and buildup can be achieved by using plaster of Paris (Figure 1-17). Blocks of urethane can also be cast in large cardboard boxes using the liquid urethane. Some of the common uses of foam are as follows:

1. The foam is carved, rasped, and sanded to arrive at finished forms, from which a negative mold is made reproducing the texture of

Figure 1-15

Hot wire cutting tool for cutting plastic foams.

ELECTRIC CUTTERS

the foam. Urethane foam has a finer texture than Styrofoam and should be used when finer surfaces are desired.

2. The foam model acts as a core or armature, and the final surface is developed with modeling clay to provide a finished work from which a negative mold is made.

3. The foam pattern is packed in sand, and directly cast in metal. The hot metal vaporizes and displaces the foam. A gating system as described in Chapter 2 must be attached to the pattern. Top gating or pouring as illustrated in Figure 2-20 is often used. (In this process plaster cannot be used for joining foam.)

4. The polystyrene foam pattern is covered with a layer of wax approximating the metal thickness desired. The wax is developed to the desired surface finish and the foam pattern is dissolved with acetone. The resulting wax pattern may then be used for lost-wax casting. This is becoming a highly successful way of doing large works; for large works, the wax pattern is cut into sections for the final casting. In some instances, the foam is left in the wax pattern until the outer mold is built.

5. The foam pattern is covered with plaster, or fiberglass, or plastic resins and fillers, resulting in a finished work.

Figure 1-17

Foam pattern being developed.
Student project, Southern Methodist University.

Figure 1-16

Cutting foam with the hot wire cutting tool.

WAX PATTERNS

In lost-wax casting, the wax model can be solid if the work is small; larger works require hollow patterns, however, because of the weight of the metal and excess shrinkage in large metal masses.

The hollow wax pattern is achieved either by building the form directly out of wax or by building the form out of another material, making a plaster piece mold or flexible mold, (as described in Chapter 2, pages 15 and 17), and casting a wax pattern. Some sculptors prefer the spontaneity of working directly with the wax, although this is somewhat risky; if the casting is unsuccessful, the work is lost and a new pattern must be built. On the other hand, it is simple to cast a new wax pattern from a mold if the metal casting fails.

Figure 1-18
Wax melting pot.

Although there are formulas (containing beeswax or paraffin) for making modeling wax, this practice is somewhat outdated, since a wide variety of prepared waxes are readily available. The wax most sculptors use today is a petroleum derivative called "microcrystalline wax." Less expensive than beeswax formulas, it is available in various hardnesses. The wax is usually tinted dark brown, almost bronze-colored, making it easy to distinguish surface texture and details as they would appear in a bronze casting. If the wax purchased is not dark brown, it can be tinted readily by adding powdered lampblack pigment to the melted wax.

Soft waxes are at times preferred for directly built patterns, whereas harder waxes are used for cast patterns, to reduce distortion in large patterns, and, sometimes, because of variance in room temperature. A wax handled easily at 70 degrees might be too soft at 90 to 100 degrees. This problem can be overcome by adding paraffin to harden the wax, vaseline or 30-weight motor oil to soften it. If you are doing a lot of wax modeling, it is more practical to purchase quantities of wax with different working consistencies.

To develop a direct wax pattern, first melt the wax and pour slabs to the desired thickness of the final metal casting (usually one-eighth, 3/16, or one-fourth inch, depending on the size of the work). The wax can be melted in a commercial melting pot. (Figure 1-18) For small quantities, less expensive devices are double boilers, electric saucepans, or electric frying pans. Heat only to the melting point—do not overheat. After the wax has

melted, pour it on a moist plaster slab recessed to the desired thickness to contain the molten wax. If the plaster is too wet, small pot marks will form on the surface of the wax slab. After they have cooled, the wax sheets are removed and are ready for use. They can be cut and bent into the desired shapes and joined with a hot metal spatula warmed over a bunsen burner. Sometimes, the wax pieces may need slight warming to make them softer and more flexible. One of the least expensive devices for this is an infrared bulb mounted over a table.

Tools for wax modeling can be metal or wood. Metal plaster-modeling tools are very adaptable, or you can fashion your own tools out of strips of sheet metal, wire, etc.

The wax pattern can be finished by tooling with a warm metal tool or textured with small pieces applied with the fingers. The possibility for surface qualities are many, and only by working with the wax can you discover its potential. (Figure 1-19)

In large wax patterns, it may be necessary to build internal supports, particularly when the pattern is cut into sections for casting. In this case, the supports should be constructed laterally, across the cut area, to prevent distortion in the handling of the pattern during the casting. Each pattern has its own design problems. Learning which areas of

Figure 1-19

Wax pattern with sprues, vents, and pouring cup attached. *Student project, Southern Methodist University.*

your wax pattern need support is, essentially, a matter of experience.

In casting a wax pattern, the melted wax is poured into a moist plaster mold or a flexible mold treated with a separator. As the wax cools, a layer of wax is formed next to the mold wall. The temperature of the wax should remain as low as possible (about 150 degrees). If you do not have a melting pot with temperature control, heat the wax until melted and then allow to cool until a thin skin forms over the wax. At that point the temperature should be approximately right. Break the surface skin and pour the wax. As soon as the layer of wax achieves the desired thickness, pour the excess wax back into the container. In some cases, the wax pattern is built up by several layers of about 1/16-inch thickness, emptying the mold several times. This practice seems desirable in complex patterns to insure a more uniform thickness of the pattern wall. For open-face relief molds or large molds that have the surfaces accessible, the wax can be brushed on until the desired thickness is achieved.

Another approach to direct wax patterns is to build the wax pattern and not be concerned with the thickness of the wax wall. In this technique, the wax pattern is covered with the investment material, the investment shell is dewaxed with steam, and outer shell is recharged with melted wax and poured off when the desired thickness is achieved. A core is then added, and the work is ready for casting after burnout. Details of

Figure 1-21

Large positive plaster pattern for direct application of fiberglass. The pattern is removed after the fiberglass has been built up. *Student project, Southern Methodist University.*

this approach are similar to the mold techniques discussed on pages 30 and 31, Chapter 2.

Principal advantages of this approach are not having to worry about the thickness of the wax wall in developing the pattern, greater rigidity in the pattern (minimizing distortion of the pattern during application of the investment material), and the elimination of pattern distortion due to wax shrinkage.

PLASTER

Plaster patterns are achieved by casting into a plaster or flexible mold or by building the plaster directly on an armature. For simple forms, special jigs or screeds can be used to contour plaster forms. (Figures 1-20 and 1-21) Chapters 3 and 4 contain basic techniques for casting or building patterns directly.

WOOD

Wood patterns can be built with basic wood-carving or wood-fabrication techniques. The wood

Figure 1-20

A simple pattern being developed from plaster using a wood template as a screed. *By sculptor James Surls.*

Figure 1-22

Wood patterns for parts of a cast sculpture. *By sculptor James Surls.*

Figure 1-23

Sculpture, cast bronze, by James Surls. (Note that the parts in Figure 1-22 can be identified in the completed work.)

pattern is used when semipermanent molds are desired or when the pattern can be constructed readily out of wood. Flat shapes or shapes that can be turned on a lathe are typical examples. (Figures 1-22, 1-23 and 1-24)

PAPER AND CARDBOARD

Patterns can be built out of paper mache (strips of newspaper and thin wheat paste) or cardboard. Patterns of this kind are particularly applicable to direct techniques with a final more permanent surface of fiberglass and polyester resin. Flat rigid cardboard patterns can be constructed as a substitute for wood forms when building simple geometric shapes. The cardboard form is sealed with two coats of shellac or lacquer and treated with a paste wax or oil based release agent if a plaster mold is to be made from the cardboard pattern.

Figure 1-24

A wood and oil clay pattern on the left with the sand mold removed on the right. *By sculptor James Surls.*

Mold-making Techniques

TWO

With traditional and present-day materials, there are many methods for mold-making. Some of the molding materials date far back into history. Early molds, undoubtedly, were earth materials such as loams or natural clays, followed by plaster sand investments. Today, technological research by industry has produced investment and molding materials to cope with almost any molding problem encountered. Generally, some of the simpler techniques serve the sculptor's needs, and conditions unacceptable to industry are often suitable in sculptural design.

Good craftsmanship and work habits are essential in mold making. Faulty or sloppy mold construction usually results in excessive time required to finish the cast positive, or irreparable damage to, or loss of, the casting. Perfect results cannot be expected on the first attempt, however, and it is advisable to keep the first project small and simple, not risking loss of a work in which considerable time has been spent.

The selection of a molding technique and material will generally depend on a variety of factors, some of which are as follows:

1. Suitability to ultimate casting media.
2. Number of castings desired from a single mold.
3. Suitability to form being cast.
4. Accuracy desired in reproduction of pattern.
5. Accuracy desired in surface detail.
6. Handling; weight of mold.
7. Cost of molding materials.
8. Availability of materials.
9. Time involved in mold technique.
10. Feasibility in relation to studio and equipment available.

Some of the more common molding processes used by the sculptor are plaster waste or piece molds, for simple casting of plaster, concrete, plastic resins with fillers and fiberglass. Sand, plaster investment, and ceramic shell molds are used for metal. Wood, cardboard, foam, and other materials can be used for simple direct molds for casting plaster, concrete, and plastics.

PLASTER WASTE MOLD

The waste mold is usually the simplest in construction and the most economical to build. It is an efficient method of achieving a negative from a clay or foam model when a single casting is desired in

Figure 2-1

Clay pattern ready for a waste mold. *Sculpture by Charles Aberg.*

gypsum cements, plastic, or fiberglass. The plaster waste mold contains the fundamental steps to building a mold. Once these procedures are grasped, it is easy to attain more complexity in mold construction.

In the waste-mold technique, as the term implies, the mold is wasted or destroyed by breaking and chipping the mold away from the cast positive.

The first step in preparing a clay pattern for a waste-mold is to divide the pattern into two or more sections. This is accomplished by inserting a wall of metal shims, or building a wall of clay strips, to section off the work. In selecting the sections, try to eliminate as many undercuts as possible. Since wherever the mold joins, it will leave a slight seam on the cast positive, try to locate the dividing lines where the seams will be most accessible. If you use the clay rather than metal shims, make several indentations in the clay wall to serve as registration marks for mold alignment.

When the clay wall is used to section the mold, the mold is made a section at a time. The edges of each mold section must be treated with a separator, such as liquid soap or vaseline, before the next section is built. The principal advantage in using a clay wall is that there is less of a seam, and the cast positive and mold alignment are usually better.

After the work is divided into sections, the next step is to spatter, spray, or brush a thin coat of molding plaster on the pattern section being molded. An R2 all-materials spray, particularly useful on large molds and surfaces, can be used for spraying plaster. U.S. Gypsum No. 1 molding plaster is used by most sculptors. This first coating should be tinted with household bluing or a small amount of colored pigment. This tinted coating allows easier

location of the cast positive in the process of removing the mold.

In mixing plaster, sprinkle the plaster into the water until the plaster floats, forming a dry film on top of the mix. Let the mixture stand for a few minutes to allow lumps to dissolve, and then complete the mixing. If a thick mixture is needed, allow the mix to sit until it reaches the desired consistency, and then very rapidly apply to the mold, or, otherwise, add additional plaster until the desired consistency is achieved.

After the spatter coat has set, additional coats of untinted plaster are applied to the mold until a thickness of about one-half to three-fourths inch is achieved. The plaster can be mixed to a puttylike consistency for this application. For large molds, the plaster would be thicker and the mold sections should be reinforced with wood strips, concrete reinforcing rod, wire mesh, burlap, jute, or hemp fiber dipped in plaster.

After the mold sections have been completed, the plaster is chipped away along the seams to expose the separation lines of the mold. A preferred method is to build the mold carefully and avoid covering the separation lines. Next, wooden wedges are gently tapped into the seam to separate the mold sections from the clay pattern. Any remaining clay is removed from the mold sections and the sections are cleaned with soap and water. If steam cleaning is available, it is an efficient way to clean molds. After being cleaned, the mold sections are ready for treatment with a separator, such as liquid soap, vaseline or paste wax, and are assembled for casting. (Figures 2-1 through 2-7)

Figure 2-2

Clay wall has been built over the mid-section of the clay sculpture; the plaster spatter coat is being applied.

Figure 2-3

Thick plaster is being applied to build up the outer layers of the mold.

Figure 2-4

Reinforcing strips have been added to the mold.

Figure 2-5

Completed mold for left section of the clay pattern. Parting seam is being cleared.

Figure 2-6

Wooden wedges are gently driven into parting seam to separate mold sections.

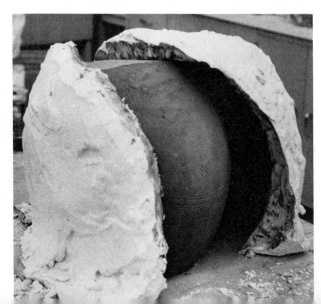

Figure 2-7

Mold sections separated showing the clay pattern inside the mold.

PLASTER PIECE MOLD

Rigid plaster piece molds are effective for several castings when the form is not too complex. Knowledge of the process is necessary, not only where multiple castings are required, but also in the construction of outer containing molds for flexible molds.

Prior to the development of flexible molds, reproduction of a complex form with the plaster piece mold was a complicated, time-consuming procedure. Generally, when a work has numerous undercuts, a flexible mold is recommended; the plaster piece-mold should be considered only where a few simple parts small enough to be handled manually are necessary.

Building a piece mold is fundamentally the same as building a waste mold. The difference is in carefully studying the pattern and building the mold of sufficient pieces to be removed without damage to the mold or pattern. Figure 2-8 illustrates a typical beginning of piece mold construction. It is easy to identify the clay wall, a completed mold section, the spatter technique for the first coat, and the three, small, light dots along

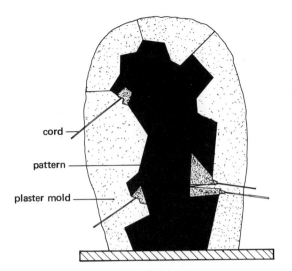

Figure 2-9

Cross section of a piece mold involving undercuts.

the seam indicating the interlocking registration points. Figure 2-9 shows a diagram of a plaster piece mold. Note how the inner section accommodates an undercut fits into the outer section of the mold. The vaseline-coated cord attached to the inner section can be pulled and tied to a wooden peg to hold the pieces in place.

FIBERGLASS PIECE MOLDS

In recent years, fiberglass piece molds have been used in place of the typical plaster piece molds. Undoubtedly, if more than one casting is desired, the fiberglass mold should be used.

The mold is essentially the same as the plaster piece mold, except layers of polyster resin and fiberglass reinforcing materials are used instead of layers of plaster. The pattern should be waxed with a paste wax. The fiberglass layup should be handled in the same manner used in laying up fiberglass positives, described in Chapter 3.

The principal advantages of the fiberglass mold are in the strength of the material and the ease of handling. It weighs less than a plaster mold, does not chip or break as readily, and can withstand a considerable number of castings.

In fact, the casting industry uses fiberglass molds for small-production runs in which the cost of metal molds is prohibitive; construction of a new fiberglass mold every several-hundred cast-

Figure 2-8

Large piece mold being constructed from a clay pattern. By author, 1958. *Photograph by Marshall Brooks.*

ings proves more economical. Wood and fiberglass molds are quite common in the boat-building industry.

Fiberglass, molds also, possess a small degree of flexibility; moreover, an elastomer can be added to the resin to produce a less-rigid mold. Although not as flexible as rubber mold materials, fiberglass with elastomer addition allows for contours that a plaster mold cannot accommodate.

DIRECT RELIEF MOLDS

There are several mold possibilities in the construction of sculptural reliefs that are not adaptable to full three-dimensional forms. In these processes, the molds are built directly as negatives and when complete are ready to receive cast media.

Frequently, these techniques have been used in the classroom as spontaneous projects and have been overlooked as serious sculptural media. How-

Figure 2-10
Direct relief mold in sand. *Student project, Southern Methodist University.*

ever, in recent years (with greater emphasis on sculptural forms in architecture), these processes have reappeared with considerable success in the execution of large-scale, sculptural wall reliefs.

Sculptor Albert S. Vrana, working in Florida, has refined the use of direct polystrene foam-molds and utilizes them on a monumental scale. He works closely with architects, engineers, and building contractors to complete and execute his designs. Figures 3-8 through 3-15, in Chapter 3, show several steps in the construction of a direct mold and completion of a large wall relief.

In addition to foam, sand, clay, and wax, direct molds have been built from wood, paper, cardboard, inflatable sections of rubber, and combinations of these materials.

Perhaps one of the most difficult problems in using the direct mold is learning to think in the negative. The student attempting this technique must realize that the deepest part of the mold becomes the furthest projection on the finished casting.

Figure 2-10 illustrates a typical direct relief mold technique, using sand as the mold material. In this case, masonry sand or fine silica sand is moistened with old crankcase oil and packed in a wooden frame. On small works, the sand can be moistened with water; on large works, the water-sand mixture dries too fast.

After the sand has been packed, the desired sculptural form is carved out of the sand, and, when completed, it is ready for casting. This technique is particularly suited to plaster or concrete castings where the forms are bold and simple. It is possible to carve directly into slabs of sand bonded with a no-bake binder. These can be used for metal casting.

If intricate or detailed forms are desired, moist modeling clay or wax can be used instead of sand. This approach lends itself to plaster or concrete casting. In exceedingly complex designs, plastic resin with filler material works effectively as a casting material.

Polystrene foam or urethane foam offer many possibilities as direct-mold material. The foam pieces are nailed or glued to a plywood or foam backing. Large-scale architectural reliefs can be produced by fastening the foam to the inside surfaces of concrete forms and pouring the relief and wall at the same time. Or, preformed panels can be constructed, as in the work of Albert S. Vrana.

Foam molds offer distinct possibilities for angular or rectangular forms or for unusual textural surfaces achieved by burning or melting the foam or using poured urethane foam.

If fiberglass or polyester resin and fillers are to be used as casting material, it is advisable to use urethane foam in building the mold. Styrofoam® will disintegrate when it comes into contact with polyester resins.

FLEXIBLE MOLDS

In complex patterns, from which more than one casting is desired, or in the preparation of complex hollow wax models for lost-wax techniques, the flexible mold is essential. Although the plaster piece mold is a feasible way of producing complex forms, it is difficult to justify the time involved in that approach. Flexible molding materials have made the production of a mold for intricate castings a relatively simple procedure.

Rubber molding compound has become the principal material used by industry and sculptors in the production of flexible molds. Early rubber molds were of air-curing latex materials. The more recent materials are silicone or polysulfide rubbers, which cure chemically at room temperature, in anywhere from 24 to 48 hours. Curing time can be accelerated by increasing the amount of catalyst, increasing room temperature, or using a curing oven. Manufacturer's recommendations should be followed on these materials.

Generally, sculptors get good results using either air cure or the chemically-curing materials at room temperature. The room temperature should be relatively warm (72 degrees or higher). Cool room temperatures may lengthen the curing time or, in many cases, result in incomplete curing and inferior molds. An inferior mold due to bad curing conditions will usually lack tear strength and, for all practical purposes, be useless.

If room temperatures are too low, a simple curing oven for temperatures up to 150° can be constructed with a wood frame covered with insulation board or foam sheet. This is lined with aluminum foil and equipped with several 100 watt light bulbs to achieve the desired temperature.

Silicone-rubber molding compounds are the costliest but produce molds of the highest quality. They generally do not need release agents or separators and withstand numerous castings before losing their shape. For the sculptor, the less expensive rubbers are more than adequate for several castings.

There are two basic approaches to building a rubber mold. The molding material can be cast around the work, or it can be brushed on and built up with successive layers. The first process is practical for small forms and is frequently used by industry, while the second method is more applicable to sculptured forms too large for the cast approach.

In the brushed layered technique, consecutive coats of the molding compound are applied until the mold reaches the desired thickness (one-eighth to one-fourth inch, depending on mold size). Undercuts can then be eliminated by bridging over the spaces with fabric or glass cloth dipped in or brushed with the molding compound. Pieces of sponge can also be fitted into undercut areas and coated with subsequent layers of molding compound. Like the plaster piece-mold, the rubber mold can be made in several sections, or the whole pattern can be covered and the mold removed by slitting the rubber with a razor blade. Air-drying latex, the least expensive, is efficient for this approach, if ample time is available to allow for the drying of each coat. I prefer the two-part chemically-curing materials, since thicker coatings can be applied and mold construction takes considerably less time.

After the rubber mold is completed, a containing mold is needed to support the rubber. This is usually a two- or three-piece plaster mold on small works or a fiberglass piece mold for larger works. To facilitate the removal of the rubber mold from the containing-mold, the rubber can be covered with a layer of wet tissue or plastic film, such as Saran® Wrap, prior to building the containing mold.

If the sculpture pattern being reproduced is other than clay, it should be covered with a thin coating of paste wax before starting mold-construction. (Figure 2-11)

When the rubber molding material is cast around the sculpture pattern, the containing mold is built first. In relief work, the process is quite simple, since all that is needed is a wooden fence or frame around the relief, with the edges sealed

plaster containing mold

Note registration peg to assure mold alignment

rubber inner mold

sponge fill

pattern

Figure 2-11

Flexible mold construction with molding compound brushed on.

hot wax seal   wooden fence   rubber mold   pattern

Figure 2-12

Poured flexible mold technique for a relief.

pouring hole

plastic tubes as vents

plaster mold

pattern

rubber mold cavity

registration points for alignment of mold

Figure 2-13

Containing mold and details for poured flexible mold.

with masking tape, hot wax, or wet modeling clay. (Figure 2-12)

With three-dimensional forms, the problem is slightly more complex. The first step is to fasten the pattern to a board and cover it with a layer of Saran® Wrap. Countersink tapered holes into the board to assure positioning of the containing mold. The pattern is then covered with about one-half inch of soft, moist modeling clay, eliminating all undercuts. Sometimes it is necessary to include several vents to allow air to escape during the pouring of the rubber. This can be achieved with plastic tubing. After the pattern is covered with clay and vents positioned, a plaster or fiberglass mold is built in the usual fashion.

After the piece mold is completed, it is removed from the pattern. The pattern and inside surface of the containing mold are then waxed when this is necessary, and the containing mold is reassembled around the pattern. The containing

mold should be tied together and the edges sealed with plaster or hot wax. The mold is now ready for pouring. (Figure 2-13)

A room-temperature-cure molding compound is used in the cast-mold (sometimes called "closed mold") technique. Manufacturer's instructions should be followed. Generally, the molding materials are two different colored parts, which should be mixed until all streaks disappear; a mixing blade on an electric drill usually assures a uniform, adequate mix. For technically perfect molds, the mixed compound should be placed in a vacuum chamber to remove air bubbles from the mixture, although this is usually not essential for sculpture. Room temperature and mold temperature should be 72 degrees or higher. After the mold is poured, it should be vibrated slightly for a few minutes to eliminate air bubbles next to the surface of the pattern. (Figure 2-14, 2-15, 2-16, 2-17, 2-18)

18

Figure 2-14

Plaster pattern for a flexible mold. *By sculptor Roger Kotoske.*

Figure 2-16

Completed cast polyester sculpture. *By sculptor Roger Kotoske.*

Figure 2-15

Flexible mold brush applied showing the pattern, flexible mold and the edges of the fiberglass containing mold. *By sculptor Roger Kotoske.*

Figure 2-17

Typical supplies and equipment for pouring flexible molds. (1) Vacuum chamber for removing air from mixture; (2) vacuum pump; (3) reusable polyethylene buckets; (4) vac-Seal grease for cover and chamber; (5) gyro plastic mixers; (6) hand cleaner. *Photograph courtesy of Plaster Supply House Industries, Inc.*

Figure 2-18

Spraying rubber molding material into a negative mold with an R-2 spray gun. *Photograph courtesy of Plaster Supply House Industries, Inc.*

PLASTIC MOLDS

When working with wood, metal, or patterns of materials that can withstand temperatures up to 400 degrees, there are several plastic materials that make suitable flexible molds. These are particularly useful for relief molds or closed molds in which the form is not exceedingly complex and maximum flexibility is not needed.

Vinyl or polyethylene materials in powder, pellet, or shredded form are melted at 250 to 400 degrees and poured in the same manner as rubber molding materials. The vinyl or polyethylene are natural-release materials and release agents are not usually needed on the patterns or containing mold. The material can be melted in a commercial melting pot, oven, an electric frying pan, or deep-fry pan; with reasonable care, it can be melted in a double metal container on a hot plate.

Flexible polyesters and polyurethane foams can be used as mold material and should yield results for the student or sculptor who wishes to experiment with them.

METAL-CASTING MOLDS

A mold for metal casting consists of two basic ingredients: a material for bulk and strength and a substance to bind the material together. The bulk investment materials can be sand, perlite, earth-clay materials such as grog, pulverized investment material from old molds called "Luto," silica sands, and asbestos fiber. Binders may consist of clay, chemicals, plaster, or any of a variety of organic or inorganic materials.

The investment material and subsequent mold must be strong enough to withstand the weight and shock of the hot molten metal. It must be sufficiently porous to accommodate gases from the molten metal, yet fine enough in texture to reproduce the detail and surface of the original pattern.

Today, a great variety of sands, fillers, and binders are available to the sculptor and foundry man. Commercial foundries have developed precise mold techniques capable of achieving high-quality castings within dimensional tolerances of a few thousandths of an inch. Materials and mold techniques vary considerably among sculptors and foundries, depending on the nature of the pattern, the quantity desired, and the metal or alloy being poured.

There are three basic molds for metal-casting sculpture: the sand mold, the plaster investment mold, and the ceramic shell.

Until recent years plaster investment and the lost-wax process were the usual procedures followed in casting sculpture. However, in the past 20 years, new materials and broad experimentation by sculptors and foundry men have resulted in the development of many simple and successful mold-making techniques. The mold technique a sculptor selects may depend on the piece he is casting, its material and size, his technical ability, personal preference, and the facilities and equipment at his disposal.

Small molds can be constructed and cast readily in the average studio; bulky, heavy molds require specialized handling equipment.

All metal-casting molds possess similar terms and features. The mold material may vary somewhat, but the essential components remain the same. The system for getting the molten metal into the mold cavity is referred to as the "gating system." Figure 2-19 is a typical example of a sand mold. Although sculptors seldom use sand molds in this precise form, many of their mold techniques are adaptations of the basic, foundry sand-mold process. A brief description of mold terms and the gating system follows.

Flasks. These are containers used to hold the mold material during the construction of the mold or during the pouring. Steel and castiron flasks are used in the foundries. Wood flasks are sometimes used for short runs or odd-sized jobs. The lower section of the flask is referred to as the "drag," the top section is the "cope," and center sections are the "cheeks." Improvised wood flasks, usually used by sculptors, may be rectangular or irregular shapes that follow the configuration of the sculpture pattern. (Sections of 25- or 50-gallon drums are also useful.) In mold techniques in which flasks are not used, reinforcing materials, such as wire mesh or steel rods, are used to hold the mold together.

Pouring basins. A basin carved into the top of the sand mold to feed metal directly into the

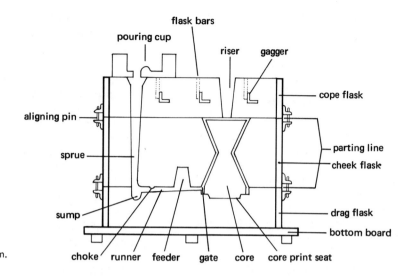

Figure 2-19
Foundry sand mold system.

sprue. It is difficult to prevent dross from entering the mold with this technique.

Pouring box or cup. In sand or plaster, the pouring box is set on top of the mold, over the sprue, or a cup is attached to the wax sprue in investment casting. The pouring box or cup can be designed with a strainer or skimmer arrangement that prevents dross from entering the feeding system. Insulating and preheated boxes and cups can be used to help maintain the metal temperature. A proper-sized pouring box or cup can assure adequate molten metal for the gating system. Pouring cups and boxes can be made from investment materials or purchased precast.

Sprues. These are the vertical shafts receiving the molten metal. In large castings, there may be more than one sprue. The sprue must be of sufficient size to handle the charge of metal as it feeds from the cup. It may be round or square; square sprues are believed to produce less turbulence in the molten metal as it is being poured. An undersized sprue may result in the metal's "freezing" in the sprue before the pour is completed.

Runners. Runners are the horizontal feeds running from the mold cavity to the sprue. These may be located on several levels, running from the sprue and feeding metal into the mold cavity.

Chokes. These may be included in the runner to control the flow of metal and to trap dross.

Gates. Gates are the openings at the end of the runners entering the cavity. Their size controls the rate at which the metal feeds into the mold.

Feed into the mold is also effected by the size of the sprues, runners, and feeders, and the pressure they provide at the gate.

Feeders. These supply additional metal to the casting as the metal shrinks and cools. They may also trap particles of dross.

Risers. Risers provide metal to compensate for shrinkage. Open risers, as illustrated in Figure 2-19, also serve as escape routes for gases formed during the pour. Blind risers do not open to the outside of the mold. They may be located at various essential points in the mold to control shrinkage.

Bottom boards. These serve as a platform on which to build the mold. Aligning pins assure correct alignment of the mold parts. Register marks are also used when the flasks consist of random stacked shapes.

Cores. Cores form the inner mass that maintains the wall thickness of the casting. Core materials may be the same as the mold material being used or may be formulated to meet special requirements. A core material must be soft enough to yield as the metal shrinks, to prevent tears in the metal. It must be porous enough to allow gases to escape. The core may be vented to allow gases to leave the core as they penetrate into the core. Venting can be accomplished by piercing the core with wire or the core can be built hollow. Large hollow cores may be filled with coke; small cores can be filled with dry sand. The gases readily penetrate the coke or sand and escape.

Pattern boards. These are used as a surface on

which to place the pattern in constructing the drag section of the mold.

Flask bars. Flask bars are horizontal crossbars in the cope, which help support the sand.

Gaggers. These consists of angular iron strips that are placed against the flask bars as additional support for the sand.

Facing. The facing is a fine sand, investment material or coating that forms the mold surface next to the pattern. It is utilized to assure maximum reproduction of the pattern surface. In sand casting it may also serve as a more resistant surface, to prevent erosion of the mold surface as the hot metal is poured. Facing materials can at times be troublesome. If the bond between the facing and the backing is not adequate, the facing may spall or chip off and result in surface defect in the casting.

Backing or backup. This is the material used on the outer portions of the mold parts. It is often a coarse and more permeable material. Pulverized or reclaimed mold material is often used to reduce mold cost.

Unit sand or unit mold. This refers to a mold in which the facing and backup are made of the same material. When possible, this is a highly desirable, as it eliminates the possibility of defective castings due to spalling or chipping of the face coat.

Dross. Dross is the accumulation of metal oxides, impurities, and fluxing materials that form on the top of the molten metal as it is melted.

Chaplets. These are used to keep the core in position if it cannot be anchored directly to the mold. They may be double- or single-headed and may vary in design. Nails can be used as core pins; they need to be removed on bronze castings, however, and the holes filled by tapping a thread and screwing in a threaded bronze rod.

Parting lines. These are the points of separation for the mold. Each mold section, as well as the pattern, is treated with parting compound to prevent the mold pieces from adhering to the pattern and to each other. In sand molds, the parting compound is talc or silica flour. It is dusted on the surfaces by shaking a porous cloth sack filled with the powder over the surfaces. The sack can also be dabbed against vertical surfaces. Parting lines may also run vertically through mold sections so that a section can be removed in pieces.

Vents. Vents provide a means for air and gas to escape the mold cavity as the metal is poured. The extent to which venting is required depends on the pattern being cast and the porosity of the mold material.

Refractory washes. These are used on sand-mold surfaces to prevent erosion and penetration of the mold surface by the molten metal. By preventing metal penetration of the sand, the surface quality of the casting is improved and the mold releases from the casting more readily. Washes consist of carbonaceous materials, such as graphite or coal dust, and refractory materials, such as zircon. Binders are added to form brushing or spraying solutions. Commercially prepared washes are available from foundry supply houses.

Draft. This is the slight angle provided on the sides of the patterns to allow the mold to be readily removed from the pattern.

There are two ways to design a gating system in a mold. Figure 2-20 illustrates bottom and top pouring or gating. In bottom gating, the metal feeds into the bottom of the mold; in top gating, which is simpler and can be used in many circumstances, the sprue gates directly into the top edge of the casting. It is vented from the other side. Additional vents may be introduced into areas where there is danger of gas entrapment. The decision to top-pour or bottom-pour may depend on the piece being cast, the mold material, or, in many cases, personal preference.

Figure 2-20
Bottom and top pouring system.

TOP POURING

Core Pins

BOTTOM POURING

SAND AND PLASTER INVESTMENT MOLDS

The sand mold, one of the oldest techniques in metal casting, is still used extensively in commercial casting.

In the commercial foundry, the sand-mold process involves packing sand around a pattern, disassembling the mold, removing the pattern, placing the core, and reassembling the mold. If the pattern is complex, the mold is sectioned sufficiently to make removal of the pattern possible. Patterns are often made to split, or of loose pieces, to facilitate disassembly of the mold. In sand molding, the material is often sufficiently porous so that venting is minimized or unnecessary.

Commercial foundry techniques are primarily developed around the reproduction of a pattern to be used in quantity. Since sculptural casting is usually concerned with a single copy or reproduction, mold techniques follow different procedures.

The sand-mold material consists of the sand and a binder to hold the sand together. Two classifications for the sand would be natural sands, with a binder such as clay present in the sand, and synthetic sands, which are dried with the binders and impurities removed. In synthetic sands, the desired amount of binder is added when preparing the mold material.

Sands are classified by grain size or mesh (number of particles per linear inch). Sand particles may be round, angular, or a composite of both. Round particles allow greater mold permeability, whereas angular particles produce greater mold strength with less permeability. Uniform particle sizes also provide more permeability; a variety of sizes produce a more compact less permeable mold.

Binders added to the sand may be natural or synthetic. Clay is a natural binder. Kaolinite and Bentonite are clay binders. Bentonite, a derivative of volcanic ash, has particularly outstanding qualities, since it produced a mold of greater strength. Silica flour, iron oxide, and portland cement also act as binders.

Small percentages of materials such as molasses, linseed oil, resin oil, dextrin, gelatine, vegetable oils, petroleum derivatives, and plastics form another group of binders.

Sand binder mixtures can be broadly defined in terms of three-mold applications. These are green sand, bake, and no-bake.

Green-sand molds utilize sand with binders such as clay. When packed in a mold, they possess sufficient strength to withstand handling and the weight and pressure of the molten metal. Moisture content of a green-sand mold is kept low. It may run from three to five percent.

Baked-dry-sand molds utilize clay, oil, or other binders. They are stronger than green-sand molds. Baking temperature may run from 300 to 500 degrees Fahrenheit. A refractory wash may be sprayed or brushed on the mold to assure a clean surface on the casting and prevent mold penetration of the molten metal.

Molds of high strength can be constructed with no-bake binders. In this process, a small amount of resin is mixed in the sand in a mixer or muller. After the resin is well-mixed into the sand, an additive or catalyst is added and mixed. The resin and additive interact, causing the sand mold mass to solidify. The action might be compared to the catalytic process that occurs when working with polyester or other resins. Sand mold resin and additive should never be mixed together without the addition of sand, as some formulations may react violently.

No-bake binders may be furan resins, vegetable oil or petroleum derivatives. The amount of resin and additive used is fractional and varies according to the product and manufacturer. In a typical sculptural application with a binder such as Aristo, 100 pounds of sand would require two pounds of resin and about six ounces of additive. The sand might be about 80 to 100 mesh. About one and a half percent (by weight) of iron oxide can be added to the sand to improve its refractory properties. For sculpture, the no-bake mold is perhaps one of the simplest and most satisfactory ways of working with sand. It provides high strength without the use of drying ovens and complex equipment. It is adaptable to a variety of sculpture and casting techniques.

Another no-bake process that is simple and inexpensive is the cement-sand mold. High-early-strength portland cement is mixed with sand in the ratio of one part cement to ten parts sand. Four to eight percent water is added to the mix. It is desirable to keep the water content as low as possible. The mold should be kept covered with a moist cloth and plastic film for the first 24 hours to allow the cement to set and cure. It is then uncovered and allowed to dry for several days. After casting, the discarded mold material can be pulverized. With a small addition of cement and water, the material can be reused as backing. New cement and sand are used for the face coating.

A no-bake mold not using resin or cement is the CO_2 process (carbon dioxide). In this technique, three to five percent sodium silicate is mixed with the sand. When carbon dioxide is passed through the sand mass, it reacts with the silicate causing it to set and harden. The carbon dioxide is introduced into the sand with a probe or lance; also, a cup, or plywood cover with appropriate fittings, can be used on top of the mold.

Plaster investment-materials consist of plaster combined with fillers such as sand, perlite, asbestos fibers, fiberous talc, silica flour, crushed brick, and grog. The fillers add bulk, strength, and porosity to the mold. Asbestos fibers add strength and increase porosity. Typical investment mixtures might be equal parts by volume of sand or grog, plaster, and perlite; two parts sand or grog to one part plaster; or grog and equal parts luto and plaster. Grog produces a better mold; it should be fine (about 80 to 100 mesh) for face coatings and a mixture of fine to 15 mesh when a face coating is not used (unit mold). Commercial investments such as U. S. Gypsum metal-casting plaster are convenient to use and fairly foolproof if their directions are followed accurately.

A relatively new, highly permeable plaster called "Hydroperm® B–32," which is available from U. S. Gypsum, utilizes a foaming agent to produce air spaces in the mold to increase permeability. With a mechanical mixer, one-hundred parts Hydroperm® is mixed with 80 parts water. The volume of the mix increases from 50 to 100 percent as the air is formed in the mix. An electric drill, with a five- or six-inch piece of one-eighth-inch rubber attached to a drill shaft, makes an excellent mixer.

Plaster ingredients should be dry-mixed and then added to the water. Water content will vary according to the ingredients and according to whether the mix is to be poured in a flask or stuccoed on the pattern.

Face coatings unnecessary for most plaster investments, can be made from a mixture of two parts silica flour to one or one and a half parts plaster; or, a proprietary facing can be purchased from a foundry supply.

The release agents for patterns and mold parts can be thin, oily, or wax films, or releases such as those discussed in Chapter 3, pages 39 through 40.

Since plaster molds are highly insulative, thinner and more intricate castings are readily made. Plaster also reproduces fine detail and surface finish. The major disadvantage is the length of time needed for burnout and the lack of permeability, which results in a need for more complex venting.

CERAMIC-SHELL MOLDS

Ceramic-shell molds achieve high strength with comparatively thin walls, because of a highly refined binder and refractory. The binder consists of sodium silicate that has had most of the sodium removed. The resulting extremely fine particles of silica are suspended in water to form a binder. A single drop of binder contains millions of particles. The refractory used with the binder is a fused silica possessing a very low coefficient of thermal expansion. Three to four hundred mesh zircon flour can be used instead of fused silica flour for a less expensive, reasonably strong mold. The grain sizes are carefully controlled to produce the desired results.

The ceramic-shell mold is one of the simplest and most practical approaches to investing wax-patterns. Some principal advantages are: the bulk of the mold is decreased, allowing maximum burnout space in the furnace; burnout time is reduced to a fraction of the time required with plaster investments; surface reproduction of the pattern is excellent; and, since the material is highly porous, venting is minimized or unnecessary. Within reason, mold size is not a problem; its limits are determined generally by the size of the burnout facility and the mechanical means available for handling large molds. Large wax patterns can be cut into sections, cast in smaller pieces, and later welded together.

The two basic ingredients for ceramic-shell molds are the refractory slurry to coat the mold and the refractory stucco material. There are several manufacturers of these materials.

The slurry is mixed in a stainless steel container or other rigid, noncorrosive container. The colloidal-silica liquid is placed in the container and the fused silica flour is added and mixed until the desired viscosity is achieved. Some variance in the viscosity can be tolerated for sculptural casting; most sculptors simply judge the mixture by weight and feel. A sort of thick, creamy consistency is needed.

If you wish to be accurate about the viscosity of the slurry, it can be checked with a Zahn viscosimeter cup. The cup is filled with slurry, and the slurry runs out of the cup through a calibrated hole. By recording the seconds required for the cup to empty, the viscosity of the mixture can be determined.

Mechanical mixing of the slurry is fairly essential. Mixers are available that mix the liquid and operate on programmed timers to keep the slurry-silica particles in suspension. For small quantities, in building sculptural molds, the liquid can be mixed with a mixer blade on an electric drill.

A few drops of wetting agent are added to the slurry to improve its ability to cling to the wax pattern. Air bubbles may form in the mix because of excess wetting agents. They should be allowed to rise to the surface and be skimmed off with a spatula covered with a defoaming agent. To prevent evaporation, the slurry should be kept covered when not in use. After mixing, it should be allowed to stand for about five hours before being used. If the mixture thickens because of evaporation, small amounts of water can be added. This is a haphazard procedure, however, since it is difficult to estimate the remaining silica content. Preparing slurries and utilizing stucco material become somewhat more complex in commercial foundries, where precise control of the casting is necessary. Information on these procedures for mixing, determining slurry-viscosity, maintaining slurries, applying stucco material, burnout, and casting can be obtained from the suppliers.

There are several other applications for ceramic-shell materials. Slurries and refractories can be used over wood, plaster, or other patterns to produce mold facings that can be backed up with sand in split molds. Colloidal silica can be used as a binder and vehicle with refractory powders for mold washes.

SCULPTURAL MOLDS FOR METAL CASTING

Having discussed three basic materials suitable for metal-casting sculpture, we might examine several applications in the actual construction of a mold. The diagrams, at best, indicate procedures. Ultimately, designing a mold and developing the ability to judge what material to use, as well as where to gate, sprue, and vent, is a matter of personal experience. It is important not to worry about losing a casting or sculpture piece. It is inevitable and part of learning mold-construction.

In many procedures, it is possible to use any of the mold materials. As an example, in Figures 2-21 through 2-25, it would be possible to use

Figure 2-21
Pattern on pattern board with flask and mold material.

Figure 2-22
Flask with pattern; sand with a no-bake binder is being packed around pattern.

Figure 2-23

Mold with clay liner.

Figure 2-24

Mold with cope and drag sections formed.

Figure 2-25

Completed mold, bottom gating.

Figure 2-26

Top gating system.

plaster investment or sand. If a burnout kiln were not available, sand with a no-bake binder would be an appropriate choice. It would be simpler and if a fine sand were used, surface detail of the pattern could still be picked up.

Figures 2-21 through 2-25 illustrates how to cast a simple relief. If this process is understood, it can be adapted readily to more complex reliefs or three-dimensional forms. Figure 2-21 illustrates a pattern without undercuts on a pattern board. A flask or wooden frame is placed around the relief. A suitable release agent is applied to the pattern board, pattern, and inside edges of the flask. Plaster investment could be poured into the flask or a sand-mold technique could be used. For plaster, strips of wire mesh would be imbedded in the plaster for reinforcement. For large sand molds, reinforcing rod might be used.

Figure 2-23 shows the mold removed from the flask and turned over. The pattern has been replaced with a layer of clay approximating the thickness of the metal. An oil base clay should be used if the mold material is to be sand with a no-bake binder. If the mold were plaster investment for lost wax, hot wax could be poured or brushed into the mold. Besides clay, any material can be used that is the right thickness and readily follows the contour of the mold. A release material is next applied to the edges of the mold.

Figure 2-24 shows the mold with the cope and drag section of the mold. The cope section of the mold has been filled with the desired mold material.

Figure 2-25 shows the completed mold. To complete the mold, the drag and cope section was

separated, the clay was removed, vents and sprues were drilled out, and the pouring basin was carved. In this case, we have bottom gating, with the metal entering the bottom of the mold. If sand with a no-bake binder were used, the mold surface would be treated with a refractory wash, reassembled, wired together—ready for casting.

A plaster-investment mold could be wired together or held together by placing a piece of wire mesh around the side and stuccoing with investment materials. For plaster, the mold would have to be heated in a burnout kiln to drive off all of the moisture.

Figure 2-26 shows the mold detailed for top gating, with the metal first entering at the top edges of the cavity. In this case, bottom gating would be preferable. Since the metal would have less distance to travel and there would be less chance for gas and air entrapment.

Figures 2-27 through 2-29 show several steps in the construction of a mold, as previously diagrammed in Figures 2-21 through 2-25. (Figure 2-30)

As patterns become more complex, molds require more pieces. Figure 2-31 illustrates how the drag section of the mold can be constructed in three pieces to accommodate an undercut on a rigid pattern. If the undercuts are on the surface, as in Figure 2-32, a separate piece is built that dowels, or fits, the inside surface of the mold. This piece can be cemented in with core paste. If the mold is being built over a clay pattern, it is possible to accommodate some undercuts without making the mold complex, since the clay will break away, or can be dug out of the areas. The under-

Figure 2-27

Pattern with flask around the pattern. *Student project, Southern Methodist University.*

Figure 2-28

Mold sections with pattern removed. Wax liner, vents, and pouring cup have been attached. Cope section of flask is in place.

Figure 2-29

Mold completed and ready for burnout.

Figure 2-30

Wax pattern in a tar paper flask ready for casting.

Figure 2-31
Piece mold construction to accommodate side undercuts.

Figure 2-32
Piece mold construction to accommodate surface undercuts.

Figure 2-33
Mold construction to accommodate undercuts through varying thickness of the casting.

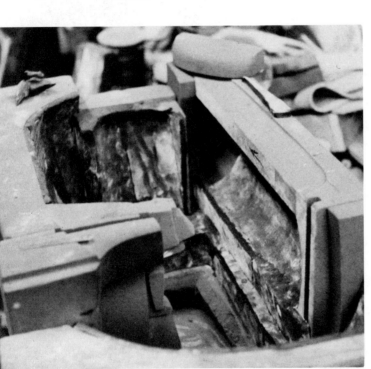

Figure 2-34
Partial sand mold in random pieces. *By sculptor James Surls.* (Mold has been lined with clay in preparation for adding the core.)

cuts can be accommodated by allowing increased metal thickness in some areas. (Figure 2-33)

Building reliefs by carving into the mold material is a spontaneous and direct approach. In this case, the drag is placed on the bottom-board and is rammed with sand or filled with plaster investment. The relief is carved into the mold material, the cavity is then lined with clay, and the procedure progresses as in Figure 2-23.

Sculptor James Surls uses this technique with three-dimensional forms. The sides are carved and the mold pieces are stacked and assembled. They can be cemented together with core paste or a refractory cement. The mold is surrounded with flasks and rammed with moist, sandy loam to give added support to the mold pieces. (Figure 2-34)

Sand mold-construction in three dimensions is, primarily, a more complex application of the relief technique. Essentially, it is still a matter of building the mold sections, disassembling, lining with clay, and reassembling. For small works, the mold is built around the pattern and turned over to ram up the core. If the mold is large and cannot be turned over, the mold is constructed as in Figure 2-35.

In this case, the core will rest on a slab of

mold material placed on the floor of a bottom board, and chaplets are not necessary. The core can be held in place with metal reinforcing rods, and rammed up progressively, as the sections are stacked. It is a good idea to use less binder and additive in the core material so that it will be softer than the mold. The core is rammed up to about one inch from the top of each section. When the next cheek section is placed, it is necessary to reach into the mold and join the two sections of clay wall. Core material is then rammed up; subsequent sections progress in the same fashion. Between sections four and five, the core is completed and trimmed. A layer of clay is placed on top of the core; it is detailed or finished, and section five is completed. The mold is then disassembled, the clay is removed, and refractory washes are applied when needed; sprues, vents, and gates are drilled or carved, and the mold is reassembled. The pieces may be cemented together with core paste, which can be made simply by mixing thinned lacquer and talc.

There are numerous variations to this approach. A simpler procedure is to build a core approximating the sculpture. The core should be about one-eighth to one-fourth-inch smaller than the finished work. Then, the clay is applied to represent the metal thickness, and the sculpture is finished with the surface qualities desired. The mold is then built around the work. (*See* Figures 2-34 and 2-32.)

In another approach (Figure 2-36), the mold is built around the sculpture pattern and core, randomly following the contour of the pattern. Registration marks or pegs must be placed on the individual pieces so that the mold can be readily realigned when it is assembled. After the mold is completed, it is disassembled. The clay is then removed, a gating system is added, a refractory wash is applied to the mold surface, and it is reassembled. The parts are cemented together with core-paste and bound with wire. After the mold has been completed and assembled, flasks are placed around the mold, and it is rammed up with backup sand or loam. Rather than using the flasks, the mold can be bound together with wire and reinforcing materials.

Yet another approach would involve building over the core with wax instead of clay. Fine detail and texture can be reproduced by coating the wax with a face coating. The mold is built in random pieces. Sprues, vents, and wax-drains are made of wax and are attached to the wax pattern as the mold is being built. Wire, wire mesh, and concrete reinforcing rod can be added for reinforcement.

If the mold is too large to handle, the melt-out furnace can be constructed around the mold.

Figure 2-35

No-bake binder sand piece mold construction built in flasks.

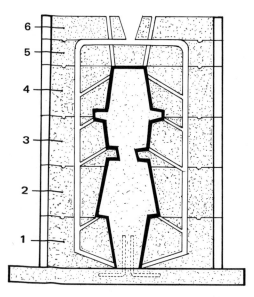

Figure 2-36

No-bake binder sand piece mold built with random pieces.

In this case, the mold should have been built on a layer of fire bricks. The temperature of the melt-out may be 300 to 500 degrees for sand, depending upon the heat resistance of the binder used.

Figures 2-21 through 2-35 discussed molds built in flasks. Molds can also be constructed without containing the material in a flask-like device. In this application, the mold material is spattered, stuccoed, troweled, or applied by hand. Plaster investment mixtures are usually used. The procedure starts out the same as in building a plaster piece mold for casting other materials. However, sprues, vents, etc. must be included as the mold is being built; or, they can be carved or drilled, as in previous techniques.

When the mold is completed, it is disassembled and lined with clay. It is reassembled, and the core is poured. It is then disassembled, and the clay is removed. The mold pieces are then reassembled; the core is held in place with chaplets. The mold is oven-cured prior to pouring.

Rather than a clay lining, the lost-wax process is often used with the plaster mold. The plaster mold can be assembled and held together with plaster and reinforcing wire. If it is small enough to handle, it can be filled with melted wax. As soon as the desired wall thickness has accumulated, the excess wax is poured out. If it is possible

Figure 2-38

Plaster investment bottom gating.

to reach into the mold, core pins can be pushed through the wax pattern into the mold wall. If the inside of the mold is not accessible, small holes can be drilled through the mold wall and wax pattern. The metal rods or core pins are pushed through the holes until they protrude into the core cavity. The core is then poured. After the mold has set for a day, it is ready for meltout or burnout.

A more traditional approach is to build the plaster investment over the wax pattern as a single homogeneous mass rather than making a piece mold. Sprues, vents, and runners are attached to the wax pattern. Core pins are pressed through the wax pattern, protruding sufficiently to anchor into the mold. After the mold is built, it is turned upside down, placed in a flask, and investment is poured around the pattern and into the core. (Figures 2-37 and 2-38) Since plaster is not as porous as sand, extra care must be exercised in locating the vents. They should be located at high points that could otherwise result in air or gas entrapment. (Figure 2-37)

If the wax pattern and mold are too large to handle, drains can be provided for melting out the wax. The mold can be built on a firebrick slab, with channels running from the drains to allow the wax to run out. The furnace can be built around the mold. The core is poured by providing an access hole on the top of the mold.

In building a plaster mold where a face coating is used, a good bond must exist between the

Figure 2-37

Plaster investment top gating.

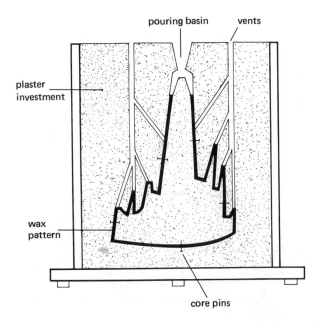

face coating and the backup material. Backup material should never be applied to a dry face coating. The surface of the coating should be roughed with a piece of saw blade or toothed scraper. Sprinkling sand on the face coating before it has set can provide additional bond.

CERAMIC SHELL

Building a ceramic-shell mold is somewhat like the building up of a plaster mold by stuccoing or hand applying the investment material. The essential difference is that the layers are thinner and correspondingly stronger.

The wax pattern for ceramic shell should be properly gated. Top pouring works well on ceramic-shell molds of moderate size. The sprues, runners, gates, and vents should be hollow, preferably, and of a lower melting point than the pattern. This will facilitate the removal of the wax during meltout. If the pattern has a deep core cavity, a hole should be cut through the end. (Figures 2-39 and 2-40) This allows for better air circulation for drying and provides an additional

anchoring point for the core shell. The piece cut out can be attached to the sprue and cast. It is welded back upon completion of the casting.

Prior to applying the first coat of slurry, the pattern should be degreased or etched so the slurry will cling to the pattern. Washing with trichloroethane, full-strength or diluted with half isopropyl alcohol, will clean and etch the surface. Another approach is to brush the pattern with Johnson's Glo Coat® floor wax. The floor wax is water-soluble and seems to produce a surface that the slurry readily clings to. Apply the slurry immediately after the wax has dried.

In commercial foundries, the wax patterns are dipped into the slurry. Most sculptors do not do sufficient volumes of work to merit the cost and justify the large quantity of slurry necessary for such application. Consequently, the most practical approach is to mix small amounts and brush it on, or pour it over the pattern. It can also be sprayed on using an R-2 spray gun. Pouring the slurry over the pattern works well if the pattern is small enough to handle. The pattern should be rotated over a shallow tray while the slurry is poured. When the pattern is covered, the excess slurry is drained off until the dripping stops.

The next step is to sprinkle the stucco ma-

Figure 2-39
Ceramic shell mold construction.

pouring cup

sprue

vent

cavity

Figure 2-40
Ceramic shell mold ready for burnout.

terial over the wet pattern until it is covered. The best stucco material is fused silica. Calcine clay (grog) can be used with a zircon flour slurry mixture. Grain size for the first two coats of stucco would be 60 to 80 mesh with subsequent coatings of 30 to 50 or 20 to 50 mesh. The stucco material can be kept in a covered, shallow tray large enough to catch it as it is being sprinkled. Occasionally, it may be necessary to sift the stucco material with a wire-mesh screen to remove investment particles.

After the pattern has been sprinkled, it is allowed to dry. The drying time depends on the temperature and humidity. With warm temperatures, low humidity, and fans to circulate the air, drying is rapid. With fused silica the pattern will appear white when dry. Since speed and production are not a major concern in sculptural casting, drying time is not critical. Application of one coat per day is a practical procedure; twenty-four hours is more than adequate to assure drying under normal room temperature. Accumulating several patterns for investing is a good practice, to economize on time and material.

Although final coatings need not be thoroughly dry, dry coatings do assure a mold of maximum strength. Ideally, it is also desirable to have consistent temperature and humidity. Drying temperatures of 80 to 85 degrees Fahrenheit and humidity of 45 to 50 percent seem to produce optimum results. If ceramic-shell mold construction is going to be a regular operation, it would undoubtedly be worth while to construct a drying room with circulating air and temperature and humidity control.

After the first coating is applied, the pattern is wetted with the colloidal silica, which can be poured over the mold in the same fashion as that used in applying the slurry. Another coating of slurry and grog is then applied, and the pattern is again allowed to dry. This procedure is repeated until the desired mold thickness is achieved.

The mold thickness is relative to the size of the work. Small works of about 12 inches, involving ten- or 20-pound pours can be produced in shells that are about an eighth of an inch in thickness. Four to six coats would produce a shell about one-eighth inch or thicker. If there is any doubt about the thickness, apply an extra coating or two. The cost is minor in relation to the risk of losing the work.

Large molds can be reinforced during the last two coatings. Strips of thin fiberglass matting or other fiberglass reinforcing fibers can be dipped in the slurry and applied to critical areas. Flat-surfaced patterns need reinforcement, particularly on the corners and edges.

DE-WAXING AND DE-FOAMING

Since de-waxed molds can be used as easily in the casting of plastics as of metals, the de-waxing or de-foaming process is included in this chapter; it can no longer be considered purely as a metal-casting problem.

With the development of foam and wax patterns comes the additional concern of pattern removal. Pattern removal can be accomplished by two methods: solvent removal or by melting or burnout.

Solvent removal of foam in plaster or ceramic-shell-invested patterns is a simple matter of a solvent such as acetone or lacquer thinner being poured on the foam. Polystyrene foam should be used, since it dissolves more readily. A good coating of a paste wax or hot melted wax on the foam will contain the solvent and minimize its absorption into the mold material. During burnout, as the term indicates, the film of wax is burned out for metal casting. Likewise, in plastic-casting, the wax film and residue from the dissolved foam should be burned out.

Solvent removal of wax is a vapor process, limited in size to the size of the vapor de-waxer

Figure 2-41
Vapor de-waxer.

lid

metal tank

drain and
drain valve

gas burner   control valve

Figure 2-42
Steam de-waxer.

used. A simple vapor de-waxer can be built out of a 55-gallon drum or large metal container and a gas or electric-heating element. (Figure 2-41) The de-waxing solvent is heated and the vapors dissolve the wax. Trichloroethylene is one of several solvents than can be used. The mold is placed in the de-waxer with the pouring cup down. It can be held above the liquid on several bricks or on a rack fabricated out of steel. About an inch of solvent is placed in the degreaser. Since trichloroethylene vapors are toxic, de-waxing should take place in an outdoor area or proper ventilation should be provided.

Vapor removal of wax is especially applicable to ceramic-shell molds. As with foam, it provides a way of eliminating the expansion problem of furnace de-waxing, since the expanding wax pattern may crack the mold before it starts to melt.

In plaster-investment molds, the wax can be melted out by the use of steam. A simple steam de-waxer can be built in the same way as the vapor de-waxer. (The gas burner can be purchased new or can often be salvaged from an old hot-water heater.) In this case, the cooling coil is not necessary. The mold is placed in the drum over about an inch of water. As the water heats and steam forms, the wax melts and floats on the water. This is a way to recover wax for reuse and achieve a partial meltout. After this meltout, the mold must

still go through the burnout process. (Figure 2-42)

Steam de-waxing cannot be used on ceramic shell molds unless it is carried out in a pressurized steam autoclave. The pressure counteracts the wax expansion and prevents the mold from cracking.

Burnout or meltout is the traditional approach for removing the wax from plaster investments. Ceramic-shell burnout utilizes a different method from plaster investments.

The burnout or meltout of plaster investments requires considerable time. In meltout, the mold is placed in the furnace with the pouring cup and vents down. The temperature is slowly raised 200 to 300 degrees. The wax melts and runs out through a trough or drops through a hole in the furnace floor, where it is collected in a partially filled bucket of water for reuse. After the initial meltout, which may take from several hours to a day, the temperature is gradually increased until the mold reaches a temperature of 1,000 to 1,500 degrees. This may take several days for a large mold. The wax and carbon must be completely burned out and all moisture expelled. The ultimate temperature depends on the investment being used. Lower meltout temperature takes more time but results in less shrinkage. The furnace temperature can be checked with a pyrometer or a visual estimate can be made on the basis of the color of the mold or the length of time the mold has been in the furnace. The mold should be a dull red if the investment is heated to 1,500 degrees. Black carbon present on the mold indicates insufficient burnout. Wax and materials still burning in the mold can be identified by the presence of a yellow-tipped flame burning out of the cup or vents.

If the wax is not going to be reclaimed, another approach is to burn out the mold with the pouring-cup and vents up and allow the wax to simply burn off.

In burning out ceramic shell, the furnace is brought up to 1,500 degrees. The shell is placed cup-down in the furnace at this temperature. The objective is to get the wax pattern to melt before it has a chance to expand. The wax is usually partially collected as in the de-waxing of plaster molds. After the wax has melted, the temperature may be kept at a level of 1,500 degrees or increased to 2,000 degrees. The burnout period runs from 15 to 30 minutes, depending on the size of the mold. When the mold is ready for removal, its condition

Figure 2-43

Typical gas burners for burnout and meltout furnaces.

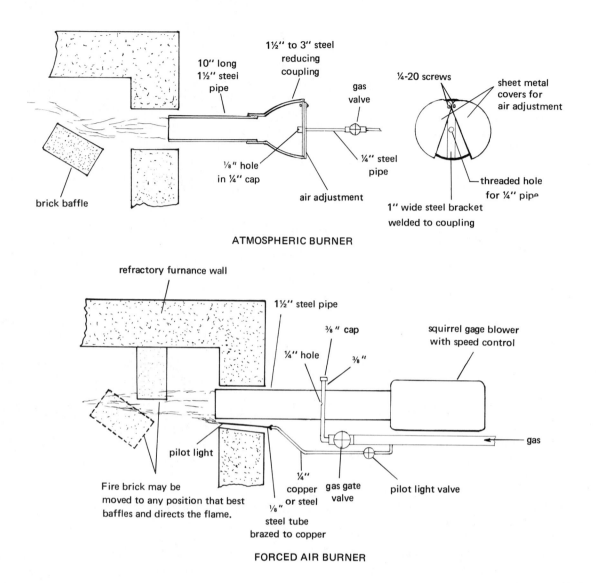

10" long
1½" steel
pipe

1½" to 3" steel
reducing
coupling

gas
valve

¼-20 screws

sheet metal
covers for
air adjustment

⅛" hole
in ¼" cap

¼" steel
pipe

air adjustment

threaded hole
for ¼" pipe

brick baffle

1" wide steel bracket
welded to coupling

ATMOSPHERIC BURNER

refractory furnance wall

1½" steel pipe

⅜" cap

squirrel gage blower
with speed control

¼" hole

⅜"

pilot light

gas

Fire brick may be
moved to any position that best
baffles and directs the flame.

¼"
copper
or steel

⅛"
steel tube
brazed to copper

gas gate
valve

pilot light valve

FORCED AIR BURNER

is easily identifiable by the dull red color or the absence of black carbon on the shell.

In order to minimize wax expansion, some sculptors will melt out some of the wax with an oxyacetylene torch or a gas burner. The mold cup is placed down on two bricks; the heat is directed into the cup. As the wax melts, the heat is slowly moved around and up the lower mold surface. Burnout is still required prior to casting.

**FURNACES
FOR DE-WAXING AND BURNOUT**

Essentially, the furnace for de-waxing or burnout can be an uncomplicated thing. A small furnace can be constructed easily out of stacked fire bricks or a 50-gallon steel drum. The steel drum can

be lined with firebricks or the refractory can be cast or stuccoed into the interior. Numerous refractories are available today. A simple refractory for burnout furnaces can be made by mixing one part aluminite cement, one part powdered fire clay, and five parts perlite. This can be cast or stuccoed into place. The burner can be an atmospheric or forced-air type burner. (Figure 2-43) The atmospheric burner draws air from the atmosphere without the use of a blower. Some space must be allowed around the burner where it enters the furnace to allow for additional air for the flame. The atmospheric burner is useful for meltout or burn-out when a slow temperature rise is desired. Several burners can be used in larger furnaces to achieve the desired temperature. The forced air burner is excellent for fast heat and higher temperatures. The squirrel-cage-type blow-

burner mounted to
side as indicated

Figure 2-44
De-waxing furnace.

Figure 2-45
De-waxing a shell mold in a burnout furnace.

er for the forced air burner has about a one-tenth horsepower, universal-type motor. The volume of air can be controlled with an inexpensive speed control. The flame from the burner should impinge on the refratory wall of the furnace if the furnace is round. It should be baffled with a fire brick if the furnace is rectangular. Both the atmospheric and forced air burner require some experimentation and experience to operate. They usually require constant attention and readjustment as the temperature of the furnace rises. Although these burners can be operated without safety controls, the practice is not advisable if the furnace is left unattended and certainly should never take place if the furnace is operated inside a building. The safety controls are attached to the burner, fan and pilot light. If the air supply stops, flame or pilot light go out, the controls shut off the gas. Johnson Gas Appliance Company is a good source for controls, and burners. Note the fans on the burner in Figure 2-47; lighting instructions and other burner designs are in Chapter 3.

Plaster molds can be placed in the furnace and the temperature gradually increased. Ceramic-shell molds can simply have a nichrome wire loop on top of the mold. A metal pole is put through the loop, and the mold is lowered into the furnace. (Figure 2-44 and 2-45) The pole can be left in the furnace with the mold hanging from it, as in Figure 2-44. If the mold is quite heavy it can be placed on the furnace bottom and the pole can be removed. More satisfactory but complex approaches involve the furnace being built high enough to have a drop bottom. (Figure 2-46) The mold is placed on the lowered bottom which is then raised to place the mold in the furnace. The furnace can also be designed with a platform or grate that drops down or is placed into the furnace. Front-loading furnaces can be loaded by moving the mold on a platform, guided by a steel track (Figure 2-47). Steel components should be of a high-temperature-resistant material.

There are an infinite number of variables in furnace design. Each sculptor seems to find a form that best suits his needs. For larger works, the 55-gallon-drum concept can be expanded to any size steel container the sculptor finds possible to build.

For de-waxing large plaster investments, the most direct and simplest approach (used for centuries) is to stack firebrick around the mold, forming a beehive shape. The cracks can be filled with

35

steel pipe to protect
cable from furnace heat

pulleys

steel
cable

2″ or 3″
steel pipe

50 gal.
steel drum

section of steel
pipe to slide on
4-pipe legs

Figure 2-46

Top and side views of a drop bottom furnace.

Figure 2-47

Front-loading a ceramic shell mold. (Note bucket for catching
wax from center trough.)

Figure 2-48

Stacked-brick furnace (furnace should be round).

Figure 2-49

Front-loading furnace.

Figure 2-50

Stacked-ring furnace.

investment material. In ancient beehive furnaces, wood was used for fuel. Today, a regular gas or oil burner with forced air can be used. (Figure 2-48)

A more permanent furnace of this kind can be designed with a removable door made of firebricks, either stacked or built in a steel frame and hinged; a refractory mortar can be used between the bricks. (Figure 2-49)

Stacked furnaces with banded rings of firebrick or reinforced, cast rings can be built so the height and capacity of the furnace can be varied. (Figure 2-50)

Casting
and
Reproduction

THREE

Today, there are many castable materials; metal casting, once thought of as primarily bronze casting, now includes cast iron, steel, aluminum, lead, magnesium, nickel, silver, and a vast number of alloys and combinations of alloys.

Clay bodies can be cast in the form of slip castings or pressed into molds.

Plaster (gypsum cement) is formulated so that a considerable choice exists as to density, strength, and permanence. Portland cement combined with aggregates has numerous possibilities as cast stone.

Emphasis today on plastics as a whole new class of castable materials has radically altered our ideas. The versatility of these materials has made it possible to produce castings with diverse physical and visual properties.

Selection of a casting material will depend on the desired visual effect and the purpose of the work. If the sculpture is to be outdoors, the choice of materials is, of necessity, limited. If it is an interior work, the more fragile materials, such as plaster or paper-mache, may very well be more suitable than more permanent materials.

Casting techniques have also become more complex. We ordinarily think of "casting" as pouring a liquid or viscous compound into a mold and removing the mold after the material has solidified. Commercially, if spray, hand layup, pressure, or mechanical means are used to place the compound into the mold or on the mold parts, it is usually referred to as "molding technique."

There is a wide variety of commercial casting and molding techniques for mass production that become highly sophisticated automated applications of the simple process of placing a castable material in a mold and removing it at the proper time. Many metal-casting techniques are automated with permanent metal molds for quantity production. Semiautomated systems for rapid production and handling of sand, plaster, and shell molds are standard foundry procedure.

Injection, extrusion, rotational, transfer, and compression molding are utilized in the plastic industry to rapidly produce thermosetting and thermoplastic parts. Semipermanent molds of wood or fiberglass are used in the construction industry for casting concrete, producing structural and decorative modular components for building.

Although the sculptor does not usually deal with high-production casting techniques, he should be aware of them, since sculptural adaptations can often be made from commercial procedures. Sometimes, sculptors or artists design for mass production. Today, mass production of sculpture or components of sculpture is feasible and, to many, acceptable.

Two obvious requirements for casting or molding are the mold or container to receive the material, and a release agent to prevent the material from adhering to the mold. Some materials are their own release agents; or release agents can be added to the mix, as in the casting of plastic.

In Chapter 2, we discussed many kinds of molds. As we have seen, the selection of a mold depends on the material to be cast, the number of castings desired, and the surface quality desired on the casting. The plaster waste or piece mold is still one of the most basic and simple molds for casting a single form of almost any material. It may not always be the most desirable or efficient, but if other materials are not available, satisfactory casting can be achieved. Clay slip, pressed clay, plaster, cast stone, and plastics can all be cast in plaster molds. With proper refractories added to the plaster, bronze, aluminum, and low-melting alloys can also be cast in plaster investments.

In many applications, when casting plaster, cast stones, and plastics, porous mold surfaces need to be sealed prior to the application of a release agent. Moist plaster, dry plaster, cardboard, and wood molds are usually treated with several coats of thinned lacquer or shellac prior to the application of the release agent. Several thin layers are preferable to thick coatings.

In handling, preparing, and applying release agents, the sculptor should be cautious if the material is toxic or flammable. This is particularly necessary when melting waxes or solids into flammable solvents. Melting these materials in electric saucepans, frying pans, deep fryers, or similar utensils having sealed heating elements and temperature controls, is the best practice. Do not overheat the mixture. Good ventilation should be provided when spraying solvent-based release materials, and toxicity should be a consideration.

Release agents should be applied in thin films, since excess buildup may eliminate fine detail, affect surface qualities, and complicate cleaning of the casting.

Release agents can be simple oils, waxes, soaps, or plastic such as fluoro carbons (Teflon®), silicones, polyethylenes, polyvinyl alcohol, or other materials. The formulation of release agents has become an industrial specialty, with formulators designing release agents for a wide variety of specific applications.

Although release problems are far less exacting for the sculptor, some care in the selection of a release agent can result in a better quality casting and fewer hours spent in finishing the work.

Some considerations in the selection of a release agent would depend on the mold surface, the quantity being produced, the temperature of the casting material and the casting operation, the material being cast, the desired surface of the casting, and the final surface finish or surface treatment.

Mold surfaces can be porous, semiporous, nonporous, and possess natural release properties, such as silicone rubber, polyethylene, or vinyl. Each requires a different release material.

Quantity of production is seldom a problem for the sculptor, since he is normally concerned with a limited number of castings. When mass production is a concern, the ability of a release agent to withstand numerous castings per application of release material is important. Temperature of the casting material and the molding process is usually important in injection-molding and other industrial molding processes. However, for the sculptor, it matters in heat-curing techniques, temperature buildup in plastic casting, or in the adaptation of industrial processes utilizing heat.

The material being cast can pose many problems. Some resins, such as polyester or epoxy, tend to have a solvent action on the release agent and tend to be adhesive. Polyurethane is particularly adhesive and often presents release problems unless special agents are used and precautions are exercised. Materials possessing natural release properties or release-property additives may not require release agents.

The surface of the casting can be affected by improper usage of release materials. They can affect the surface-curing of resins and foams. For rough textured sculptural casting this may not be a problem. However, when casting smooth or pre-finished surfaces, it becomes a matter of critical concern. If the surface is to receive posttreatment, the choice is also important.

A good example of this is in casting plastic,

plaster, or concrete, when the surface is to receive further coating or treatment. Wax or oil-based separators may combine with the surface of the casting, providing an undesirable surface or conditions that may make removal of the release agent difficult and time-consuming. In this case, the use of a release agent that permits painting or surface treatment with minimal cleaning or preparation is desirable. Silicone, water-soluble polyvinyl alcohol or other plastic release agents are often used in this application. Water-soluble release agents are easy to remove.

Aerosol spray cans, liquids, pastes, and powdered release agents designed for specific applications are available today from plastic suppliers, molding suppliers, or companies specializing in these products. These are preferable to the simpler soaps, oils, and waxes the sculptor customarily uses (although soaps, oils and waxes still have practical economical usage in some casting techniques or where surface results are not critical).

Release-agent materials can be classified in some of the following categories:

Soaps. Liquid soap, or bar-soap shavings dissolved in hot water, are used on moist plaster molds. The soap is brushed on the mold and polished with a soft cloth. Several layers are necessary for good release. Soaps are primarily used in plaster casting. The mold does not require a lacquer or shellac sealer.

Fatty compounds. Thin films of tallow and animal fats can be used on sealed wet or dry plaster molds and on wood or sheet-metal molds, in the casting of concrete or plaster. Stearic acid, dissolved at the rate of about one-quarter pound per pint of kerosene, is an excellent fatty material that has been used extensively as an inexpensive release agent for many years. It is carefully melted in a container, and the kerosene is stirred into the melted stearic acid. Stearic acid (zinc and aluminum stearate) release agents are commercially available.

Oils. Vaseline thinned with kerosene, lightweight-petroleum lubricating oils, and vegetable oils are used on sealed plaster and wood or nonporous molds (such as fiberglass) in the casting of plaster and concrete. Aerosol spray cans of vegetable oil are convenient for the application of thin films on small molds.

Waxes. Paraffin, melted into kerosene or mineral spirits at the rate of about four ounces of wax to one pint of solvent, provides an inexpensive release agent. Commonly used are commercial paste floor-waxes, in their existing paste form or diluted with mineral spirits or other solvents. Waxes can be applied hot or cold, depending on the desired thickness of the film or porosity of the mold. The wax is usually wiped or brushed on the mold surface. The excess is wiped off, the mold is polished, and a second coat is applied and polished. Porous molds of wood, plaster, or cardboard can be saturated with a hot application of diluted wax—without prior sealing for plaster, plastic, and concrete castings, when postsurface treatment is not critical. Excess wax should be wiped off. Thin films of wax are used on metal, sealed plaster, and fiberglass molds, for the release of plastic castings. These thin films are often applied along with water-soluble release agents such as polyvinyl alcohol. Commercially-formulated wax release-agents are available in aerosol spray cans and paste forms.

Plastics. Fluorocarbons (Teflon®), silicones, polyethylene, and polyvinyl alcohol are the most commonly used plastic release-agents. For limited usage, small quantities are available in aerosol spray cans. Flurocarbons and silicones are longlasting and highly desirable in quantity production. To the sculptor, these are of principal interest when wax- or grease-free release is desired. Polyethylene film or sheet can be used as a separator when casting on flat surfaces. Sprayed films of polyethylene or polyvinyl alcohol are excellent release agents for reinforced or cast polyester and epoxy resins.

Internal release agents. In this application, fatty, wax, or other compounds are mixed in with the resin to provide separation from nonporous molds.

Three basic casting or molding techniques ordinarily are used in sculptural application. Pouring the material into the previously assembled and treated mold is the simplest and, as mentioned, is associated with the term "casting." It is applicable to most materials. Slush or rotational molding is a technique in which the material is poured into the mold and the mold is turned or tumbled. Some of the material clings to the wall of the mold, and the excess material is poured out. This procedure is repeated several times, until the desired thickness is achieved. In casting plaster and thermoplastics, small molds can be rotated and tumbled by hand. A simple rotational-molding machine can be constructed out of an old cement mixer, allowing for a more uniform, continuous rotation of the mold. Slip casting in ceramics is a simple and typical example of this approach. Plaster and plastic resins with fillers or hot, melted thermoplastics can be cast in this fashion. Open-face molding techniques involve placing the material into the mold sections and assembling the mold before or after the material has solidified. The simplest version of this is the relief mold. A moist clay body, such as terra cotta, pressed into a dry-plaster mold, is typical of this procedure and has been used for many years. Plastic resins with fillers, paper mache, or plastic-reinforced fiberglass are also molded in this way.

CLAY

Clay can be either slip-cast or pressed into a dry plaster mold. Either technique is suitable only if the forms are relatively simple. Since the clay shrinks upon drying, complex mold surfaces hold the shrinking clay in a rigid position, causing cracks in the clay wall as it dries. In fact, designing clay forms for either technique requires some experience and judgment in the design of the sculpture, the mold, the viscosity of the slip being poured, and the proper removal of the mold.

Dry, powdered clays suitable for slip casting can be purchased from ceramic suppliers. The dry clay is sprinkled into a rust-proof container of clean, cool water and mixed until a thick, creamy consistency is achieved. The container should be covered, and the slip should be allowed to age for several days. Prior to pouring the slip, it can be sifted through a 40-to-60-mesh screen to eliminate lumps or foreign particles. It can be thinned if the mixture seems too thick, although it should not be too thin, as a high water content will mean greater shrinkage of the cast form.

In slip casting, the slip is poured into an assembled dry plaster piece mold. Normal procedure is to wire the mold together or hold it together with large rubber bands made from strips of old inner tubes. The seams on the mold are sealed with moist clay. Separators or release agents are not used, since the plaster mold must absorb moisture out of the slip. As the plaster absorbs the water, a clay wall is formed. This may take ten to 30 minutes, depending on the water content of the slip, the size of the work, and the absorbency of the mold wall. The mold should be kept filled with slip while the wall is forming.

When the wall has reached the desired thickness (one-fourth to three-eighths inches), the slip is poured out of the mold and is placed with the opening down to allow the mold to drain. In another slip-casting approach, the slip is poured in and out of the mold several times, until the desired wall thickness is achieved. In either case, after the mold has been finally drained, the moisture is allowed to evaporate out of the slip wall, causing the slip wall to shrink away from the plaster mold. When the clay has reached a fairly firm consistency, it is trimmed around the opening, and the pieces of the mold are carefully removed. The clay casting is then tooled, finished, and allowed to dry.

In the pressed-clay technique, the mold parts are sprinkled lightly with talc, and pieces of moist clay are pressed into the mold, forming a wall thickness of one-half inch or more. The wall thickness is a matter of personal judgment and depends on the size of the piece. The clay must be wedged and firmly pressed and bonded so that no air pockets exist in the pressed-clay mass.

The moist clay should be of firm dough-like consistency. 10 to 15 percent Grog (a pulverized fired clay) is often added to the clay to improve its properties during drying and firing. Terra cotta, a reddish-colored clay with grog added, is ordinarily available. It has been used for centuries as a sculptural media in cultures as diverse as ancient Greece and Mexico. If the pressed-clay sculpture parts are in a piece mold, sufficient clay surplus is allowed along the edges so that they will press together when the mold is assembled. Prior to assembling, the edges should be wetted with a small amount of slip made from the clay being used to assure bonding of the edges.

After the mold has been assembled, moisture is allowed to evaporate until the clay wall is reasonably firm. The mold is then removed and the clay casting is tooled, finished, and allowed to dry. Drying of either slip cast or pressed forms should be rather slow, to allow internal stresses to equalize somewhat as the clay dries and shrinks. Dried-pressed or slip-cast clay bodies called "greenware" need to be baked or fired to develop their full strength.

Normal procedure is to first soak the clay for a couple of hours at a very low temperature (100 or 200 degrees), to be certain that all moisture has been removed. Firing normally takes place in an electric or gas-fired kiln. The work is placed in the kiln and the temperature is slowly brought up to about 1,800 degrees, over a period of about 18 hours. At this point, the clay matures or vitrifies.

In ceramics, this first firing is called the "bisque firing." After the bisque firing, the work is usually glazed and fired at a higher temperature to mature the glaze and fuse it to the clay body.

To achieve color in ceramic sculpture, there are three basic approaches. The natural color of the clay, or the color-producing pigment added to the clay, produce limited colors, from white to buff to brown or reddish tones. Thin-colored slip or glaze materials painted on the clay prior to firing (green ware) can extend the color range. The broadest color range is achieved by glazing the bisque ware and subjecting it to a second firing.

Glazes mature at varying temperature ranges, which are controlled by placing three pyrometric cones, set in a piece of clay, in the kiln. Allow the clay to dry prior to placing the cones in the kiln. Observing the melting or bending of these cones through a peephole in the kiln door makes it possible to determine the approximate temperature range.

Glazing is a complex and highly refined art in itself, requiring considerable experimentation in order to obtain consistent desired results.

PLASTER

The casting plaster or gypsum cements available today range from soft to exceptionally hard, durable materials. They are still among some of the most basic, simple-to-handle, and inexpensive studio materials. Sculpturally, plaster has been used for centuries, dating back to ancient Egypt; plaster death masks have been found in tombs dated around 2,500 B.C.

Today, plaster applications include casting temporary models and experimental works, patterns for metal-casting, thermoforming, and permanent-cast interior works. The natural white finish on plaster still has much appeal; or castings can be painted or surfaced with plastic or metallic coatings.

The softest gypsum cements are those we refer to as "molding" or "art plasters." Selected grades of gypsum rock are used to produce high-strength plasters. U.S. Gypsum's trade-named products "hydro-stone" and "hydrocal" are two of the most readily available high-strength gypsum cements.

The ratio of water to plaster determines its consistency, setting time, density, and ultimate strength. Plaster usually requires 67 to 80 pounds of water; hydrocal requires 30 to 50 pounds of water, and hydro-stone requires 32 to 40 pounds per 100 pounds of material. In casting, it is desirable to keep the water content as low as possible and yet have a creamy, pourable mix.

If consistent results are to be achieved in determining mixtures, the best practice is to weigh the plaster and water proportions. In nonproduction sculptural casting, however, it is quite common to estimate the mix visually.

In preparing the casting mix, the plaster is sprinkled into the water and allowed to stand for several minutes, until fully dissolved. It can then be mixed by hand or with a mixing blade on an electric drill or drill press; or with a specially designed mixer. (Figure 3-1)

Sculptural gypsum-cement castings are usually simple solid castings with wire mesh, hardware cloth, or reinforcing-rod armatures. Reinforcing materials can be held in place, and away from the mold walls, with an occasional dab of plaster on the reinforcing materials, which are positioned in the mold as it is being assembled. The liquid mix is poured into the mold, which has been treated with a release agent. The mold is then vibrated to work out air bubbles and assure a dense surface. Vibration is achieved by tapping the mold with the hand, by placing the mold on a vibrator table, or by inserting an air-operated vibrator into the plaster mass for a few seconds. Hand tapping the mold is the simplest and most common approach. The mold is supported while casting in a bucket of sand, wooden or cardboard box; or, in the case of large molds, supports are built into the mold to make it self-supporting.

Plaster can also be molded in a layup or slush-molding technique in molds treated with appropriate release agents. The layup technique is

Figure 3-1

Small batch mixer for plaster and plastics. *Photograph courtesy of Plaster Supply House Industries, Inc.*

usually used only in relief molds, or if the inside of the form is accessible after the mold has been assembled. In this case, a layer of plaster is brushed or spattered on the inner facing of the mold to a thickness of about one-fourth inch. Subsequent coatings are built up by dipping strips of burlap or pieces of long fiber hemp in the plaster mix and applying it to the surface until the desired thickness is achieved. The edges of the built-up sections should be kept at a 45-degree angle to allow for joining the parts when the mold is assembled. If an exceptionally strong wall is desired, the final layer is reinforced with wire mesh such as hardware cloth or expanded metal. In this buildup technique, to assure good bonding, the layers should be moist. If a layer has been allowed to dry, it should be wet thoroughly before the application of the next layer.

After the plaster has been built up to the desired thickness on the mold parts, the mold is assembled, tied together with wire or twine, and held firmly with some dabs of plaster on the mold seams. The layup is completed by reaching into the mold and applying plaster along the seams, followed by layers of hemp and a final wire reinforcement. If the piece is so large that it is impossible to reach all the way into the mold, the

parts are joined as the mold is partially assembled.

Slush-molding with gypsum cements is only practical if the mold is small enough or light enough to handle. In this procedure, a small batch of plaster, hydrocal® or hydro-stone® is poured into the mold, and the mold is tumbled and rotated.

CAST STONE

Sculptural cast stone, a refined version of concrete, has excellent physical properties for interior and exterior works. In recent years, it has had wide aesthetic appeal to both sculptors and architects; the natural, warm, grey color has been used successfully in many sculptural and architectural applications. With color and aggregate additives it is possible to create a diversity of colored and textural effects. (Figures 3-2 through 3-6)

The ingredients in cast stone consist of portland cement, sand, and aggregates of varying size. A good distribution of particle size is desirable in the concrete mixture to produce a dense casting of maximum strength. (Figure 3-7) Rough concrete may have sand particles up to one-fourth inch in diameter and gravel particles up to one and a half inches. Fine cast-stone mixtures, consisting of marble dust and marble aggregates, at times do not exceed one-eighth inch for their largest particles. Large works obviously need larger particles to achieve the desired strength. Fine mixtures need a larger proportion of cement than coarse mixtures. The proportion of the coarse aggregate is usually larger than the proportion of fine aggregate as the aggregate size increases. With a maximum aggregate size of three-eighths inches the proportion would be about equal parts, coarse to fine. With maximum aggregate size up to one and a half inches the proportion would be about one-third fine to two-thirds coarse. One part Portland cement by weight is added to three or four parts of the fine-coarse aggregate mixture for a typical cast-stone mixture when the maximum aggregate size is around three-eighths inches. Mixtures with aggregate size up to one and a half inches would use four or five parts of the aggregate mixture. Very fine mixtures for small works have been mixed with proportions of equal parts cement and fine aggregate. Small batches of concrete can be hand mixed

Figure 3-2

Cast stone sculpture by author, 1958. *Lakeside Shopping Center, Denver, Colorado.*

Figure 3-3

Concrete being placed into plaster piece mold. (Note mechanical vibrator behind worker on the right. Sections of the mold are added as the mold is filled.)

Figure 3-4

Separator being applied to a mold section prior to the section's being placed on the mold. (Note that registration points on the edge of the mold are to insure alignment.)

Figure 3-5

Mold sections being removed.

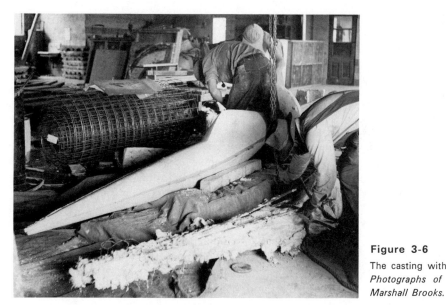

Figure 3-6
The casting with the final mold sections removed.
*Photographs of the casting process courtesy of
Marshall Brooks.*

A

Figure 3-7
Concrete sand and aggregates. (A) A well-graded
coarse aggregate mixture; (B) aggregate separated
showing sizes 1/4 to 3/8 inch, 3/8 to 3/4 inch and
3/4 to 1-1/2 inches; and (C) sample of well-
granded sand before and after separation. Particles
vary from dust to those passing the number 4 sieve
(approximately 1/4 inch.) *Photograph courtesy of
Portland Cement Association.*

B

C

with a shovel, whereas larger batches require a mechanical concrete-mixer.

In hand mixing with a shovel, the dry ingredients are first mixed in a mortar box or on a clean, flat surface, such as a piece of plywood or sheet metal. The water is then added while mixing until the mix reaches a pourable consistency.

In machine mixing, an appropriate amount of water is placed in the mixer, and the dry mix is added to the water until the desired consistency is achieved.

In the construction industry, the ratio of water to other ingredients is carefully measured to insure optimum results. Sculpturally, the primary concern is a matter of the pourability of the mix. Mold cavities with thin cross-sections and surface detail obviously need a thinner mix and smaller aggregates than large, open molds. Water-to-cement ratio can vary from .40 to .70 percent water (by weight) per pound of cement, depending on the aggregates, moisture content of the aggregate, and the desired consistency of the mix. Portland cement should be stored in a dry place. If it has lumps that cannot readily be crushed with the fingers, the cement should not be used.

Water content should be kept to a minimum to insure maximum strength in the casting. The mixture should not be watery; it should be like a thick paste or thicker. If the mixture is too thin, the aggregate will settle to the bottom of the mold, and the result will be a weak casting and poor distribution of the aggregate.

A cast-stone casting should not be allowed to dry out too quickly. Moisture is essential in a cast-concrete mass, in order to effect fully the chemical action in the setting of the concrete (hydration process) and to allow the mass to cure and reach full strength. Spraying the mold with water and keeping it covered with plastic film is advisable. After the casting is removed from the mold, it should be kept covered with damp cloths and wrapped with plastic film for a week to ten days.

Portland cement is produced by applying heat to a wet or dry material such as limestone, marl, chalks, clay, silica, blast-furnace slag, slate, etc. The ground material is passed through rotating kilns. The resulting discharged clinkers are cooled and ground to a fine powder to produce the finished sacks of cement.

A sack of Portland cement weighs 94 pounds and is one cubic foot in volume. Portland cement is available in several forms. Most commonly used is Type 1 Portland cement, a general, all-purpose material—most likely found at the lumber yard or builder's supply house when you simply ask for cement.

High early-strength Portland cement, as the name suggests, is used when it is desirable to have concrete reach its maximum strength quickly. Although more expensive, it is recommended if the cast material cannot be allowed adequate curing in the mold. White cement is available for white or light-colored castings.

Low-heat Portland cement is used in casting large masses in which the heat produced by hydration may need to be controlled. Air entraining cements are used for producing frost-resistant concrete. Portland Pozzolan cements are used largely for underwater structures and dams.

General-purpose, white, and high early-strength Portland cements are generally used for casting small and moderate-sized works in the studio and classroom. Large, outdoor works, formed and cast in place, may require special cements and mixtures. In works of this scale, the sculptor should rely on competent architectural and engineering advice, and the work should be cast by a recognized concrete contractor.

Accelerators, retarders, and air-entraining agents are added to concrete to alter physical properties and working conditions. Hot water or calcium chloride (one to two pounds per sack of cement) are utilized as accelerators. Retarders are used to lengthen the working time and delay the stiffening action of the concrete. When an exposed-aggregate surface is desired, they can be brushed on mold surfaces to prevent surface setting of the concrete. Manufacturer's recommendations should be carefully followed in the use of retarders. Excess quantities of a retarder in a concrete mixture can seriously affect the ultimate strength and quality of the casting.

Air-entraining agents are used to produce solider, weather-resistant concrete castings with blemish-free surfaces. Requiring less water and possessing better workability, these materials should be investigated for casting large architectural outdoor sculpture.

Aggregates can be sand, natural rocks and pebbles of varied sizes, or rocks crushed and graded to size. Sands are available as concrete- or masonry-sand, with a good distribution of particle sizes, as illustrated in Figure 3-7. In cast sculpture, finely graded white silica sands are often used. Finely pulverized marble is often used as a substitute for sand in cast-stone mixtures. Crushed marble aggregates provide a wide choice of color in cast sculpture, when combined with colored, pigmented cast-stone mixtures. Cinders, haydite, perlite, and vermiculite are used as lightweight aggregates.

Aggregates should be clean and free from organic contaminates. The selection of an aggregate depends on the visual and physical properties desired in the cast sculpture. For exterior work in which finely finished, smooth surfaces are desired, abrasion and moisture resistance of the aggregate must be considered. Surfaces with soft aggregates can be affected by wind and abrasive particles in the atmosphere. Soft aggregates that absorb moisture can easily deteriorate in freezing temperatures. Soft surfaces can be protected with appropriate sealers.

A limited range of colored pigments (cement colors) for coloring concrete is available from building-materials suppliers. A broader range of color can be achieved by using standard powdered pigments provided by paint distributors and manufacturers. Colors are best determined by mixing sample of the material, prior to casting. Proportions of pigment, cement, and aggregate should be determined by weight or volume. The sample should be allowed to set and dry, to determine its true color. If a sealer is used on the casting, it will darken the color somewhat and should be applied on the sample to determine the final results.

Graded particle-size is determined by passing the materials through wire-mesh sieves and counting the number of openings per linear inch. For example a "100-mesh silica sand" means that 100 particles, placed edge to edge in a row, measure approximately an inch.

Permanent, versatile, and inexpensive, cast stone can be cast in almost any mold material. Plaster, wood, reinforced fiberglass, sheet metal, plastics, rubber, sand, clay, earth, and cardboard have all been used to contain poured cast-stone mixtures. Besides molds produced from formed patterns, direct molds built out of earth, sand, clay, styrofoam, cardboard, wood, and sheet metal provide an opportunity to work spontaneously and directly. (Figure 3-8 through 3-15 show the procedure involved in casting a large-scale architectural work by Albert S. Vrana.)

Figure 3-8

Preparation for large-scale concrete casting. Drawing from cartoon to full-scale work on polystrene foam backing.

Figure 3-9

Negative mold being developed with sheets of polystrene foam.

Figure 3-10
Grinding and hand-sanding mold to finish the form.

Figure 3-11
Mold being placed in wooden concrete forms to prepare for casting.

Figure 3-12
Concrete being placed in the forms.

Figure 3-13
Picking up panels and stripping off molds.

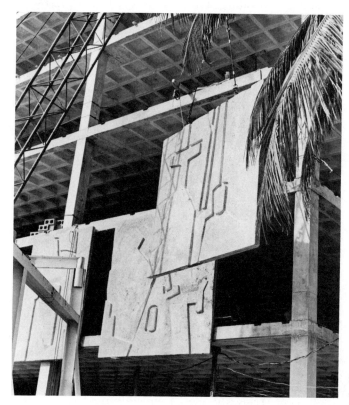

Figure 3-14
Erection of the pre-cast panels.

Figure 3-15
Front view of building, installation completed. *Sculpture relief by Albert S. Vrana. Photographs courtesy of Albert S. Vrana.*

Normally, mold surfaces should be nonporous for reproducing smooth cast-surfaces. Porous surfaces can absorb moisture, weakening the casting, and can produce defective surface qualities. Plaster, wood, and cardboard molds can be saturated with oily or waxy release agents without the use of a sealer. The excess release agent should be wiped off. This technique provides good separation, with a minimum amount of release agent transferred to the cast surface.

When pouring concrete into direct relief-molds of earth, sand, and clay, the mold material is kept sufficiently moist to prevent excessive moisture absorption from the mix. The cast-stone mixture is also poured slightly wetter, to compensate for some moisture absorption. These techniques produce a rough textural surface, with some of the mold material adhering to the casting and adding to the surface texture of the cast. Coarse aggregates, metallic pieces, and other materials are often placed on the mold surface and adhere to the casting to produce textural effects.

Nonporous mold materials, such as rubber, plastic, reinforced fiberglass, and metal, will readily release from cast stone, with the application of a thin film of oil or wax.

Since concrete does not possess high tensile strength, steel reinforcing-materials are included in the cast work. The reinforcing is usually deformed rod or wire mesh. Deformed rod has slight projections, or lugs, which provide a mechanical bond to the cast stone.

The problems encountered in pouring a concrete mass are relative to the size of the casting. Small works can be cast readily with a single batch of material, whereas large works may require several or many batches. When more than one batch is required, it is necessary to mix all the needed dry ingredients at one time or to measure carefully each batch to assure uniformity in the mix; this is particularly essential with colored or exposed-aggregate mixtures.

For a dense mixture, the poured mass needs to be packed and vibrated to eliminate air entrapment. For small molds, hand tapping the mold, or vibrating the table the mold is on, is sufficient. A mechanical vibrating table is advisable if casting becomes a daily operation. On large molds, mechanical, air-operated vibrators are inserted into the poured mass to disperse air entrapment, and air-driven tamping devices are sometimes used to compact the material.

Concrete surfaces can be left in their as-cast condition, coated with paints and metallic coatings; or the aggregates can be exposed. Aggregates are exposed by wirebrushing, acid etching with diluted solutions of muriatic acid, mechanical grinding, polishing, or sandblasting. If a rough-aggregate surface is to be exposed, special retarding compounds can be brushed on the mold surface. These compounds prevent the concrete surface from hardening. The surface is then simply brushed or washed with water to expose the aggregate.

PLASTICS

Commercially, a large volume of plastic articles is cast by injection molding, rotational molding, and match-die molding. Large, reinforced-plastic articles such as boat hulls are often formed in open molds with spray application of resin and reinforcing material. Cast resins and fillers are used for large industrial castings.

The two plastic-casting methods used in sculpture are reinforced plastics in open-faced molds and cast resin, or resins and fillers, in closed molds. Slush molding and rotational molding are used to produce hollow castings in closed molds.

Casting of any resin should not be attempted without first becoming familiar with the safety precautions outlined in Chapter 15.

SOLID CASTINGS

In solid plastic casting we will consider casting in clear and tinted pure resin and resins with filler additives.

In recent years, considerable interest has developed in the visual properties and possibilities of clear and tinted solid-castings for sculpture. Polyester resins, the most frequently used, are the simplest to handle, inexpensive, reasonably clear, and nonyellowing. Acrylic resins are being cast with dramatic results by some sculptors. For clear castings, the optical properties of this material are superior to any other plastic. However, the technique and equipment necessary for casting are far more complex than for casting polyester.

SOLID CASTING POLYESTER

In clear-casting with polyester resins, the selection of a good quality, clear-casting resin is of prime importance. These resins are formulated to accommodate some of the problems unique to casting thick layers and masses, and are different from laminating- or general-purpose resins. They usually contain less or different promoters and are more flexible.

The principal problem in casting large masses of resin is in controlling excess heat and thermo-expansion as the mass polymerizes. Fractures and discoloration are the result if polymerization is too rapid. A fixed ratio of catalyst to resin does not exist. Room temperature, mold material, and the size of the casting are always relative to the amount of required catalyst. The best starting point is the manufacturer's recommendations. Most sculptors working with large cast forms have found it necessary to experiment to arrive at workable percentages of catalyst to resin. The amount of catalyst can vary from .01 percent to a small fraction of that amount. Large castings of ten to twelve inches in thickness may simply require about one hundred drops per gallon of resin. A reasonable starting point at 72 degrees room temperature is 3 or 4 drops per ounce for one inch thickness and 2 or 3 drops per ounce for 2 inch thickness. An 8 inch cube would require 150 to 180 drops per gallon. Methyl ethyl ketone peroxide is normally used for the catalyst.

A few guidelines for controlling temperature on thick castings follow:

Use a minimum amount of catalyst and allow a maximum amount of curing time. A huge mass of resin can be allowed several days to a week to cure. If the cure is not complete, post-curing can be accomplished with heat. A simple oven can be constructed of insulation board with several 150 watt light bulbs mounted inside to produce a low temperature. This low-temperature postcure may take from several hours to a full day or more, depending on the size of the casting. (Postcuring is also a good way to accelerate the dissipation of the styrene-monomer solvent from the cast mass.)

Work at room temperature (72 to 75 degrees Fahrenheit) when possible, increasing the catalyst for lower temperatures and decreasing it for higher ones. Ninety-to-100-degree summer temperatures can require considerable reduction in the quantity of the catalyst.

If a cast resin mass has gelled and appears to be curing too fast, it can be submerged in cold water to assist in the dissipation of the heat.

When possible, molds with low-insulating qualities should be used. Water cooling a fiberglass mold would be more effective than water cooling a plaster, wood, or rubber mold.

If possible, cast large masses or blocks in layers of one-half to one inch. This should be done in a relatively dust-free environment. The block for the cast sculpture in Figure 3-16 was cast in this fashion.

From one to ten percent flexible resin can be added to the general-purpose resin, increasing flexibility and allowing greater expansion before fracturing occurs. However, when possible, start with an appropriate resin designed for casting.

Solid castings in polyester, or epoxy resins with fillers, pose less problems than clear castings; the fillers act as reinforcement and absorb some of the heat; catalyzing is less critical.

To receive fillers, resins should be thinner than laminating resins if they are to receive large amount of filler. Resins are not thick enough to hold coarse fillers in suspension without the addition of fine-grade fillers. Thick (thicksotropic) resins with fine grade fillers are available from sup-

Figure 3-16

Cast polyester sculpture. *By Roger Kotoske.*

pliers or fine-grade fillers can be added to the resin. Fillers in resin are like sand and gravel in concrete mixtures. A reasonable distribution of particles, sizes, or fibers is essential for optimum strength. If the resin is not thick enough to hold the largest particles in suspension, they will settle to the bottom of the mold, resulting in an unsatisfactory casting. Heavy fillers, such as crushed rock, need thicker resins (or a more appropriate balance of fine particles) than lightweight fillers, such as milled fiber, asbestos, or perlite.

Filler particles vary in size from powders measured in microns (millionths of a meter) to coarse fibers and crushed rocks.

Aerated silica (Cab-O-Sil®) is an excellent fine-grade filler that is often used. Tripoli, diatomaceous earth, Kaolinite, aluminum silica, magnesium silica, mica, wood flour, shell flour, calcium silicate, and calcium carbonate are other fine-grade fillers. Pigments and metallic powders act as fillers, besides producing desired visual effects.

Fibrous fillers can be asbestos, cotton flock and linter, chopped cotton cord, jute, rayon fibers, nylon flock and chopped fabric, polyester fibers, and chopped glass fibers.

Granular fillers may be sand, crushed rock, saw dust, vermiculite, perlite, glass spheres or nodules, and plastic materials. With an appropriate resin water can be used as an extender instead of a filler. Water-extendable resins that increase the volume of resin by 50 percent are available. The water is blended into the resin with a mechanical mixer, resulting in a cream-like emulsion. (Figure 3-17)

One of the simplest, most available fillers is perlite, which can be mixed with a resin. About 90 percent resin and 10 percent perlite by weight are used. About one cup of Cab-O-Sil® per gallon of resin can be added to help keep the perlite in suspension. The Cab-O-Sil® should be mixed with a small amount of resin and blended (with a mixer blade on a drill) into a paste before it is added it to the mixture.

Fillers may serve the sole purpose of reinforcing the casting, or may be exposed to form decorative finishes. Fillers may be exposed by casting transparent or translucent forms, or the surfaces can be abrasive-finished. Abrasive-finishing procedures are similar to the finishing methods outlined in Chapter 10.

Resins should be cast in nonporous molds. Any mold material is adequate as long as it will withstand the weight and pressure of the cast material. Mold cavities produced through the lost-

Figure 3-17
Typical fillers left to right. Top row: asbestos fibers, glass nodules, perlite. Bottom row: chopped fiberglass strands, sand, Cab-O-Sil®.

wax process can be filled with resins to produce hollow castings. In this case, the release agent is poured into the mold and then poured out. In casting resins, separation can be accomplished by using wax-based, release agents, if the casting is to be abrasive-finished. For cast surfaces that are to be polished or coated, the mold can be coated with a thin layer of wax, which is subsequently buffed. A layer of water-soluble release agent (polyvinyl alcohol) is sprayed over the wax coating. This is easily washed off the casting after it has been removed from the mold. Silicone, flurocarbon, polyethylene and other plastic release-agents can be used as well. Paintable silicone, or polymer release-agents that do not require removal, can be used when the casting is to be painted.

ACRYLIC CASTING

Acrylic (methyl methacrylate monomer) is available in forms of resin, powder, small beads, and pellets.

Resins are available as inhibited and uninhibited, syrupy liquids. Inhibitors are added to some resins to prevent them from polymerizing before they are used. The uninhibited resin is normally used by sculptors for clear casting, to produce the best optical clarity. Inhibitors can be removed from acrylic resins by means of chemical washing or by a process of distillation. When optical properties are of less concern to the sculptor, the action of the inhibitor can be overcome by the catalyzation process.

Pigments, dyes, ultraviolet absorbers, destaticizing agents, plasticizers, and other additives are present in resins or powders, or they can be added prior to casting. Powders, beads, and pellets are often supplied in color.

As stated earlier, casting acrylic is far more difficult than casting polyesters and epoxies. Heat, pressure, and precise control are necessary for casting masses exceeding one-half inch in thickness. Controlling exotherm (heat), shrinkage, and stresses is difficult and requires complex and expensive equipment.

When exotherm becomes excessive in atmospheric pressure in acrylic casting, the monomer begins to boil, causing a bubbly and foamy appearance to the casting. This can only be controlled by casting under pressure and in a pressure autoclave. Shrinkage can be controlled by mold design and partially reduced by prepolymerizing the resin prior to casting.

Shrinkage problems are simple in casting flat sheets and tubes, since the mass can move as it is shrinking. In sculptural molds with projections and undercuts, stresses must be relieved. Shrinkage and polymerization should occur at the slowest possible rate. Molds that will move with the shrinkage, or break as shrinkage occurs, should be considered. Stresses are relieved by proper annealing.

Benzoyl peroxide is the catalyst ordinarily used. If colored pigments or dyes are used, a catalyst such as azo diisolbutyronitrile might be used since benzoyl peroxide can produce bleached effects in colored castings. The quantity of catalyst is minute in large, massive castings and may require only a few drops or one- or two-thousandths of a part per gallon of resin.

Industrially, sheets are cast between glass sheets; rods and tubes are cast in aluminum tubes. As the acrylic shrinks, it separates naturally from the mold surface. Any nonporous mold material can be used for sculptural castings. Sealed porous molds, such as plaster, must be dry. Thin coatings of stearic acid, fluorocarbon, or silicone release-agents can be used when necessary.

Besides cast resins, monomer-polymer slurries can be made. Fine acrylic powders are added to their monomers at about a 50-50 ratio. As the powder is added to the liquid monomer,, the powder dissolves and swells, forming a thick liquid or slurry. Dyes, pigments, etc. can be added, or colored powders can be used. Shrinkage and exothermic heat are less of a problem in cast slurries than in cast resins.

In casting a large mass, the sculptor prepares the resin or slurry mixture. A vacuum is applied to the mixture to remove air; the mixture is poured into the mold, and the mold is placed in an autoclave. Heat and pressure is then applied. The autoclave should be professionally designed, with proper safety controls; pressures may be as high as 100 pounds per square inch and are hazardous if attempted in inadequate equipment; also, fumes from resins can be highly flammable; necessary precautions should be taken.

Polymerization for large castings may require

from one day to several weeks. Temperatures are started low (90 to 115 degrees) and slowly increased to 150 to 250 degrees. The final temperature cycle may also serve as an annealing process, after which the temperature is gradually reduced until the casting reaches room temperature. Programmed timers are used to control temperature.

If a casting receives postmachining and finishing, it is necessary to give it a final annealing to remove the stresses produced by these operations. This is accomplished by slowly heating and cooling, as in the polymerization process. Pressure is not necessary for annealing. The maximum annealing temperature can be 230 degrees, or the work may be annealed at a lower temperature by extending the annealing time. (Figures 3-18 and 3-19)

Figure 3-18
Cast acrylic sculpture. *By Mac Whitney.*

FIBERGLASS-REINFORCED PLASTICS

Polyester resins are usually used in fiberglass-reinforced plastic. Epoxy resins can be used when their physical properties are considered more desirable. In fiberglass-reinforced plastics, the glass fibers bond with the resins to form a strong, homogeneous sheet or part. Ultimate tensile strength of glass-fiber laminates can be from 30,000 to 50,000 pounds per square inch.

The catalyst used, as with polyester-resin casting, is normally methyl ethyl ketone peroxide. The catalyst is added to the resin at the rate of one-half to one and a half percent. As the amount of catalyst added to the resin is increased, the setting-time decreases. The amount of catalyst should not exceed two percent. Ideally, the tem-

Figure 3-19
Acrylic casting by Mac Whitney. Surfaces being planed with a power plane prior to abrasive finishing and polishing.

perature of the room should not be less than 70 degrees. Cooler temperatures can affect the curing of the resin, unless catalyst is added to compensate for the lower temperature. General-purpose resins for fiberglass layup are readily available from plastic supply companies. Cab-O-Sil® can be used to thicken the resin when needed; styrene monomer can be added if the resin needs to be thinned.

Fiberglass reinforcing-materials are available in veil, matt, roving, woven roving, and cloth. Veil is a thin layer of glass fibers about ten mils thick. It is often used as the layer next to the gel coat to assure the absence of air bubbles between the gel coat and the subsequent layer of glass fiber. Matt is made of chopped strands of glass fiber up to two inches long, and has less strength than cloth. Standard thicknesses are from three-fourths to three ounces per square foot. Roving, untwisted strands of glass fiber available in cylindrical packages, is used in the sprayup process, in which it is chopped and fed into the stream of sprayed resin. Woven roving, a coarse weave of untwisted strands of glass fiber, is stronger than matt and conforms more readily to contours. It weighs from 13 to 27 ounces per square yard. Cloth is the strongest woven material and comes in weights from two to 40 ounces per square yard. It is available in different types of weaves, such as twill, crowfoot, or satin. Satin is the strongest and conforms most readily to curved surfaces. (Figure 3-20)

The two most common methods of working with fiberglass are hand layup or spray application. Hand layup, most often used sculpturally, is one of the simplest and most inexpensive ways of producing reinforced fiberglass in sculptural molds.

HAND LAYUP

For fiberglass layup, if the mold is porous, it is sealed with two coats of lacquer or three-lb. cut shellac. Aerosol spray cans of lacquer are convenient for small molds. After the lacquer or shellac has dried, the mold should be coated with paste wax, such as Johnson's, or a wax separator designed for plastic molding. Do not apply the wax too thickly. After the wax has dried, it should be buffed with a soft cloth, and a second coat should be applied. After it has dried, it should again be

Figure 3-20

Fiberglass mat, (left); fiberglass cloth (right).

buffed lightly. If the final molding is to be painted, the mold should be coated with a separating film of polyvinyl alcohol. This can be washed off easily with water after the molding has been removed. It is also possible to use paintable release-agents rather than the wax and polyvinyl alcohol.

The first coating on the mold is called the "gel coat." It is slightly more flexible, has better impact strength, and keeps the glass fiber from showing on the surface of the casting. Prepared gel coats can be purchased in a wide variety of colors from resin suppliers, or it is possible to add your own coloring agents. In industrial application, the gel coat is sprayed on. A DeVilbiss-JJA502 spray gun with an E-fluid tip and 704 air cap can be used. An R-2 all-material spray gun also works quite satisfactorily. If spray equipment is not available, the gel coat can be brushed on, but the results are not as satisfactory. For simple beginning castings in which there is not a great concern for technical perfection, a gel coat can be made by adding Cab-O-Sil® to the general purpose resin used for the layup. Mix the resin with the CaB-O-Sil® with a mixing blade on an electric drill. Mix a rather thick paste first (this assures good blending of the Cab-O-Sil® and the resin) and then thin with additional resin until the desired brushing con-

Figure 3-23

Roller for working out air bubbles in fiberglass layup.

Figure 3-21

Fiberglass layup into a negative mold. Note explosion-proof fan with enclosed motor in background, also protective mask and rubber gloves on worker.

Figure 3-22

Fiberglass layup over a positive mold. *Student project, Southern Methodist University.*

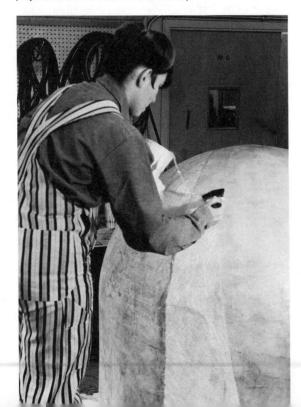

sistency is achieved. Then add two percent catalyst per volume of mixture and brush on the mold surface. Be certain that the mold surface is at a room temperature of at least 70 degrees, or the coating may not set. As well as coloring agents, metallic powders can be added to the gel coat (from 150 to 300 mesh). After the casting is removed, the surface can be made metallic by light sanding and polishing. In this case, apply two layers of gel coat to be certain that the abrasive finishing does not go through to the fiberglass backup material.

After the gel coat has set, mix a container of resin with catalyst and brush part of the resin onto a section of the mold surface (about one square foot). Stick a piece of three-fourths-ounce mat or veil (two inches by two inches or larger depending on the contour of the mold) on the wetted mold surface and dab with brush and resin until the matting is saturated. Repeat this process, overlapping the matt or veil pieces until the mold is covered. Be certain to work out all the air bubbles as the matt and resin are applied. For larger, flat surfaces, greater areas of the surface can be wetted with resin and larger pieces of matting can be used. A special roller can be used to roll down the

57

resin-saturated matting to squeeze out all the air bubbles.

The next layer should be three-fourths or one and a half-ounce matting, depending on the thickness desired. For small moldings of no more than two square feet of surface, an additional three-fourths ounce is adequate for a lightweight casting. For larger works, the second layer should be one and a half ounce. This might be two layers of three-fourths ounce, if the contours are complex. The next layer should be woven roving or six to ten-ounce cloth. If it is the final layer, cloth should be used. For extremely large layup in which additional strength is required, the remaining layers should be alternating layers of matt and woven roving. The molding will release more readily from the mold if it is removed as soon as the resin has set or polymerized. Some of the heat from the polymerization process tends to soften the wax release-agent that facilitates the removal of the molding.

Resins can be mixed in paper-disposable containers or cups. Do not use polystyrene cups, as the resin will dissolve the styrene. A container can be used more than one time, if the film of resin left in the cup is allowed to set before it is used again. Acetone can be used for cleaning brushes and equipment. Rubber gloves or disposable plastic gloves should be worn. It is best to work in a well-ventilated area, as resin solvents and catalysts are toxic. (Figures 3-21, 3-22, and 3-23)

SPRAYUP MOLDING

In the sprayup process, a spray gun with a chopper is used to apply the resin and glass fiber over the gel coat. The chopper cuts the glass fiber and propels it toward the mold surface. The chopped fiber converges with the stream of catalyzed resin from the gun and is deposited on the mold surface. The roving is fed to the chopper from spools mounted on the machine. The air supply to the machine should be at least 5 H.P. and should be able to maintain a working pressure of 100 p.s.i. Figure 3-24 illustrates a typical sprayup machine.

METAL CASTING

Metal casting (often referred to as founding) is one of the oldest of metal crafts practiced by many; nonferrous casting dates back to the Bronze Age (3,000 to 5,000 B.C.). Although casting and the related metallurgy are handled industrially with great precision, the principles remain essentially the same.

A mold is needed to receive the metal. The metal must be contained in a crucible, or the furnace itself, for melting, and a refractory material is needed for construction of the furnace. A fuel is needed to produce heat, and an air supply is

Figure 3-24
Fiberglass spray equipment. *Photograph courtesy of Glas-Craft of California.*

needed to increase the rate of combustion and elevate temperatures.

Mold materials, metals, and refractories are all natural, earth materials. Early melting furnaces were constructed easily out of clay, stone, or fired ceramic blocks. Wood was used as a fuel, and simple bellows were used for delivering the air.

Metal for casting may be classified as ferrous or nonferrous. Ferrous metals are those primarily containing iron and generally susceptible to corrosion. Nonferrous metals are more corrosion-resistant. We ordinarily think of copper-based alloys and aluminum as nonferrous metals. Zinc, lead, tin, nickel, silver, manganese, gold, platinum, and cadmium are also nonferrous materials. Many of these are used as additives or alloying agents to alter the properties of copper or aluminum.

In copper alloys, lead increases tensil strength and ductility. A small amount of lead exists in almost every alloy. Zinc improves fluidity and hardness. Nickel and silicon increase structural density, strength, and corrosion resistance. Tin increases strength and hardness.

Today, hundreds of alloys meet specific performance needs in metal casting and fabrication. Few sculptors need to become overly involved in these complexities. Suitable alloys are readily available for casting and fabrication. Ordinarily, it is better to purchase new ingots for casting than to attempt to use scrap; with this approach, it is possible to know the precise characteristics of the metal being cast and casting requirements. Suppliers should be able to supply specification sheets on their alloys. Descriptions of some of the most common metals follow.

Aluminum. Principal alloying elements are copper, magnesium, silicon, zinc, and tin in small percentages. In casting aluminum, alloys specifically designed for casting should be used.

Bronze. Tin is the principal alloy, with additives of zinc and lead. Seventy to 90 percent copper, ten to 20 percent tin, and the remainder zinc and lead is a typical bronze. However, in traditional bronzes, such as "statuary bronze," "bell bronze," and "art bronze," it is more likely that there would be close-to-equal portions of tin and zinc.

Commercial bronze. This is actually a brass, with ten to 12 percent zinc as the alloying agent.

Muntz metal. This is a brass with about 40 percent zinc and 60 percent copper.

Silicon bronze. This alloy is one to three percent silicon, 94 to 98 percent copper, and one to two percent additives of aluminum or manganese.

Tobin bronze. This is 60 percent copper, about 39 percent zinc, and the remainder, tin.

Manganese bronze. This is 58 percent copper, about 39 percent zinc, one percent tin, and a fractional amount of manganese.

Aluminum bronze. This alloy is 82 to 95 percent copper, with the balance in aluminum; some aluminum bronzes have fractional amounts of tin or manganese.

Brass. Any copper-based material that has zinc as its principal alloy is classified as brass. At times, these may be called "bronze," but metallurgically they should be classified as "brass." Brasses vary considerably as to zinc content. Copper content may be as high as 95 percent, with the zinc content varying from five to 40 percent. Pure brass is a copper-zinc alloy. Leaded brasses make up a whole area of brasses, with lead added in fractional amounts up to about three or four percent. Special brasses have fractional percentages of tin, lead, aluminum, phosphorous, or manganese.

Phosphor bronzes. These are up to 98 percent copper, with the balance in tin and a fractional amount of phosphorous. In some cases, one to four percent lead is included.

Pewter. This is comprised of lead and tin, or tin, copper and antimony; the percentage of tin is about 80 percent.

Nickel-bearing copper alloys. These are 45 to 65 percent copper, 17 to 42 percent zinc, and ten to 18 percent nickel, with a fractional amount of manganese. At times they are referred to as German silver, monel, iconel, or nickel silver.

Low-melting-point alloys. These consist of cadmium, tin, bismuth, and lead, and melt at temperatures of 140 to 180 degrees Fabrenheit. Lipowitz alloy consists of three parts cadmium, four parts tin, 15 parts bismuth, and eight parts lead. It softens at 140 degrees and melts at 158 degrees. Woods metal consists of four parts lead, two parts tin, five to eight parts bismuth, and one to two parts cadmium. It melts at between 140 to 161 degrees.

Cast iron is the ferrous metal usually cast by sculptors. It has a reasonably low melting point of 2,100 to 2,200 degrees Fahrenheit and is melted readily in a cupola furnace. Steel has enjoyed less aesthetic appeal than bronze and other nonferrous metals. The need for higher working temperatures and, subsequently, more costly equipment has undoubtedly discouraged wider sculptural use of it as a casting material.

Steel is available in a wide variety of alloys. The carbon content largely determines the physical properties of steel. Carbon lowers the melting point and the steel becomes harder, stronger, more brittle, and wear-resistant. Other alloys such as nickel and manganese improve toughness. Tungsten and chromium carbide improve wear resistance; chromium provides corrosion resistance, as in stainless steel. Copper provides resistance to the atmosphere, and silicon acts as a deoxidizing agent and adds to its strength.

Principal factors involved in metal casting are the properties and characteristics of the metal being poured, the molds and dewaxing of the molds, the furnace and melting procedures, the pouring of the metal, mold removal, and final finishing of the casting. (Figure 3-25)

FURNACES

A furnace is a heat-producing device operating at temperatures above 1000 degrees Fahrenheit. Furnaces for melting metal may be classified as to the method of metal removal, the kind of heat energy, and the method of containing the metal during the melting process.

The metal is either melted in a refractory crucible placed in the furnace or directly in the refractory-lined furnace. A major distinction exists between the two approaches, since, in the second approach, the melting metal often comes directly into contact with the combustion.

The heat energy may be coke, coal, natural or butane gas, oil, or electrical energy.

Molten metal is removed from a furnace by liftout, baleout, tapout, or tilting. Liftout is associated with the crucible furnace from which the crucible of molten metal is removed. Baleout is a matter of ladling or scooping out quantities of metal from a crucible- or other-type furnace. In tapout, a plug is removed from a tap hole allowing the metal to flow out into a receiving ladle. Tilting furnaces tilt to discharge the metal into the ladle.

Aluminum	1225
Aluminum Alloys	900–1250
Anitmony	1160
Brasses	1550–1875
Bronzes	1300–1900
Cast Iron	2050–2200
Chromium Nickel Cast Iron	2100
Chromium	2925
Copper	1980
Cobalt	2690
Gold	1950
Hard Steel	2560
Iconel Metal	2475
Lead	625
Lead Alloys	150–650
Manganese	2300
Manganese Bronze	1590
Magnesium	1200
Magnesium Alloys	650–1200
Mild Steel	2725
Monel Metal	2475
Nickel	2650
Nickel Steel & Iron	2150–2775
Pure Iron	2800
Red Brass	1860
Silver	1760
Silicon	2580
Silicon Bronze	1850
Stainless Steel 12% Cr.	2760
Tin	450
Tin Alloys	375–650
Tobin Bronze	1640
Wrought Iron	2700–2900
Zinc	790

Figure 3-25

Melting points of metals (degrees Fahrenheit).

The blast furnace is used to produced iron from iron ore. The open-heart furnace processes the iron into steel. Reverberatory furnaces are used in producing copper.

The fuel-operated cupola furnace is used in the production of cast iron and in melting large quantities of copper or copper alloys. It is a relatively simple device. Art-department foundries and sculptors doing large castings often use the cupola for melting bronze or cast iron. A simple drop-bottom cupola furnace can be built out of 55-gallon steel drums welded together. (Figure 3-26)

The cupola furnace is essentially a refractory-lined, vertical-steel cylinder. The lining may be brick or a refractory that is stuccoed, troweled, or rammed in place. A drop door is located at the bottom of the furnace, in order to clean out ashes and unburned coke. The other parts of the furnace

stack

charging door

metal charges

charging floor

limestone charges

coke charges

air

air chamber

tuyeres

slag spout

molten metal

rammed sand bottom

drop bottom door

prop to hold door closed

clean out door

bott (clay plug)

tapping spout

DIAGRAM OF CUPOLA FURNACE

Figure 3-26
The cupola furnace.

consist of a tap hole to discharge the metal, a slag hole to draw off slag, the tuyeres (or holes to introduce air into the furnace), a bell-shaped enclosure or wind chamber around the tuyeres to direct the air, and a charging door.

In the operation of a cupola furnace, the bottom is lined with green sand and a coke fire is built up to the level of the tuyeres. (The tuyeres may be anywhere from 12 to 48 inches from the bottom of the furnace, depending on the furnace size and whether the metal is collected in the bottom of the furnace or is continuously discharged.) Blowers or gas burners may be used to start the fire. As soon as the coke fire is burning freely, the tap hole is plugged with a lump of earth clay; the

fire is built up above the tuyeres. An initial charge of metal is placed on the fire, followed by alternating layers of metal, coke, and limestone. The initial charge could be anywhere from 100 to 150 pounds or more, depending on the size of the furnace. The proportion of metal to coke can vary from seven to ten pounds of metal per pound of coke. The limestone is added as a fluxing agent at the rate of about 20 to 30 percent.

After the furnace has been charged through the charging door, the air is turned on and, as the coke burns, the metal melts and flows to the bottom of the cupola. Additional charges of material can be added as the charges burn and melt.

The metal is allowed to accumulate in the

bottom of the furnace, or it is allowed to flow out continuously into receiving ladles as the melt proceeds. In a continuous melt, the tap hole would not be closed. If the metal is allowed to accumulate, the tap hole would be closed at the time the furnace door was closed. Another practice is to leave the tap hole open until the metal begins to run. This procedure is used as a safeguard to prevent the metal from freezing around the tap hole. To close the tap hole and stop the flow of metal, a clay lump is rammed into the hole with a bott stick. The bott stick is a steel rod with a small, flat metal disc on the end. The clay is fastened to the metal disc.

Periodically, slag may need to be tapped off through the slag hole. This is accomplished by letting the molten metal build up to the level of the slag hole. At this point, the slag hole is unplugged and the slag flows off the top of the molten metal.

After completion of the melt, the ashes, slag and unburned coke are immediately removed from the furnace.

Electric furnaces are most prevalent in steel foundries. Lack of contamination enables the foundry to alloy and process metal with a great deal of precision in these furnaces. In electric-induction furnaces, current passes through coils surrounding

SIMPLE CRUCIBLE FURNACE

Figure 3-28

Simple melting furnace.

Figure 3-27

Small crucible furnace with controls. Note ingots on top of furnace being preheated.
(Other views of furnace in figures 3-32, 3-33.)

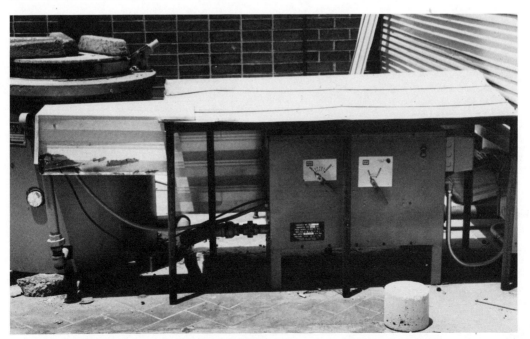

the metal-charged crucible or furnace. Electric energy passing through the charge melts the metal. Electric-arc furnaces are of several varieties. The electrode may be submerged in the metal; it may be above the metal charge, with the arc occuring between the metal charge and the electrode; or the arc may be over the metal charge, between two electrodes.

The gas-fired, liftout-crucible furnace is the type most frequently seen around sculpture departments and studios. Used primarily for melting nonferrous metals, it is simple to build and operate. In this furnace, the flame enters at an angle at the bottom of the furnace and travels in a circular pattern around the crucible to a hole in the lid. These furnaces either stand upright on the floor or are pit furnaces, buried in the floor. Crucible furnaces may melt quantities of metal up to several thousand pounds. (Figures 3-27 and 3-28)

Since most melting by the student or sculptor would be in a crucible-type furnace, further discussion of metal casting will focus on this technique For the average sculpture studio, a furnace of 100- to 200-lbs. capacity is more than adequate. Cast sections of that weight can be readily welded together. Some sculptors, however, prefer a single casting and some techniques require it. In this

case, far larger melting and handling facilities are essential. Whenever possible, it is perhaps advisable to put the job of large castings into the hands of competent art foundries.

From the small crucible furnace, the crucible is lifted with a one- or two-man crucible tong. The tongs should be designed so that they can be adjusted to hold the crucible firmly without applying excessive pressure on it. Large crucibles are removed with a lifting tackle attached to an overhead hoist on a monorail. The pour may take place directly from the crucible, or the metal may be transferred to a pouring ladle. Large quantities are also bailed out, or, in the case of a tilting furnace, poured. For large amounts of metal, the ladle may be preheated, or heat from a ladle warmer may be directed on the ladle to maintain the temperature of the metal. A ladle warmer can be built in the same fashion as the building burners seen in Figure 3-29.

Although commercial furnaces with manual or automatic controls are expensive, they are well worth the investment. Many sculptors construct their own melting furnace by improvising or buying the necessary components. A simple, inexpensive furnace would consist of a refractory-lined

Figure 3-29

Simple burner design.

FORCED-AIR BURNER FOR SMALL CRUCIBLE FURNACE
IN FIGURE 3-28

steel container, a lid, a burner, and an air supply.

Refractories are available as bricks, preformed shapes, castable material, or material that can be stuccoed, or rammed in place. These materials are readily available in any major city. The castable, or stucco materials are less expensive than brick and are very adequate in the studio where firing is only occasional. The lid for the furnace can be cast, or properly shaped bricks can be held together with a steel band. Precast lids and furnace linings can be purchased.

The burner can be as simple as a piece of steel pipe or it can be a complex mixing chamber. Figure 3-29 illustrates a burner-mixer that can be built readily out of steel pipe. The burner should be positioned in the furnace so that the flame impirges on the refractory wall so that the wall produces a slight baffling action for the flame. The refractory will then rapidly develop a few red hot spots that will help keep the burner ignited. Since the melting furnace is not left unattended as the melt proceeds, safety controls are less important than with the burnout furnace. A simple, manually operated burner is often quite adequate.

The air supply can be an old vacuum-cleaner motor or an appropriate fan. Often it is advisable to buy a burner fan unit, which is available with all the components preassembled. Considerable savings are still realized in the building of the furnace.

The size of the burner and the blower is relative to the amount of heat desired. Heat is estimated in terms of b.t.u. per hour. It takes approximately 250,000 b.t.u.'s per hour to melt approximately 90 pounds of bronze in a number-30 crucible. A one and a half-inch gas line is usually necessary to deliver the desired amount of fuel. The size of the gas line depends on the distance the line must travel from the meter to the furnace. It is also important that the line from the street to the meter, the meter, and the pressure regulator be the right size. These requirements can be checked with the local utility company.

Crucibles are made of graphite or silicon carbide. Standard sizes run from 6 to 800. (The number indicates the approximate number of pounds of aluminum the crucible will hold. Multiplying the number by three gives the pounds of brass or bronze.) A new crucible should be heated slowly the first time to temper the refractory material. It should be kept dry and not subjected to rough handling. Metal should not be wedged, forced, or dropped into the crucible. The crucible is placed in the furnace on a base block.

To start the furnace, the lighting procedure may vary with the manufacturer and the kind of controls. If an automatic ignition system is used, the starter button is pressed. As soon as the ignition strikes or sparks, the gas and air are turned on. After the mixture ignites, the burner is adjusted to the desired flame. Ignition is usually identified by a buzzing sound.

For manual lighting the lid is removed and a small piece of rag moistened with charcoal lighter fluid is placed in the furnace in front of the burner (and lighted). Adding a pilot light to the burner (as seen in Figure 3-29) is simple and is far more convenient than using the rag. After the rag is placed in the furnace, or the pilot is lighted, the gas is turned slightly on. The air is kept off or as low as possible during the lighting of the burner. If the air is controlled at the intake, the intake is closed. For blowers with variable-speed control, the air is kept at as low a speed as possible. The burner in Figure 3-30 is relatively easy to light. A match, burning stick, or a burning soda straw is placed in front of the pilot light, and the pilot valve is turned on until the pilot ignites. (The pilot light is a piece of one-eighth-inch steel tube brazed to the copper tube) In this case I prefer to light the burner and get a flame started prior to turning on the air. The gas control valve is slowly turned on until the burner lights. This can be determined readily by the yellow flame in the furnace. At this point, the air is turned on low, and gas and air are slowly increased until the desired flame is achieved. As the flame is increase the amount of air is increased much more than the gas. If the burner does not ignite, the pilot may have gone out, in which case, the gas valves to burner and pilot should be turned off. The fan should be turned on to clear out the gas and the procedure should be repeated.

It is advisable to seek the assistance of another sculptor or student familiar with burners when trying to light a furnace; lighting it and judging the proper amount of gas and air takes some experience. Above all, care must be exercised, since a furnace that has accumulated a lot of gas can be explosive.

The burner should be kept on low for a few

Figure 3-30

Simple burner with pilot light. (A) Pilot valve; (B) gas control valve; (C) blower;
(D) blower control; (E) pilot light tube; and (F) main gas cut-off valve.

minutes, until the crucible and furnace have a chance to preheat. The air and gas are then increased. The preheating is important, since sudden, intense heat exposes the furnace and crucible to thermo-shock and results in more rapid deterioration of the refractory materials.

The flame should be kept adjusted to a moderate-to-slight oxidizing atmosphere for bronze and a slight oxidizing atmosphere for aluminum. An oxidizing atmosphere is rich in air and lean in fuel. The flame can be identified by its bluish-to-clear pale color. A reducing atmosphere is rich in fuel and can be identified by its yellow-tipped flame.

The crucible is usually charged with metal after the first preheating with the furnace on low heat or prior to lighting the furnace. Aluminum may be charged into the crucible at a higher furnace-crucible temperature to reduce gas entrapment.

The metal should be clean and free from moisture. A slight preheating of the metal is a good practice when possible. Metal added to melted metal in the crucible must be moisture-free. For preheating, the pieces to be added can be placed on the top of the furnace lid, around the opening. It is important to realize that moisture or contaminants on a cold piece of metal, or ingot dropped into a molten-metal mass, can cause spattering or violent reaction. The metal being added should be picked up with a tongs and gently lowered into the crucible. Protective apron, goggles, and gloves should be worn.

If alloys are being added to the molten metal, they are added in order of their melting point, with the lowest melting-point alloy being added last. For example, in adding tin or zinc to copper,

the copper would be brought to a molten state before the addition of either alloy. Conversely, a higher-melting-point alloy, such as silicon, would be melted before the copper. In commercial foundries, alloying is a precise practice. For the sculptor or student, it is far more practical to buy ingots of the desired metal.

When the metal is charged into the crucible or, as the metal begins to melt, a flux may be sprinkled on the metal to act as a protective cover for the molten metal. This protective cover helps prevent oxidation and gas absorption, which are the result of the molten metal being exposed to combustion and the moisture of the atmosphere of the furnace.

Many nonferrous metals, such as those with a high zinc content, produce a natural, oxide protective cover as they are melted. In this case, a flux may not be necessary. In fact, if clean, new metal is used, a flux is probably unnecessary for most copper alloys.

Fluxes also clean and remove unwanted agents and impurities by direct action with these particles in the molten mass. They may also act as degassing agents, removing and dispersing gases such as hydrogen. Multipurpose fluxes that combine to form protective covers, clean, and degas are readily available.

Fluxing oxidizing-agents are frequently manganese dioxide or copper oxides; deoxidizing agents may be phosphor copper, silicon, boron, magnesium, and others. For aluminum, degassing is also accomplished by inserting a hollow metal tube attached to an appropriated nitrogen source and bubbling the nitrogen into the molten-metal mass prior to pouring. The nitrogen is available in a cylinder equipped with pressure gauge. Degassing agents may also be included in the initial flux, or they can be sprinkled and stirred into the molten-metal mass after it has been removed from the furnace and skimmed. A typical degassing would consist of stirring in two percent phosphor copper. This can be stirred in with a metal rod.

The metal should not be stirred during the melting, or the protective cover of oxides and flux will be broken. If the cover is broken during the addition of more metal to the crucible, it may be necessary to add a small quantity of flux.

When the metal reaches a molten state, the temperature should be checked with a pyrometer. A hand pyrometer (as in Figure 3-31) is a convenient method of checking temperature. The pouring temperature is 100 to 200 degrees above the melting point of the alloy. The temperature of the

metal in the furnace should be about 100 degrees higher than the actual pouring temperature. This allows for the cooling of the metal that occurs between the removal of the crucible from the furnace and the actual pour. The pouring temperature varies according to the alloy. In some cases, if the temperature is raised too far above the melting point, alloying agents can start to disintegrate. This happens readily in materials such as brass that have a high zinc content. The ideal pouring temperature is as close to the melting point as possible.

After the metal reaches the desired temperature, it should be removed immediately. The furnace is first turned off (gas first, then air); the crucible is lifted out of the furnace and placed in a pouring shank. (Figure 3-32 and 3-33) The two-man pouring shank is used, typically for pouring

Figure 3-31
Using the hand pyrometer to check metal temperature.

Figure 3-32
Crucible being lifted from the melting furnace.

Figure 3-33
Crucible being placed over lifting tongs.

by hand. It is placed on the floor with a few inches of dry sand around the shank opening; a refractory block is placed in the center of the shank to insulate the hot crucible from the floor.

At this point, slag and flux are skimmed off the top with a skimming bar or small hand ladle, and the metal is poured. The skimming bar is a small piece of perforated steel welded to a rod (as in Figure 3-36). An assistant may also use the skimming bar and hold back any particles of flux and slag during the pour.

Pouring is a matter of some skill. The pour must be continuous, steady, and even; metal must always be present in the pouring cup, keeping turbulence in the cup to a minimum.

Molten metal can be poured into sand, plaster, ceramic shell, or permanent metal molds. Molds are often placed in a wood or metal flask. Most loam is rammed around plaster or sand molds; dry sand is used with ceramic shell. If the mold should crack during the pour, the sand or loam may prevent a runout and loss of the casting.

Adequate cooling time must be allowed after the pour. Breaking away the mold is a simple matter; most mold materials readily fracture and fall off in large sections when tapped or struck with

Figure 3-34
Sand mold ready for casting. The first flask has been placed around the mold.

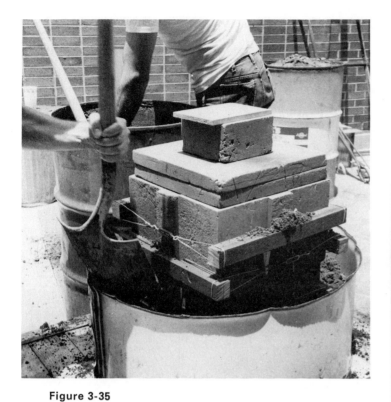

Figure 3-35

Moist sandy loam is being placed in the flask. It is being rammed or packed in place. Flasks are stacked until the top of the mold is reached. Note cover over pouring cup and vent to prevent ramming material from getting into the mold and how strips of wood, wire, and turn buckles were used to hold the mold together.

Figure 3-36

Metal being poured into the mold. Skimming bar is being used to hold back the slag as the metal is poured.

Figure 3-37

Flasks being removed from the mold.

Figure 3-38
Mold has been partially removed revealing the completed casting.

a metal hammer. Final investment material is carefully scraped off or removed with small chisels, wire brushes, etc. Sandblasting can be used for cleaning; however, this may alter the surface appearance of the casting. (Figures 3-34 through 3-39)

After the removal of the mold materials, sprues, vents, etc. are sawed off. This can be accomplished with a hack saw, band saw, cutting air-arc, or abrasive cutoff wheels. Powder cutting or using a cutting bar are fast and efficient ways of removing sprues. Final finishing is accomplished with small cold chisels and punches for chasing. Abrasive coated belts and discs, grinders, and polishing wheels or buffs are used for final finishing.

Imperfections in the casting may be due to any number of errors occurring during mold construction: the meltout in lost-wax molds, the melting of the metal, and the pour. Some common defects in metal castings and their cause would be as follows:

Flashings, runouts. These are caused by mold failures, improper materials, inadequate reinforcement, insufficient bulk to the mold, or poor mold design.

Porosity. Porous castings are usually the result of gases accumulated during the melting of the metal or gases entering the molten metal in the mold. Proper degassing agents should be used during the melt or prior to pouring. Mold conditions such as excess moisture, gas-releasing agents in the mold, or turbulence in the pouring of the metal may produce porosity.

Pinholes. These are caused by moisture in the mold or gases that the molten metal absorbs during the pour. Better venting and mold permeability may remedy these problems.

Cold shut. This is usually observable as a thin, hairline on the surface of the casting. It is caused when the metal is fed into the mold, or flows in several directions, and has cooled to the extent that the two meeting flows do not mingle or bond together. Metal temperature, mold temperature, and mold design (in terms of gates, sprues, etc.) are some of the causes. Insulated feeders may assist in maintaining metal temperature.

Blowholes. Internal or external defects in the casting are caused by trapped gases. This is due to lack of mold permeability or inadequate venting.

Figure 3-39
Ceramic shell molds being poured. (Note protective gloves, leggings and face shield.)

Inclusions. Slag, oxides, mold particles or other materials are present in the castings. This can be due to careless assembly of the mold, careless handling, improper melting of the metal, inadequate slag and flux removal, or poor mold materials or construction (resulting in sand or mold particles breaking away from the mold as the metal is poured). Bottom-pour crucibles can be used to minimize slag- or flux-inclusions.

Hot tears and Cold cracks. These are caused as the metal shrinks in cooling. They are controlled by the choice of the proper mold material and mold design. Too rigid a core or mold material may prevent the metal from shrinking without tearing. A core or mold material should tend to collapse as the metal shrinks.

Misruns. Poor pouring techniques, improper gating and sprueing, poor mold design, and improper mold- or metal-temperature may result in defective or incomplete castings. In sculpture, if a misrun is not too severe, it is repaired. Small holes and cracks are filled by welding. New patterns for missing sections can be cast and welded into place.

Warping. Uneven cooling and irregular thickness of wall or metal mass may cause distortion during cooling, particularly if the casting is cooled too fast. Mold design may also be a factor. Exercising care in the design of the wall thickness of the casting and allowing adequate, slow cooling can minimize this problem. Do not be in a hurry to remove the mold after the casting.

Carving

FOUR

Carving is one of the oldest methods used to shape materials; simple stone tools and implements date back to primitive man. Ancient Egyptian craftsmen were expert at wood and stone carving and possessed excellent metal tools for carving.

The simple tools and techniques for carving are not much different today from those of ancient times. We have a greater variety and the aid of mechanical and electrical tools to make the task easier. However, the steps, from roughing out a wood or stone form to finishing it, remain essentially the same and can be accomplished with relatively few tools.

The materials for carving are still, basically, wood and stone. There are some blocks of synthetic materials that have specialized usage for student projects and temporary patterns.

Some of the soft synthetic materials, such as blocks of foam or concrete, or plaster mixed with vermiculite or perlite, are excellent for beginning students. These materials are easily carved and can rapidly acquaint the student with the problems of thinking subtractively and visualizing form in a mass of material. A few practice carvings of this kind can help considerably in building con-

fidence and minimizing error in subsequent wood or stone carvings.

In recent years, emphasis has been placed on the newer, industrial materials, and some sculptors do not favor carving techniques for contemporary sculpture. For the young sculptor or student, however, exploring this traditional technique can produce worthy and satisfying results.

If carving is approached spontaneously and each material is explored for its own unique qualities, carved forms, or combinations of carved forms with other materials, still have fresh and creative potential.

WOOD-CARVING

Selection of wood for carving is a matter of personal choice: any wood can be suitable for carving. Some woods possess fine, even grain and can be carved with greater ease than others; however, the woods that are less desirable possess unusual grain and coloration and can be of equal merit. (Figures 4-1 and 4-2)

Figure 4-1
Carving wood with a chain saw. *By sculptor, James Surls.*

Figure 4-2
Completed carving, "We're Stumped," 1971, by James Surls.

There is usually an adequate supply of native wood available in any geographic area. Landscape and construction companies, park departments, and public utility companies are always busy trimming or removing trees. In the normal process of driving around a city, logs can be obtained from the work sites of these firms. It is also possible to find the city dumping area for these materials. Firms selling fire wood frequently have logs of fireplace length that can be used for small carvings. Exotic and uncommon woods can be obtained from wood suppliers. As a last resort, dimensional lumber available at any lumber company can be laminated together.

Ideally, it is desirable to collect logs, seal the ends by painting with oil paint, and dry or cure them in a dry, sheltered area. Curing can take several years for a large-diameter log. Uncured logs can be carved, although cracks or checks will develop. These can be filled with pigmented beeswax; or, after the log is completely dry, slivers of wood or wood fillers can be used.

First carvings can best be done in soft to medium-hard woods. Cedar, white pine, redwood, aspen, basswood, soft maple, cottonwood, spruce, cypress, and poplar are easy to carve. Birch, butterwood, olivewood, and fruitwoods such as apple, cherry, pear, and plum are good medium-hard woods for carving. Domestic medium-hard to hard woods are ash, beechwood, dogwood, elm, sycamore, maple, oak, walnut, and hickory. Excellent imported hardwoods are cocabola, ebony, koko, lemonwood, mahogany, rosewood, teakwood and *lignum vitae.*

Identifying woods is a matter of recognizing the texture and color of the bark, or the color of the wood and its grain configuration, in a rough or finished state. *Knowing Your Trees,* by G. H. Collingswood and Warren D. Brush, published by the American Forestry Association, Washington D.C. 1955 is an excellent reference.

It might be said that carving undergoes three phases: the roughing-out, intermediate carving, and final finishing. In some cases, the work may be

Figure 4-3
Hand tools for wood carving. Left to right: carving mallet, parting tool, bent gouge, straight gouge, straight flat carving chisel, straight gouges.

Figure 4-4
Pneumatic tools for wood carving.

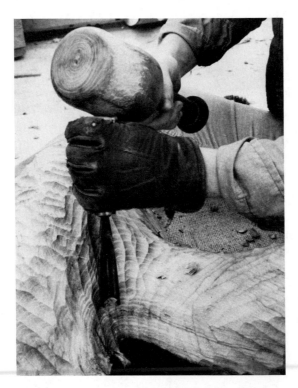

Figure 4-5
Roughing out a carving with a straight gouge.

carried to completion with roughing-out or intermediate carving as the final desired effect.

Figures 4-3 and 4-4 illustrates some of the typical gouges, chisels, and other tools used in carving. The shapes of wood carving tools are flat (chisels), slightly curved to half-round (gouges), or V-shaped (parting tool). Tools should be kept sharp while working. Chisels can be honed on a flat oilstone, whereas gouges are sharpened with specially shaped slipstones.

Small logs or blocks of wood need to be held in a vice, bolted, or clamped to the table. Butting the end of the log or wood block against a 100-pound canvas bag of sand placed on the workbench works exceptionally well, allowing the log to be turned and manipulated easily as the carving is developed on all sides. Large logs are usually supported by their own weight.

Roughing-out on moderate-sized work is accomplished with a half-round gouge, which is struck with a wooden mallet. The width and curvature of the gouge and the weight of the mallet (16 to 32 ounces) depend on the size of the log and the preference of the sculptor. The gouge is held at approximately 45 degrees and is struck with the mallet. (Figure 4-5) As the gouge bites into the wood, the angle of the chisel is decreased and a piece is gouged out of the material. Always carve in the direction of the grain, since working against the grain, or attempting to gouge out too large a piece, may result in imbedding the chisel in the wood and breaking the tool.

Large sections can be sawed or chiseled out of a log; hand saws or chain saws can be used. Cavities or holes can be drilled and carved out. Hand axes and adzes are also used for roughing-out. Pneumatic hammers can be used to drive the gouges and accelerate the carving.

After the initial roughing-out is accomplished, a shallow or slightly curved gouge is used to cut down the ridges left by the gouge. In the intermediate carving, lighter-weight mallets are often used. The chisel is either struck with the mallet or pushed and tapped with the palm of the hand. After the gouge ridges have been reduced somewhat, flat chisels are used to further flatten the surface.

Surfaces can also be rasped or worked down with rifflers. In fact, a good variety of rifflers (Figure 4-6) is essential for getting into otherwise inaccessible areas when finishing by hand. Mechanical rotary rasps can also be used instead of hand rasps. (Figure 4-7) These can be used in an electric or air drill, or on a flexible shaft. The flexible

Figure 4-7
Rotary rasp for wood finishing.

Figure 4-6
Two rasps and rifflers for rough finishing of a wood carving.

shaft or the air drill is more compact and highly desirable when finishing in holes and negative spaces.

If a carving is to be given a smooth finish, the normal abrasive finishing procedures can be followed. Unusual-shaped sanding drums and discs can be used to finish rapidly the difficult-to-reach areas.

STONE CARVING

Stone for carving is fundamentally of three geological origins. The very hard igneous rocks, such as granite and basalt, were formed by heat, volcanic action, and the subsequent cooling of the molten masses. The moderately soft materials, such as sandstone and limestone, are sedimentary rocks formed by layers (strata) of sediment resulting from erosion by chemical and physical action. Metamorphic rocks, such as quartzite, slate, shist, soapstone, marble, and gneiss, were formed through heat, pressure, and chemical action on igneous and sedimentary rocks.

Marble has been one of the most preferred materials for sculpture, whereas granite, valued for permanence and weather resistance, has been used extensively in large monumental works. Porous rocks, less resistant to erosion, moisture, and freezing temperatures, should be treated with a sealer if permanency is desired.

The selection of stone is a personal matter, and the choice of stone is extensive. The ease with which it can be carved varies from the soft materials, such as soapstone and alabaster (which, when wet, can be scraped and carved with a knife or coarse rasp) to granite (which requires sharp, well-tempered chisels and a pulverizing action to break down the hard, granular material).

Since permanence, in the sense of a century or centuries, is of less concern to many sculptors today, any material is worthy of experiment. Every

Figure 4-8

Moving large stones with rollers and levers. *St. Margarethem Sculpture Symposium, Austria. Sculpture by Paul Aschenbach. Photograph courtesy of Paul and June Aschenbach.*

Figure 4-9

Hand tools for stone carving. From top: cutters, hand hammer, bush hammer, hand set or pitching tool, hand tracer and hand point, hand plug drill, hand chipper, and hand chisel.

Figure 4-10

Pneumatic tools for carving. Top: pneumatic hammer and ripper. Left vertical row, top to bottom: two carvers drills, 4, 9, and 16-point chisel and carvers drill. Horizontal row, left to right: hand point, 1/2-inch clean-up chisel, marble cutting chisels, 3-tooth marble chisel, 5-tooth marble chisel, ripper and carvers drill.

rock has its own unique form and structure. Traditionally, only well-formed, even-grained stones with minimum defects were considered suitable for statuary. Today, however, we should not hesitate to explore previously unacceptable materials.

As in wood carving, a stone carving is developed by roughing-out, intermediate carving and final finishing. The final finish may be quite rough revealing the chisel marks of the intermediate state, or it may be finished to a smooth or polished surface with the use of abrasives.

During carving, large blocks of stone will support themselves; small blocks should be placed on a sturdy wooden stand or a 50-gallon steel drum filled with sand. Large blocks of stone can be moved by hand, using rollers, levers, A-frames, or block and tackle. Mechanical equipment, such as fork-lifts and cranes, should be used when available. (Figure 4-8)

Figures 4-9 and 4-10 illustrate the basic tools and equipment used in stone-carving. Stone-carving tools of the proper design, steel, and temper can

Figure 4-11

Using a hand set or pitching tool to break off edges in roughing out limestone.

best be purchased from a reliable supplier. These may be hand, pneumatic, or thermal tools. The tools should be kept sharp and in proper condition. Any mushrooming that occurs on the striking end of the chisel should be ground off immediately to avoid injury. Appropriate safety goggles and dust masks should be worn at all times.

In the roughing-out stage, it is important to visualize the general outline or essential, simple

Figure 4-12

Spliting stone. *Proctor, Vermont Sculpture Symposium, 1968. Photograph courtesy of Paul and June Aschenbach.*

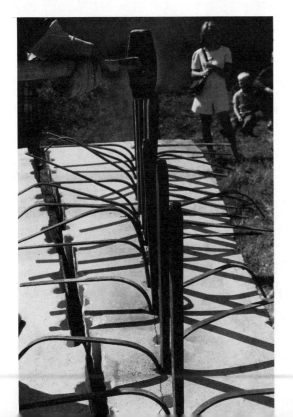

shape of the form to be carved. If the stone is a block of material, the first roughing-out is accomplished by hand carving with a hand set or pitching tool. The rough corners and edges are broken off by striking the tool intensely with a relatively heavy striking hammer; the heavier the hammer the sculptor is capable of handling, the easier the task will be. (Figure 4-11)

Large pieces can also be removed, or blocks can be split, by drilling a series of holes and driving wedges into them. Holes are drilled with an electric drill with carbide-tipped masonry bits or an air-hammer-driven carver's drill. For cutting negative spaces or holes it is simplest to drill into the stone and then chisel out the pieces. (Figure 4-12)

After the initial roughing-out, subsequent material is removed with the point. (Figure 4-13) The point for marble is rather slim and tapered, whereas the point for granite is rather blunt. The point is held at an angle and is struck with the cutter's hammer. The point should not be buried in the stone. For carving soft stones such as sandstone and limestone, frequently the hand tracer and chipper work more satisfactorily than the point.

Intermediate carving is achieved with toothed or flat chisels for soft stone. (Figure 4-14) Granite is finished with the four- or nine-tooth chisel. Intermediate carving is best accomplished with machine-operated chisels; however, hand finishing, although tedious, is also possible and, in fact, is considered more desirable by some sculptors. In hand-finishing granite, the bush hammer is often used in place of the four- and nine-tooth chisel, at this stage. Since granite is granular, the action pulverizes the surface, wearing it down to within about an eighth of

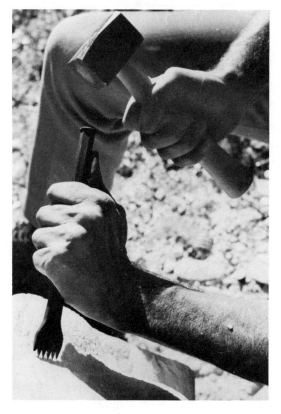

Figure 4-13
Sculptor, Paul Aschenbach, using a point in carving marble. *Photograph courtesy of Paul and June Aschenbach.*

Figure 4-14
Hand finishing marble with the toothed chisel. *Photograph courtesy of Paul and June Aschenbach.*

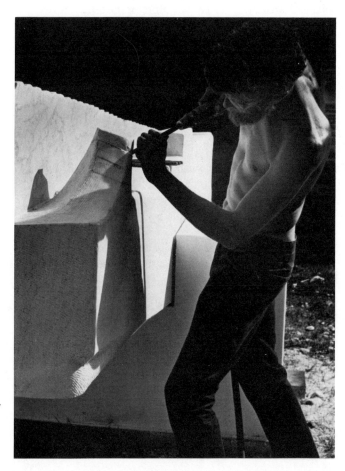

Figure 4-15
Sculptor, Paul Aschenbach, carving with a pneumatic hammer. *Photograph courtesy of Paul and June Aschenbach.*

Figure 4-16

Completed sculpture. *Proctor, Vermont Sculpture Symposium. Sculpture by Paul Aschenbach. Photograph courtesy of Paul and June Aschenbach.*

an inch of the desired surface. (Figures 4-15 and 4-16)

If the stone is not to receive a polished finish, the final surface is usually achieved by working down with fine, sharp flat chisels. These chisels are struck lightly with lightweight hammers or, in the very final stages, pushed or tapped with the palm of the hand. A variety of smaller chisels is used to do fine detail and to get into difficult places. Although some sculptors might object to the practice, machine-operated air- or electric-rasps and abrasive grinders can be used at this stage. It is really a matter of personal choice as well as a matter of what is intended for the final surface finish.

The sculptor may desire a smooth or polished finish rather than a tooled one. After working down with the flat chisel, the surface can be finished abrasively in the same manner as other materials, by starting with a coarse grit of about 20 and working up to 200 or 300. Vitrified-bond, silicone-carbide cup wheels are best used on flats and planes. Wet or dry silicone-carbide discs are used on curved and irregular shapes. Any of the variously shaped and coated abrasive wheels can be used for difficult-to-reach areas, some of which may require hand polishing. This can be accomplished by breaking off small pieces from abrasive wheels, using pieces of hand bricks, or other abrasives glued to desired shapes.

In wet finishing, an air grinder is preferable. If an electric grinder is used, it should be properly grounded. Even then, I would hesitate to recommend its use in any wet-finishing operations. In dry abrasive finishing, a good fitting mask is absolutely essential as stone dusts are hazardous.

If a polished surface is desired, the final buffing is accomplished mechanically with a felt buff using tin oxide or cerium oxide buffing compound. Hand buffing is possible if mechanical equipment is not available.

Carving with thermal torches is a relatively new process for carving spallable stone such as granite. It involves spalling off thin layers of material by thermally induced expansion of the surface. The thermal torch employs a high-velocity flame produced by burning a mixture of oxygen and vaporized fuel such as kerosene. The flame size can be controlled by reducing the fuel-flow. A jet of water alongside the flame washes away the spalled off material and gives the operator better control of the spalling action. The torch can be used for the rapid removal of material and more delicate surface finishing. (Figure 4-17)

SYNTHETIC CARVING BLOCKS

Many materials can be purchased in cast-block or slab form, or can be cast into blocks in the classroom or studio. I consider these synthetic blocks, versus the natural blocks of wood or stone.

Besides their above-mentioned value as an introduction to carving, synthetic blocks can be used for patterns, as forms on which to build fiberglass, or, in some cases, as a permanent media for interior or exterior work.

The usual procedure for casting blocks or slabs is to build a wooden box or frame the size of the desired form, or to pour the mixture into a corrugated cardboard box, which can be greased, lacquered, waxed, or lined with polyethylene film to make it waterproof.

Another interesting approach is to build the container to roughly approximate the shape of the desired piece. This reduces the amount of material and somewhat eliminates the first roughing-out stages of the carving.

PLASTER

Plaster carving blocks have existed for some time. In recent years, perlite or vermiculite has been added to produce a softer material. Three parts vermiculite, one part plaster, and one and one half parts water produces a soft block; these proportions can be varied to achieve softer or harder material. To prepare this mixture, the dry ingredients should be mixed and sprinkled into the water mix, and should keep on being added until the mixture reaches a firm, dough-like consistency. Too much water will result in excessively soft material. Dry pigments or cement-coloring can be added for tinting. Marble chips, sand, sawdust, or fine gravel can be added for texture; or these materials can be mixed with plaster, without vermiculite. The addition of these ingredients, or the elimination of ver-

miculite will result in harder blocks of material.

When vermiculite is added to plaster, complete the rough carving within the first few days, while the block of material is relatively soft; after the block dries, it becomes harder, and finer detailing is possible.

The tools for carving plaster or plaster and vermiculite can be the regular plaster tools and rasps. If sand or other abrasive materials are added, stone-carving tools should be used.

The finished carved pieces can be sealed with a clear lacquer or masonry sealer.

PORTLAND CEMENT

Portland cement mixed with vermiculite in the ratio of three parts vermiculite, one part cement, and one and one half parts water produces a block harder than the plaster mixture. A distinct advantage in the use of the cement instead of the plaster is that the cement mixture allows far more time in preparing and pouring the mixture.

Generally, the same method is used for carving and mixing this material as is used for the plaster mix, although the cement material does become hard more quickly; it is, therefore, advis-

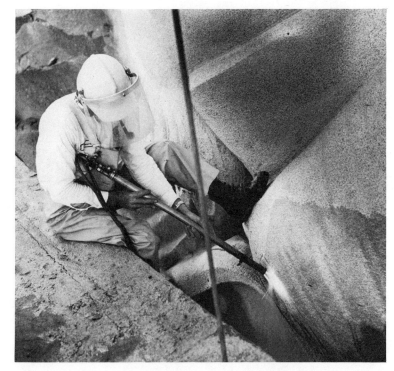

Figure 4-17

Cutting with a thermal torch. *Stone Mountain, Georgia. Photograph courtesy of Frank Rippetoe and Union Carbide Corporation, Linde Division.*

able to do the first rough carving as soon as the mix has set. This is usually from 12 to 24 hours after pouring the mixture.

This material can be used outdoors if it is treated with a clear sealer for concrete or masonry.

Portland cement and sand- or gravel-aggregate mixtures can be carved immediately after setting or when cured and dry—a difficult process, demanding essentially the same tools and approaches as stone-carving. One of the principal disadvantages is that the concrete does not fracture as does limestone or marble. However, its own unique chipping and fracturing qualities can be exploited when the desired form is bold and direct.

A spontaneous and direct approach to concrete is to carve it immediately after it sets to the point at which the mass will support itself and the mold can be removed. As with plaster-block molds, it is preferable to design the mold in wood roughly approximating the desired form. If the mixture is poured in the late afternoon or early evening, it will reach a desirable carving condition by early the next morning. This allows a full day for the rough carving, with subsequent finishing taking place as the material hardens and becomes more resistant to the tools.

The concrete mixtures are usually one part cement to three or four parts aggregate. The aggregates can be masonry, sand, graded silica, mixtures of sand and gravel, selected-size gravel, or crushed rock.

FOAM

Blocks or slabs of polystyrene or polyurethane foam are easily carved. The material can be purchased in densities ranging from two to 35 pounds per cubic foot.

Preformed blocks or slabs are available from plastic suppliers or marine supply houses, where they are sold as flotation billets. Several companies market blocks of high-density, colored foam for carving. The foam can also be purchased as a two-part mixture, which, when mixed and poured into a box or mold, forms a block.

An ordinary carpenter's hand saw or hot-wire cutters can be used. The material can be carved with ordinary wood-carving tools or can be cut down very rapidly with a coarse wood rasp. Finer rasps and sandpaper are used for finishing.

Usually, foam is used as practice material for students, or for patterns to receive subsequent treatment (as described in Chapter 1). Specially formulated, colored, low- and high-density carving foams have been used for finished sculpture in interior applications.

Figure 4-18

Sculptor Roger Kotoske carving a cast polyester form using a rotary file.

PLASTICS

Blocks of acrylic, polyester, or epoxy can be cut with ordinary woodworking saws, drills, rasps, and files. The process involves sawing, drilling, rasping, filing, and abrading, instead of chipping and gouging. If abrasive fillers are present in the plastic material, stone-carving tools and techniques should be used.

Sheets of acrylic up to three inches thick can be purchased and laminated into blocks. Blocks of polyester or epoxy can be cast clear or with fillers (following the casting procedures in Chapter 3).

When possible, it is advisable to cast blocks in the approximate shape of the desired form, since this reduces material cost and expedites carving. (Figure 4-18)

Direct Modeling

FIVE

Building directly with a doughlike or soft material, or applying it over a previously prepared armature is a spontaneous and satisfying approach to some forms of sculpture. It is particularly useful for students wishing to experiment with form, without investing much time and expensive materials in a single work.

Direct sculpturing with clay has existed for centuries as a practical approach to pottery and statuary. Direct paper-mache, plaster, and concrete have been used by sculptors for many years. Plastics such as polyester or epoxy resin mixed with sand, fine crushed rock, perlite, saw dust, metal powders or combined with fiberglass have provided us with a new group of materials that possess greater strength and permanence than paper, plaster, or concrete.

Direct materials may be thought of in relation to their characteristics and methods of manipulation; some materials can support themselves, whereas others require internal armatures for structural support.

Armatures may be constructed of metal lathe, screening, hardware cloth, wire and rods. Figure 5-1 illustrates a typical large-scale armature being constructed out of concrete-reinforcing rod and hardware cloth. As a wire-mesh material for armatures, hardware cloth is preferred; it can be cut and formed easily. Metal lathe is satisfactory for large, flat surfaces; it tends to be more rigid and gives more reinforcement support for the material. More difficult to shear, its sharp-wire ends may cut the hands or fingers. Protective leather gloves should be worn when handling any wire mesh. (Figures 5-2, 5-3, and 5-4)

When twisted wire, concrete-reinforcing rod, welding rod, or metal piping is used for linear forms, it should be wrapped with a fine wire, string, or fiberglass strands to provide additional bond between the armature and the material.

For direct-sculpture techniques for plaster or concrete, the armature must be carefully planned and constructed. It should be built to the precise proportions of the piece, with reasonable space allowance for the material that is going to be applied. Internal supports should be sufficiently rigid to carry the weight of the material and stresses developed within the form. An armature that is constructed too hastily—with the attitude that strength can be achieved simply by adding bulk

Figure 5-2

Plaster build-up of armature.

Figure 5-1

Armature for a plaster pattern being constructed out of reinforcing rod.

Figure 5-3

Detail showing wire mesh, steel armature, and applied plaster.

Figure 5-4

Completed plaster pattern by Charles Aberg.

to the work—results only in failure; the increased bulk merely increases the weight and often compounds the problem.

Polystyrene or polyurethane foam is an excellent armature material. It can be sawed, rasped, carved, and sanded (as described in Chapter 1). For plaster and concrete, the foam armatures must be bulky enough to withstand the weight of the material. Wire mesh and steel are often applied over the foam to give additional support to the concrete or plaster. Foam armatures to receive fiberglass can be quite linear and delicate, since as soon as a thin layer of fiberglass and resin is applied, the surface becomes strong enough to support itself.

Wood frames with cardboard or stretched-muslin surfaces make suitable armatures for paper mache or fiberglass construction. For paper mache construction the armature should be waterproofed with lacquer or shellac.

There are several methods for applying materials directly over armatures. Puttylike materials are best applied with spatulas and trowels. Materials such as plaster and concrete are sometimes applied with the fingers for initial roughing-out. Sometimes materials can be thinned for brush application. Specialized equipment has been developed for spraying plaster, concrete, plastics, and metal.

PLASTER

Since plaster does not posses much tensile strength, armatures must be well-constructed for direct-plaster techniques. Whereas linear forms can be constructed better in other materials, plaster is good for simple, massive, or bulky forms. For additional performance, high-strength plasters such as U. S. Gypsum Hydrocal® and Hydrostone® can be used.

Although plaster is seldom thought of as a very exotic material, it is still one of the most versatile, most adaptable, and least expensive materials the sculptor has to work with. In direct modeling for patterns, or for interior works, it is a highly suitable material; students can quickly fashion direct models at very little expense. Plaster is simple to handle and requires very few tools.

To build up plaster directly, small quantities of plaster are mixed in plastic bowls and are applied with spatulas and other tools. The plaster is mixed in the same fashion used in building plaster molds. (See Chapter 2, page 13) On large works, the plaster is often applied with the fingers. The plaster-water ratio may vary. Less water increases the strength of the plaster. If the surface of the work is to be sanded to a smooth finish, a soft surface may be desirable. In this case, the final application may be a mixture with a higher water ratio. Conversely, if a hard surface is desired, the water ratio can be reduced. Any patching or additional buildup should be made with the water-plaster ratio remaining the same as that used in the surface coatings; patching with mixes of lower water ratio results in hard spots, which often prevent sanding a surface to a smooth, homogeneous finish.

Whatever method of application is used, the work should be carefully developed. The layers of plaster should be applied evenly, allowing the form to progress slowly to completion. To assure bonding, each layer should be kept rough until the final layer is applied; surfaces that have dried should be moistened before applying new layers. The kind of final surface texture developed is a matter of personal choice; many sculptors have explored the rough, troweled look that goes with the hand application of material. A wide variety of tools is available for the application of plaster and for producing surface finishes. (Figure 5-5)

Rather than applying plaster with a trowel or spatula, loose-textured, bold forms can be achieved by dipping burlap strips, hemp fiber, or

Figure 5-5

Plaster modelling tools.

Figure 5-6

Large plaster wall relief being constructed of plaster and burlap. *Student project, Southern Methodist University.*

Figure 5-7

Figure composition out of plaster and burlap. *Student project, Southern Methodist University.*

Figure 5-8

Plaster being sprayed with an R2 spray gun using a siphon hose. *Student project, Southern Methodist University.*

Figure 5-9

R2 spray gun with disposable container for spraying small batches of plaster, resins and other materials.

strips of fiberglass mat into the plaster and applying the pieces over the armature. (Figures 5-6 and 5-7)

Plaster can also be applied directly over foam armatures. If the form has sufficient bulk, wire reinforcing may not be necessary; the first layer might be reinforced by mixing hemp fiber or other fibrous material with the plaster.

Plaster can be mixed thin and applied with a brush, which should be cleaned and rinsed in water quite frequently to prevent the plaster from setting in the brush.

Spray applications of plaster can be achieved with a spray gun (as illustrated in Figures 5-8 and 5-9).

For finishing, wet plaster is usually chiseled, scraped, sanded, and rasped. Ideally, if a work is developed carefully, chiseling should not be necessary; it is undesirable, since chiseling off lumps and projections due to careless application of the plaster may result in fracture of the work.

Fillers such as marble dust, sand, marble chips, stone aggregates, vermiculite, glass spheres or nodules, and pigments can be added to the plaster for final surface application, to produce decorative results. Sanding or wire brushing the surface will expose the filler. Plaster can also be painted, coated with plastics, plated, or sprayed with metals.

CONCRETE

Direct application of Portland cement and aggregate mixtures on metal lathe have been used in the building industry for many years. Stucco and terrazzo surfaces are frequently built this way; the disc shape in Figure 3-2 was fabricated in this manner by a commercial terrazzo company.

Direct sculpturing with Portland cement and aggregate mixtures is fairly similar to working with plaster, as far as armature construction and method of application are concerned. As mentioned earlier, it is important that the armature be designed to carry the full load of the applied material; otherwise, cracks will result.

Cement and sand-aggregate mixtures do not stick as easily to the armature as plaster; for flat surfaces expanded metal lathe, rather than hardware cloth, should be used, concrete mixtures adhere more readily to it.

Marble dust, brick dust, marble chips, fine gravel, sand, and vermiculite are used as aggregates. A typical mixture of cement and aggregate would be one part cement, one or two parts masonry sand, and one or two parts aggregate, with a particle size of one-eighth to one-fourth inch. Fine mixtures might be one part cement to one or two parts marble dust, masonry sand, or other fine material. A small amount of hydrated lime (five to ten percent of the weight of the cement) can be added to the mixture to increase its plasticity and to produce a mixture that sticks more readily to the armature. Commercially available mortar mixes with the appropriate proportions of ingredients can also be used. High early-strength cements can be used if a fast curing of the material is desired. Concrete-coloring agents can be added to the mix. The description in Chapter 3 of the strength of cast concrete in relation to aggregate-particle size also pertains to directly applied cement-aggregate mixtures. Extremely coarse aggregate mixtures are seldom used in direct build-up, since the weight of the aggregate makes application of the material impossible on vertical surfaces. As in cast mixtures, the cement and aggregates are mixed dry prior to addition of the water.

In a typical application, the cement-aggregate mixture is applied with a spatula or trowel, working from the bottom up. A layer up to one-half inch thick is applied. It is kept comparatively rough in order to provide a mechanical bond for the subsequent layers. A good practice is to scrape or roughen the surface with a toothed tool, such as a piece of saw blade, after the cement has partially set and is firm enough to withstand the scraping. To reduce costs, the first coating can be a cement-sand-fine-gravel mixture. Since coarse mixtures possess greater strength than fine mixtures, as coarse a mix as is feasible should be used on the first coating. Generally, as the work develops, it should proceed from a coarse layer to finer layers, with refinement of detail taking place in the second and third layers.

Total thickness need not be more than an inch, unless the work is extremely large. For large works or for added strength additional layers of metal lathe or hardware cloth can be used along with the layers of fine cement-aggregate mixture.

Throughout the buildup, the work should be kept moist and covered with a plastic or airtight cover. Surfaces that have been allowed to dry should be moistened with water before applying the next layer. Under ideal circumstances, the work should be completed as quickly as possible, or a layer a day.

Upon completion, the work should remain covered with moist cloths and a plastic or airtight cover for at least two weeks. This allows the concrete to cure and reach full strength. High early-strength cement would require less curing time.

Grinding and finishing for smooth surfaces and to expose aggregates are accomplished upon completion of the curing. For rough, exposed aggregate surfaces, the work may be lightly wire- or fiber-brushed after the final coating has partially set to the point at which it can withstand the brushing. After the work has thoroughly dried, it is a good practice to treat the surface with a clear sealer for concrete or terrazzo.

A commercial spray technique for concrete called "gunite" is available. Extensively used in the building of swimming pools, this process can be adapted to large-scale sculptural forms. (Figure 5-10) In this method, a cement-sand slurry is sprayed directly onto a wire mesh and reinforcing-rod surface. The mixture is compacted by the pressure of the mixture hitting the surface. Some spray apparatuses use a dry mixture to which water is added at the nozzle; in others, the cement and sand are mixed before the nozzle is reached. A typical mixture consists of one part cement to four parts sand.

PLASTICS

Plastic resins such as polyester, epoxy, or other thermosetting resins can be mixed with fillers, or applied with other reinforcing materials, and built up over armatures. These materials have substantially more tensile strength than plaster or concrete, and can be applied in thinner layers to produce relatively lightweight sculpture.

Armatures may be clay, wire mesh, polystyrene or polyurethane foam, paper mache, earth, wood, cardboard, or plaster. If the forms are such that the armature can be dug out, the plastic can be built over a clay form. Foam armatures are among the most desirable due to their light weight. When using polyester resins, polystyrene-foam armatures should be sealed with several coats of a water-based latex paint, an epoxy coating, or a layer of tissue paper and white glue. Although plaster armatures are quite common, their weight is a distinct disadvantage. Rough armatures of wood, cardboard, or foam can be built to more accurate dimensions by using plaster, wood fillers, or commercial spackling compounds. The fillers and reinforcement materials described in Chapter 3, page 55 can be used in these buildup processes.

The reinforced plastic materials are applied to the armature in several different fashions, depending on the desired surface qualities, strength in the material, fillers, and resins used. Fine powders and granules can be mixed in small quantities with a catalyzed resin to form puttylike modeling pastes. They can be applied with a

Figure 5-10

Concrete being sprayed for a pool structure. *Photograph courtesy of Travis "S" Gunite, Inc., Dallas, Texas.*

trowel or spatula. With polyesters, the amount of filler must be considered as part of the total volume, in determining the required amount of catalyst. The fillers may be added until a paste-like consistency is achieved. Some commercial putties have concentrations of filler to resin that reach 90 percent of the total volume. The amount of filler that a resin will take depends on the viscosity of the resin, the particle size of the filler, and the oil-absorption qualities of the filler. Low-viscosity resins with nonabsorptive, maximum-dense particles allow for the largest amount of filler. Metallic powders, such as aluminum, brass, steel, and copper, of from 150 to 300 mesh, are often used as fillers to produce fine, durable, metallic-like surfaces. Coloring agents can also be added to the mixtures. Glass nodules or perlite make excellent filler for bulk and lightweight buildup.

Prepared modeling pastes of epoxy or polyester with metal or other fillers are available from sculpture supply houses. High-quality commercial plastics with metal fillers designed for repair are also available and are excellent for direct modeling.

Another method of direct modeling is to place the pieces of reinforcing material on the armature and saturate it with resin by applying the resin with a brush. Fiberglass mat or cloth is usually used. It is applied in several layers, as in layup techniques, into an open-face mold. Strips of fabric, paper towels, or burlap can also be used; however, the strongest and most durable form is achieved using glass-fiber reinforcement. In this approach, an accurate armature is necessary. Clay, foam, plaster, or paper mache is usually used in this application. (Figures 5-11 through 5-17)

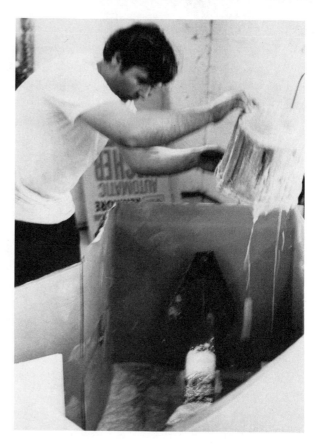

Figure 5-12
Sculptor Mike Cunningham pouring foam into the mold.

Figure 5-13
Urethane foam beginning to rise.

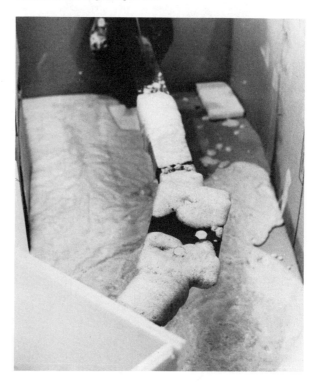

Figure 5-11
Cardboard container for casting foam shapes. Note armature in the container.

Figure 5-14

Mold filled with foam. Note that some scraps of sheet have been used as additional fill material. *Figures 11 through 14 photographs by Don Schol.*

Figure 5-15

Foam shapes completed, assembled, and covered with Dynel fabric and resin.

Figure 5-16

Mechanical detail on method used to join foam sections. Mechanical sections were covered with a sheet metal detail in the finished work.

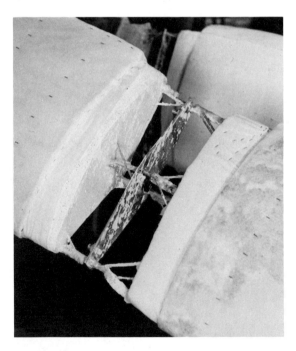

Figure 5-17

Epoxy resin being applied over the Dynel fabric. Note use of protective mask and gloves. *Sculpture by Mike Cunningham.*

Working with modelling paste and fiberglass cloth or matt might be combined in many applications. When a form is built up with putty or paste it may be desirable to include a layer of fiber glass-reinforced plastic for maximum strength. In a typical procedure, working with paste over a rough armature, it would be desirable to use a lightweight filler, such as perlite or glass nodules mixed with resin and Cab-O-Sil® to build the form out to about one-fourth inch less than the desired form. A layer of glass cloth or matt would next be applied and saturated with resin. The final surface would be putty with a fine-grade filler.

Another approach, which requires paper, fabric, fiberglass cloth or matt, is to dip pieces into the resin and apply them over an armature, as in the plaster and burlap technique. Some sculptors place pieces flat on a nonabsorbent surface, saturate them with resin, and then shape the piece (as in Figure 5-18). This is a rather spontaneous approach that presupposes a certain amount of waste and modification as the work is developed.

There are several spray applications for applying resin and fibrous reinforcing material. Industry uses a spray gun that sprays a mixture of resin and chopped-glass fiber for the rapid buildup of fiberglass forms. Since this equipment is costly,

Figure 5-19

Spray equipment for foam. *Photograph courtesy of Glas-Craft of California.*

Figure 5-18

Plastic reinforced fiberglass relief. *By Roger Kotoske, 1964.*

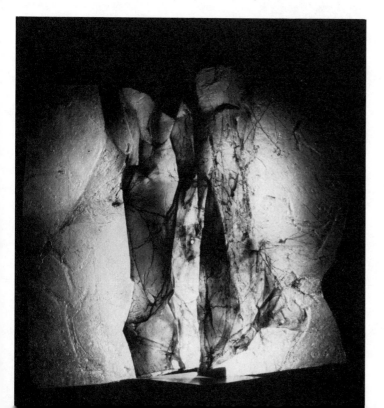

a likely approach for a sculptor would be to build the armature and have an industrial firm apply the reinforced plastic. The inexpensive all-material spray gun can be used for spraying resins and slurries.

In another method, using the R-2 spray gun, a layer of resin is sprayed, followed by a layer of short aluminum or steel fibers sprayed with a flocking gun. The alternating layers are repeated until the desired thickness is achieved. Pieces of fiber projecting after the final coat are removed by abrasive finishing.

Spraying urethane foam is another direct technique for spontaneous forms or for building up rough armatures. Although the equipment used (as with fiberglass) is costly, some art schools and individual sculptors are using it. Inexpensive spray-foam kits are now available that are practical for smaller works. (Figures 5-19 through 5-22) Some sculptors have worked directly with poured urethane foam to produce reliefs. The rough form might be poured and left as is or finished with carving techniques. The foam can also be contained with mold sections made out of cardboard or wood. The urethane foam is a two-component system. When the liquids are mixed in

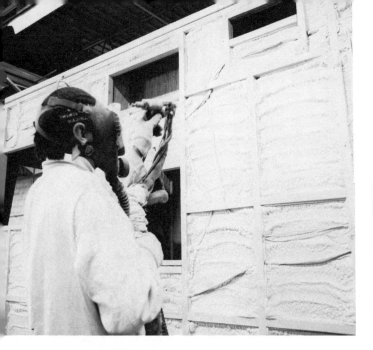

Figure 5-20
Commercial application of foam insulation with spray equipment.
Photography courtesy of Cook Paint and Varnish Co.

Figure 5-21
Sculptor Roger Bolomey pouring foam for a relief panel, 1964.
Photograph courtesy of Roger Bolomey.

Figure 5-22
Hoboken Number 13, a completed
foam relief. *By Roger Bolomey.
Collection: University of California
Museum of Art, Berkeley, California.*

equal proportions, a reaction occurs that causes the material to foam and increase in volume. Good ventilation or protective face masks should be used when working with this material.

Direct sculpture in plastic is most adaptable for spontaneous forms where the surface is textural and minor irregularities are acceptable. To build a form directly with the intention of producing a precise, highly finished surface is tedious and almost impossible. Filler and plastic often do not lend themselves to machining or abrasive finishing. In this case, as a rule, it is far less time-consuming to build a smooth clay or plaster pattern, make a mold, and use a molding technique.

CLAY

Today ceramicists build directly with clay to achieve dramatic sculptural results. The approaches in handling the materials are fundamentally the same as in the construction of other ceramic objects. Wheel-thrown forms are no longer thought of as simple, cylindrical shapes, but are cut, distorted, or manipulated. Slabs are cut and assembled, and rolls or pieces are pinched together. Ceramic units are combined with welded metal, plastic, or cast metal to produce visual contrast between materials.

Assembly of the pieces may entail simple joining with a slip mixture while the clay is still moist, or finished fired sections may be joined with adhesives or mechanical fasteners. The material and procedures for the handling of clay, firing, and glazing discussed in Chapter 3 relate as well to direct clay techniques. (Figures 5-23 and 5-24)

SPRAY METAL

Spray-metal equipment, discussed in Chapter 9, pages 174 and 175, on coatings, can be used in direct buildup. Armatures covered with fine screening, or material that will provide a good mechanical bond with the sprayed metal, should be used.

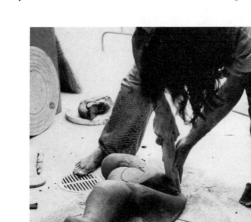

Figure 5-23

Direct clay form using wheel thrown parts. *By Pat Hollern.*

Figure 5-24

Completed direct clay form. *By Pat Hollern.*

Wood Fabrication

SIX

Visually, wood is diversely rich. Amidst the clamor for new materials, it is refreshing to see sculptors and students who continue to explore the visual texture and forms that only wood can produce.

Wood-carving is distinct in itself. Fabrication and construction with wood perhaps offer greater diversity and spontaneity in producing sculpture than almost any other material. Readily cut and shaped with hand tools and inexpensive mechanical-shop equipment, wood pieces are easily assembled by bolting, gluing, and nailing.

In observing some of wood's visual properties, we find that carefully polished, stained, or laminated woods reveal the beauty of the grain, the growth rings, and the inner structure. Weathered timber and planks bolted together boldly express the unusual structural nature of wood. Assembled boards and strips assume their own forms and attitudes. Band sawing readily produces a limitless variety of shapes and configurations. Massive monolithic forms are easily constructed out of plywood. Properly coated or painted, they are reasonably durable.

Imported and domestic woods are available in a wide variety of textures, colors, shapes, and sizes.

Selecting a piece of wood is a matter of personal choice, intent, and common sense. Some woods left untreated are more weather-resistant and less susceptible to decay than others. Some possess better structural properties. The grain, as a result of the way a log is cut, may affect the wood's structural properties, surface treatment, or paintability. Each specie of wood has its own unique color and grain configuration.

A wide variety of used and weathered old lumber can be found in wrecking-company yards; two other principal sources for wood are lumberyards dealing in construction-grade materials, a few hardwoods, and specialty items, or lumber companies which specialize in fine grades of domestic or imported woods or plywoods.

Wood for fabrication may be classified as hardwood or softwood. This is a botanical distinction. There are some soft hardwoods. Hardwoods are those woods produced from broadleaf-bearing trees. Needle-bearing trees, such as pine, produce soft woods.

Some of the soft woods ordinarily available are cedar, redwood, fir, cypress, hemlock, pine, and spruce. Some of the common hardwoods are basswood, beech, cherry, gumwood, hickory, mahogany, maple, oak, poplar, walnut, and willow. Lumberyards usually handle only soft woods for general construction and a few hardwoods such as oak and walnut. Some lumber companies specialize in a wide variety of domestic and imported hard-wood boards and plywoods.

The grain in a piece of lumber depends on the way it is cut in relation to the annual growth rings of the log and the kind of growth ring. Growth rings may vary in thickness. (Figure 6-1) Each annual ring usually consists of a spring wood, with a soft, light-colored ring and a summer wood, with a harder and darker ring. In some woods, there may be less distinction in hardness and color between the spring-wood and summer-wood rings. These factors, as well as the manner in which the wood is cut, determine the boldness of the grain and the machining and finishing characteristics of the wood.

If slabs are simply cut off a log, the grain is more open and wavy. This is called "plain sawed" or "slash grained." Cutting into the log parallel to the radius produces a straight grain and is referred to as "quarter sawing." Quarter-sawed lumber has less shrinkage, warpage, and grain rise. It is more paintable and does not surface check or split as much as plain-sawed. (Figure 6-2)

Plywood grain configurations also vary according to the method of cutting the veneer. If a log or half log is mounted on a lathe and revolved against the blade of a knife, the result is a rotary or half-round veneer. If the log is sawed into halves or sections and the sections are mounted on a slicer after having been softened by steam, boiling or soaking, a sliced veneer is produced. Rotary, half-round, and plain-sliced grains are often wavy and bold. Sliced plain-quartered grains are straight. In some instances, veneers are sawed rather than being sliced.

Selecting a piece of wood for sculpture is a matter of personal choice and common sense. Any surface or texture has aesthetic potential. However, if the wood is to be painted and a smooth, grain-free surface is desired, boards or sheets should be selected with this application in mind.

Material for wood fabrication may be thought of in terms of "boards, planks, dimensional lumber, timbers," and "sheets." In rough dimensions, boards are usually cut to one inch or less in thickness and

four inches or more in width. Narrower pieces would be classified as strips. Dimensional lumber may be two to five inches in thickness. Timbers are at least five inches. Sheets consist of plywood or pressed-wood products such as masonite and particle board.

Lumber is classified according to the degree

Figure 6-1
Growth rings on a Bois d-arc log.

Figure 6-2
Plain sawed (A) and quarter sawed (B) wood grain.

A   B

of manufacturing at the saw mill, its use, and the quality of the material. The degree of manufacture would be "rough," "dressed" or "worked." Rough lumber is as it appears after being cut from the log, with the edges trimmed. The nominal size or rough-cut dimension is usually in increments of an inch. Rough-cut lumber can be readily identified by the presence of saw marks and its rough appearance. Dressed lumber is surfaced (planed smooth) on one or two sides, one or two edges, or all surfaces. Common boards and strips purchased at the lumber yard are normally dressed thicknesses of one-fourth, three-eighths, one-half, three-fourths, or 13/16 of an inch. In surfacing or dressing dimensional lumber, it loses about one-fourth to three-eighths of an inch of its original dimension. Timber loses about one-half inch. For example, if you order a one-by-four-inch piece of lumber at a lumber yard, it will be three-fourths to 25/32 inches thick and three and five-eighths inches wide. An ordinary two-by-four piece of dimensional lumber would be one and five-eighths inches thick and three and five-eighths inches wide. Worked lumber receives additional milling after having been dressed. Tongue-and-groove lumber and moldings are typical of worked lumber.

Use classifications of lumber are "yard," "factory," "shop" and "structural" grades. Yard lumber is the type stocked at most lumber yards. Factory and shop grades are a better class of material, produced for wood-product manufacturing. Structural grades are large-sized pieces selected for their strength and durability.

Yard lumber is classified as "select" or "common." Common lumber is graded from one to five. Grading is based on the number of knots, the soundness of the knots, pitch pockets, spots of decay, and other defects. Number one lumber has a few sound knots but is relatively clear. As the number becomes larger, the number of defects increases. Select lumber is a finer grade than common. It is classified "A, B, C" or "D." A type is clear and relatively free of all defects. Grade B is clear but permits minor defects. Grades A and B are used when a nearly perfect natural or stained finish is desired. Grades C and D are used for painted surfaces. Grade C is often used for molding and for other millwork.

Factory and shop lumber is graded on the basis that it is going to be cut into pieces that are clear and sound. It is supplied to manufacturers of furniture and other wood products. The grade of lumber, inspection agency, kind of lumber and conditions of lumber (green or dry) can be identified by the grade mark on the end or surface of the board.

Structural lumber consists of dimensional lumber or timbers. Lumber yards normally stock dimensional lumber such as two-by-four, two-by-six, two-by-eight, two-by-ten, and two-by-twelve. They also stock some four-inch-thick material. Timbers are usually specially ordered from the sawmill.

When lumber is purchased, it is ordinarily measured in terms of board-feet. A board-foot is 12-by-12 inches by one inch thick. To compute board-feet in inches, the thickness is multiplied by the width and then by the length; the resulting figure is then divided by 144. If the length is in

Figure 6-3

Typical grade markings for plywood. *Courtesy of American Plywood Association.*

feet, the thickness is multiplied by the width in inches, then multiplied by the number of feet and divided by 12. Normal lumber widths are two, four, six, eight, ten, and 12 inches and from four to 20 feet in length in increments of two feet. Strips of lumber are purchased by the lineal foot. Boards and sheets are sold by the square foot.

Sheets of plywood are made from thin strips or sheets of veneer that are glued together with the grain of each layer running at right angles to the previous layer. This cross-laminating produces sheets with high strength in both directions. The number of layers in a sheet may vary from three to seven ply. We are most familiar with plywood as four-by-eight sheets. However, one-fourth-inch plywood is available in sheets up to 12 feet in length. Three-eighths-inch plywood can be obtained in lengths up to 16 feet. Plywood is available in thicknesses of one-eighth to one and 3/16 inches.

Plywood is manufactured in two types: exterior with waterproof glue and interior with moisture-resistant glue. The grade of a veneer sheet is designated as "N, A, B, C," or "D." N-grade is the best, and D is the poorest. Grades N, A, and B are used as the face of the plywood or on both sides where both sides are exposed. Grades C and D are used as inner layers or as backing when the back is not exposed. Besides the grade or quality of the veneer, the kind of wood used in the veneer is designated "1, 2, 3" and "4," with "1" being the most desirable.

The quality of the sheet of plywood can be recognized by the marks on the sheet and on the edge. (Figure 6-3) Ordinarily we might go to a lumberyard and ask for a piece of plywood, interior or exterior, good on one side or good on both sides. If the plywood were for staining or natural finishing, it ideally should be N-grade. If it were for painting, and a smooth finish were desired, it should be A-grade or a plywood with a special surface for painting.

There is a wide variety of plywoods available in both exterior and interior forms. One group is plywood with fine surface appearance; another is used by construction and industry, in which case, it is assumed that the surface of the plywood is to be covered by another material, or that the plywood is selected for unusual structural needs or other properties.

The first group is perhaps of most interest to the sculptor. Interior plywoods are available with

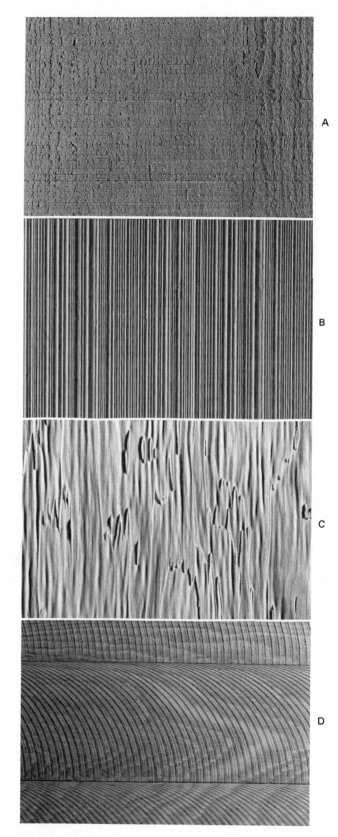

Figure 6-4

Plywood decorative textures. (A) Rough sawn; (B) striated; (C) brushed; and (D) circular sawn. *Photographs courtesy of American Plywood Association.*

Figure 6-5
Fabrication of a plywood sculpture with framework out of dimensional lumber.

Figure 6-6
Detail showing gussets and bracing. (Note grade marking on plywood.)

Figure 6-7
Sections completed prior to installation.

Figure 6-8
Completed sculpture. *Denver Sculpture Symposium. By author.*

various-grade surfaces, veneers, and decorative treatment. Decorative treatment may consist of the veneer being brushed, scored, grooved, or rough-sawed. (Figure 6-4) Interior plywoods are available with hardboard, plastic, or other precoatings. Of the exterior plywood, the most weather-resistant and most paintable would have greatest sculptural appeal. Marine plywood is often used. High-density overlaid plywood and medium-density overlaid plywood with a fused resin-fiber overlay is particularly durable and paintable. The fiber overlay prevents grain raising and problems often associated with plywood and the deterioration of coatings. The painted sculpture in Figure 6-8 was constructed of medium-density overlaid plywood. (Figures 6-5, 6-6, 6-7, and 6-8)

Sheets of pressed wood (masonite) or particle board are the result of the processing of wood chips or fibers. In pressed wood, the chips are treated and expanded into fiber with steam; the fibers are pressed together in heated hydraulic presses for forming sheets. Pressed wood is available in tempered and untempered sheets. The tempered sheet is harder, more abrasive, and moisture-resistant. It is available in four-by-eight-foot sheets, in thicknesses of one-eighth, 3/16, one-fourth and 5/16 inches. Larger sheets are available or can be specially ordered.

Particle board is made from resin-impregnated wood chips that are pressed into sheets under high pressure. It is available in four-by-eight, four-by-ten, and four-by-12-foot sheets, in thicknesses from one-fourth to one and one-eighth inches.

TOOLS

As stated earlier, lumber is easily fabricated with hand or power tools. In fact, a few hand tools can accomplish the majority of cutting and detailing operations that are achieved with power tools. The major distinction is in the time and effort involved. Some basic power tools are relatively inexpensive, however, and there would be very little merit or justification in using only hand tools in daily wood-fabrication problems. We might think of tools for wood fabrication in three basic groups: hand tools, hand power tools, and floor or bench-mounted power tools. Some tools in each of these categories would be essential for any complex wood fabrication.

Hand tools. There are a few basic hand tools that are essential for occasional work or for tasks not performed by power tools. These should be of good quality. With proper care, good quality hand tools will not only outlast inferior tools but will insure greater tool life and ease in performing the desired work. Some of the basic tools needed are as follows. (Figure 6-9)

Squares. Framing, try squares, and miter squares are used for drawing or checking angles of 45 to 90 degrees. The T-bevel square is used for angles other than 90 degrees, by setting the desired angle from a reading on a protractor.

Gauges. Marking gauges are used to mark off a specific width along the edge of a board. The sliding adjustable combination square can be used for this purpose by placing a pencil along the outside edge of the ruler as the square is moved along the board. (Figure 6-10)

Levels. Vertical and flat horizontal surfaces are checked for their accuracy with the level. When a level is placed on a flat or vertical surface, the air bubble in the liquid should be between the two lines in the glass indicator. (Figures 6-11 and 6-12)

Saws. On occasions it becomes necessary to cut a piece of material with a handsaw. To cut across the grain, a cross-cut saw with eight teeth or points per inch is used. For fine-finish cuts, a saw with ten and a half points to an inch is preferable. To rip a piece of wood along the direction of the grain, a saw with five and a half points per inch is used. In handsawing, small pieces may be placed in a vise, whereas large pieces are placed on a low table or on sawhorses and held in place with the knee. The saw is gripped with the right hand, with the thumb and index finger along the sides of the saw. The cut is made along the outside of the line, leaving a trace of the line as cutting proceeds. It is best to start with a few short strokes to get the cut started and then apply even, full strokes. If the wood binds the saw blade, drive a wooden wedge in the crack or kerf to slightly spread the wood and relieve the pressure. For cutting inside holes, a starting hole is drilled and a keyhole saw is used. For scroll work and odd contours, a coping saw may be used if an electric saber or jig saw is not available. When cutting with a coping saw, the blade is placed in

Figure 6-9

Basic woodworking hand tools: (1) handsaw; (2) keyhole saw; (3) coping saw; (4) wrecking bar; (5) nail puller; (6) chisels; (7) brace; (8) calipers; (9) bit set; (10) draw knife; (11) wood rasps; (12) rafter square; (13) combination square; (14) sliding "T" bevel; (15) steel measuring tape; (16) folding ruler; (17) level; (18) scratch awl; (19) flat blade screw driver; (20) bull nose rabbet plane; (21) bench plane; (22) tack hammer; (23) claw hammer; (24) rubber tipped mallet; and (25) rasplane.

Figure 6-10

Marking lumber using a combination square.

Figure 6-12

Detail of level showing air bubble between lines.

Figure 6-11

Level being used to check a vertical edge.

the saw with the teeth pointing toward the handle. The cutting is done as the saw is pulled. The material being cut may be placed in a vise or clamped to a table. Coping-saw blades may have anywhere from ten to twenty teeth per inch and are suitable for fine, delicate scroll work.

Clamps. Clamps are the principal holding devices in wood work. C-clamps are used to clamp stock of a few inches in thickness. Bar clamps, designed to span greater distances, are for holding and gluing in the assembly of materials. The adjustable hand-screw clamp is designed for holding and exerting pressure on material. The miter clamp is essential for holding square-mitered corners while nailing and gluing. There is a wide variety of miter clamps. Spring clamps are particularly helpful in holding flat-sheet material while gluing it to wood frames or supports. (Figure 6-13)

Hammers. The claw hammer, the principal tool used for driving, setting, or pulling nails, is available in weights from five to 20 ounces. For finishing and average work, a 12 to 16-ounce hammer is used. Twenty-ounce hammers are used for heavy construction and for driving spikes or large nails. A good-quality hammer is important. It should be well-balanced and of a good-grade, properly tempered steel. The face or striking surface, polished and hard-tempered, is not simply flat but slightly convex. A woodworking hammer should not be used in metalworking; The face should be kept clean.

Hand plane. The hand plane is used for smoothing or beveling surfaces and edges if a power planer or jointer is not available. The bench plane, eight or nine inches long, is often used by hobbyists for this operation. It is however, a more professional approach for planning long surfaces or edges to use the 22-inch jointer, 18-inch fore, or 14-inch jack plane to produce better results. Under ideal circumstances, the jointer or fore plane would be used for rough removal of wood, followed by the jack plane for further finishing. The jack plane can be used as a general-purpose plane for both operations if another plane is not available.

The bench plane is normally used for finish-planing of short surfaces and edges. The block plane has its cutting edge set at a less acute angle (20 degrees) and is used for planing end grain. Normal blade angle for most planes is 45 degrees. Special-purpose planes are available for cutting rabbets, planing concave and convex surfaces, dadoing, cutting tongue and grooves, scraping, and other shaping and finishing operations.

In planing, the depth of cut is controlled by adjusting the adjusting nut. The lateral adjustment

Figure 6-13
Clamps for working with wood and metal: (1) corner clamp; (2) "C" clamp; (3) gluing clamp; (4) spring clamp; and (5) pipe gluing clamp.

lever is used to tilt or move the blade to adjust for a uniform cut. The depth of cut may vary, depending on the hardness of the wood and the amount of wood to be removed. For finishing, the plane is set to shave off slight amounts. All planing should be in the direction of the wood grain, to avoid tearing or gouging the wood. In the planing of end grain with the block plane, the plane is moved at a slight angle to the direction of travel. The wood should be clamped or held securely in a woodworking vise while planing. In planing flat surfaces, the wood can be butted up against a stop fastened to the work bench. For planing edges on strips, a V-shaped guide can be nailed to the workbench as shown in Figure 6-14.

Planes should be stored with the blades adjusted so they are not protruding from the surfaces of the planes. The plane blade should be kept sharp by occasional honing on an oilstone. In planing old wood, care should be exercised to be certain all nails are removed. If the plane blade becomes nicked, it is necessary to grind it down

Figure 6-14

Edge planing with the bench plane. (Note jig for holding lumber.)

on a bench grinder and resharpen or hone it on an oilstone.

Chisels. The flat chisel is used for chopping or paring out dovetails, lap joints, and other detail. For special purposes there is a variety of chisels, such as the mortice chisel for morticing; the butt chisel, with a short blade for working in awkward places and for finishing; the offset chisel, for working close to a surface; and the paring chisel, for fine finishing. The firmer chisel is a rugged, general-purpose chisel. A set of these would be adequate for most work. Chisel widths are normally sold in increments of one-fourth inch up to two inches. The blade lengths may run from three to six inches.

Chisels should be sharpened periodically on an oilstone, to maintain a good cutting edge. For chopping out wood, the chisel is struck with a wooden mallet. The wood should be securely clamped to a workbench or held in a vise, to free the hand for working the chisel. The usual position of the chisel is with the bevel down. For paring or finishing, it may be tapped with the palm of the hand or simply held firmly and pushed with a slight side-to-side motion, to cut the material.

Screwdriver. In woodworking, since the slotted screw is usually used, the flat-tipped screwdriver is the principal tool for driving or removing screws. Sometimes, Phillips screws and Phillips screwdrivers may be used.

The flat-tipped screwdriver is available in many sizes. Selecting the proper size is essential for efficient work. A good set of screwdrivers with sufficient variety in tip size is necessary to avoid damaging the wood, the screw, or the screwdriver. Inexpensive screwdrivers should be avoided, since their metal tips are usually inferior and are readily worn and damaged; The handles moreover, are usually too small in diameter, reducing the leverage and making driving the screw more difficult.

As well as the common screwdriver, special-purpose screwdrivers are available. The offset, stubby, and ratchet offset are used for driving screws in spaces inaccessible to the common screwdriver. The spiral ratchet screwdriver makes it possible to drive or remove screws more rapidly. Screwdriver bits that fit a bit brace make it possible to apply more leverage and pressure. Electric and pneumatic screwdrivers are used for fast-production work.

Rasps and files. When the plane or chisel cannot be used, a rasp or file may be needed for shaping and finishing. Rasps and files are available in a

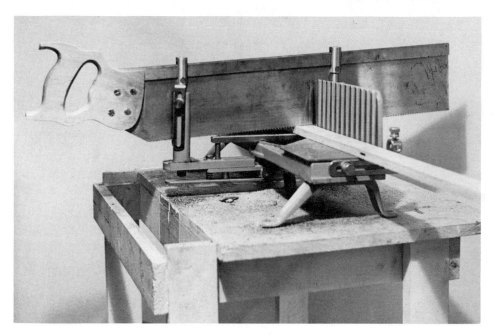

Figure 6-15
Miter box for cutting 45° and 90° cuts.

variety of shapes and degress of coarseness. A useful version of the rasp is the rasplane. It has an open-mesh, serrated, removable blade that cuts rapidly and is self-cleaning. A drum variety of this is available for use with an electric drill. Rotary files and rasps are also made for use with a drill. In handrasping and filing, the cutting is done on the forward stroke; pressure should be released on the backstroke. Files can be kept clean with a wire brush called a "file card." Separate files should be used for wood and metal. All files should be fitted with proper handles, for ease of handling and proper manipulation of the tools.

Wood bits. Devices for cutting holes in wood are turned with the bit brace, hand drill, or the electric drill. Today, the bit brace and the hand drill are used only when electric power is not available.

Twist auger bits, expansion bits for large holes, twist drills, and the countersinks are used with the bit brace. Small twist drills and countersinks are used with the hand drill. Twist drills, bits, countersinks, plug cutters, hole-cutting saws, and woodscrew bits are available for use with the electric drill. The woodscrew bits are designed to drill a pilot hole and countersink or counterbore to the desired depth.

Miter box. The miter box is a device used for hand cutting 45 degree angles and for squaring the ends of wood pieces. Inexpensive wood miter boxes can be purchased or built; however, they easily wear out and lose their accuracy. A good-quality miter box consists of metal parts and adjusts from 0 to 45 degrees, right or left. It also

adjusts for depth of cut. On the top edge, the saw has a rigid metal strip, which rides on two metal guides that support the saw blade. Miter clamps are available with saw guides, and bench-mounted miter clamps are used for framing and mitering strips. Miter attachments are designed for hand planes, for controlling the planing of bevelled edges. (Figure 6-15)

Nail sets. In finished-wood fabrication, it is often necessary to drive the nail beyond the surface of the wood and fill the hole with wood putty, to conceal the nail. Since it is also desirable to avoid denting the wood with the hammer, the nail is driven into the wood, allowing it to protrude 1/16 to one-eighth of an inch. A nail set is placed with its point on the nail, and the nail is driven in the remainder of the way by striking the nail set with the hammer. Nail sets are available with point diameters of 1/32 to 5/32 of an inch. (Figure 6-16)

Figure 6-16
Setting a nail with a nail set.

Figure 6-17
Left to right: portable jig saw, circle saw and 3/8-inch drill.

Portable electric tools. Portable electric woodworking tools were designed to ease the workload normally associated with hand tools and to supplement stationary power tools. With a portable electric drill, plane, sander, portable circle saw, saber or jig saw, and router, it is possible to perform most of the tasks ordinarily carried out by large stationary equipment. Power equipment purchased should be of good quality. For an occasional job, an inexpensive power tool may be satisfactory; however, it is a better practice to purchase something of good quality, with sturdy, accurate construction and ample power to do the job. (Figure 6-17)

Dull drills, cutters, and saw blades should not be used. Besides doing an inferior job, they place an excessive load on the tool's power supply and shorten the life of the tool. Portable power tools can be extremely dangerous if improperly handled. All tools should be equipped with a three-prong plug that provides for proper grounding of the tool. When changing drills, saw blades, and cutters, the tool should be unplugged from the extension cord or wall socket. This may seem troublesome, but many accidents have been caused by the accidental hitting of a switch while working on a power tool. The tool cord, fingers, and hands should be kept clear of the cutting edges of the tool. Goggles should be worn when operating all power tools.

Drills. Electric drills are classified according to the size of the drill bit the chuck will accommodate. Standard chuck capacities are one-fourth, three-eighths, one-half and three-fourths inches. Larger industrial sizes are available up to one and one-fourth inches. The three-eighth-inch drill is the most popular standard size tool for moderate and occasional heavy-duty jobs. The one-half-inch drill is used for heavy work. Motor size is rated by amperage. Typical amperage is from 2.4 amps, 115 volts, for a one-fourth-inch drill, to around 11 amps, 115 volts, for a three-fourths inch drill. Drill speeds are rated on the basis of the drill's being run with or without a load. Small drills operate at higher speeds than large drills. A one-fourth-inch drill may have a load speed anywhere from 750 to 3,300 r.p.m.; three-eighth- and one-half-inch drills run with load speeds between 300 and 700 r.p.m. The three-fourth-inch drill runs at a speed of 200 to 300 r.p.m. Variable speed drills are available with the speed varying from zero to the maximum speed of the motor. Some drill motors are reversible.

Available for electric drills are attachments that convert the drill to other small woodworking tools. Saber saw, circle saw, drill press, sander and router attachments are the most common. These may be satisfactory for extremely light work, but normally they are not capable of the capacity a sculptor demands of a tool.

Power Plane. The power plane is normally used in construction for planing and fitting wood doors, windows, and cabinet work. For the sculptor, it can be useful when a jointer is not available. As a shop or studio tool, a moderate-sized jointer, which costs no more than a power plane, is preferable. The cost is about two hundred and fifty dollars for either one. A good-quality power plane has a motor capacity of three-fourths or one H.P., with plane speed of 18,000 to 23,000 r.p.m. The shoe or plane surface, adjustable for planing angles, is 16 to 24 inches long and two to two and a half inches wide. It can be mounted on a workbench with bench brackets and serve as a jointer. Grinding arbor and attachments are also available. (Figure 3-19)

Router. The router cuts and performs shaping and detailing otherwise accomplished with the shaper. It is pushed over the surface or along the edge of the board, which must be securely clamped or held with a bench vise, leaving the hands free to operate the router. Adjustable guides and the shape of the cutters determine the depth, width, and configuration of the cut. Cutter blades are designed for molding cuts, rabbets, inserts, dovetails, fluting, dados, grooves, and beading. There are also trim saws, grinding wheels, power planes and other attachments. Gouging and routing out for relief carving can be successfully accomplished with the router, followed by hand finishing.

The size of the router is based on the horsepower or amperage and the diameter of the cutter shaft. For very light, delicate work a one-fourth-H.P. router is adequate, whereas three-fourths or one-H.P. router is more reasonable for general studio work; for heavy-duty continuous work, one and one-fourth to two and one-half-H.P. routers should be used. Router speeds are normally from 18,000 to 27,000 r.p.m. Blades must be kept sharp, operating at these high speeds. Burn marks on the finish cut indicate dull blades or too slow a travel speed for the router. The router can be mounted with special bench brackets for use as a shaper.

Saber saw. As mentioned in Chapter 8 on metalworking, the saber saw or portable jig saw is one of the most versatile tools in use. Although not as accurate as bench-mounted equipment, it can do much of the work normally associated with the jig saw, band saw, circle saw, and radial-arm saw. The blade on the saber saw operates with a reciprocal action similar to that of the jig saw. A larger, all-purpose version of the saber saw takes blades up to 12 inches in length and can be used for rough-cutting thick-dimension lumber and timber up to eight or ten inches thick. The normal saber saw blade is from three to four inches in length. A heavy-duty saber saw can cut two-inch material and with the proper oversized blade can do small amounts of cutting in thicknesses up to four inches.

Guides for ripping, mitering, and crosscutting mount on the saw for greater accuracy. The saw tilts for 45-degree cuts and other angles. In some models, the saw motor and housing can be turned independently of the blade mechanism, for greater maneuverability. Variable-speed saws are available. Although these are not essential for wood, it is advisable to purchase a variable-speed saw, taking into account possible future needs for cutting other material. Typical amperage ratings on a saber saw are 2.5 to three amps, whereas the all-purpose saw are rated at about five amps.

In operating the saber saw, a starting hole is usually drilled for inside cuts, For many saws it is possible to start a cut without drilling a hole: by tilting the saw and gradually bringing it into an upright position as the blade cuts into the wood. The saw should be pressed lightly against the surface of the wood as it is moved forward. Upon completion of the cut, the pressure should be maintained until the saw is stopped; blades are frequently broken when downward pressure is released before the saw has completely stopped.

Normal blades for cutting wood with a saber saw have from six to ten teeth per inch. The design and set of the teeth in the blade determine whether the saw is used for rough or finish cutting. Special blades are manufactured with fewer teeth for rough cutting dimensional lumber, for cutting at right angles to the normal position of the blade, and with a knife edge for leather.

Circle saw (portable). The circle saw is classified according to blade size and motor capacity. Blade sizes are six, seven, eight, nine, and 10 inches. Motor capacity or amperage rate from 7 amps, 115 volts, for home workshops and light construction, to ten- to 14-amp saws, for heavy-duty construction and fabrication.

The circle saw is equipped with a tilting surface for cutting angles, a rip gauge or guide for ripping, and an adjustment for depth of cut. The capacity or depth of cut depends upon the saw blade sizes. At 90 degrees, a ten-inch saw will cut to a depth of about four inches. A sliding safety guard keeps the blade covered when the saw is not in use.

When cutting with the circle saw, the blade should be adjusted to extend about one-fourth inch beyond the material. The saw should be grasped by the handle and front knob, held firmly, and moved with moderate forward pressure. As the saw is moved forward to start the cut, the guard is pushed back by the edge of the board. The saw should not be forced. Blades should be kept sharp. The material should be placed on

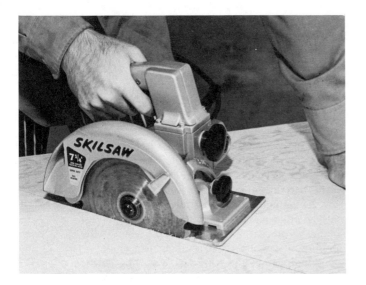

Figure 6-18
Portable circle saw cutting plywood.

sawhorses or on a low cutting table. Special-purpose blades for cutting material other than wood, tables for converting to a table saw, and other attachments are available. (Figure 6-18)

Stationary power tools. Power tools ordinarily used in wood shops are the table circle saw, radial-arm saw, band saw, scroll or jig saw, jointer, planer, sander, lathe, and drill press. Stationary power tools are rated according to size of the blade, cutting capacity, and horsepower of the motor. Motors in excess of one H.P. should be operated at 220 volts, single or three-phase for maximum power and efficiency. They should be equipped with some form of overload switch or device to prevent overheating and burning out of the motor. Motors, wheels, and shafts on the tools should have bearings instead of bushings, if long life is expected of the tool. Equipment should be kept clean and oiled at required intervals. Manufacturer's instructions should be carefully studied and followed for required maintenance, operation, blade-changing, and adjustment. Recommended safety precautions should be followed.

Bandsaw. The wood-cutting band saw has a continuous steel blade mounted on two rubber-tire wheels. Adjustments are provided for centering the blade on the wheel. Adjustable guides hold the blade straight and support the back of the blade during working pressure. A typical blade speed is about 3,000 surface-feet per minute. The working table on the saw is designed to adjust for cutting various angles as well as cutting straight cuts. A slot in the work table

allows for the use of a miter-gauge guide for straight cuts and angles. With the miter gauge and the table tilted, compound cuts are possible. Attachable guide bars for the table allow for the use of a rip fence for cutting strips. The table size is about the same width as the diameter of the wheels holding the blade.

Band saws are in many sizes. The size is based on the wheel size, which determines the approximate cutting capacity, or distance between the cutting edge of the blade and the rear of the blade, minus about one-fourth inch for the rear blade guard. For example, a saw with a 14-inch wheel would have clearance of 13 and a half inches for cutting a piece of wood. Wheel sizes are from 12 to 40 inches. A typical small-shop or studio band saw would be 14 inches and would cut wood up to six inches thick. Ideally, a studio should have a saw of at least 20 inches, which would allow for cutting thicknesses up to 13 inches. The motor size is usually one-half H.P. for a 14-inch saw and may be up to two H.P. for a 20-inch saw. (Figures 6-19, 6-20, and 6-21)

The saw should always be kept in proper adjustment: tension on the blade should be appropriate to blade size; blade guide-pins should be adjusted so that they clear the blade by about the thickness of a heavy piece of paper. The saw teeth should project slightly in front of the guide pins. The back guide or blade support holds the blade in this position when working pressure is applied to the front of the blade.

Saw blades come in widths from one-eighth to three-fourths inches. The one-half-inch blade is a good, all-purpose width, unless fine scroll work is being done. Standard and skip-tooth blades are most common in wood cutting with a raker or alternate set. (See Figure 8-36, Chapter 8.) The kind of blade used and the number of teeth depend on the cutting operation to be performed. For fine cutting and scroll work, a standard blade with a wavy or alternate set and six teeth to an inch might be used. For cutting through thick stock, a skip-tooth blade with a raker set would provide the widest possible kerf, freedom from binding, and the best cutting action.

In a wood shop, the band saw is primarily used for cutting curves. Straight cuts and ripping can be accomplished more efficiently and more accurately with the circle saw. Cutting on a band saw is relatively simple: the upper guides are raised to a height to just clear the material; the wood is fed through the saw blade with moderate to light pressure. If excessive pressure is needed, it probably indicates a dull blade, which should

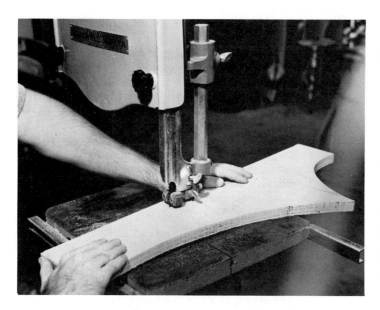

Figure 6-19
Cutting free forms on the band saw.

Figure 6-20
Cutting on the bandsaw using the miter gauge as a guide.

be changed. In sawing, it is important to be aware of the position of the fingers, keeping them clear of the path of the blade. Particular caution should be exercised when completing a cut.

In complex cuts, it is often advisable to make several short cuts into the material or to rough out the material. For duplicate pieces, the material can be stacked and tacked together and sawed at the same time. Rounds can be ripped by using a V-block or special jig. The rip fence can be used as a guide for sawing short lengths of dowels or other stock, ripping or resawing a thick board into two thin boards, diagonal cutting of square stock (from corner to corner), and cutting off corners of square stock for turning. Jigs can be constructed for cutting circles, rounding corners, kerfing, arcs, tapering, and many other special problems.

Table Circle-saw. The table saw is classified by blade size. Blade sizes for shop and fabrication are eight, ten, 12, 14 and 16 inches. The ten-inch saw with a two- to three-H.P. motor is the most popular size; it can handle most shop and studio work. The standard motor for the ten-inch saw operates at about 3,450 r.p.m., with a cutting speed of about 9,000 surface feet per minute. Its depth of cut is three inches, and it can readily handle boards, sheets, dimensional lumber, etc., up to two inches in thickness. If the saw is expected to rip large quantities of dimensional lumber in thicknesses exceeding two inches, a 12

or 14-inch saw should be used with a five- to seven and a half-H.P. motor. The small eight-inch saw may be all right for occasional light work, but it should not be considered for the classroom, shop, or professional studio.

Figure 6-21
Constructing a wood relief using the bandsaw for cutting. *Student project, Southern Methodist University.*

Inexpensive table saws are available with tilting tops. The stationary top with the tilting arbor is the better machine, since it is safer, easier to operate, and more accurate. The tilting arbor saw and the tilting top saw both adjust for 45 degrees and other kinds of angles.

Besides sawing, the table saw can dado and groove, by virtue of a dado head consisting of

Figure 6-22

Basic saw blades.

novelty combination

rip

cross cut

plywood

carbide tipped
wood cutting

metal cutting

abrasive metal cutting

dado blades

Figure 6-23

Ripping a piece of plywood on the table saw. Note saw blade height and position of fingers over the rip fence as an added precaution to prevent the hand from getting too close to the blade.

two outside blades and four inside cutters. By varying the number of inside cutters, or by using only one of the saw blades, grooves and dados can be cut from one-eighth to 13/16 inches in width. When equipped with a special molding head and appropriate blades, the table saw can function as a shaper and can cut a variety of molding shapes. Standard blades for the circle saw are the crosscut, rip, and combination. (Figure 6-22) The combination can be used for ripping and crosscut. A carbide-tipped combination saw blade, although initially expensive, is perhaps one of the best investments that can be made for wood-sawing operations. The initial high cost is soon offset by the fact that it seldom needs sharpening and the fact that only one blade is needed. The proper combination blade will cut plastic as well as wood.

In all sawing operations, the blade is raised to a height to project about one-fourth inch above the surface of the material. (Figure 6-23) Higher settings are unnecessary and hazardous. Hands should be kept clear of the blade, and proper devices should be used to hold material that is close to the blade. Loose clothing, particularly partially rolled-up shirt sleeves, neckties or hanging items, should be avoided.

Ripping, grooving, and cutting molding involves cutting the board lengthwise. For this operation, the board is placed flat on the saw table and is guided by the rip fence, to maintain the proper width being cut. The rip fence slides along a front and rear guide. The front guide is calibrated in inches, to indicate the width of the cut. The fence is equipped with a front and rear locking device, to hold the fence parallel to the saw blade. When ripping strips narrower than three inches, a push stick should be used to complete pushing the material through the saw. (Figure 6-24) A common and safe practice is to pull the remaining material through the saw rather than to use a push stick. When the material being ripped is long, an extension table or other support should be provided for the material as it feeds off the saw table. Ideally the saw should be equipped with an antikickback device and a splitter for ripping; the splitter spreads the board, preventing it from binding on the saw blade.

The miter gauge is used as a guide for the material when the cut is made across the board. Attempting a crosscut without the support of the miter gauge is dangerous and should never be attempted. In a typical crosscut of strip material or boards, the wood is held against the miter gauge with one hand and is pushed across the table; it is not necessary to hold on to the free end with the other hand. If a wood facing is fastened to the miter gauge (as in Figure 6-25), crosscutting operations are easier for long strips. Short pieces can be held down with a small block of wood, to avoid getting the fingers close to the blade.

A stop or the rip fence should never be used against the free end of the wood for measuring exact lengths. For measuring exact lengths, the safest method is to fasten a stop to the facing board on the miter gauge. With the miter gauge and saw set at an angle, compound angles can be cut. A wide variety of jigs can be constructed for sawing unusual details and joints.

Radial-arm circle saw. In the radial-arm saw, the saw is mounted on a track, over the work. For crosscutting, this has distinct advantages over a table saw, since the cutting operation and layout marks can be observed more easily. Woodworkers and fabricators many times disagree over the merits of the radial-arm saw and the table saw. Ideally, it is desirable to have both—using the table saw for rippings and the radial-arm saw for crosscutting, or using each saw according to which seems to provide the greatest ease, accuracy, and safety in the particular operation being performed. The distinct advantage in using the radial-arm saw for crosscut operations is that the material remains in a stationary position while the saw is moved across the work to make the cut. If a studio or shop is to be equipped with one saw, it would be advisable to consider the radial arm saw, which is also more versatile than the table saw; with attachments, it can be used for dadoing, molding, drilling, sanding, shaping, and routing.

For cutting operations, the radial arm saw is placed into the desired position in relation to the table and ripping fence. The saw is never operated without the blade guard, in normal ripping and crosscutting operations. For ripping, the saw is turned parallel to the rip fence. The guard is adjusted to just clear the material, allowing the sawdust to be collected and discharged away from the worker. For maximum cutting width, the rip fence can be moved all the way to the back of the table. A calibrated scale (in inches) on the over arm provides a convenient means of setting the width to be cut. An antikickback device on the guard prevents the material from being kicked back by the blade. This is adjusted to rest on the board. For ripping, the lumber is placed on the table against the rip fence and is pushed through the saw from the back side

Figure 6-24
Using a push stick to guide material.

Figure 6-25
Cross cutting with the miter gauge, a wood facing is attached to the miter gauge to help guide the material.

of the blade; feeding from the front results in pulling the board into the blade, making the rate of feed difficult to control; moreover, front-feeding is a dangerous, since, at the completion of the cut, the saw could easily pull the hand or fingers of the operator into the blade. In ripping, the same precautions should be observed as when cutting on a table saw. A push stick should be used for narrow cuts, or the work should be pulled through to complete the cut.

For crosscutting, the rip fence is in a position in front of the blade. The wood is placed and held against the rip fence with the left hand. The saw is grasped with the right hand and is slowly pulled across the wood to execute the cut. Hold the right arm rather stiffly, and hold back on the saw slightly as the saw is moved slowly forward. An abrupt forward movement may cause the saw to jam. If the saw is held securely by the proper handle, and care is exercised in being certain that the left hand (holding the material) is not in the path of the blade, crosscutting on a radial-arm saw can be safe and efficient. Material should never be crosscut unless it is held securely against the rip fence. For crosscutting a number of strips the same length, it is a simple matter to clamp a stop on the rip fence. For crosscutting 45-degree angles with the saw traveling at right angles to the rip fence, the saw is raised and tilted to a 45 degree setting. For a 45-degree angle from the rip fence, the overarm is moved 45 degrees. For compound angles, both adjustments are made. As well as for 90- or 45-degree cuts, the saw can be set for any other desired angle. The location for the adjustment knobs for making the settings on the saw will vary according to manufacturer. The manufacturer's instructions should be followed for cutting adjustments and maintenance of the saw. (Figure 6-26)

Radial-arm saws, as table saws, are rated by blade sizes, which may run up to 20 inches for an average fabrication shop or studio. Larger blades are used industrially. Motor speeds are usually 3,450 r.p.m., with surface feet per minute depending on the blade size. The average small shop or studio would use a ten- or 12-inch saw, with a motor rated at one H.P. for the ten-inch and three H.P. for the 12-inch. Saw blades and recommendations would be the same as for the table saw.

With the saw guard removed, the shaft pointing down, and the saw positioned behind the rip fence, the saw is in position for molding, routing, sanding, shaping, dadoing, and grooving along the edge and length of the material. With a drill-chuck attachment, it can be used as a vertical or horizontal drill press. Cove cutting and many other special cuts and details can be accomplished with the proper technique and the saw in the proper position.

Scroll saw. The scroll saw or jig saw is primarily used for cutting fine patterns and scroll work in thin stock. Intricate inside cuts can be made by drilling a hole through the sheet of wood, attaching the blade, and proceeding with the cutting. A principal advantage the scroll saw has over the band saw is its ability to make shorter-radius cuts, being able to cut from the inside of the material and having clearance for making wider cuts. A 24-inch scroll saw is able to cut to the center of a four-foot-wide piece of material.

The scroll saw operates on the basis of the blade moving up and down with a reciprocal action. Most saws are equipped with step pulleys or with a variable speed control to alter the speed from 600 to 1,700 cutting strokes per minute. A one-fourth- or one-third-H.P. motor is usually sufficient power. In thickness, the cutting capacity of the saw rarely exceeds two inches. The table of the saw tilts for bevel cuts. (Figure 6-27)

In cutting with the scroll saw, the upper guide (with the hold-down) is lowered on the material. The spring tension of the hold-down holds the material against the surface of the saw table. Feeding the work through the saw is a matter of moderate feed pressure.

The saw blades for the scroll saw consist of two basic types: the jeweller blade and the saber blade. The jeweller blade is held from both ends; the saber blade is mounted in the lower mount.

Figure 6-26

Cross cutting with a radial arm saw.

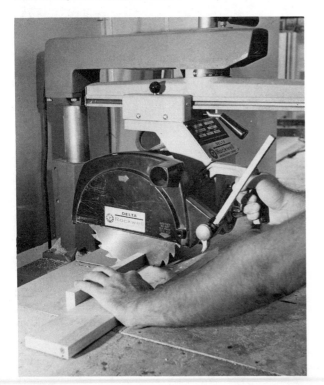

alignment. The day-to-day adjustments for cutting depth are made by adjusting the front half of the table. The fence can be tilted for planing angles or for beveling.

In planing on the jointer, the wood is held firmly against the fence and the table. The right hand is placed to the rear of the board and is used for feeding; the left hand leads and guides the material. The wood is pushed slowly over the cutting head; the wood should be fed so that the blades cut with the grain and in the direction of the rotation of the cutters. The guard should always be in proper position, covering the cutting edges. Particular attention should be directed to the position of the right hand and fingers feeding the material. They should not be resting on the table surface as the cut is completed. This is the point at which accidents usually occur. Fingers of both hands should always be clear of the table surface. For planing small strips or flat pieces, a push stick as shown in Figure 6-28 should be used.

Planer. The planer is used for the surfacing of boards and dimensional lumber. There are two basic types of planers: they either surface one side at a time or both sides at once, as the material is fed through. Planer sizes range from small machines, accommodating stock four inches thick by 12 inches wide, to large machines handling material eight inches thick and 48 inches wide. Motor sizes start at two or three H.P. for the smaller machines, and correspondingly increase as the machine becomes larger.

In operating the planer, the machine is set for the desired depth of cut (about 1/16 inch or less) and the rate of feed. The board is fed into

Figure 6-27
Sawing on a scroll saw.

The blades are mounted with the teeth pointed downward, since the cutting takes place on the down stroke. Saber blades are used for coarse cuts and for cutting larger radii. Jewellers blades are used for fine and extremely intricate cuts. Fine, spiral jewellers blades, with cutting surfaces on all sides, make it possible to change the direction of the cut with minimum movement of the material.

Jointer. The jointer is used as a planing machine, primarily in the surfacing of edges and some flat work. Some models are also used for rabbeting. The jointer uses a rotary cutting head with three or four blades turning at about 4,000 r.p.m. The material is planed as the board is moved across the table surface of the jointer. Jointer tables and blades vary in width from four to 16 inches. The six- or eight-inch model with a three-fourths or one-H.P. motor is usually sufficient for average wood shops and studios.

For planing, the jointer is set so that the rear half of the table is even with the highest point of the cutting knife. This is easily adjusted by placing a flat piece of wood flat on the rear half of the table extending over the blade. The blade is moved back and forth as the table is raised or lowered until the blade clears the strip of wood. All of the blades should be checked in this fashion. After the adjustment has been made, further adjustment should not be necessary until the knives are sharpened or appear to be out of

Figure 6-28
Surfacing on a jointer using a push stick.

the machine so that the blades cut with the grain. An infeed roller grasps the board and feeds it through the machine. An outfeed roller carries the stock out. Friction rollers hold the board in alignment with the cutting head.

Planers are relatively expensive in comparison to other shop equipment. For the shop or studio that does not wish to invest in a planer, lumber companies with mills, or shops doing commercial mill work, will plane material at a modest cost.

Shaper. The shaper is used primarily for shaping edges of boards in the production of molding or for cutting grooves, rabbets, and glue joints. When equipped with small sanding drums it can also be used for edge sanding, sanding inside contours and short-radius curves.

The shaper is essentially a machine with a vertically mounted spindle that can be raised and lowered. A cutter or cutting head with knives is attached to the spindle. It is equipped with a 3,450 r.p.m. motor. Power is transferred to the spindle by means of a belt and pulley. The ratio is usually three to one providing a spindle speed of about 10,000 r.p.m. The average shop shaper requires a one to two-H.P. motor.

Straight stock is cut by running the stock along a fence, past the projecting cutter blades. A hold-down device to hold the material against the table and the fence is highly recommended. For shaping ends of stock, a miter-gauge guide that fits into a slot on the table top is used. The stock is guided and pushed past the cutters. A sliding jig with miter gauge and hold-down clamps is a good device for this operation.

Figure 6-29

Shaper with three knife cutting head. Note hold down device.

Figure 6-30

Some typical knife shapes for cutting molding and detailing edges of material.

In shaping curves or material that cannot be guided against the fence, the wood is guided along a pin projecting from the table top and a collar on the spindle. Patterns can also be fashioned to act as guides. The material is clamped into the pattern guides and the pattern is guided along the guide pin and collar.

There are three basic types of cutters for the shaper: the three-lipped solid cutter, the open-face knife clamped between two slotted collars, and the three-knife cutter head with changeable blades. The three-lipped solid cutter is the safest and most convenient to use. (Figure 6-29 and 6-30)

Drill press. The drill press is primarily used for accurate drilling or sawing of holes, countersinking, circle cutting, plug cutting, and boring mortices. (Figures 6-31, 6-32, and 6-33) With attachments and jigs, it can be used for contour sanding, routing and shaping with the three-lip solid cutters. However, if a large quantity of this work is to be done, the appropriate piece of equipment should be used. The drill-press shaft is not designed to take continuous heavy side loads as are the router and shaper.

A particularly useful device for woodworking is the morticing attachment. It consists of a bit that cuts inside a square chisel; as pressure is is applied, the drill cuts out most of the material and the chisel squares the corners.

The standard drill press is the single spindle, 14- or 15-inch model, powered by a one-half or three-fourths H.P. motor. A variable speed machine is desirable so that it can be used for both wood and metal work. Typical speed ranges from 300 to 5,000 r.p.m. Drill presses are classified in terms of the distance they will drill into the center of a circle. In other words, a 14-inch drill press will drill into the center of a 14-inch circle, and the center of the drill chuck would be seven inches from the back-supporting column.

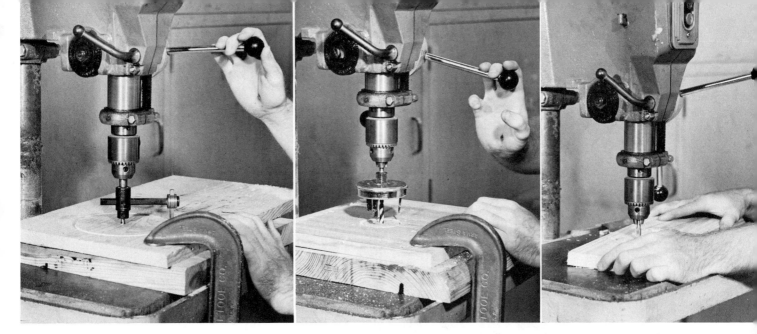

Figure 6-31

Circle cutter on a drill press.

Figure 6-32

Holecutting with a drill press.

Figure 6-33

Routing with the drill press.

In many cases, the work should be securely clamped to the drill press table for drilling operations. If material is hand held and a drill binds or catches in the material it can easily be pulled, from the hand and result in injury to the worker. Proper fences and jigs should be used for morticing, shaping, etc.

Lathe. Although many sculptors or students would seldom find a lathe applicable to their needs, it is an indispensable tool when round wood or spun-metal parts are needed. Turned wood parts can be used in wood constructions or as patterns for metal-casting. Spun-metal parts are occasionally needed in metal fabrication. Buffing wheels, grinding wheels, sanding wheels, sanding attachments, and drill chucks for horizontal drilling can be used with the lathe. (Figure 6-34)

Wood-turning is a relatively simple operation. For long turnings the piece of wood is placed between the spur center on the headstock spindle and the cup center on the tailstock spindle. The wood is first marked for the center on both ends by drawing two diagonal lines from

Figure 6-34

Wood turning lathe with wood pattern: (1) headstock spindle; (2) spur center; (3) tailstock; (4) cup center; (5) tailstock spindle; (6) tailstock spindle handle; (7) tailstock spindle clamp; (8) tool rest; (9) speed control.

Figure 6-35

Wood turning tools: (A) spear; (B) skew; (C) gouge; (D) round nose; (E) parting; (F) gouge; (G) skew; and (H) gouge.

corner to corner. A center hole is punched or drilled in the case of hard wood. Slight sawing of the crosslines on the band saw helps to position the spur center. The spur center is placed on the end of the material and is struck with a wood mallet, to seat it. Spur center and wood are then picked up and placed in the lathe. While holding the piece in position with one hand, the operator moves the tailstock up and locks it in place with the cup center pressing against the other end of the wood. The tailstock-spindle handle is then turned, pressing the cup center slightly into the wood. A moderate amount of pressure is applied; then, back off about one-fourth turn and lock the tailstock spindle in place with the tailstock-spindle clamp. The tool rest is then positioned to be about one-fourth inch away from the work.

Figure 6-35 illustrates the typical wood-turning tools. The gouge, used for gouging out, is the most used tool. The skew is used for smoothing, cutting shoulders, and other details. The other chisels are used when their shapes suit the desired contour to be cut. There are two basic procedures in wood turning: if the chisel is held horizontally on the tool rest and moved straight in, it is a scraping position; if the handle is dropped ten to 15 degrees, the chisel slightly turned toward the work and moved slowly in the direction of the cut, this is a shearing or cutting action. (Figure 6-36) The depth of cut should be slight—controlled by the forefinger of the left hand pressing against the tool rest, the chisel being held between the thumb and forefinger. The tool handle is grasped with the right hand well to the rear of the handle, to provide maximum leverage and control during the roughing-

out. In later finishing, it may be desirable to take a shorter grip on the handle. The gouge is held with the curve resting on the tool rest and the concave surface pointing up.

For turning shapes that cannot be held between the two centers, the wood is mounted with screws or cemented on a face plate attached to the headstock spindle. Many lathes have an outside spindle to allow for turning larger than the normal inside capacity of the lathe. This turning technique is always a matter of using a scraping position for the chisel; cutting or shearing would gouge into the wood. The tool rest is positioned on the center line of the piece being turned.

Figure 6-36

Wood turning a pattern for metal casting. Note position of gouge.

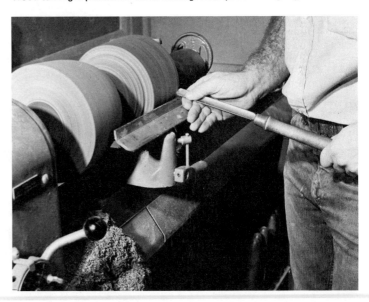

Normal turning speeds are 600 to 1,000 r.p.m., for roughing out the cylinder; 1,200 to 1,600, for further shaping; and up to 2,400, for final finishing and sanding.

The lathe size is determined by the maximum diameter of material it can turn. An average shop lathe would be an 11 or 12-inch machine with a one-half- or three fourth-H.P. motor. Limited variable speeds may be obtained by a series of step pulleys on inexpensive models; or a more complex variable speed unit, with speed choices anywhere between 300 to 3,600 r.p.m., is available on higher priced machines.

WOOD JOINTS

The essential goal in any wood joint is to achieve maximum strength between two or more pieces of material. If the wood structure is an internal frame to be covered with plywood or other material, wood or metal gussets (as in Figure 6-6), brackets or glue blocks often can be used to achieve the desired results. If the wood structure is exposed and joining occurs on finished surfaces, other means must be employed. Wood-joining problems may be classified as four basic types: end-to-end, edge-to-edge, end-to-surface other-than-end, and surface-to-surface. (Figure 6-37)

The simplest end joint for end-to-end fabrication is the end butt-joint. This may be satisfactory for internal structures with gussets or other bracing; however, when exposed, the joint can readily separate, and the exposed-end grain is often objectionable. A plain miter on the joint improves the appearance, and since it can be nailed from both directions, it is less likely to separate. Ideally, for the best joint, the miter should be splined; or, if the end grain is not objectionable, it can be dove-

Figure 6-37

Typical wood joints.

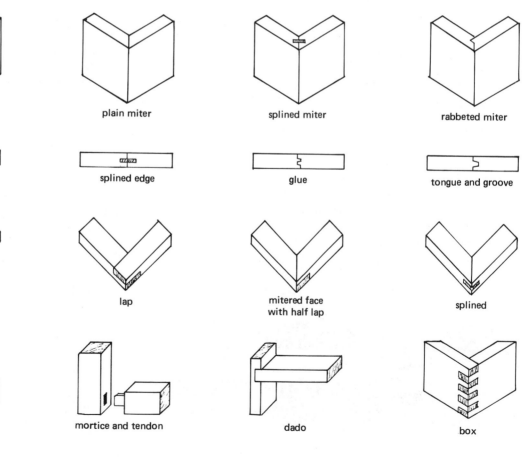

tailed or box-jointed. If the corner joint is surface-to-surface, a simple end joint is the end lap joint. The end lap joint can also be handled as a miter, or the end joint can be mitered and splined. A mortice tenon joint can also be used.

Edge-to-edge is often used when several boards need to be joined to form a wider board or surface. The tongue and groove, spline, or glue joint are the three usual methods of joining. Edge-to-edge corner joints can be joined at 45 degree angles, as just described for end-to-end stock.

For end-to-surface, the joint can be dado, half lap, dovetail lap, or mortice tenon.

Any woodworking book will illustrate many variations of these joints. Any joint can be fashioned with simple hand tools or with appropriate stationary equipment.

BENDING

Wood can be bent by steaming, cutting relief kerfs, or laminating. In steaming, the wood is placed in a steam vessel or container, such as a metal tank large enough to hold the wood part. The tank can be covered but should not be sealed to the extent that steam pressure is built up. The wood part is placed on supports in the tank so that it does not touch the water. Steaming time is approximately one hour per inch of thickness of the wood. After the wood has been steamed and becomes pliable, it is clamped in place, or in a jig to the desired shape.

Cutting relief kerfs, one of the simplest methods of curving wood when maximum strength is not needed, is done very efficiently on the radial-arm saw. Cutting across the board to a depth of about three-fourths of the thickness of the wood allows the board to be bent. The closeness of number of cuts depends on the sharpness of the desired bend. Cuts or kerfs should be uniformly spaced if an even bend is expected. (Figure 6-38)

Laminating consists of clamping together thin strips of wood bent to the desired shape and clamped in a jig, or held in place until the glue has set. Thin strips of plywood or veneers are readily shaped in this fashion.

Wood to be bent should be clear and free of knots or defects. The grain of the wood should run parallel to the length of the material. Asbestos or leather gloves should be worn when handling the hot wood parts, if they are being steam bent.

FASTENERS

Nails, screws, bolts, and adhesives are the principal means used for fastening or holding parts together. Fasteners are often accompanied by the use of adhesives for added strength and rigidity. In close-fitting joints, the adhesive and bonding of the surfaces may provide the major portion of the joint strength, with the fastener merely serving to hold the parts together during the curing or drying of the adhesive.

The kind of fasteners used in wood depend entirely on joint design, performance required, and surface appearance. Exposed nails, bolts and screws can add a dramatic and effective detail on fabricated wood sculpture. (Figure 6-39). If fasteners need to be concealed, nails may be driven below the surface with a nail set as discussed on page 101. The hole is filled with a wood putty. Screws and bolts can be countersunk by drilling appropriate holes (as in Figure 6-40). Countersunk holes may be filled with putty, or wood plugs can be used if the hole is counterbored. Wood plugs can be made with a plug drill. For filling holes, prepared wood putty can be used. Epoxy paste is an excellent filler; or a plastic filler can be made by thickening catalyzed polyester resin with Cab-O-Sil®. The kind of filler used depends on the hardness of the wood and whether the wood grain is to be exposed or the material is to be painted.

Figure 6-38
Strip of wood relief kerfed for bending.

Figure 6-39
Bolted sculpture by Harvey Phillips. *Photograph courtesy of Harvey Phillips.*

COUNTER SUNK   COUNTER BORED

Figure 6-40
Countersunk and counterbored holes.

NAILS

Nails used for wood fabrication are essentially round lengths of metal with a head and a point. Although ordinarily made of steel, copper, aluminum, and other metals also may be used. Metallic coatings such as galvanizing are also applied to nails. Common nails and spikes have flat heads and are used in rough construction. Box nails are flat-headed nails made of a small diameter wire; they are less likely to split the wood than the common nail. Finishing nails have a small, tapered head designed to countersink into the wood. (Figure 6-41) The casing nail is similar to the finishing nail, except it has a slightly larger head for more holding. Common nails, finishing nails, box nails, and casing nails are all classified according to wire gauge and numbers. When ordering nails, it is good to remember that larger numbers indicate larger nails, both in diameter and in length. Figure 6-42 indicates common-nail lengths. The small-wire nails and brads are ordered by length and gauge or diameter. The wire nail has a flat head; the brad has a tapered head like the finishing nail's.

Besides the nails just described, there is a variety of nails designed for special purposes. Nails with grooves, rough, or coated surfaces are designed for extra holding or mechanical bonding in wood. The ring-lock-scotch nail and grip-screw nail are typical examples of this form of fastener. On the ring-lock nail, the projecting ridges prevent the nail from being pulled out. For any large permanent sculpture, nails of this kind should be used. Ring-lock nails were used for fastening the plywood to the wood frames, on the wood sculpture at the Denver Sculpture Symposium. Nail points may vary in shape to provide easier driving, prevent wood splitting, etc. Obviously, a fine-pointed nail will drive into the wood with less tearing and will have more holding quality than a dull or blunt point. Nail heads are available in many shapes to serve many purposes. (Figure 6-43) These are of particular interest to the sculptor wishing to use the head of a fastener as a decorative detail on the work, heads may be round, flat, oval, square, or diamond-shaped, and will vary in thickness. Diamond-headed boat spikes, drive spikes, track spikes, oval-headed beer-case nails, hoop fasteners and duplex-headed nails are just a few of the unusual nails not ordinarily considered.

In driving nails, if there is any possibility of splitting the wood, a pilot hole should be drilled. In driving finishing nails, the nail should be driven to about 1/16 to one-eighth inch from the surface and the driving and countersinking completed with a nail set.

A

Figure 6-41

Some basic nails. Nail code follows: (A) *Right:* Oil quenched hardened concrete nails—flat countersunk head, smooth shank, diamond point; *Left:* Oil quenched hardened masonry nails—flat countersunk head, fluted shank, diamond point; (B) Perfect shingle nail—flat head, smooth shank, blunt point; (C) Asbestos shingle nail—large flat head, barbed shank, long diamond point (usually galvanized); (D) Duplex head nail—diamond point, smooth shank; (E) Non-leak nail—large knobbed convex head, smooth shank diamond point; (F) Large head barbed roofing nail—large flat head, barbed shank diamond point; (G) Checkered head perfect roofing nail—large checkered head, smooth shank, diamong point; (H) Scotch finishing nail—bead head, cupped scotch shank, diamond point; (I) *Left:* Scotch common—flat head, scotch shank, diamond point; (J) *Right:* Common nail—flat head, smooth shank, diamond point; (K) Common nail—flat head, smooth shank, diamond point; (L) Finishing nail—brad head, cupped diamond point, smooth shank; and (M) Barbed dowel pin nail—headless, cupped end, diamond point. *Photographs courtesy of Bethlehem Steel Corporation.*

B   C   D   E   F   G   H   I   J   K   L   M

Figure 6-42

Basic nail lengths.

Designation	Length, inches
2d	1
3d	1-1/4
4d	1-1/2
5d	1-3/4
6d	2
8d	2-1/2
10d	3
12d	3-1/4
16d	3-1/2
20d	4
30d	4-1/2
40d	5
50d	5-1/2
60d	6

Figure 6-43

Different heads, shanks and tips of nails. *Photograph courtesy of Bethlehem Steel Corporation.*

116

DRIVER TYPES

slotted

phillips

HEAD STYLE

oval

round

falt

ACTUAL SIZE

24 20 18 16 14 12

11 10 9 8 7 6 5 4 3 2 1 0

Figure 6-44
Wood screws actual size.

WOOD SCREWS

The round, oval, and flat-headed, slotted wood screws are ordinarily used in wood fabrication. Assembling with screws is more costly and more time-consuming than nailing. However, in many circumstances it is preferred in wood sculpture fabrication. It provides a permanent, positive method of fastening, with little possibility of the fastener working loose (as is the case with nailing).

Screws are classified as to the thickness or diameter and length. The diameter of the screw is based on sizes from zero to 24. The 24-gauge is the largest size. (Figure 6-44)

For good craftsmanship and to prevent splitting the wood, it is a good practice to drill a pilot hole for the screw. If the head is to be countersunk, the pilot hole must be drilled out with a countersink, or counterbored. A set of drill bits that drill a pilot hole, extra diameter for the screw, shank, and countersink or counterbore all in one operation is an efficient way of drilling holes for setting screws.

If the head is countersunk, a putty filler is used to cover the head, unless the head is to remain flush and exposed. If it is counterbored, a wood plug is used. Round- and oval-head screws are used where the head can be exposed as a decorative element in the fabricated work.

BOLTS

When assembling with bolts, appropriate holes need to be drilled in the wood to the same diameter as the bolt. The round, oval-head carriage bolt with a square neck is generally used in wood-to-wood fabrication. The square neck of the bolt is seated in the previously drilled hole by striking the bolt with a hammer. The square neck prevents the bolt from turning while the nut is being tightened on the bolt. In the use of a lag bolt, a pilot hole is

117

Figure 6-45

Typical bolts: (A) carriage bolt; (B) lag bolt; and (C) machine bolt.
Photograph Courtesy of Bethlehem Steel Corporation.

drilled. The lag bolt has a screw-like thread that is turned into the material in the same fashion as a wood screw. Machine bolts can also be used in wood-to-wood or metal-to-wood fabrication. Washers may be used with bolts to increase the surface contact between the bolt and the material. Bolts can be recessed by counterboring and plugging or filling the hole. (Figure 6-45)

Plastic Fabrication

SEVEN

Since 1950, plastic has gained increased recognition as a sculptural material. Its acceptance suffered many of the prejudices that industrial use of plastics experienced in its infancy. Manufacturers, accustomed to metal and metal fabrication or other materials, were reluctant to use plastics; often considering plastics to be cheap substitutes for metal and other materials, they failed to recognize the unique, and sometimes superior, qualities of plastics.

In many sculptural or industrial applications, plastics can be superior to metal and metal fabrication techniques. However, the principal aesthetic merit of plastics in the arts, as in industry, is not only as a substitute for metal and other materials, but rather as a vast new array of materials suitable for many purposes.

For the sculptor, artist, and designer, it has opened the door to many form possibilities not previously feasible. For the first time in history, the sculptor has a selection of colored dimensional materials comparable to the painter's palette. Pigments and dyes added to plastic-sheet materials or resins to form coatings have given the sculptor an

acceptable and durable range of color with a high degree of permanency. Plastic has contributed new dimensions in the scale as well as the visual and tactile qualities, of the sculptural object. For example, soft inflatable works are one of the many approaches to sculpture made possible by plastic. (Figure 7-1)

This chapter deals primarily with a brief description of plastic materials and the basic fabrication and forming techniques of sheet, film, tube, rod, and slab material. Further discussion relating plastics to other techniques will be found in Chapters 2, 3, 4, 5, and 9, dealing with casting, carving, direct modeling, mold-making, and coatings. General safety procedures, as discussed in Chapter 15, should be observed in the handling of plastics. Solvent fumes, resins- and catalyst-fumes, dusts, and fumes from plastic heated to a point of decomposition are often toxic.

Plastic-like materials, such as wax, clay, rubber, and glass, have existed for centuries in a natural state. Today, the materials we think of as plastic are synthetic and can be divided into two basic groups of materials: thermoplastic and thermoset-

Figure 7-1

Inflatable sculpture. *By Betty Voelker; photograph courtesy of Betty Voelker.*

ting; thermoplastic materials can be remelted and reformed, whereas thermosetting materials cannot.

The chemical elements forming plastics are relatively few. Carbon is usually the principal element along with others such as hydrogen, oxygen, nitrogen, chlorine, and fluorine, which are linked to the carbon atoms to form molecules. These molecules are combined to form monomers, the primary combining units, or building blocks, in the formation of plastic. When subjected to heat, pressure, catalyzation, or a combination of these processes, polymerization occurs. The result is the finished material or object consisting of complex groups of polymer molecules.

The final material can take on many forms. In other words, the arrangement of molecules can be such that a material is thermoplastic, thermosetting, hard, soft, flexible, brittle, dense, cellular (such as foams), adhesive, or nonadhesive (such as in mold-release agents).

Although it is not essential to be a chemist or to have a complex understanding of chemistry. To work with plastics, it is important to know that a chemical process is occurring. Polymerization of a plastic is often the result of specific conditions and is usually dependent on temperature, humidity, mixture proportions, and other working conditions.

Plastic is not as stable as metal, having a higher degree of thermal expansion, a lower range of operating temperatures, and rigidity and fatigue strengths below that of metal.

High degrees of thermo expansion often re-

quire special fabrication techniques. Lower range of operating temperature may render some materials useless in direct sunlight. Degree of chemical resistance, moisture absorption, and resistance to abrasion may limit the suitability of a material for a particular use. Physical properties vary to such an extent in plastics that each material must be considered in relation to its use and expected performance. Specification sheets on individual materials can be obtained from suppliers. *Modern Plastics Encyclopedia,* published annually by McGraw-Hill Book Company, Inc., is an excellent source for information of this kind.

Plastics as an industry is still developing at such a rate that each year new variations of plastics with improved physical properties develop. In fact, it might be safe to say that for any problem the sculptor or designer envisions, he can find a plastic which will do the job. Tensile strengths of plastic tend to increase each year. With glass reinforcement, polyester layups can reach strengths of 50,000 pounds per square inch. Other glass-reinforced resins can also reach high-performance levels. Development of exotic reinforcing fibers promises to dramatically increase tensile strength up to 250,-000 p.s.i.

Impact strengths also increase each year and can be varied by fillers and additives in plastic formulations. Although these factors are not of major concern in small works and wall reliefs, they do become of concern in large-scale sculpture: play sculpture, works in parks and public places, and kinetic and environmental forms subject to impact.

Top-service temperatures concern the sculptor working with materials exposed to sunlight and special conditions, such as heat buildup in light sculpture. Moisture and chemical conditions are perhaps of major concern to those sculpturing outdoor works or forms relying on fluids encased in plastics for visual effects.

Beyond chemical and moisture resistance, another major concern in outdoor work is the stability of the material in sunlight. Ultraviolet stabilizers can be added to many plastic formulations to improve their properties under these conditions.

Flammability can be a major concern in large-scale interior installations, particularly in environmental forms where the viewer may be surrounded by the materials. Many plastics are relatively slow-burning or self-extinguishing, and flame-resistant substances can be added to plastic formulations to make them less flammable.

Machinability is primarily a concern in mass-production and is not of prime importance to the sculptor in most instances.

Although plastics exist in great abundance, many forms of plastics are unavailable to the sculptor or design student; small quantities are often unavailable from suppliers whose principal customers are large industrial formulators and fabricators. For the practicing sculptor who is serious about a material this is less of a problem; he is often prepared to buy minimum quantities such as 50-gallon barrels, 100- to 500-pound lots, full sheets, or quantities of sheet, rod, or tube. In large cities, a student can often find a sympathetic formulator or fabricator who will sell him small quantities of the materials that are difficult to obtain.

Material such as granules, pellets, powders, and flakes—usually used as molding materials in injection, extrusion, and other forms of molding—can also be melted and cast, used as mold materials, as fillers with resins, or in other experimental forms. Powders are also used in fluidizing bed, flocking, and other coating operations.

Filaments are most often used as continuous strands. They are machine-wound on a mandrel and treated with resins. After the resin is cured, the mandrel is removed or destroyed.

Resins are used in producing high-pressure and low-pressure laminated materials in sheet, rod, and tube form or finished products. Formica® is a common high-pressure formed material familiar to most of us. Fiberglass-reinforced polyester sheets and products are usually the result of low-pressure laminating. Resins combined with fillers are also popular as castable materials or adhesives. With the addition of colored pigments they become excellent coating materials.

Foams are available to the sculptor in a liquid form, such as urethane two-part systems; foam solids are available in blocks, sheets, and special shapes. Polyurethane and polystyrene materials are the most readily available foam materials. Sheets may be from 12 to 48 inches wide and up to 12 inches thick, in lengths up to 12 feet. Blocks may be up to 48 inches wide, 18 inches thick, and 12 feet long. (Figure 7-2)

Foams, formulated in both rigid and flexible forms, may be as light as one pound or as dense as fifty pounds per cubic foot.

Films, sheets, rods, and tubes are available in an unlimited array of sizes, colors, and materials. (Figure 7-3) Films are usually heat-sealed, sewn or cemented. Sheets, rods, and tubes may be rigid or flexible; thermoplastic forms may be heated and bent or thermoformed. They can be fabricated by

Figure 7-2
Typical foam materials.

Figure 7-3

Some common plastic materials. From top: plastic rods, rigid plastic tube, flexible plastic tube, transparent acrylic sheet 1/4 and 1 inch thick, opaque sheet, flexible foam, and vinyl film.

adhesive bonding, solvent cementing, welding, and with most conventional fastening and fabricating techniques. They are available in a wide variety of surfaces, textures, and decorative patterns. Films and thin sheets are often laminated to backing of plastic, fabric, wood, metal, paper, and other materials.

Many plastics are available in a wide variety of custom shapes. Angles, tees, L's, U's, and shapes common to metal can be found in plastic.

Fabrication and forming techniques exist for all plastics. Forms of adhesive bonding and methods for painting or plating most plastics also exist. Many thermoplastics can be welded with heat devices in techniques similar to welding metal.

There are approximately fourteen major thermoplastics and seven thermosetting plastics. ABS (acrylonitrile-butadiene-styrene), acetals, acrylics (polymethyl methacrylate), cellulosics (cellulose acetate, cellulose nitrate, butyrate, cellulose propionate, and ethyl cellulose), chlorinated polyether, fluorocarbons (tetrafluorothylene, chlorotrifluoroethylene, and others), polyamides (nylon), polycarbonates, polyethylenes, polymides, polypropylenes, polystyrenes, urethanes, and vinyls are the thermoplastics. The thermosetting materials are epoxides, furane, melamine, phenolics, polyesters, silicones, and ureas. ABS, polyethylene, polystyrene, and vinyls are of more recent usage and interest to the sculptor. Where solid colors are used, ABS is less expensive than acrylics. It is highly serviceable

upon exposure to weather, although it is subject to slight yellowing and color changes. ABS is actually one of the newer plastic concepts and is an alloy of a styrene-rubber combination.

THERMOPLASTICS

Acetals, a high-strength, tough plastic of recent origin are to some extent competitive with die cast metals. At present, they are of limited interest sculpturally, due to the complex equipment necessary for the forming process.

Acrylics, resins, pellets, powders, films, sheets, rods, tubes, and blocks, are clear or available in a wide range of colors; colorless acrylic, one of the clearest plastics available, has a white-light transmittance of 92 percent. Acrylic, whose major constituent is methyl methacrylate, has superior physical properties; it is exceptionally stable against light discoloration and has good resistance to weather and chemicals.

Acrylic has enjoyed wide sculptural use for many years. Sheets have been fabricated into a wide variety of forms. It is easily sawed, cemented, welded, finished, and thermoformed. Some sculptors have cast resins into exceptionally optically-clear castings. Rods have been used as light transmitting devices. (Figure 7-4)

Cellulosics are some of the oldest of the plastic family; cellulose nitrate dates back to 1869 when it was patented as celluloid. Other cellulosics are cellulose acetate, cellulose acetate butyrate, ethyl cellulose, and cellulose proprionate. Cellulose nitrate has the disadvantages of being flammable and it lacking stability in heat and light. Cellulose acetate butyrate, a weather-resistant material, has been used by sculptors in thermoforming. Although chemically resistant, cellulosics are not resistant to solvents such as alcohol, acetone, lacquer thinner, paint removers, strong alkalis, and paints with similar solvents.

Polyether, particularly known for its excellent chemical-, corrosion-, and thermo-stability, is chiefly used in corrosion-resistant pipes, valves, fittings, coatings, and linings for handling chemical materials. Coatings and linings are usually applied with a conventional spray apparatus, fluidizing-bed process, or flock coating. Commercial application of polyether coatings to sculptural fountain compo-

nents, or in situations demanding exceptional corrosion resistance, would have merit. Size limitations would exist in relation to available commercial facilities.

Fluoroplastics, tough, nonflammable, high-temperature and chemical-resistant plastics, are used, for example, in the familiar Teflon® coating on cookware. Fluoroplastic coatings are available in spray cans as mold-release agents. Gasket materials, bearings, and coated parts may be useful in fountain construction and motorized assemblies. Coated wires are excellent as lead wires to ovens and heating devices, or in areas of heat buildup in forms, such as light sculpture.

Fortified with glass fiber, fluoroplastics are as tough as aluminum.

Polyamides are most common to us in the form of nylon-brush bristles and fabric. Films are utilized in food packaging. Gears, pulleys, non-corrosive fasteners, and coated wire should have sculptural application in mechanical and electrical

Figure 7-4

Memorial scultpure, acrylic plastic, 1969. *MACH PELAH Cemetery, Flint, Michigan. By sculptor Mon Levinson. Photograph courtesy of Mon Levinson.*

forms. Nylon tubing is used as venting material in mold construction. Fluidized-bed coating may come into use. Fabrics coated or impregnated with nylon, or all-nylon fabric, can be sewed into forms and stuffed with shredded foam or stretched over rigid frames. Paper and other materials are also impregnated or coated with nylon and are laminated to rigid surfaces. These materials and techniques have been used in display design and sculpture.

Polycarbonates are relatively new; the first products in polycarbonate were introduced about 1960. Polycarbonate, a high-performance, tough material, is transparent, with good optical qualities. Highly heat-resistant (up to 250 degrees Fahrenheit), it should prove useful for light-boxes and sculpture needing a heat-resistant, transparent material.

Polyethylene is one of the most familiar plastics in our day-to-day life; in excess of three billion pounds per year is used in the manufacture of industrial and household materials and products. Packaging containers, housewares, and toys are the most common items. Polyethylene has excellent weathering properties when treated with ultraviolet stabilizers and is available in both a flexible and rigid form. With good fatigue strength, it could be valuable in sculpture where flexing of a surface is desirable. Melted pellets, powders, or molding compounds can be used in relief molds or they can be cast into conventional rigid and flexible molds.

Sheet material can be thermoformed, welded, and assembled with mechanical fasteners. Film can easily be heat-sealed for inflatable or stuffed forms.

Polyimides, developed to fill the need for plastic meeting high-temperature requirements, can withstand temperatures up to 900 Fahrenheit for sustained periods of time. Resins, combined with glass fibers to produce high-strength components, are also used to produce heat-resisting adhesives. Polymides are not commonly available except from industrial suppliers.

Polypropylene, a result of the experimentation for a high-density polyethylene, is more heat-resistant and stronger than polyethylene. Fiber products such as yarn and rope, auto-upholstery material, ribbon, and piping may have sculptural possibilities. Polypropylene is a plastic that can be metal-plated easily if plating-grade resins are used. Sculptural suggestions for polyethylene also apply to polypropylene.

Polystyrene, although it has excellent potential as a sculptural material, has not enjoyed the popularity of acrylic.

We are most familiar with polystyrene-foam materials and products. Styrofoam®, a favorite with hobbyists and for small classroom projects, has been on the market for many years in small slabs, blocks, and other forms. As containers such as ice chests, and in other applications, it can be found in almost every home.

In recent years, large blocks and sheets have been particularly popular with sculptors. The material is carved, sealed, and coated with plaster, paint, or fiberglass. In another technique, the foam serves as a pattern and is placed in dry or green sand and cast in metal. The hot metal burns out the foam as the casting takes place.

Polystyrene is relatively inexpensive and is available in exceptionally diverse forms. Its water-clear resins are castable. Glass-filled resins possess high strength. Medium-, high-, and extra-high-impact grades of sheet material can be thermoformed and fabricated with all common fabrication techniques. Available in an unlimited range of color, it does not possess good weather resistance and tends to become brittle and to discolor under ultraviolet exposure.

Styrene-butadiene, an elastomer available in pellet form, should be useful as a hot-pour mold material or in castings where rubber-like properties are desired.

Urethane is the result of reacting polyester or polyether resins with diiocyanates, water, or fluorocarbon blowing agents. It is primarily available in resins, coatings, adhesives, rigid and flexible sheet or blocks, and shredded material. We are normally acquainted with foams of a light density, such as one and a half to four pounds per cubic foot. However, urethane can be formed into densities of 50 pounds or more per cubic foot.

In the past fifteen years, there has been considerable sculptural application of polyurethane. Preformed sheets or blocks are carved or constructed into patterns and handled in the same manner as polystyrene foam. If the foam pattern is to be covered with polyester-reinforced fiberglass, urethane is preferred, as it does not react to the solvent nature of the polyester resin.

Castable urethane foams, usually a two-part liquid mixture, can be foamed into molds for flexible or rigid foam castings. Dyes can be added to the mixtures for tints and coloring. Urethanes have been poured in a free-form technique to fashion sculptural reliefs or for the buildup of textural surfaces. Prefabricated building panels surfaced with thin-gauge metal or paper should be useful for large-scale fabricated sculpture.

Industrial spray applicators for foam can be used to construct large-scale sculpture. Recent development of thin layers of foam laminated to other plastic sheet has resulted in thermoforming sheet-material.

Although the toxicity of liquid-formed foams has been reduced considerably, caution should be exercised when working with these materials.

Vinyls, the most versatile of the thermoplastics, can be compounded in an infinite number of ways. Vinyl chloride and vinyl acetate are the principal compounds in many formulations. Other materials are polyvinyl alcohol, polyvinyl acetals, and polyvinyl chloride acetate. We are familiar with vinyls as finished products in commonplace items such as fabric, film, floor covering, and house siding.

Flexible and rigid materials can be fabricated and formed by most known processes. Vinyl fabric, film, sheet and special shapes, building products, and coatings have been used sculpturally and show promise for further application. Melted-vinyl molding compounds are castable in certain mold techniques. Polyvinyl chloride should lend itself to hot-pour mold applications or slush molding for rigid or soft sculpture.

THERMOSETTING PLASTICS

Epoxides in many commercial forms have sculptural application as they possess highly desirable physical properties. In sculpture, as in industry, epoxy adhesives often make exceptional replacements for mechanical fasteners and weldments. Coatings are desirable on metal and other surfaces. Resins combined with fillers make outstanding castings with good weather resistance, as do epoxy-fiberglass laminates.

Colored glass, epoxy bonded to glass, and glass set in epoxy-resin-sand mixtures have had extensive application in decorative, stained-glass windows.

Epoxies are usually two-part systems, involving a mixture of the resin and a catalyst or curing agent. Polymerization occurs at oven or room temperatures. Normal precautions observed in handling toxic materials should be followed when working with epoxies.

Furane, through a complex formulation process, originated in furfuraldehyde and furfuryl alcohol, which is processed from vegetable wastes such as corn cobs and rice hulls. Sculpturally, its primary use has been as a no-bake binder added to sand in metal casting.

Amino plastics are usually melamine-formaldehyde or urea-formaldehyde formulations. Melamine-plastic dinnerware and high-pressure laminated melamine-phenolic-sheet material, such as Formica®, are most familiar to us. Urea-formaldehyde formulation has been used in products such as electrical components for many years. Fabrics treated with amino formulations produce permanent-press fabrics.

Most amino-plastic products are formed by compression molding. Resins are combined with fillers and processed to form molding compounds. Products are formed under pressure and heat.

High-pressure, laminated-sheet material such as Formica® has been used for durable final surfaces on simple flat-surfaced sculpture.

Phenolics were the first synthetic thermosetting resins to be developed; Dr. L. H. Baekeland discovered the first material in 1909. The tradename Bakelite has been a household word for many years. First application of this phenol-formaldehyde plastic was in the automotive and electrical industries.

Sculpturally useful would be phenolic resins that can be poured and heat-cured in cheap molds, resins mixed with fillers for molding compounds, resins for shell mold and foundry processes, laminated materials, and phenolic foams that can be carved with ordinary hand tools.

Polyesters are among the most promising of plastics to find application in the arts. Fiberglass-reinforced polyesters and cast polyesters, exceptionally useful to the sculptor, can be handled easily in a variety of molds and direct-buildup techniques, resulting in exceptionally strong and durable works. Resins with color additives and fillers have been used for textural paintings since 1950.

Industrially, polyester has been used since about 1942. Furniture, boats, car bodies, corrosion-resistant tanks, pipes, and containers are a few of the many products produced with reinforced plastics. The remaining applications are in such areas as fabrics, coatings, corrugated and flat sheets, and castings.

In reinforced plastic, fiberglass matting, cloth, or fiber is placed in a mold and saturated with catalyzed polyester resin. This may be a hand layup, spray, or match-dies-mold procedure.

In casting, the resin is catalyzed and poured into the mold. The resin may be clear, colored, or reinforced with fillers; the casting may be solid or hollow, utilizing a slush-mold technique.

Catalyzing the resin is a simple matter of adding from one to two percent catalyst to the resin. The catalyst is usually MEKP (methyl ethyl ketone peroxide).

Polyester resins are as various as their uses: laminating resins for hand layup, resins for match-die molding, spray applications, and casting resins are all formulated to suit the particular process. Precautions pertinent to handling of toxic materials should be observed when working with resins and catalysts.

Silicone is an inorganic plastic. Sand, when heated with carbon, is the basic raw material that produces the silicones that are compounded chemically to produce silicone formulations. These are usually in the form of liquids, oils, resins, and elastomers.

Silicone-rubber molding compounds and silicone mold-release agents are used extensively in sculpture and in industry. Castable-silicone elastomers could be used for flexible sculptural components. Coatings may be useful in situations where high-service temperature is needed.

FABRICATION

Industrial fabrication of plastics may involve extremely simple techniques or complex and sophisticated machinery. Many wood- and metal-fabrication techniques can be adapted to plastic fabrication. Simple hand and electric tools can be used. Inexpensive versions of complex industrial machinery can be built, since the sculptor seldom needs the accuracy and high-production rate required by industry. Ovens and forming machines are easily built from simple materials and components.

We can think of plastic fabrication in terms of two basic categories: cold forming and thermoforming. In cold forming, the material is sawed, sheared, stamped, machined, and carved. Assembling is achieved through adhesive bonding, welding, bolting, riveting, or other mechanical means. In thermoforming, the material is heated until flexible, and held in the desired form until cooled. At this point, the thermoplastic material retains the desired shape. Thermoformed parts are also assembled by the techniques just mentioned. Plastic forms are often a combination of cold-formed and thermoformed parts.

SAWING AND CUTTING

Since we are dealing primarily with flexible or rigid sheet, rod, tube, or custom shapes, our first concern would be cutting the material to the desired form. Since plastic tends to be soft and easily scratched, the surface often needs protection. Plastic is often purchased with protective paper or film covering; when possible, these should remain on the material during sawing and fabrication. If the material is purchased without a protective covering, surface paper can be taped on to sheets or rods, and tubes can be wrapped and taped.

Small quantities of plastics can often be cut with simple hand tools. Tin shears or scissors can be used on film and thin materials. Thin, flexible material can often be cut with a razor blade in an appropriate holder or with a linoleum knife. Paper cutters and sheet-metal foot-squaring shears can also be used on flexible and semiflexible material.

For handsawing, a handsaw, keyhole saw, hacksaw, or coping saw can be used. The handsaw should have 10 to 12 teeth per inch and moderate set. Eighteen teeth per inch is a fairly standard and desirable size for the keyhole saw and hacksaw. A coping saw should have from 15 to 20 teeth per inch. Sheet material should be clamped to a table and cut with the handsaw for straight cuts; the coping saw can be used for curves and free forms. In fact, it is advisable to build a slotted table for clamping materials, if much cutting is to be done with hand and portable electric tools. This table is indispensable for the hand cutting of plastic, wood, or metal. (Figure 7-5) Rods, tubes, and other straight stock should be wrapped with carbdoard, clamped in a vise, and cut with the hacksaw.

In sawing, use moderate pressure on the

Figure 7-5
Slotted table for cutting materials.

cutting stroke and ease up on the return. On hard, somewhat brittle plastics, side movement of the saw blade should be avoided as much as possible, as this can result in minor chipping or fracturing. The saw blades should be kept sharp and clean, to prevent excess friction and to insure clean, smooth cutting action.

Teeth per inch in sawing is relative to the thickness of the material. General guidelines call for having two to three teeth in contact with the cutting surface.

Plastic materials appropriately clamped can also be cut with a hand electric jig or saber saw. Metal-cutting blades with 18 to 24 teeth per inch and a fairly wide set are usually recommended. A straight edge can be clamped to the plastic to guide the saw when making straight cuts.

If the saw is a variable-speed saw, a slower speed, such as 1,000 to 2,000 strokes per minute, is advisable, to reduce friction and heat. In fact, cutting plastic with a portable jig saw, stationary jig saw, or band saw all have one thing in common: if the saw teeth are too fine or too dull, the set too narrow and the speed too fast, heat can build up to the point of setting up undesirable stresses in the material. This is particularly true when working with acrylics or fairly rigid plastics with relatively low service temperatures. A partial remedy for this is to work with the fewest number of teeth and the lowest speed practicable. One thousand to 2,000 strokes per minute for the portable and stationary jig saws and 3,000 feet per minute for a band saw are reasonably acceptable speeds.

When cutting on the band saw, use metal-cutting blades. Materials over an inch thick can be cut with blades having three or four teeth per inch, with slight set.

The blade width should be as wide as the nature of the cut will permit. One-half-inch wide is a good all-purpose width for straight cuts and for cuts with a large radius. Short-radius and intricate cuts call for blades with widths of one-eighth to one-fourth inch; or spiral-edged blades can be used for exceptionally intricate cuts. The spiral-edged blade can readily change direction of cut with minimum movement of the material.

When the jig saw is being used for cutting, the hold-down should be set down on the plastic, exerting sufficient pressure to prevent vibration of the material. On the band saw, the upper guide should be set down to within about an inch of the material. Rollers and guides should be adjusted to as close a tolerance as possible.

The feed pressure on the material, when cutting with either the bandsaw, table saw, jig saw, or other power saws, should be moderate to light; it should be such that the cut proceeds at a reasonable speed. The normal tendency when first cutting materials on a power saw is not to apply sufficient pressure; the result is usually excess friction, heat, and gumming of the blade. This can also occur if pressure, or rate of feed, is too fast. Proper rate of feed is gained by experience. It is possible to get manufacturers' recommendations on inches-per-minute recommended for a particular material under certain conditions, as a check for your cutting speed. If compressed air is available, a jet of air can be directed toward the cutting zone, to cool and remove dust. Industrially, liquid cooling is also used in production cutting. A small amount of wax on the blade can help reduce friction and prevent the blade from gumming. The blade can be cleaned with alcohol, mineral spirits, acetone, or other suitable solvents.

In cutting plastics on a table saw, or with a skill or radial-arm saw, metal-cutting blades or carbide-tipped blades should be used. Hollow-ground, eight-to-ten-inch-diameter metal-cutting blades with six to eight teeth per inch are suitable for cutting thin material. Material over one-half-inch thick requires blades with three to four teeth per inch. Some fabricators prefer a small amount of set in the teeth when cutting thick stock. On a table saw, the blade should be set up so that it barely projects above the material.

If a table saw, radial-arm saw, or skill saw is a permanent piece of studio equipment, the best practice would be to equip it with an all-purpose carbide-tipped blade suitable for cutting both plastic and wood.

The table saw and radial-arm saw can be used for straight cuts, grooves, miters, and all cuts normally associated with woodworking equipment. Special jigs can be constructed to hold pieces of rod, tube, or custom shapes while cutting.

In sawing or cutting plastics that have fillers added, carbide-tipped, diamond-tipped, or abrasive cutting-wheels should be used. Glass and other filler materials are often so abrasive that they can ruin a metal saw blade in just a few cuts. For highly abrasive-filled materials, the abrasive cutoff-wheel should be used.

To prevent scratches when ripping material on the table saw or with a radial-arm saw, the material should have a protective piece of paper on it. If cutting quantities of long, straight cuts is going to be a daily routine, it would be advisable to purchase a special traveling saw; since the plastic remains stationary while the saw blade moves, the danger of marring or scratching the material is eliminated.

MACHINING PLASTICS

In machining plastics, woodworking or metalworking equipment such as shapers, routers, jointers, lathes, drill presses, and milling machines, can be used. Since plastics are usually fairly abrasive, carbide-tipped cutters, blades, and tools should be used.

With routers and shapers, shapes such as half-round, coves, corner beads, and other shapes common to woodworking can be achieved. Spindle speed should be from 10,000 to 20,000 r.p.m. for cutters under one and a half inch in diameter. Edges can be planed on the jointer in the same fashion as handling wood as discussed in Chapter 6 on page 109. Shapes can be turned on a lathe at surface speeds of about 500 feet per minute, with a moderate rate of feed. Surface speed is circumference in inches multiplied by r.p.m. and divided by twelve.

Drilling holes with portable drills or on the drill press can be accomplished with standard metal-cutting twist drills. However, if fabrication of plastic is a usual studio procedure, it would be advisable to purchase a set of drills designed for drilling the desired kinds of plastic. Metal-cutting

small flat
on cutting
edge of drill

Figure 7-6
Modified twist drill for cutting holes in plastic.

drills can be modified. Using a hand stone or fine grinder a small flat should be ground on the cutting edge of the drill. Since plastics are soft, the flat side on the cutting edge produces a scraping rather than a cutting action and prevents the drill from digging into the material. (Figure 7-6) Drill speed is about 3,500 r.p.m. for 1/16-inch drills to 1,000 r.p.m. for a one-half-inch drill. Quarter-inch drills require 1,800 r.p.m. and five-eighths-inch drills run at 700 r.p.m. Precise recommended speeds and drills can be found in a source such as the *Plastic Engineering Handbook* (Allen F. Randolph, ed. New York: Reinhold Publishing Corp., 1960, 3rd ed.) or in machining handbooks. For drilling, the plastic should be backed up with a piece of wood. Pressure should be eased up as the drill cuts through the material. In cutting deep holes, the drill should be backed out several times to remove chips, and a coolant should be used. The coolant can be simply a small amount of soapy water applied with an eye dropper, or commercially prepared solutions. A jet of air is one of the most desirable methods for cooling.

Problems common to sawing also apply to machining operations. Cutting tools should always be sharp and clean; rate of feed should be moderate, and materials should be at room temperature. With a small amount of experience in handling plastic, the right technique to minimize heat and friction is soon developed. Stresses developed in plastic by sawing and machining can be removed by annealing the parts before assembling them.

TAPPING AND THREADING

Plastic rods can be threaded and holes can be tapped with dies and taps used for metal. In soft

Figure 7-7

Loose fit joint to allow for thermo-expansion of plastic to plastic or other material.

plastics, coarse threads are preferable. The tap or die can be lubricated with wax or soap to facilitate the cutting. The tap should be backed out frequently to remove chips. A slightly oversized hole is advisable for threads in deep holes, to prevent the tap from binding or freezing in the hole. Self-threading screws that cut their own mating thread as they are inserted are also available. Additional information on tapping and threading procedures can be found on page 166 in the following chapter dealing with metal fabrication.

SANDING AND POLISHING

Plastics can be sanded and polished by following the normal abrasive-finishing procedures outlined in Chapter 10.

ASSEMBLY OF PLASTICS

Plastic parts can be assembled with either mechanical fasteners, adhesive bonds, solvent cementing, or welding.

Mechanical fasteners may be screws, bolts, or rivets. For plastics with a high rate of thermo-expansion, loose-fit arrangements are the most desirable. Tapped holes for threaded screws should be slightly oversized, and Class 1 taps should be used. In many cases, self-tapping screws can be used; special self-tapping screws for plastic are available. Plastic screws can be used in all plastic assemblies, or screws can be made from threaded dowel. On solvent, sensitive materials, pieces of threaded or unthreaded dowel can be inserted and permanently set, by touching the top of the insert with a drop of appropriate solvent. (Figure 7-7)

In setting screws into plastic, pressure on the

screw should be moderate. In some cases, it may be necessary to back out the screw and start again. Soft plastic screws are particularly difficult to set and easy to break.

In fastening plastic to other material, or bolting two pieces together, oversize the hole slightly to allow for expansion. The most ideal screw or bolt arrangement is round-headed, with a metal or rubber washer or both to distribute the pressure over a wider area of the material. From a decorative standpoint, this is often not desirable, however, and devices with less optimum results may be necessary.

Many kinds of rivets can be used on thermo-setting plastics of high tensile strength and relatively low rates of thermo-expansion. Rivets are fairly ineffective in most soft materials unless washers are used to distribute the pressure over a larger area. Riverting is also less desirable in stress-sensitive materials such as acrylics. Pressures produced by rivets can produce stresses that result in crazing or cracks in the material.

Blind riveting using the pop-rivet tool is one of the simplest riveting techniques and is acceptable in many decorative applications. It is preferable to use back-up washers on both sides to distribute the pressure. The holes should be slightly oversized. Squeeze the riveting tool handles together until the rivet has spread out and set. Do not continue to apply pressure until the mandrel pin is cut. Rather, release and remove the tool by spreading the handle, and cut off the mandrel pin with a wire cutter. This will minimize the pressure on the material.

WELDING

Many thermoplastics can be welded in a fashion similar to welding metal. Using a welding torch containing a gas or electric heating unit, a jet of hot air is directed at the welding zone. As the plastic softens, a filler rod is pressed and melted into the softened zone. (Figure 7-8)

Joint designs are first beveled as in Figure 8-25 illustrating metal fabrication techniques. On thick material, multiple passes with the welding torch are made into deep bevels. Pieces can be tacked together and then welded, as in metal fabrication. Rate of feed from the rod and speed of welding will depend on the plastic being welded. As in any welding technique, some practice on

rod fed to
weld zone

torch

torch tip

Figure 7-8
One of several plastic welding techniques.

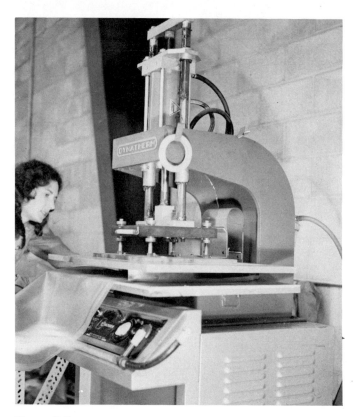

Figure 7-9
Dielectric heat-sealing vinyl film for an inflatable sculpture. Note curved die between the two platens. Dies are designed to meet the seam configuration of the individual sculpture.

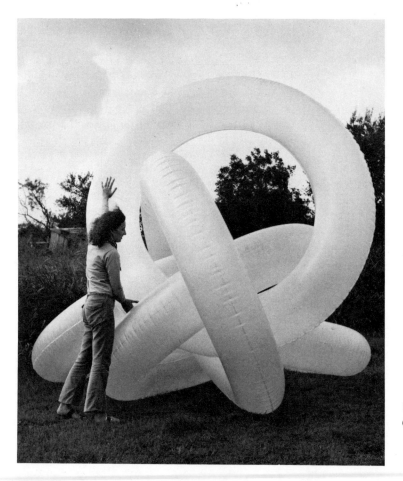

Figure 7-10
Completed inflatable sculputre. *By Betty Voelker.*

scrap material is essential and is the most appropriate way to learn and establish the desired technique for a specific material.

In another version of welding, the metal tip of the welding tool comes into contact with, and melts and fuses, the material. A filler rod can be used for added fill.

An unusual welding process not too commonly known in the arts is spin welding, which is applicable only to small, round parts that can be placed in the chuck of a lathe or drill press. In this process, the piece is rotated at a high speed against the desired weld spot on the material. Friction builds up heat until the plastic softens enough to bond to the part. At the fusion temperature of the material, the drill press or lathe should be stopped as quickly as possible. To stop the chuck quickly, it is possible to grasp the chuck with a gloved hand, and slowly apply pressure.

In welding, fumes from heated plastic can be toxic. Knowledge of toxicity levels and required safety procedures should be obtained prior to welding a plastic.

HEAT SEALING

Heat sealing is another form of welding thermoplastic together. Industrially, the four basic methods are dielectric, induction, ultrasonic, and thermal sealing.

In dielectric sealing, a radio frequency produces molecular disturbance at the point where the die contacts the plastic, producing heat and a resulting softening and bonding of the material. (Figures 7-9 and 7-10)

Induction heat-sealing involves metal membranes or powders placed in the plastic material at the point of bonding. The metal carries the necessary energy to produce heat and bond the material.

In ultrasonic welding the bond is accomplished through high-frequency vibration and the resulting friction between the two surfaces to be bonded. Plastic can be bonded to dissimilar material in this process.

Thermo-sealing is a process in which the thin film or sheet is melted together by directly applied heat.

Thermal sealing is simple, and equipment is less expensive. The process involves pressing the surface or surfaces of the heated die or tool against the material until the points of material contact, melt, and bond together.

Processes such as dielectric sealing are most satisfactory if a superior, leakproof seal is needed on seams in works such as inflatable scupture. Since equipment is extremely expensive, the most practical approach is to work with a commercial plastic-fabricator that has sealing equipment.

Adhesive bonding of vinyl and polyethylene film is reasonably successful if the design is such that the seams can be clamped while the adhesive sets. Solvent-based, heavy-bodied adhesives are usually used.

THERMOFORMING

Thermoforming is a simple process of heating thermoplastic sheets to their softening temperature and forming them while they are in this soft, flexible condition. When the plastic cools, it retains the molded shape.

The common thermoforming methods utilize air-blowing, vacuum, or mechanical pressures to shape the softened sheet. Plastic bottles, signs and letters, skylight bubbles, toys, and many household bowls and containers are formed in this manner.

Equipment for forming plastic in the studio or classroom need not be expensive or complex, if the forms are moderately sized and the artist is concerned with one of a kind or limited production. For small works, an ordinary household over can be used to soften the plastic, and a vacuum cleaner can be used as an air supply. This, however, is quite inadequate for anything more than a few small experiments; the serious sculptor or art student obviously needs a larger-capacity machine.

The essential components for thermoforming are a heat source and air compressor for pressure or vacuum. There are many variations in thermoforming, depending on the desired configuration and its size. For thin material (up to about one-eighth inch), it is best to heat the plastic in place, and minimizing the handling time. The plastic can be heated from one side with radiant heat. Thicker materials retain their heat longer and should be heated from both sides to insure uniform temperature of the material. This is usually accomplished in

Figure 7-11

Free blowing technique for plastic.

Figure 7-12

Simple vacuum forming technique.

a circulating-air oven that is either gas- or electrically-heated. The material is either hung in the oven or placed on metal trays that have a drill cloth or flannel covering. An oven can be built easily out of cement asbestos board and angle iron. Kaowool®-blanket insulation can be used to insulate the inside of the oven. Simple gas or electric burners can be used as a heat source. The metal casing from an old electric dryer or washer is easily converted into a small oven. Temperature controls can be salvaged from old ovens, or they can be purchased new.

One of the simplest techniques, which has sculptural appeal but little commercial value, is free forming. In this approach, the previously cut and oven heated parts are formed by hand and held in the desired position until cool. Insulated gloves must be worn to protect the hands. The parts can be assembled by adhesive bonding or mechanical means.

Figure 7-11 illustrates another relatively simple technique. Here, the plastic and template are clamped to a board having an inlet for air, and the shape is free-blown. This is the process ordinarily used for forming skylight bubbles. Thin plastic can be clamped in place and heated with a radiant heater from one side; thick material may need to be heated in an oven and then clamped and formed. Formed shapes can be further modified by heating selective areas with a heat gun; or air pressure can be applied to flat sheets and selective areas can be formed in this fashion. In addition to free blowing, forms can be free-vacuumed into a suitable vacuum chamber.

From simple free forming and free blowing, the techniques become more complex and often require positive or negative molds or plugs. Figure 7-12 illustrates typical vacuum forming into a negative mold. In this case, the plastic is placed in the forming position and is heated from the top. As it softens, it will partially drape into the cavity. When

the desired temperature is reached, the vacuum is applied and the material is drawn into the mold. In another version of this technique, the top is sealed and air pressure forces the plastic against the mold walls. Mold walls must be smoothly finished as imperfections may transfer to the soft plastic.

Drape forming is an application in which the plastic is draped over a positive mold and vacuum is applied from the bottom, or air pressure is applied from the top. (Figure 7-13) In some simple forms, the weight of the plastic is sufficient to conform to the mold shape and vacuum or air pressure is not needed. A desirable aspect of this approach is that the exposed surface of the finished work does not come into contact with the mold surface. (Figure 7-14)

In another forming process, a plug is used to press the soft plastic into shape. A variation of this approach is vacuum snapback, in which the plastic is vacuum-drawn into a bubble, the plug is lowered into place, and the cooling plastic snaps back and forms around the configuration of the plug. (Figure 7-15) Match dies and mechanical pins or rams can also be used to force the soft plastic into the desired shape. (Figure 7-16)

The amount of time it takes for a piece of plastic to reach the forming temperature depends on the thickness of the material and the intensity of

Figure 7-13

Air pressure forming technique.

Figure 7-14
Drape forming.

Figure 7-15
Vacuum snap back technique.

Figure 7-16
Vacuum formed sculpture. *By Steve Wilder.*

the heat source. Several experiments with scrap material are advisable to gain experience in estimating time requirements. Estimating proper forming time is also partially visual. If the plastic is hanging free in a frame over the positive or negative mold, the softness of the plastic can be judged by the extent to which the material sags as it softens.

Visual qualities, such as a change in the surface appearance of the material, also indicate temperature. If the material is heated in a thermostatically controlled oven, the oven can be set to hold the desired temperature, and obtaining the proper temperature will not be a problem. Most plastics for thermoforming soften at temperatures of 300 to 400 degrees Fahrenheit.

On complex mold configurations, it may be desirable to preheat the mold to about 125 to 150 degrees to prevent the plastic from chilling too quickly as it comes into contact with the mold surface. Preheating can be done in an oven; or, if a radiant heat-source is used, the heat can be directed on the mold prior to insertion of the sheet of plastic. After the plastic has been formed, fans can be used to blow air on the formed part to accelerate cooling.

The design of a simple thermoforming machine can vary considerably. Figures 7-11 through 7-14 indicate the basic principles, the application of which is often a matter of the personal needs and objectives. If a large quantity of pieces is needed, as in a modular design, it may be desirable to have them formed commercially. Figures 7-17, and 7-18 illustrate an excellent example of this approach. Sculptor Roger Kotoske, who visualized a sculptural module that could be arranged in many configurations, collaborated with the Samsonite Corporation to produce commercially 700 pieces in five hours. However, design- and engineering-time far ex-

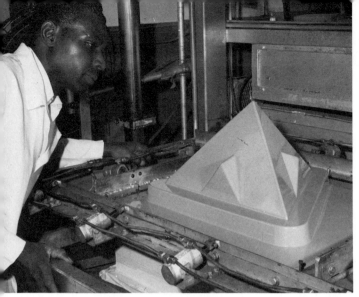

Figure 7-17

Drape forming on an industrial forming machine. *Photograph courtesy of Samsonite Corporation.*

Figure 7-18

Completed sculpture of drape-formed modules. By Roger Kotoske. *Photograph courtesy of Samsonite Corporation.*

Figure 7-19

Basic design for a strip heater.

electric heating element   plastic sheet

asbestos board

Figure 7-20

Forming plastic over a pattern or jig.

ceeded the production time. Often, what appear to be simple shapes may require complex engineering in order to be vacuum-formed.

Bending of thermoplastic simply requires a strip heater placed between strips of asbestos board, as shown in figure 7-19. The sheet of plastic should be turned several times to thoroughly heat the area to be bent. Sheets can be heated and bent over simple forms, as in Figure 7-20. They are clamped in place until the plastic has cooled.

Metal
Fabrication

EIGHT

Metal-fabrication techniques, such as riveting, forge welding, and other simple mechanical devices, are ancient. Egyptian statuary of riveted sheet copper dates back to 2300 B.C. Somerian craftmen working around 2500 B.C. were particularly skilled in many forms of metal work.

Most fastening or fabrication devices used today are products of the last one hundred years. Both welding (which started around 1900) and adhesive bonding developed considerably during and immediately after the Second World War; high-performance requirements in rocket design and space travel resulted in new and more sophisticated fabrication techniques. The development of these processes has contributed significantly to materials and techniques in sculpture and three-dimensional designing.

Among twentieth-century industrial techniques, the welding torch undoubtedly offered the greatest challenge and fascination. Direct, spontaneous manipulation of metal suited the sculptor, just as direct, spontaneous application of paint suited abstract expressionist painters.

Properly conceived, usage of industrial materials and techniques can produce striking visual effects. Rich surface qualities are achieved with brazing and bronze welding. Bolting devices can take on an honest and dramatic effect. The welded bead can be a strong visual-surface device (as in Figure 8-1). David Smith explored the noncorrosive qualities and appearance of stainless steel in his cubi series. (Figure 8-2)

Complex processes are usually prohibitively expensive for scupture and, usually, simpler approaches are sufficient for the sculptor, who seldom needs the high-performance fabrication processes demanded, for example, by the aerospace industry.

The basic methods of metal fabrication can be divided into three groups: fabrication with fastening devices, adhesives, and welding.

Selection of the proper fabrication technique depends on the nature of the form and the equipment available. Although, ideally, it is always desirable to select the best process, this is not always feasible for the sculptor, who solves the problem in relation to the tools and equipment available.

For example, in fabrication of large-scale metal sculpture with thick material or large parts, an arc-welding process would be the most desirable in terms of cost, time involved, and quality of the

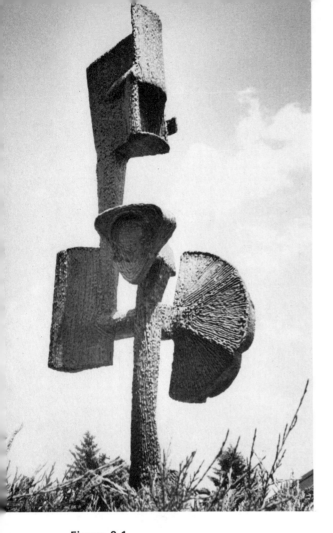

Figure 8-1

Welded steel sculpture. *By Robert Mangold.*

Figure 8-2

Cubi VIII by David Smith. *Collection of Elizabeth Meadows Sculpture Garden, Southern Methodist University, Dallas, Texas.*

weld. If arc-welding equipment were not available, the work could be accomplished with oxyacetylene welding but would be more difficult, more time-consuming, and more costly.

Another example is in the use of adhesives, in which there are techniques involving pressure and heat curing that can approach or surpass the strength of welding. These procedures are usually inaccessible to the sculptor became of the need for special ovens and precise temperature control. Consequently, the sculptor would probably use an adhesive involved air drying or room-temperature chemical curing.

Although welding offers the greater number of possibilities for metal fabrication, it is often overused because of its problem-solving ease. Technically and aesthetically, there are many instances when an adhesive or fastening device would meet particular needs more satisfactorily.

Welding also has some disadvantages: there is always the problem of thermo-expansion and the possibility of distortion due to heat input in the weld zone; undesirable stresses may be set up in the metal; change in color and appearance of the metal may be unacceptable. Prefinished metallic or plastic-coated steel or aluminum usually require other fabrication technique, since the coating would be damaged next to the weld zone.

Ordinarily, oxyacetylene welding are used on lightweight steel and for brazing nonferrous metals to each other or to steel. Other welding processes prove more satisfactory for welding thick sections of steel or matching alloys in nonferrous metals. The higher heat input of the electric arc makes it particularly desirable for large volumes of metal or for metal such as copper or copper alloys that possess a higher rate of thermal conductivity. Nonferrous metals are most easily welded with shielded-arc processes, since the inert-gas shield protects the welding zone from oxidation as the metal fuses together.

WELDING METALS

Steel. Steels may be classified as hot-rolled or cold-rolled. Hot-rolled steel is easily identified by the oxide scale present on the surface. Cold-rolled steel has the scale removed prior to being rolled to its finished size. Rolled steel up to one-eighth-inch thick is referred to as "sheet." Over one-eighth-inch thicknesses are called "plate." Further classification is based on the alloying element. Plain carbon steels are identified as "low," "medium" and "high" in carbon content. Low-carbon steel is ordinarily about 0.15 percent carbon and is easily weldable with oxyacetylene or arc-welding processes. Most common varieties of steel sheet and shapes are low-carbon. As the carbon content increases, the metal becomes less weldable. Other alloying elements are used to increase the toughness and strength. Nickel and manganese improve toughness, tungsten and chromium carbide improve wear-resistance. Chromium provides corrosion resistance, molybdenum provides hardness, and copper provides atmosphere resistance. Low-alloy steels alloyed with chrome-molybdenum, nickel-chrome-molybdenum and manganese-chrome-nickel can be welded by oxyacetylene or shielded arc. Tool steels alloyed with tungsten, molybdenum, or cobalt require special welding techniques. Cast steels such as cast or gray iron can be welded with oxyaceylene or arc techniques. Low-carbon steels and cast iron are the materials most often used by sculptors. Copper-alloyed steel, which has been used on exposed architectural components and sculpture, aquires a deep brown protective patination in several years.

Stainless steel. Shielded arc-welding processes are preferred for welding stainless steel, although coated electrodes can also be used. Of the high-alloy steels, stainless steel is perhaps of most interest to sculptors because of its high corrosion resistance. Stainless steels are heavier than carbon steels, and some have up to a 30-percent-higher rate of expansion. Thermal conductivity is lower. Low-carbon chromium-nickel stainless steel possesses the greatest corrosion resistance; although more difficult to weld, it should be considered for exterior works. Carbon-chromium steels can be identified by A.I.S.I. (American Iron and Steel Institute) numbers in the 400 series; chromium-nickel steels are identified with 200- or 300-series numbers.

Copper and copper alloys. These materials can readily be brazed with the use of a bronze rod and the oxyacetylene torch. Fusion welding is best accomplished with the shielded arc, although a few alloys are easily fusion-welded with oxyacetylene or the carbon arc. Generally, copper alloys are used instead of copper; the alloys are easier to weld and possess far less thermal conductivity. Brasses with relatively high zinc content, bronzes alloyed with zinc and tin, phosphor, aluminum, silicon or nickel are usually used. High-zinc-content materials are easily brazed or can be fusion-welded with the oxyacetylene torch. They are difficult to weld with arc-welding procedures, since the high temperature of the arc and low melting point of the zinc cause rapid decomposition of the zinc and excessive zinc fumes. It is important not to be misled by the term bronze, since sometimes a brass with a high zinc content will be called "bronze." Brasses called "commercial bronze" have a low zinc content, whereas brasses called "architectural bronze," "tobin bronze," or "manganese bronze" have high zinc contents.

Silicon bronze is particularly weldable and consists primarily of copper alloyed with one to three percent silicon. It has a very low rate of thermal conductivity and requires far less heat input than many of the other alloys or pure copper. It can easily be welded with the oxyacetylene torch or with the carbon arc using direct current. A silicon-bronze welding rod would be used as the filler material. Nickel-alloyed copper can be easily brazed of fusion-welded with the oxyacetylene torch. Phosphor and aluminum bronzes are best welded with shielded-arc processes.

Aluminum. Rapid oxidation, high thermal conductivity, and no color change during heating make welding aluminum with conventional arc and oxyacetylene torch difficult. However, with the use of shielded-arc processes, these conditions are easily controlled. If shielded arc welding is not available, aluminum can be oxyacetylene welded, using an appropriate flux with the aluminum rod; since heat input is slower, the heat is distributed over a wider area and there is a greater tendency toward distortion or slumping of the metal. A backup plate should be used on the back side of the weld joint to prevent slumping and provide support for the soft metal around the weld zone. Flux-coated electrodes are available for use with the conventional arc welder. Some aluminum can be soldered with special aluminum solders.

Aluminum consists of a whole group of aluminum alloys, some of which are more weldable than others. Alloys 1100, 3003, 5050, 6053, 6061, 6062, and 6063 can be welded with all welding processes, and can also be soldered. Alloys 5050, 6062, and 6063 are more difficult to solder. Alloys 2011, 2014, 2017, 2024, and 7075 are not very weldable. A few casting alloys that are most easily welded are 43, 355, A355, and 356.

OXYACETYLENE WELDING

This process is based on the principle that an acetylene flame combined with oxygen will burn at a temperature sufficiently hot to melt almost any metal. The temperature of the flame depends on the mixture of oxygen and acetylene. An excess acetylene flame is a maximum temperature of 5,550 to 5,700 degrees Fahrenheit; a neutral flame is 5,850 and an oxidizing flame is 6,000 to 6,200 degrees. Essentially, the oxyacetylene process is used for the joining or cutting of the metal. As a heat source, it is also used in bending, forging, forming, scale- and rust-removing, and other metal preparations.

With the use of a wide variety of welding rods and fluxes, most metals can be joined with the oxyacetylene process. These metals would include cast iron, wrought iron, carbon steel, alloy steel, stainless steel, copper, brass, bronze, aluminum alloys, nickel, nickel alloys, and magnesium alloys.

The decision to use, and desirability of using, the oxyacetylene process with some metals depends, of course, on the nature of the material and on the other processes available.

The oxyacetylene equipment consists of a cylinder of oxygen, a cylinder of acetylene, regulating gauges, hoses, torch body, welding tips, cutting tip, cutting attachment, gloves, goggles, and friction lighter. Figure 8-3 illustrates a typical portable setup. To avoid any possible error in assembling the equipment, the acetylene fittings are equipped with left-hand threads and the oxygen fittings are equipped with right-hand threads. Acetylene is further identifiable by a red hose and the oxygen by a green hose.

In the assembly of the equipment, before attaching gauges, the oxygen and acetylene tanks are turned on one-quarter turn, one at a time, momentarily (on and immediately off) to blow out dust or dirt that may have accumulated in the valve seat. Never look at the tank valve or stand in the stream of released oxygen or acetylene. Examine gauge fittings for dust, dirt, or grease before attaching them to the cylinder. Since they are highly combustible and explosive, oil or grease must never come into contact with oxygen or oxygen fittings. It is after gauges are attached to cylinders, hoses to gauges and torch body, the desired-size tip is attached, that the equipment is ready to be turned on.

Figure 8-4 illustrates a typical oxyacetylene regulator setup. The first step is to be certain that the pressure-adjusting screws (A and B) are turned out counterclockwise until loose. The remainder of the procedure is as follows.

1. Turn on oxygen valve (c) counterclockwise, opening valve all the way. Gauge (e) indicate tank contents.
2. Turn on acetylene value (d) counterclockwise one fourth to one half turn. Gauge (f) indicates tank contents.
3. Turn in oxygen pressure-adjusting screw (B) until oxygen gauge (g) reads desired pressure —generally around seven to ten pounds for moderate work, higher readings for large tips and cutting, lower readings for very small tips.
4. Turn in acetylene pressure-adjusting screw (A) until acetylene gauge (h) reads desired pressure—generally around five to seven pounds for moderate work, higher readings, not exceeding 15 pounds, for large tips and heavy cutting, lower readings for very small tips. (Refer to pressure settings and tip sizes

Figure 8-3
Oxyacetylene portable welder.

Figure 8-4
Oxyacetylene pressure regulators: (A) acetylene adjusting screw; (B) oxygen adjusting screw; (C) oxygen tank valve; (D) acetylene tank valve; (E) oxygen tank pressure gauge; (F) acetylene tank pressure gauge; (G) oxygen working pressure gauge; and (H) acetylene working pressure gage.

Figure 8-5
(A) Acetylene torch adjusting knob; (B) oxygen torch adjusting knob; (C) friction lighter; and (D) tip cleaners.

Figure 8-6
Acetylene flames.

EXCESS ACETYLENE FLAME

NEUTRAL FLAME

EXCESS OXYGEN FLAME

recommended by manufacturer of specific equipment, for more precise setting in relation to metal thickness.)

To turn on torch, open acetylene valve [A] (Figure 8-5) on torch body counterclockwise one eighth turn to a quarter turn and oxygen valve [B] (Figure 8-5) counterclockwise about one-quarter turn. Light torch with friction lighter [C] (Figure 8-5), and adjust to neutral flame. A simpler approach (perhaps preferable until one is familiar with the equipment) is to open the acetylene valve one eighth to one quarter turn, light the acetylene and adjust it until the flame stops smoking or shows a tendency to leave the end of the tip; then, open the oxygen valve slowly and adjust until excess acetylene cone [A] (Figure 8-6) disappears, and you have a "neutral flame," with a pale blue inner cone [B] (Figure 8-6). If the oxygen is further increased—with a slightly shorter inner cone—the flame becomes an excess-oxygen flame. (Figure 8-6) The principal disadvantage of this method igniting first the acetylene, then the oxygen is that the smoke from the burning acetylene is dirty and settles on work and shop equipment. When lighting the torch, be certain it is not pointed toward the cylinder, other workers or flammable material.

To turn off the torch, turn off the acetylene torch-body valve and then the oxygen. If work has been completed for the day, turn off the acetylene cylinder-valve and then the oxygen. Then, bleed the system by turning on the acetylene torch-body valve, releasing the acetylene in the system. When released, turn off the acetylene valve and repeat the same procedure for the oxygen. To complete the procedure, turn out the acetylene and oxygen gauges adjusting screws until they are loose.

Good work habits and safety practices are of continuous concern while welding: always wear proper goggles—available in light, medium, or dark shades; always wear leather gloves and other protective clothing when cutting and when welding on large work requiring large amounts of heat; keep the work area clean and clear of flammables; never exceed recommended working pressures, and periodically check equipment for leaks with soap suds; always be alert to metal properties for toxicity of fumes during welding—good ventilation is essential.

In oxyacetylene welding, the three common methods for joining metal are fusion, fusion with a filler rod, and brazing. In fusion, the metal is melted and the molten metal flows to join the two parts. When a filler rod is used, a rod of metal similar to the metal being welded is added to the weld as it is being developed. In brazing, a nonferrous metal (usually bronze) is used to join materials.

FUSION WELDING

Most welding operations require a neutral flame. In fusion welding, the tip of the neutral flame is directed at the joint to be welded. As the edges of the metal start to melt, the tip of the flame is moved in a series of overlapping ovals (Figure 8-7), allowing a molten puddle to form, joining the two pieces. If a filler metal is added to the weld, the filler rod is directed at the edge of the molten puddle in front of the flame, working from right to left, melting off small amounts of rod as the weld proceeds. This is referred to as a "forehand technique" (Figure 8-8) and is most commonly used. When the rod is fed behind the flame, working from left to right, the procedure is referred to as a "backhand technique."

There is a number of very common problems that occur when welding is first attempted. If the tip of the flame (inner cone) is not close enough to the metal, it may be difficult to get the metal to a melting point; when the melting point is reached (particularly on thin sheet metal), the heat is distributed over too large an area, and the molten metal will separate, forming a hole in the metal. To confine the heat to the weld area, it is essential to work with the tip of the flame next to the metal; there should be about a 1/16-to-one-eighth-inch gap between the tip of the flame and the metal.

Figure 8-7

Oval welding pattern for torch movement.

FOREHAND TECHNIQUE

BACKHAND TECHNIQUE

Figure 8-8

Basic oxyacetylene welding techniques.

A   B   C

Figure 8-9

Typical welding bead and welding faults: (A) good bead; (B) overheating welding zone; and (C) insufficient heat, rod applied too soon with very little fusion of the base metal.

Selection of proper tip size is also important. If the tip of the flame is being directed properly at the metal and the molten puddle does not readily form, the tip may be too small. If the puddle separates and holes appear, the tip may be too large, or you may not be using the overlapping or oval motion to assist in formation of the puddle.

Another common problem involves feeding the filler rod in too soon. This results in deposits of metal before the molten puddle has formed. These deposits tend to overheat and burn, resulting in a porous and brittle weld. (Figure 8-9)

In welding an edge of a material to the center of a piece of metal, or a small piece to a large piece, the small piece or edge may tend to melt away. Here, it is necessary to direct the heat to the largest amount of material or area, first, until a molten spot starts to form; then, by moving back and forth in the overlapping, oval pattern, favoring the thicker or larger section, you can complete the weld.

Overheating of the weld can also be a problem. Since metal will chemically change to an oxide in the presence of air or oxygen, and heat and oxygen accelerate this process, overheating of the weld results in a porous and brittle weld. The speed at which the torch is moved and the weld developed, as well as learning to recognize the shiny, molten puddle, are important.

Dirty tips can also cause problems; tips should be kept clean with a proper tip cleaner. Figure 8-5 illustrates a standard tip cleaner. The proper-sized cleaner is moved back and forth in the tip opening and is not twisted or turned.

BRAZING

Brazing or bronze welding generally involves the use of a nonferrous filler metal with a melting point above 1,000 degrees Fahrenheit but lower than the melting point of the metal to be joined.

The bronze welding rod is used principally in the fabrication of copper or copper alloys, or in the joining of dissimilar metals, such as copper or bronze to steel. The brazing technique is also used extensively in producing decorative surfaces on copper, brass, bronze, and steel; bronze rod is used for these effects, producing a golden brasslike surface that can be oxidized to a variety of color. Silver colors can be achieved with the use of nickel-silver rod. Eutectic Corporation produces a variety of rods with distinct variations in color due to the varied alloys.

In bronze welding, if the metal is properly cleaned and the proper rod and flux are used, bronze welds with excellent tensile strength can be achieved. The metal can be cleaned with solvents, steam, sand blasting, wirebrushing, or abrasives as discussed in Chapter 9, pages 182 to 184 and Chapter 10.

The welding procedure consists of heating the base metal from dull to cherry red, at which point bits of bronze rod are melted and fused to the base metal, forming a bead, as in fusion welding. Care must be exercised in letting the base metal reach the proper temperature; if the temperature is too low, the weld will not be properly bonded to the base metal; if it is too high, the bronze will burn and fume, producing an improper weld.

In using the brazing technique to develop textural surfaces, a small area about the size of a half dollar is heated to a dull red, at which point the rod is introduced into the weld area. The tip of the flame is directed to the rod, melting off a small portion which flows over the preheated area. As the torch is moved from rod to metal, the brazing continues. If more heat is directed to the rod, the texture becomes rather thick and bumpy; if more heat is directed to the metal, the bronze will flow out and produce a thin surface texture.

Figure 8-11 illustrates a studio assistant applying bronze to a brass piece for a large metal relief.

In bronze welding or brazing, a proper flux must be used. The end of the rod is slightly heated and dipped into the flux. As the rod is melted, the flux flows over the metal and protects the metal from oxidation as the weld develops. Flux-coated rods, obtainable at a slightly higher cost, are far more convenient to use and assure the proper amount of flux being present on the rod. On large quantities of brazing, considerable time is saved with the coated rod.

In most instances, the surface brazing of metal is performed prior to assembly of the pieces. The distortion that occurs during brazing can be removed by hammering and forming. (Figures 8-10 through 8-17 illustrate the fabrication steps, from the basic metal to the finished relief, using the brazing process.)

Good ventilation should be provided when bronze welding or brazing, as the zinc fumes from bronze can be irritating.

Figure 8-11
Texturing brass sheet with the brazing process.

Figure 8-10
Brass sheet being sheared into strips on an industrial power shear.

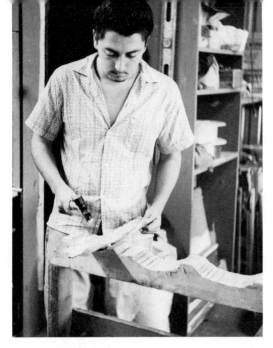

Figure 8-12
Hammering the metal into curved shapes.

Figure 8-13
Hammered pieces ready for assembly.

Figure 8-15
Sections mounted on studio wall for final detailing.

Figure 8-14
Pieces being assembled into sections to form a wall relief.

Figure 8-16
Final detailing of relief panels.

Figure 8-17
One of four relief panels installed. *Citizens National Bank, Lubbock, Texas, 1965. By author.*

SOLDERING

Soldering consists of using a nonferrous, low-melting-point metal to join metal to metal. Solder is a tin-lead mixture with a melting point of about 420 degrees Fahrenheit. The mixtures are from 40 to 60 percent tin to lead. Larger amounts of tin result in a lower melting point. Hard solders consisting of silver alloys can be used where greater strength is required. These are classified as "easy flow," with a flow temperature of 1,300 degrees Fahrenheit; "medium," with a flow temperature of 1,360 degrees; and "hard," with a flow temperature of 1,460 degrees. Aluminum solders are also available for soldering aluminum.

With proper conditions, soldering is a simple process. Normally, a soldering iron, electric soldering gun, or flame produced by air-acetylene or air-propane, is used as a heat source. (Figure 8-18) With silver solder, an air-acetylene torch or oxycetylene torch is usually used because of the higher melting temperature of the material. It is important that the metal be clean. Steel wood, emery paper, or sandpaper are usual cleaning tools. After the

metal has been cleaned, its surface is coated thinly with an appropriate flux. The metal is heated to a temperature that will melt the solder, at which point the solder is introduced into the solder area. The solder should melt when touching the heated

Figure 8-18
Soldering iron, top. Electric soldering gun, bottom.

metal. In soldering parts like copper fittings for fountains, the solder will draw into the space between the parts by capillary action, if the parts are clean and have been properly fluxed.

Since flux is often corrosive, it should be cleaned from the metal with soap and water or other suitable cleaners. Care should be exercised in preventing flux and solder from splattering into the eyes. Wearing protective goggles can be a good practice. Lead fumes from solder (particularly if it is overheated) can be toxic. Silver solder fumes can also be toxic, particularly if the alloying element is cadmium. Use good ventilation when soldering any appreciable amount.

ARC WELDING

Arc welding is essentially a process using heat formed by electrical energy—produced by a short circuit, as electrons meet resistance in the circuit and travel from rod to work piece or the reverse. Both alternating current (A.C.) and direct current (D.C.) are used.

There are virtually dozens of welding procedures using electrical or other forms of energy; the electron beam, the plasma arc, the laser beam, and atomic hydrogen welding are all processes used today by industry. In most cases, the equipment is expensive, highly sophisticated, and not practical as studio equipment. In the event that the sculptor or designer has a welding problem that cannot be solved with conventional welding equipment, he should seek the advice of a large industrial fabrication shop with more specialized equipment. Moderately-priced equipment (such as MIG and TIG) that is still too expensive for the small studio can be leased or rented from welding suppliers.

The principal advantage of arc welding is in the high rate of heat input, which not only results in considerable savings in fabrication time, but also minimizes distortion and makes the welding of thick or large metal sections more feasible.

Three of the most useful electric welders available today are: metal arc with consumable electrode, tungsten-inert-gas welder (TIG) and metal-inert-gas welder (MIG). Virtually any welding problem the sculptor encounters can be solved with these three pieces of equipment.

METAL ARC (CONSUMABLE ELECTRODE)

Undoubtedly the first electric welder the average sculptor purchases will be a simple arc-welding machine, consisting of the power supply, cables, ground clamp, and electrode holder (Figure 8-19 and 8-20). Protective leather gloves, helmet with appropriate lens (about number ten), and protective apron or jacket are also necessary equipment.

Figure 8-19
Electrode holder, left. Ground clamp, right.

Figure 8-20
180 amp. A.C.-D.C. electric arc welding machine. Cables are plugged into the receptacles for welding.

For the studio a good first welder capable of handling considerable work would be a 180-amp, combination A.C. and D.C. welder. The power supply required for a machine this size would be a single phase, 230 volts, 50-amp. circuit—the standard power service supplied by utility companies. Larger machines ideally operate off, three-phase, 220 or 440 volts. This is more efficient but usually available only in commercial or industrial locations.

The purpose in selecting the A.C.-D.C. machine is that it offers a wider choice of welding processes. Since the inexpensive, smaller A.C. welding machines seldom have a sufficient duty cycle for sustained operation, they should not be considered unless welding needs do not go beyond an occasional small welding job.

The duty cycle is the amount of time the machine can operate efficiently at a particular amperage. A machine rated at 40-percent duty cycle at 180 amps. could be operated for four minutes out of every ten. As the amperage decreases,

the performance factors increase, so that a machine with 40-percent rating would have around 90-percent duty cycle at 100 amps., or could be operated nine out of ten minutes of time.

The 40-percent rating is reasonably adequate for small shops and the studio. In general fabrication, the four out of ten minutes is seldom exceeded. Surface texturing of metals for sculpture requires high-duty cycles. However, amperages are usually low enough so that the machine can stand the near-to-continuous operation needed.

In many welding operations with the consumable stick electrode, direct current is preferred, since it provides more stable and precise current and a far wider choice of electrodes and welding procedures. However, there are many A.C. rods available that are of equal merit.

In are welding, two common terms are important: "direct current–straight polarity"; and "direct current–reverse polarity". (Figure 8-21) In straight polarity, the electrons flow from the electrode to the work; the heat is concentrated on the work and penetration into the metal being welded is deep. In reverse polarity, the concentration is on the electrode. It is consumed at a greater rate and penetration is shallow. Obviously, the selection of polarity would depend on the kind of metal, the type of weld, and the thickness of the metal. For example, in welding rather thin sheet metal, reverse polarity would be used in order to prevent burning holes in the metal.

Operation of the welder is relatively simple: the machine is plugged into a proper wall receptacle and the cables are plugged into the proper jack-plug receptable to select the process desired—such as direct current–straight polarity, alternating current, or direct current–reverse polarity. The proper amperage is selected and the machine is ready for operation. Figure 8-20 illustrates a typical machine. The design of these will vary in terms of the manufacturer and his instructions should be referred to at all times.

The amperage selected will depend on the rod size and the thickness of the metal. Figure 8-22 indicates some typical amperage settings in relation to rod size when welding steel.

After the amperage has been set, the ground clamp is fastened to the work table or work piece, and the rod is placed in the electrode holder, generally at right angle to the holder. The power is

Figure 8-21

Straight and reverse polarity.

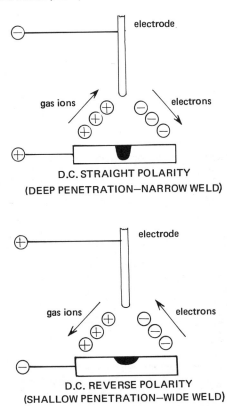

D.C. STRAIGHT POLARITY
(DEEP PENETRATION—NARROW WELD)

D.C. REVERSE POLARITY
(SHALLOW PENETRATION—WIDE WELD)

ELECTRODE DIAMETER	AMPERAGE	
	min.	max.
5/64	20	50
3/32	40	80
1/8	65	125
5/32	90	160
3/16	120	180

Figure 8-22
Current requirement for mild steel electrodes.

Figure 8-23
Proper rod postiion.

Figure 8-24
Rod movement pattern in arc welding.

turned on, and the welding is ready to proceed. The rod is positioned a few inches from the work; the helmet is lowered, and the arc is started.

The arc is started with a motion like striking a match or with a slight tappinglike motion. If the rod is not lifted quickly, it will stick or freeze to the metal. The distance between the end of the rod and the metal is generally about the diameter of the rod. The position of the rod as the weld develops will depend on the type of weld being executed; generally, the rod is at a 90-degree angle with the direction of the weld seam and about five to 15 degrees from the direction of travel. (Figure 8-23) As the rod is moved in the direction of the weld, it is usually manipulated in a zigzag, sideward or semicircular fashion. (Figure 8-24)

When welding thick metal and optimum strength is desired, the joint to be welded is "V"-grooved and multiple passes are made to fill the joint. The flux must be cleaned off each welded bead prior to application of the next bead. (Figures 8-25 and 8-26)

Figure 8-25
Typical weld joints: (A) butt joint "V" grooved from one side and filled with multiple passes; (B) simple butt joint welded from one side; (C) butt joint "V" grooved and welded from both sides; (D) lap joint welded from both sides; (E) tee joint "V" grooved and welded from both sides; (F) simple tee joint welded from both sides; (G) "V" grooved corner joint; and (H) simple corner joint welded from one side.

Figure 8-26

Arc welding sculpture. *Student project, Southern Methodist University.*

With direct, current, a carbon electrode can be used for welding with a carbon arc. In this case, the electrode is not consumed but simply provides an arc for melting the metal. A rod is fed into the weld zone, as when welding with an oxyacetylene flame. This process is used in welding some nonferrous metals; silicon bronze is easily welded with this technique.

Two typical problems when learning to weld are that the travel speed will be too fast and the arc too long. With a reasonable amount of practice on scrap material, this can usually be controlled in a short time.

The arc-welding procedure is relatively simple. However, what occurs metallurgically in the forming of a weld is complex. Any serious student of welding should read and own a good reference on arc welding and metallurgy.

As outlined for oxyacetylene welding, Safety precautions concerning metal, protective helmet and clothing, and general shop practice should be observed. Eyes should never be exposed to even a flash of the arc. Any exposed skin will burn after a few minutes of exposure and continued exposure can result in severe burns.

ARC-WELDING RODS

Rods, available for a wide variety of applications for both ferrous and nonferrous metals, should be selected on the basis of the metal to be welded, the degree of penetration desired, the profile of the welding bead, welding position, deposit rate, and for special problems such as thin material or filling in around poorly fitting parts.

Although welding rods vary to some extent in terms of alloys, some of the greatest differences are in the flux employed. The flux on the rod protects the weld zone by cleaning away oxides and providing inert atmospheres. Alloying and special elements are added to the flux to provide special welding conditions.

Rods are identified by the manufacturer as to their special purposes and characteristics. American Welding Society classifies carbon-steel rods by a four-digit system. The first two digits indicate the tensile strength; the third digit indicates rod position, and the fourth indicates a variety of rod characteristics such as power supply, coating, and type of penetration. As an example, a rod numbered 6011 would indicate a tensile strength of 60,000 p.s.i.; the third digit," "one," indicates all positions and the fourth digit, "one" indicates deep penetration. Color codes on rods indicate the type of rod and serve for further quick identification. Number 6011 is a good general-purpose rod for A.C. or D.C. welding, either polarity, and all positions. Number 6012 is about the same as 6011, but it is more suitable for poor fitup or high buildup. These rods are used on mild steel. Number 7010 is a direct current–reverse polarity, all-position rod for welding alloys and high-strength steel.

TIG WELDING

Tungsten-inert-gas welding (TIG) is somewhat similar to oxyacetylene fusion-welding or fusion and use of a filler rod. A tungsten electrode, which is not consumed, is used to form an arc for the heat source, and the metal is fused or a filler rod is added to the weld.

The principal advantage of the TIG process is in the welding of nonferrous metals, such as stainless steel, copper and copper alloys, nickel, magnesium, and aluminum. Welding of these metals has always been difficult because of the rapid formation of protective oxides when these metals are exposed to the atmosphere.

In TIG welding, a protective wall of inert gas (usually argon) around the arc and the weld zone protects the weld being formed from the atmosphere, thus preventing oxides from forming. The end result is a sound, clean weld, without the danger of flux, slag, or oxide entrapment that can occur with the simple arc or oxyacetylene processes. (Figure 8-27 illustrates TIG welding.)

Contrary to popular opinion, welding of aluminum or other nonferrous metals is not difficult. If the metal alloy is properly identified and the right rod is used, these metals can be welded with greater ease than using more conventional welding means. The power unit for the TIG torch is a precision piece of equipment (Figure 8-28) designed to provide a wide range of welding currents, current control, and shielding-gas control. The power-unit settings have been predetermined as to the metal being welded, and if manufacturer's recommendations are followed, TIG welding can be mastered easily. (Figures 8-29 and 8-30)

Figure 8-27

TIG welding process.

Figure 8-28

TIG welding machine. Note water cooler on top of machine; pump circulates water through the torch to keep it cool. Argon tank with pressure control regulator in foreground.

Figure 8-29

TIG welding aluminum. *Student project, Southern Methodist University.*

Figure 8-30
Completed aluminum sculpture. *Student project, Southern Methodist University.*

Figure 8-31
TIG torch.

Typical manufacturer's recommendations include kind of gas, rate of gas flow, type of current (A.C., direct current–reverse polarity or direct current–straight polarity) setting, amperage, electrode size, welding speed, welding rod, and gas cup size.

The TIG torch is compact and easy to handle. (Figure 8–31) It is necessary to change the gas cup and the collect and collect body inside the torch, when changing electrode sizes. Power should be off when changing or adjusting the electrode. The torch is cooled with a water supply system.

Unlike work with a consumable electrode, it is unnecessary to strike an arc with the TIG torch. The high frequency current allows the current to jump the gap between the torch and work, and the torch can simply be lowered to the right arc length.

MIG WELDING

Metal-inert-gas welding (MIG) is similar to TIG in that it utilizes a gas shield to protect the welding zone. In the MIG process, the electrode is in the form of wire which is fed from a spool mounted on the machine when the torch switch is pressed. The wire emerges through the torch body and is fed into the weld zone at a predetermined rate of speed. The process utilizes a special D.C. power supply. Most welding is done with reverse polarity. Steel, aluminum, stainless steel, and bronze can be welded, using wire similar to the metal being welded. One of the principal advantages in MIG-welding steel rather than using coated electrodes is that it produces a high-quality, clean weld that does not require postcleaning. (Figures 8-32, and 8-33)

A standard welding helmet and other protective clothing should be worn, and safety procedures should be observed with both TIG and MIG welding.

METAL CUTTING

There are a wide variety of cutting procedures in metal fabrication. Selecting the proper one often not only saves considerable time, but improves the quality of the final product. For example, the rough cut of an acetylene torch might suit the job in one instance, and yet if a close fit is required or finished edges, it would be preferable to saw or shear the metal.

The basic cutting techniques practical for the sculptor and generally used by industry fall into two categories: flame cutting, using the oxyacetylene process or arc process, and cutting by mechanical means, which includes sawing, shearing, and friction cutting.

FLAME CUTTING (OXYACETYLENE)

Flame cutting is based on the fact that metal in the presence of air changes chemically to an oxide. This process can be accelerated with the use of heat and oxygen. An oxyacetylene cutting-torch attached to a torch body is normally used, although other fuels, such as propane or natural gas, can be used with the proper torches.

Figure 8-33
MIG welding machine.

Figure 8-32
MIG torch. Note torch switch and wire protruding out of gas cup.

Oxyacetylene cutting, although commercially considered costly, provides the sculptor with a simple, portable means of cutting steel when a fine finish to the cut is not necessary. (Figure 8-34) In fact, the sculptor often prefers some of the rough qualities of a cut that is not too expertly done.

Any thickness of steel can be cut with oxyacetylene cutting. Industry uses large cutting machines to produce precision-cut parts. These machines could be useful to the sculptor if he needed a quantity of similar parts.

In the oxyacetylene process, the metal is heated to an ignition temperature with the preheating flames, at which point a stream of oxygen is introduced; the iron and oxygen combine to form iron oxide and are blown away from the flame, thus forming a narrow kerf, or slit, in the steel.

This process, limited principally to low-alloy steel, is not possible with stainless steel or nonferrous metals such as copper or aluminum. This is due to the higher ignition temperature of the oxides in these metals or alloying agents.

In flame cutting, the first step is to adjust the acetylene and oxygen pressures. For routine cutting of plate up to three-eighths-inches thick, the acetylene pressure would be three to five pounds, and the oxygen pressure would be twenty to thirty

Figure 8-35

Oxyacetylene cutting torch: (A) cutting torch oxygen adjusting valve; (B) torch body acetylene valve; (C) torch body oxygen valve; and (D) cutting torch oxygen valve to increase oxygen for cutting.

pounds. Pressure and tip sizes would increase with increased metal thickness.

The oxygen pressure is considerably higher than in welding, to provide the necessary oxygen for the cutting process. It is possible to cut a range of thicknesses with a smaller number of tips. In fact, most acetylene-equipment sets come with a limited number of cutting tips that are adequate for the average cutting done by the sculptor when clear, precision cuts are unnecessary. For optimum results, manufacturer's recommendations should be followed as to tip size and pressure required.

Figure 8-35 illustrates a typical cutting-torch attachment. To light the cutting torch, open the oxygen valve (c) on the torch body all the way. Open the acetylene valve (b) one eighth turn and light the torch with the friction lighter. Increase the acetylene until the flame stops smoking. Then, turn on the oxygen valve (a) until a neutral flame is obtained. Press down on lever (d), and if excess acetylene appears, readjust the flame by increasing oxygen or decreasing acetylene until a neutral flame is achieved.

To proceed with cutting, heat the edge of the metal with the preheating flames (tip of flames not quite touching metal). As soon as a bright red spot appears, depress the lever (d) and slowly move the torch in the direction of the cut. It will take some practice to develop proper cutting speed, which will depend on the thickness of the metal.

Although the position of the cutting torch is usually perpendicular to the metal, thin material may prove easier to cut if the torch is angled slightly away from the direction of the cut. This is particularly necessary if the supply of cutting tips is limited and you are trying to cut with a larger tip than would normally be used.

Figure 8-34

Cutting with the oxyacetylene cutting torch.

In cutting, if the travel speed is too slow, the tip too large, or the torch held too far from the metal, the metal will tend to melt and fuse together after the cut has been complete. If travel speed is too fast or the tip is too small, the cut will be incomplete.

FLAME POWDER-CUTTING

Another flame-cutting procedure, which is less-commonly-known but more expensive, is powder cutting. In this process, air pressure introduces a stream of iron or other metallic powder into the cutting zone. The powder fluxes the metal oxides in the cut, lowering the melting temperature of the oxide mixture, making the cutting possible.

One of the few practical ways of cutting thick stainless steel when a clean precise cut is needed, powder cutting is also used in cutting alumium, copper, brass, nickel, and other nonferrous metals, as well as concrete and ceramic materials.

ARC CUTTING

Steel can be cut with an ordinary steel stick electrode or cutting rod designed for the purpose. For an occasional cut, an ordinary steel rod, operating at amperage higher than welding ranges, will suffice. However, in most cases, it would be advisable to purchase rods for the specific purpose.

The principal disadvantages in cutting with the arc are the rougher cut produced and the need for higher volumes of air removal due to smoke and fumes produced in the cutting operation. In some instances, the decorative quality of the rough arc-cut is desirable and useful to the sculptor.

As well as for cutting steel, cutting rods have been developed that will cut cast iron and nonferrous metals. These rods are usually for either A.C. or D.C. operation.

Cutting with the arc is relatively simple. The machine is set at the recommended amperage, an arc is started at the edge of the metal, and a cut is produced by moving the rod up and down through the kerf in a sawing action. Typical amperage setting for one-eighth-inch rod would be 250 to 350 amps.; for 5/32-inch rod, 300 to 400 amps.; and for 3/16-inch rod, 350 to 500 amps. Available are special air-arc cutting torches that use compressed air to blow the metal slag out of the kerf as the cut is developed. These are particularly useful in cutting nonferrous metals.

If the MIG process is available, it can be used for cutting nonferrous metals. In this technique, the wire speed is such that it penetrates to the bottom side of the metal to be cut. The starting position is about one-fourth inch from the edge of the metal, with the wire protruding slightly beyond the bottom edge of the metal. Shielding gases are helium, argon, or special mixtures. The TIG welder can also be adapted to cutting by using a thoriated tungsten electrode and direct current.

SAWING

Sawing of metal is usually accomplished by hand hacksaw, power hacksaw, band saw, circle saw, or the jig saw. It has advantages over flame cutting when precise fits and angles are required, and in the absence of distortion normally associated with shearing or flame cutting; it is also one of the easiest and most preferable methods for cutting soft, nonferrous metals.

Saw blades are manufactured to cut almost any metal. The most important factors in successful cutting of metals are blade speed, number of teeth, tooth design, and rate of cut. The blade speed is determined by strokes or feet per minute; the rate of cut, in inches or feet per minute.

The tooth design in a cutting blade is usually alternate, raker, or wavy. (Figure 8-36) The set in

Figure 8-36

Three basic saw tooth settings.

ALTERNATE   RAKER   WAVY

the tooth depends on the material to be cut. Alternate set, with one tooth left and one tooth right, is common for wood-cutting blades. A straight tooth between each left and right tooth is a raker set and is used for coarse and precision-cutting band saw blades. The wavy set has two or more teeth alternately bent to the left or right at a graduated degree. This set is common to hacksaw blades and blades for band-sawing thin metal, thin tubing, and thin structural shapes.

HACKSAW CUTTING

There is a wide variety of hacksaws for hand cutting. Besides the standard hacksaw, keyhole saws, to hold a blade for working in close quarters, and shallow frame, saws for precision hand cutting of pipe and bar stock are available. (Figure 8-37)

Hand hacksaw cutting, tedious, time-consuming, is inadvisable, except for occasional cuts. However, if there is no other cutting tool available, hand sawing can be simplified with the proper cutting techniques.

Of prime importance is a good-quality blade with the right number of teeth. A poor-quality blade will be dull after a few strokes and, from that point

on, cutting is possible but is tire-some and difficult.

The common blades are the standard semi-flexible, generally used by maintenance men and for home utility; the standard flexible, for working in awkward positions and when the work cannot be held firmly; and the standard all-hard blade, when the work can be held in a vise and for hard-alloy steels. The premium flexible blade, all-hard molybdenum, and all-hard tungsten are higher-quality blades used for considerable cutting of hard materials.

The number of teeth per inch depends on the thickness of the material—thicker materials needing less teeth per inch. Approximate requirements for hand-hacksawing most materials would be 14 teeth per inch for materials one-half inch and thicker, 14 to 18 teeth per inch for 7/16- to one-fourth-inch material, 18 to 24 teeth per inch for one-fourth- to one-eighth-inch material, and 24 to 32 teeth per inch for materials one-eighth-inch thick or thinner.

Softer materials such as aluminum and copper require fewer teeth per inch.

The saw blade must be mounted on the hacksaw frame with the teeth pointing forward. The blade tension should be set so that the blade feels tight.

A moderate pressure is applied on the forward

Figure 8-37

Handsaws for cutting metal: (A) close quarter saw; (B) keyhole saw; (C) jewellers scroll saw; (D) shallow frame hacksaw; and (E) standard hacksaw.

Figure 8-38

Power hacksaw for cutting pipes, angles, bars and flat stock.

stroke when sawing. Relieve pressure on the back stroke, as it is the most common cause of tooth wear. The rate of speed for hand cutting is about 45 to 60 strokes per minute.

If frequent hacksawing is to be done, it is advisable to invest in a moderately-sized power hacksaw, which is inexpensive and performs many cutting chores. (Figure 8-38)

If occasional thick sections need to be cross-cut, metal shops with heavy-duty eqipment will perform this service at reasonable prices.

BAND-SAW CUTTING

For the sculptor, the variable-speed band saw is one of the most useful pieces of equipment (Figure 8-39). This versatile machine, properly used, is indispensable in the cutting of metal, plastic, and wood. In metal cutting it is used on both ferrous and nonferrous metal.

Cuts can be produced with speed and precision if the machine is properly adjusted and the right blade is used. The blade tension, support, and guides must be properly adjusted. Manufacturer's instructions should be followed on blade changes and adjustments.

Band-saw blades are most commonly raker or wavy-toothed. Raker teeth are preferred for general use and for thick material.

As well as the tooth-set design, band-saw blades come in several tooth patterns: standard, skip, and hook. (Figure 8-40) The standard blade is used on hard materials, whereas the skip and hook are used on soft materials such as aluminum.

Proper blade-speed (feet per minute) and rate of feed (inches per minute) is of utmost importance; excessive blade speed can ruin a blade in a single cut, when cutting ferrous metal. In fact, when using a band saw, always examine the saw for proper blade adjustment and speed, since the previous operator may have been using the saw for a different material than you intend to cut. Figure 8-41 lists blade and saw requirements for various metals.

In the rate of feed, the pressure on the material being fed into the saw should be moderate to light. Excess pressure will produce friction, heating, and subsequent blade wear. If excess pressure is needed, chances are the blade speed is too slow or is worn and in need of replacement. A wax

Figure 8-39

Variable speed bandsaw. (Note pulley arrangement for changing speed.)

Figure 8-40

Basic tooth design for bandsaw blades.

STANDARD TOOTH

SKIP TOOTH

HOOK TOOTH

REGULAR BLADES						
	under 1/2 inch		1/2 to 3/4 inch		over 1 inch	
	teeth per inch	feet per minute	teeth per inch	feet per minute	teeth per inch	feet per minute
Angle iron	24	160	14	160	10	40
Carbon steel	24	85	14	60	14	40
Cold rolled steel	18	220	14	220	14	160
Machinery steel	18	160	14	160	14	160
Stainless steel	24	40	14	40	10	40
Structural Steel	24	160	14	160	14	115
Cast iron	18	115	14	80	10	16
Bronze, Brass & Copper Alloys	18	300	14	250	10	200
SKIP TOOTH BLADES						
Aluminum	3	3000	3	3000	3	3000
Copper	6	3000	4	3000	4	3000

Figure 8-41

Bandsaw blade speeds for cutting metal.

Figure 8-42

Special jig being used for cutting pieces of aluminum tubing.

lubricant can be used on the blade to facilitate the cutting.

Blades are available in widths from one-eighth inch to one inch. The narrowest blade is primarily used for scroll work or for cutting a short radius. The widest blade practical should always be used on a job. A one-half-inch blade is a good, all-purpose width for general shop work.

Straight cuts on a band saw should be guided by a rip fence. Pipes and bar stock should be clamped and guided with a miter gauge. Special jigs are often designed for unusual cutting operations. (Figure 8-42)

Safety precautions in operating a band saw are few: protective goggles should be worn at all times; fingers and hands should be kept out of the path of the blade; the saw should be unplugged from the wall receptacle when changing blades. The most common accident results from excess pressure on the blade as a cut is completed, in which case, the workpiece moves suddenly, pulling fingers or hands in the path of the cut.

SCROLL OR JIG SAWS

The scroll saw or jig saw is available as a table model, or as a portable model called a "saber saw" or portable jig saw.

The scroll saw differs from the band saw in that the blade has a reciprocal action rather than a continuous one. It is an excellent tool for fine, intricate cuts and curves in wood, plastic, or sheet metal.

The saber saw or portable jig saw, which should be one of the first pieces of equipment acquired (Figure 8-43), should be a heavy-duty, variable-speed model of good quality; it can do much of the work, on a limited basis, that stationary band and scroll saws can do when the production needs are light and low in volume.

Even when stationary equipment is available, the saber saw performs chores that the band- and scroll-saw cannot accommodate—especially cutting into centers of large pieces of material. For example, the cutting clearance on moderate-sized band saw is 14 inches; if wider clearances are needed, a saber saw can be used.

In cutting metal, it is essential to use reduced speeds; under high-speed reciprocal action, a blade simply will not stand the excess friction. Therefore, only variable-speed saws should be considered as permanent pieces of shop equipment.

In sawing, the saber saw should be held firmly against the material. Travel-speed, as with a band saw, can be determined on the basis of a moderated forward pressure. When possible, the material should be clamped to the workbench or cutting table.

Saw-blade selection, as with the band saw, should be fine blades for thin material and coarser blades for thick. Blades are usually packaged with recommended usage provided by the manufacturer.

A hand version of the scroll saw is the coping saw or jeweler's scroll saw (Figure 8-37), which are useful for occasional work or when a cut is needed in an area inaccessible to the power tool. In handsawing on small pieces, the work is usually clamped in a vise or clamped to a work table.

CIRCLE-SAW CUTTING

Circle-saw cutting blades for metal, available for table saws or radial-arm saws, are usually of a friction-cutting type or are fine-toothed hard steel. (Figure 6-22)

A steel-slicer blade, not used on nonferrous metals, cuts steel with friction; other friction-cutting blades consist of abrasive materials embedded in fiber discs. Nonferrous metals are generally more satisfactorily cut with fine-toothed steel blades.

Figure 8-43
Portable jig saw cutting aluminum sheet.

Figure 8-44

Metal working tools: Top row, left to right: compound action tin shears, aviation pattern shears, straight pattern shears, dividers. Bottom, left to right: hole cutting saw, cold chisel, center punch, rivet or pin punch, two high-speed drills, countersink; top, wire and sheet metal gauge, drill gauge, and scratch awl.

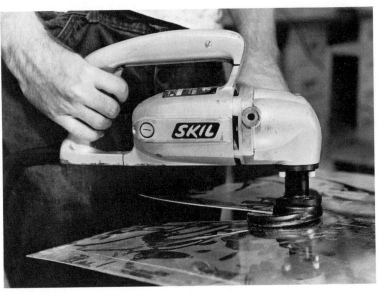

Figure 8-45

Portable electric metal cutting shears.

Figure 8-46

Foot squaring shears.

The material is generally handled on a table saw in the same fashion as working with wood— ripping by guiding against the rip fence, and cross-cutting by using the miter guide. For crosscut work, it is a good practice to have a miter guide with a hold-down device. Goggles should always be worn and a blade guard should be used when cutting with abrasive wheels. If the saw being used is used in wood work, all sawdust must be cleaned up around the equipment, since sparks from the blade can ignite the sawdust. A small amount of lubricant, (either a tallow candle or a wax stick designed specifically for the purpose) should be used on metal-cutting blades.

SHEARING

One of the simplest and most economical methods of cutting metal is by shearing. We are all familiar with the hand shears used in occasional cutting of tin or sheet metal. The most common shearing device is the foot-squaring shears, which are foot-operated. We are generally less familiar with motor-operated shears and punch presses operated by industry.

Hand shears, available in a variety of designs, are versatile, very adequate in the fabrication of light-weight sheet material, and are designed for straight, left-hand or right-hand cuts. Blade designs are also available that will accomplish all three cutting operations, and special shears are available with compound leverage for cutting thick and difficult materials or difficult angles. Electric hand shears are also available. (Figure 8-45) Figure 8-44 illustrates a variety of hand shears which are commonly used in metal shops and which are of possible use to the sculptor or designer.

The foot-squaring shears (Figure 8-46), used primarily for shearing light-gauge materials, are particularly useful when a quantity of similar-sized pieces is needed. The principal advantage over hand shearing is the ease with which the cutting can be accomplished, moreover, there is less distortion of the metal.

Power shearing or stamping is normally used for large quantities of cuts and for the cutting of thick metal when manual shearing is not possible. Usually expensive, power shears are used only by large metal suppliers or fabricators. (Figure 8-10)

If a quantity of shearing is needed, the firm supplying the metal will usually be able to shear to your specifications at a reasonable cost. For example, the 8,000 lbs. of Everdur® silicon bronze for the fountain in Figure 13-18 was supplied in presheared strips.

Metal stamping is a cutting process using a hydraulic press and cutting dies. Many shapes are available in terms of standard dies that a metal-stamping firm would have in stock. To have a die custom-designed is, of course, expensive and, for the sculptor or industrial designer, usually limited to precontracted work.

EXPLOSION FORMING

Recently new to industry is the process of forming metal with explosives. In this technique, the mold, metal, and explosives are submerged in a tank of water. A vacuum is drawn on the mold and the explosive charge is released, forcing the metal into the mold contour. In many cases, the metal form will be partially formed by a fabrication technique such as welding and completed with explosion forming.

The amount and kind of explosives, distribution, and distance from sheet are all important. Expert engineering advice is needed when attempting to use this process.

For industry, explosion forming has proven to be highly successful for pieces too large to handle in conventional forming processes.

Sculpturally, variations of the process have been used.

COLD FORMING

Cold forming involves the shaping of sheet, bar, or strip metal, using dies, punches, forming blocks, bending brakes, and rollers. Both ferrous and nonferrous metal can be cold-formed.

One of the simplest methods of cold forming is the bending of metal strips, small bars, or rods in a bench vise. The hammering of sheet metal over or into wood-forming blocks, forming over steel stakes or bending over the edge of a work-

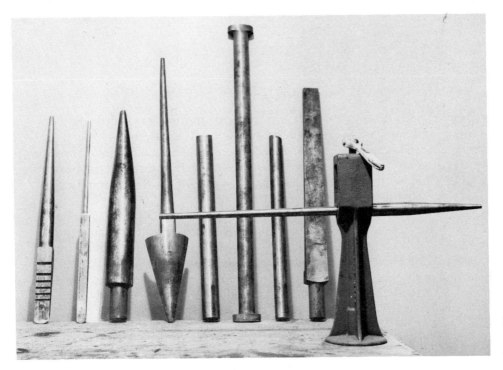

Figure 8-47
Steel forming stakes for working sheet metal.

Figure 8-48
Typical bends with a universal iron bender. *Adapted from Hossfeld Manufacturing Co. literature.*

Figure 8-49
Hydraulically operated Universal Iron Bender. *Photograph courtesy of Hossfeld Manufacturing Co.*

bench are other examples. (Figure 8-47) Bent-wire sculpture is a simple and typical example of cold forming.

Beyond the simple practice of bending materials mechanically, hand- or power-operated tools have been designed to produce almost any configuration imaginable. Angles of any degree, circles, zigzags, folds, and bends are all mechanically possible in thin-to-thick steel plate.

One of the simplest devices for bending tube, bar, angle, and strap is a universal iron-bender (Figure 8-49) Using a variety of forming dies, this hand-operated or hydraulically-operated machine performs a wide variety of bends. It is typically used in decorative wrought-iron work but has potential use for the sculptor when bending is needed. (Figure 8-48)

Bending of flat sheet can be performed readily on a bending brake, and cylinders can be formed on roll-forming machines. (Figure 8-50)

Versions of the typical sheet-metal shop equipment exist on a large scale in industrial fabrication shops. Bending, folding, and rolling are feasible for monumental sculptural works and can be performed by these shops.

Metal-forming using punch presses, draw presses, and roll forming have sculptural possibilities in the event that the sculptural design is modular. A sculptural commission with a large number of modular units could conceivably merit the cost of a punch- and die-forming operation.

FORGING

Heating and forming metal through forging dates as far back into history as many other metal fabrication techniques. The Egyptians and Sumarians (2300 to 2500 B.C.) mentioned earlier utilized forging. The blacksmith of the fourteenth and fifteenth centuries made tools and decorative metal forms. The armourer of that time produced weapons and armour. Sheet metal was hammered and forged out of spongy lumps of hot metal called blooms. Essentially, forging is still the same process although industry uses mechanical means to shape or hammer the metal and temperature of the metal is more precisely controlled in heating the metal for forging and during annealing or tempering.

The sculptor of today is more concerned with hand forging as a method for shaping metal. Metal can be heated with the oxyacetylene torch or a simple furnace can be built out of fire bricks using a small burner simular to the burner used for melting metal. (Figure 3-29) Metal can also be heated in the melting furnace. Rods, pipes, bars, and strap material can be readily bent by heating the piece of material with a torch to a bright red at the point at which the bend is to be made. For pieces of carbon steel that are to be hammered and shaped the metal is heated to a bright yellow. It is heated as rapidly as possible to prevent the grain of the metal from becoming too coarse. Heating the metal

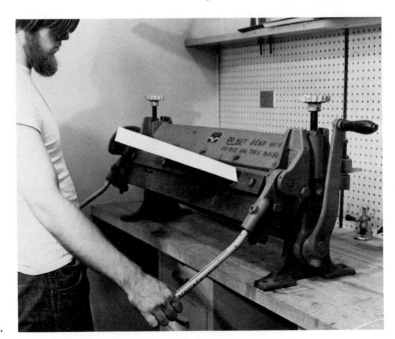

Figure 8-50
Bending brakes bending sheet metal.

softens it, and as it is hammered the grain becomes fine and the metal becomes harder and more brittle. The carbon content of the steel also effects its hardness; more carbon means a harder steel. The metal is held with a tongs and hammered on an anvil. A 30 to 40 ounce ball peen hammer can be used. The metal is hammered until is becomes a dull red. If additional shapping is necessary the metal is reheated and the process continues until the desired form is achieved.

In forging or hammering cold metal such as copper or bronze, the metal is hammered on blocks of pitch or on bags of sand. The metal is heated to a dull red and allowed to cool slowly prior to the hammering. Heating metal and cooling slowly (annealing) softens it while cooling rapidly (tempering) hardens it. Copper is easier to hammer and shape than bronze. If the metal starts to become brittle because of the hammering it can be heated and softened again as the work progresses.

On some occasions, it may be desirable to restore the temper in tools such as those used for stone carving. To temper a chisel, the cutting end is heated to a cherry red and then quenched in cold water. The tool end is then polished with a piece of emery paper and reheated to a temperature that will produce the desired temper. By polishing the steel it is possible to distinguish various color changes as the metal is heated. The desired temper can be achieved by quenching the tool in cool water when the desired color is reached. Tools for granite are heated to a straw-yellow (400 to 425 degrees Fahrenheit), marble tools are heated to a bluish-violet (550 degrees Fahrenheit).

HAND TOOLS

A variety of hand tools is basic to metal working. In hammering on metal, to begin with, plastic or rubber mallets are used to prevent marring the material. Hammering for forming or chasing is done with the ball peen hammer or with special metal-working hammers.

Hand finishing may involve the use of hand or rotary files for working down edges or surfaces and reaching area inaccessible to grinding or abrasive finishing. A hand file should be used as a hacksaw, with pressure being applied on the forward motion of the stroke and released on the back stroke. A file card is used to clean the file. Special files are designed for special needs, such as saw files, machinists files, pattern files, and silversmith riflers. Pattern files and riflers are excellent for fine detail work and for finishing in small areas. Rotary files are used with electric drills, drill presses, and with the flexible shaft. Small rotary files on a small flexible shaft can get into extremely small cavities and areas inaccessible to other finishing tools. (Figure 8-51)

Metal sculpture involves many typical mechanical devices and tools: nippers and diagonal cutting-pliers are used for cutting wire; pliers are used for holding material, twisting wire, or for holding round stock, nuts, and bolts. Nuts and bolts are more appropriately held and fastened with proper fitting wrenches; socket, open-end, adjustable, and box wrenches can be used. Pipe wrenches are used for holding pipe and round stock; flat or phillips screwdrivers are used for driving machine screws; offset screwdrivers are designed for work in close quarters. Select the proper-sized screw driver for the job to be done; the tip should be as wide as the screw slot and should fit in the slot snugly; working with an undersized screwdriver can damage the screwdriver or the screw. Allen wrenches are used to drive allen screws. The allen screw has a hexagon-shaped, recessed hole. (Figure 8-51, 8-52, 8-53, and 8-54)

In Figure 8-44, a variety of other tools useful to metalworking is illustrated. The calipers measure diameters and widths. Hole-cutting saws cut holes through sheet metal. The cold chisel, used for cutting off metal burrs and projections, can also be used for cleaning up metal castings. A center punch is used for making a center indentation in metal for starting a drill in the desired spot. Rivet or pin punches drive out rivets and pins. The countersink reams out a hole that is to receive a screw with a countersinking head. Wire and sheet-metal gauges are indispensable for quick, accurate readings in estimating wire size and metal thickness. Drill gauges check screw and drill sizes when drilling holes that are to be threaded. The scratch awl is for marking metal accurately. High-speed twist drills are used for drilling holes in metal. Use small drills up to one-fourth inch at 600 to 800 revolutions per minute. As the drill size increases, decrease the speed. Use about 250 revolutions per minute with a one-half-inch drill. Hard metals, like tool steel, need much slower speeds than soft, nonferrous metals.

HAND FILE SHAPES

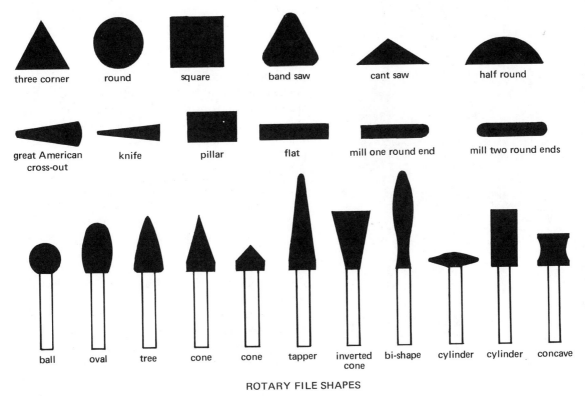

three corner round square band saw cant saw half round

great American cross-out knife pillar flat mill one round end mill two round ends

ball oval tree cone cone tapper inverted cone bi-shape cylinder cylinder concave

ROTARY FILE SHAPES

Figure 8-51
Hand and rotary files.

Figure 8-52
Hammers from left to right: rubber mallet, ball peen, metal working, metal chasing. Phillips screwdriver bottom left; flat blade screwdriver, bottom right.

Figure 8-53
Top: arch joint pliers. Middle row, left to right: vice grip pliers, linemans pliers, nippers, diagonal cutting pliers, extra long nose pliers, regular nose pliers, and long nose pliers. Bottom left: file card. From top right: half round, round, and flat files.

Figure 8-54

Top center down: socket driver speed handle, ratchet reversible socket wrench, adjustable wrench, and offset screwdriver. Left to right bottom row: pipe wrench, allen wrenches, socket driver, open end and box end wrench, open end wrench, and adjustable wrench.

FASTENERS

In some instances it may be desirable to fabricate using fasteners instead of welding or adhesive bonding. Riverts, bolts, or screws would be used in these circumstances. Riverts are either solid, semitubular, tubular-split or drive-pin, and have either flat, round, or oval-shaped heads. (Figure 8-55) For fastening with solid rivets a rivet bar is held against the head of the rivet, and the rivet is

struck with a riveting hammer on the opposite end. Semitubular and tubular rivets use a punch to spread the walls of the rivet. The drive-pin rivet is struck on the pin to cause the rivet to spread. Pneumatic hammers are used for setting rivets in production work. The drive-pin rivet is one of several forms of blind rivets that can be installed working from one side of the material; another with that advantage is the pop rivet, which is excellent for joining sheet metal. As the handle of the pop-rivet tool is squeezed, it pulls up a pin that causes the hollow rivet to spread out and flatten against the back side of the metal. The pin is sheared off with the tool after the rivet has flattened. (Figure 8-56)

Screw-type fasteners are either machine, thread-forming or thread-cutting screws. (Figure 8-57) A screw is normally thought of as a small bolt used in a threaded hole without a nut. Machine screws require the cutting of a mating thread to match the screw thread. Thread-forming or thread-cutting, self-tapping screws are used to join two pieces of thin sheet metal or are used in soft metals such as copper or aluminum. The pilot hole for the self-tapping screw must be drilled to the proper diameter to receive the screw. Typical screw heads are designed to accommodate a flat or phillips screwdriver or hexagon allen wrench. Screw threads are classified as Unified National coarse (U.N.C.), Unified National fine (U.N.F.), and Unified National extra fine (U.N.E.F.). Threads per inch decrease as the diameter of the screw increases. Screws are identified as "2, 3, 4, 5, 6, 8, 10," and "12" up to one-fourth inch in diameter; number 2

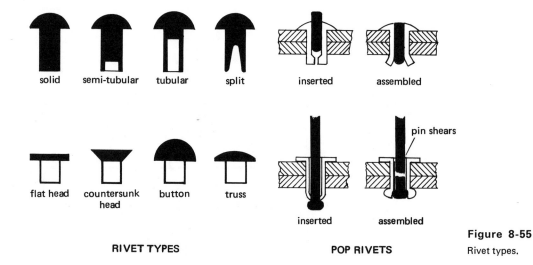

solid   semi-tubular   tubular   split   inserted   assembled

flat head   countersunk head   button   truss   inserted   assembled   pin shears

RIVET TYPES   POP RIVETS

Figure 8-55
Rivet types.

Figure 8-56
Using the pop rivet tool.

thread forming   thread cutting   machine

SCREW TYPES

Figure 8-57
Screw types.

ACTUAL SIZE MACHINE SCREWS

3/8-16   5/16-18   ¼-20   12-24   10-24   8-32   6-32   5-40   4-40   3-48   2-56

flat   round   oval   flat fillister   oval fillister   oval binding   hexagon   round washer   pan   knurled   acorn

Figure 8-58
Screws (actual size) and typical screwheads.

TYPICAL HEAD STYLES
(STANDARD AND NONSTANDARD)

is the smallest; from one-fourth inch on they are identified by inches or fractions of an inch. The second number in screw identification designates the number of threads per inch. For example, a screw identified as "8-32" would have 32 threads per inch; a 1/4-20" would have 20 threads per inch. (Figure 8-58)

A bolt is a threaded device that can be inserted through a hole in two or more pieces of material to hold the material together. A threaded square or hexagon nut is used on the opposite end of the bolt. Thread sizes are classified in the same manner as screws; a further classification designates the fit between the bolt and the nut; bolts are classified "A" and nuts are classified "B"; "1A" and "1B" designates a loose fit; as the numbers increase up to 5, the fit becomes tighter. Besides standard machine bolts and stove bolts found in most hardware stores, a variety of bolts designed for the construction industry is available from special suppliers dealing solely in fasteners. Ordinarily, the 6-32, 8-32, 1/4-20 and 3/8-16 screws and bolts are readily found and meet most of the needs of sculptors.

FASTENERS FOR INSTALLATION

Mounting or installing metalwork often requires special fasteners other than screws or bolts. If a wall consists of wood panelling, lag or wood screws can be used to fasten mounting brackets; the wooden framework or studs behind the panelling can often be located for additional support. For plaster walls, Molly® bolts or toggle bolts can be used, which spread out and hold from the backside of the wall surface. For concrete walls or floors, an appropriate sized hole is drilled in the concrete with a masonry bit, and expansion-type fasteners are inserted into the hole; machine screws or lag screws turn into the fasteners and expand the fastener to fit tightly into the hole. Threaded studs can also be driven into concrete using a special gun with an explosive charge. Studs can also be anchored into concrete by cementing with epoxy or other adhesives. Fasteners used for mounting metal works are also appropriate for works in other material. Figure 8-59 illustrates some basic mounting techniques for walls and bases.

THREAD CUTTING

Thread cutting is often required in installing sculpture, mounting it on a base, joining sections, or fabrication using screws. Dies are used to cut threads on round stock; taps are used to cut threads into holes. They are available in thread sizes corresponding to nuts and bolts. Taps, more often needed and used, are available in three basic types: taper, plug, and bottoming. The taper, easiest to start, is best used when threading through a piece of material; when threading into a hole with a bottom, a bottoming tap should be used.

In cutting a thread with a tap, the proper-sized hole is first drilled. This is easily determined by reading the drill gauge illustrated in Figure 8-44, which gives the drill size in relation to the hole needed for the threaded portion of the bolt (tap size) and the unthreaded portion (body size). Taps also have the required drill size indicated in fine lettering on the upper portion of the tap. Drills are sometimes also marked. Otherwise, the size is

Figure 8-59

Methods of mounting for walls and bases: (A) Molly® fastener used on a wood panel wall; (B) toggle fastener through a plaster wall; (C) expansion anchor in concrete; (D) stud cemented into a concrete wall; (E) metal sculpture mounted on a base using a threaded hole in the work (if the work were wood, a lag screw could be used); and (F) threaded bolt cast into the work.

Figure 8-60

Left: thread cutting tool with tap mounted in tool.
Top row, left to right: tapered tap and bottoming tap.
Center row: thread cutting dies. Bottom: die tool.

checked by inserting the drill into the proper hole on the drill gauge. For example, the 1/4-20 screw requires a number 7 drill. Pick out a number 7 drill or if the drill is not marked, select a size that you think will correspond to the number 7 hole in the gauge. If the drill fits the number 7 hole but not the number 8, it would be the proper size. The screw size, when not known, can also be determined by simply inserting it into the holes until the proper size is found and then reading the tap-size list of figures on the drill gauge. (Figure 8-60)

After the hole has been drilled, a small amount of thread-cutting oil or wax is placed on the tap to provide a better cutting action. The tap must be started straight. It is turned several turns until the turning becomes difficult. Then back up about a half turn and proceed again. In tapping into a bottom hole, it may be necessary to remove the tap several times and remove the fine metal cuttings. It might also be advisable to tap the hole first with a tapered tap, followed by a plug tap, and completed with a bottoming tap. (Figure 8-61)

Figure 8-61

Cutting a thread using a tap.

Coating
and
Finishing

NINE

Conveniently, just as experimentation with mixed materials and colors for outdoor sculpture has increased the sculptor's need for coating materials, so has industry produced a wide variety of coating materials and techniques adaptable to sculpture.

A coating material can serve more than one function, its purpose, as with clear finish, may be solely to protect the finish and surface-appearance of a material; or it may be used to protect, color, or alter the surface through the uses of pigmented enamels, lacquers, and metallic surfaces.

Historically, coating dates back at least to ancient Egypt; as early as 1,000 B.C. the Egyptians possessed a form of varnish, probably developed from the resin extracted from the sandarac tree. Still earlier, the paint used in early cave painting can be thought of as a coating. Ancient Greece and Crete made extensive use of pigments and binders such as glue, egg albumin, and natural resins. Venetian turpentine was used as a thinner. On weapons and armor, ancient warriors used protective coatings of olive oil, linseed oil, or natural fats.

There are four types of coating that are of principal interest to today's sculptor: organic and inorganic coatings, conversion coatings and metallic coatings. Although some of these materials are available to the sculptor and are easily applied by him, others must be applied commercially.

The coating and metal-finishing industry is expanding rapidly, with new materials and processes being developed each year. At best, this chapter can present only a sketchy view of the diverse methods that exist in so comprehensive an area. Two of the best sources of detailed current information are *Metal Finishing Magazine* (Nathaniel Hall, ed. Westwood, N.J.: Metals and Plastic Publications, Inc. Published monthly.), and the *Metal Finishing Guidebook and Directory*. The *Guidebook*, which presents about 900 pages of information on all aspects of metal finishing, can be obtained free of charge by subscribing to *Metal Finishing Magazine;* it is an indispensable reference in the solving of finishing problems.

Sculpturally, the use of coated materials depends on the desired degree of permanency for the work as well as on its surface appearance. For interior locations, the majority of coatings have an adequate life-span and can be used with little concern. For exterior applications, however, the choice becomes narrower and limited performance of the coating must be taken into account.

Another attitude would be to accept the fact

that if a coating material can be replaced easily, and if the life-span of the coating is reasonable, refinishing is not a major factor. Organic painted surfaces vary considerably. The life expectancy of painted films for wood or masonry may be from five to 25 years. Zinc or red lead organic primers on aluminum or steel are considered to have exceedingly long service. Zinc-powdered organic coatings have histories of at least thirty years to date. Nonorganic coatings, such as porcelain enamel, have indeterminate life expectancies.

ORGANIC COATINGS

This area of coating materials is undoubtedly the most familiar, since all of us have worked with some form of paint since early childhood. Organic coatings are clear or pigmented; the essential difference between a varnish and paint or enamel is the addition of a pigment to the latter. An organic coating consists simply of a binder (or vehicle), a thinner, and other additives, such as pigment for color, dryers or catalysts to accelerate drying, and fillers to thicken.

Modern coatings consist of complex combinations of resins, solvents, and additives, mixed to produce particularly desired results. Formulations may be directed toward flexibility, stability under temperature change, drying time, methods of application, appearance; resistance to corrosion, acid, moisture, sunlight, abrasion, and impact. Organic coatings can also be in the forms of thin sheets of paper, or plastics glued or bonded to surfaces. Some plywoods are finished with this kind of coating to prevent checking and grain rise in exterior applications. Plastic films laminated to metal or wood are also available.

Early binders consisted of natural materials such as glue, egg albumin, and resins from plants and trees; linseed and tung oil were used next; synthetic binders are the most recent in origin. The majority of resins or binders used today are synthetic. The patenting of nitrocellulose in 1869, and its development in the lacquer industry, paved the way for a wide range of synthetic resins. Some modern paint formulations consist of cellulose acetate, ethyl cellulose, acrylic, vinyl, and alkyd, phenolic resins, epoxies, styrene, polyesters, urethanes, and silicones. Early solvents were water and turpentine. Today, although a wide variety of solvents is used in relation to particular binder formulations, the most common solvents are still water, turpentine, alcohol, mineral spirits, acetone, and lacquer thinner. Coatings using water as a solvent have been particularly popular in recent years, since they eliminate the complex and undesirable practice of cleaning equipment with flammable solvents.

The drying process in early organic coatings such as oil paints and lacquers is a relatively simple process of the thinner or solvent evaporating and the binder material oxidizing to form a film. New, synthetic resins involve more complex systems of polymerization resulting in the change from a liquid to a solid film. During polymerization, chemical reactions occur not only within the coating material but they may take place in relation to the surface on which the application is made.

In paint or coating formulations, critical concerns are as follows: the method of application, the solvent or thinner and the quantity used, the quantity of catalyst or proportion of total mixtures used, the temperatures at which coating is applied, the temperature of the coating material, and the condition of the surface on which the coating is applied. Remember that the films or residue from cleaning or finishing may not be compatible with the coating material.

Reliable manufacturers will usually base their formulations on the results of extensive testing. Strict adherence should be given to specific directions for the preparation of surfaces, use of primers and to the application as recommended by manufacturers. In using coatings select a reputable paint dealer who represents a major paint- or coating-manufacturer. If permanence is desired, use the finest grade of materials offered; bargains in coatings are not bargains; the random purchase of low-priced paints cannot assure good results. Generally, a low-priced paint will mean a cheap or an inadequate quantity of the desired ingredients.

CLEAR COATINGS

There is a wide variety of clear coatings for finishing or sealing wood, metal, concrete, and other materials for interior and exterior applications. A clear finish on sculpture poses no problem when the work is to remain indoors. For exterior use, however, although great advances have been made, a totally permanent coating still does not exist. Refinishing or periodic renewal of the coating remains inevitable.

Some of the readily available clear-finishing materials are as follows:

Shellac. The purified resinous material from which shellac flakes are made is obtained from lac. Lac is a resinous substance obtained from southern Asia. It is deposited on the twigs of certain trees by the lac insect. The flakes are dissolved in alcohol, most often at the rate of three or four pounds to a gallon (commonly referred to as a three- or four-pound cut). In its simplest and least expensive form, it is known as orange shellac, when bleached, it is called white shellac.

Orange shellac is an excellent, inexpensive sealer for plaster molds, wood, modelling boards, wood armatures, and applications in which surface-appearance is not a consideration.

As a finishing material, white shellac should be used; it is an excellent sealer for stained wood or plaster. Since it is not highly stain- or moisture-resistant, it is usually used as an intermediate sealer, with the final finish being lacquer, varnish, or wax. White, pigmented shellac is available today as a sealer-primer for wood and other surfaces when the surface is to be painted.

Lacquer. When spray equipment is available, lacquer sealers and finishes are still one of the best ways of finishing wood and metal for interior and exterior use. Lacquer produces a good, highly durable film. Of the clear coating systems, lacquer films tend to be the least prone to yellowing or discoloration. It is available as a finishing material in gloss, semi-gloss, and flat. Small quantities are available in pressurized spray cans.

Nitrocellulose resins were originally the first synthetic resins used in lacquer. Most lacquers today, however, are a blend of resins; many contain alkyds, vinyl, acrylic, or rubber derivatives. Lacquer sealers tend to have better sanding characteristics and are often more preferable to shellac.

Varnishes. Originally, natural resins from trees were dissolved in turpentine or other solvents to produce varnishes. Later, binders became linseed oil, chinawood oil, and others. Today, synthetic resins, which are beginning to dominate the market, have been developed to minimize some of the problems of early varnishes. The life-span of natural-resin varnish as an exterior material had always been limited, discoloration of the varnish film upon aging also proved undesirable. Synthetic varnishes today equal or surpass lacquers and natural-resin materials. Although urethane-resin varnishes are proving to be some of the most reliable coatings for exterior and interior use, discoloration or yellowing in sunlight is still a problem with them.

Waxes. Natural waxes, such as beeswax, and synthetic wax, such as paraffin thinned with turpentine or mineral spirits, can be used to seal or protect surfaces. Brushing-wax solutions are prepared by melting the wax in a double boiler, which is removed from the stove after the wax has melted, and the solvent is added; it is then placed back on the stove and warmed until the wax and solvent have blended. Proportions of one part wax to five to eight parts solvent can be used to seal plaster, concrete, or vermiculite, and plaster or concrete mixtures. Care should be exercised in warming solvent-based materials: it is best to heat the solutions in a double boiler on an electric stove that has a sealed heating element. Commercial paste waxes and liquids can also be used to protect varnished, lacquered, and painted surfaces. Wax can also be used to dull the shine on surfaces. Oxidized surfaces can be protected with paste waxes.

Epoxy. Clear epoxy resins for coating are continuously being developed. As a metal coating these are, in some cases, considered to be superior to urethane. The principal disadvantage is a tendency to chalk after prolonged exposure to sunlight and atmosphere.

PIGMENTED COATINGS

Pigmented coatings can be classified in two categories: primer and finish coatings.

Primer coatings. These are usually design to act as an intermediate coat. They may act as a sealer or are used to increase or maintain the mechanical bond and render the surface more susceptible to finishing and final application; in which case, the appearance of the surface is of small concern, and pigment is selected in terms of other properties that are desired. This coating is of utmost importance since it determines the effectiveness of the final finish or top coating.

If the primary function of the primer is to

seal the surface and reduce porosity, a pigmented oil, shellac, lacquer, vinyl, or alkyd primer is used. These will serve the purpose on plaster, wood, or concrete. Some pigmented primers also contain fillers to assist in filling pores in the material. If the surface is to be sanded, preparatory to developing a fine finish, lacquer-based primers often prove most sandable.

Acrylic-based lacquer primers should be used on fiberglass surfaces.

White primers are used by sculptors if a translucent appearance is desired in the finished coating. If the coating is to be opaque, colored pigmented primers can be used to assist in hiding surface grain or blemishes. Tinting the white primer with a universal coloring agent is a common practice.

In addition to performing some of the functions just discussed, primers on metal have a further role in preventing corrosion. Addition of some pigments to a suitable binder inhibits electrochemical reaction, or corrosion, on the surface of the metal. This form of primer is absolutely essential if a coating is expected to adhere and have a reasonable life-span on ferrous metal.

Red-lead primers have been recognized for many years as providing superior protection on steel. Zinc-chromate primers, equally effective on steel, are used also on zinc, magnesium, and aluminum. Metallic zinc dust, in organic or non-organic vehicles, provide coatings with an extremely long life-span in protecting steel.

Finish coatings.   In finish or top coatings, appearance is often as important as the performance factors of the pigments and binders. Binders and thinners are essentially the same as those used in clear finishes. However, a greater variety exist and formulation is different, with synthetic resins predominant in pigmented coatings, today.

Some common formulations are alkyd resins, straight and modified, which produce excellent finishes with quick-drying and setting qualities. These, as well as vinyl and latex coatings, are used extensively in household and industrial finishes. Phenolic resins, which adhere well to metal, are some of the most durable for exterior use. Cellulose esters, and ethers used in lacquers modified with other resins, are extensively used on automobile finishes.

Heavy-duty coatings based on polyvinyl, epoxy, urethane, polyester, coal-tar epoxy, chlorinated rubber, acrylic, and alkyd have been developed for long life and extensive service.

Although requirements for interior and exterior finishes are similar, exterior coatings must

Figure 9-1

Painted plywood sculpture. *By Roger Kotoske, 1968 Denver Sculpture Symposium.*

obviously withstand more rigid conditions. A coating must possess elasticity, since it must accommodate temperature change and subsequent thermo-expansion, and contraction, of the material onto which it is applied. It should resist atmosphere moisture, chemicals, and abrasion. In some cases, the top coating may be dense and highly moisture-resistant; yet it may have breathing characteristics to allow moisture to escape, as in formulations for masonry and wood.

Pigments used in coatings are natural and manufactured. In addition to imparting color, pigments help exclude ultraviolet light and retard deterioration of the binder. The hiding power of a coating may be due to the color, density, or particle-size of the pigment. At times, pigments or fillers are also added to give body to the coating. The ratio of pigment to vehicles is usually about 25 to 35 percent by volume.

A wide variety of the pigmented coatings produced for household and, particularly, for industrial use should be of interest to the sculptor. Vinyl and latex exterior paints with water solvents designed for wood and masonry should prove effective on wood and concrete sculpture. (Figure 9-1) Epoxy, polyurethane, vinyl, and phenolic-resin coatings designed for ship hulls, bridges, and steel structures (where the corrosive environment of salt water and salt air are factors) should prove effective on metal sculpture. These resins are also used in exterior paints for wood and masonry. Some epoxy paints are excellent on fiberglass.

Automobile lacquers, utilizing nitrocellulose combined with alkyd or melamine resins and acrylic lacquers, are excellent for finishing metal and fiberglass. Pigmented gel-coating polyester resins are available for fiberglass fabrication as well as resin-based paints for wood, metal and masonry. Polyvinyl coatings such as those applied to dish-drain racks, etc. could have excellent sculptural application, if a commercial source for applying the material is available. Zinc-powder-filled coatings would provide long-life corrosion-protection on steel, if the sculptor can accept the limited color; or they can be used as primers. Chlorinated-rubber coating materials, available in a limited range of colors, could be serviceable on outdoor sculpture of wood or metal.

POWDER COATINGS

Fine-powdered plastic, metallic, and ceramic coatings can be applied to metal or other surfaces. In this procedure, the metal or material is heated to a temperature slightly higher than the melting point of the powder. As the powder is applied, it sticks to the surface. Post heating is used to fuse the particles into a coating, which can be built up to a thickness of 30 millimeters.

There are several methods for applying

Figure 9-2

Fluidizing bed coating technique.

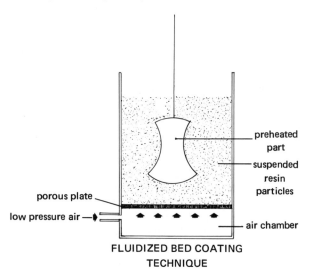

FLUIDIZED BED COATING
TECHNIQUE

powder. Moderate-sized objects may be suspended in a fluidizing bed, which is essentially a container in which the powdered particles are suspended by a cushion of low-pressurized air. (Figure 9-2) Flocking guns can be used to spray the powder on the article; electrostatic powder-spraying negatively charges the powder particle, which is attracted to the grounded object by electrostatic force. In some applications, the material does not have to be preheated when electrostatic spraying is used. The electrostatic process is also used in some powder applications using the fluidizing bed. In another process, a thermospray gun is used to spray powdered metals and ceramics.

Surface preparation of the materials to be powder-coated is the same as in other coating systems. In some cases, such as in spraying vinyls, an adhesion-promoting primer is needed.

Sculpturally, powder coating could produce highly durable coatings on moderate-sized work. Since the equipment is expensive and some experience is required in applying the coatings, however, it is advisable to find a commercial firm to do the powder coating.

METALLIC COATINGS

Materials with metallic coatings can be classified in two ways: materials coated prior to fabrication and objects coated after fabrication. Although the latter is of the greatest interest to the sculptor, the possibility of fabricating sculpture from prefinished or coated material should not be ignored.

The most common metallic-coating processes for metal are cladding, electroplating, electroless plating, hot-dip plating, metal spraying, and vapor-depositing metals through vacuum metallization.

Metal cladding. This process consists of bonding two layers of metal together under heat and pressure, or casting the cladding material around the core material, and subsequently rolling it into strips, sheets, or bars. Although other core materials are used, the most common form of cladding consists of a layer of nonferrous metal applied to one or both sides of a mild-steel core. Aluminum, copper, stainless steel, nickel, lead, and other alloys are used. The finished clad sheet is usually considered to have the corrosive-resistant qualities of the cladding material.

Sculpturally, the most practical use of clad sheets of steel would be in metal fabrication, when the fabrication technique is riveting, bolting, or adhesive bonding. Welding clad steel is possible; however, it is a problem to find a coating for the welded area that will match the clad surface.

Hot dipping. In this process, the clean metal material or object is dipped into a container of molten metal, resulting in a coating being deposited on the dipped article. Methods of application become quite complex in the industrial application of these coatings on large quantities of sheet or other forms. Low-melting-point metals such as zinc, lead, and aluminum are used, with steel as the base metal. Most familiar, perhaps, is the long-established practice of galvanizing or zinc-coating steel sheet and objects to render them corrosion-resistant.

In recent years, the steel industry has developed a complex dip procedure to aluminum-coat steel sheeting. Highly recommended for metal buildings and numerous other applications, the aluminum coat contains about eight percent silicon, and is considered to be four times more corrosion-resistant than zinc coatings.

Zinc-, aluminum-, and other-coated materials could be used in fabricated sculpture, for the visual properties or when corrosion resistance is needed. These coated materials can be left in their natural colors, modified with mild chemical oxidation, or used as undercoatings for painted surfaces. Fabrication techniques would be similar to those suggested for clad materials. Spray-can- or brush-applied aluminum and zinc organic coatings are available to cover welds in welded fabrications.

Hot zinc dipping, readily available in most major cities, should be particularly useful to sculptors desiring a silvery, noncorrosive finish on steel works. In this case, the work is simply sandblasted to produce a clean mechanical surface and is dipped in the molten metal. The resulting zinc finish can be preserved with a clear finish, chemically colored; or the natural dark gray that occurs as it is exposed to the atmosphere can be used.

Electroplating. Electroplating deposits a coating of metal onto metal or other material. The object to be coated is suspended in a solution related to the desired coating process. An anode of the plating metal is attached to the positive side of the current and the work is attached to the negative side. As the current passes through the solu-

Figure 9-3
The electro plating process.

tion, metal is deposited on the workpiece. (Figure 9-3)

The kind of solution, the rate of the current, the time submerged, the position of the anode, the temperature, and the shape of the object all determine the density, thickness, and uniformity of the coating. Cadmium, zinc, silver, gold, tin, copper, nickel, chromium, and their alloys are used as plating materials.

Nonmetallic materials require special surface-preparation prior to plating. Platable plastics are available. Wood, plaster, or other nonmetallic materials can be coated with a conductive paint. Porous materials must be thoroughly sealed. The conductive paint consists of a lacquer or varnish heavily pigmented with a graphite, copper, or silver. The piece can then be plated in conventional plating solutions.

Plating on metal often involves several dissimilar coatings applied to achieve the desired results. For example, chrome coatings usually have undercoats of copper, nickel, or cadmium. Cadmium, chromium, and zinc platings are the most corrosion-resistant, but do not perform as well as some of the dipped zinc and aluminum coatings. Copper or copper-alloy coatings on steel are generally not very satisfactory for corrosion resistance because of their particular electrical-chemical reactions with steel.

The plating processes can be performed for the sculptor at fairly reasonable costs. Modern electroplating plants have both cleaning and plating facilities, and can offer advice on the process most desirable and the necessary thickness of the coating. It is usually advisable to determine the tank size of the plating facilities in your area. If need be, a work can be designed in sections to accommodate the tank-size and can be assembled later.

An electroplating process that has been used

Figure 9-4

Brush plating : a typical selective plating installation, which includes a power pack, solutions, anodes, stylii, and accessories, can be used for plating any conductive surface regardless of shape or size. *Photograph courtesy of Selectron, Ltd.*

Figure 9-5

Gold plating a component with the Selectron process of high speed selective plating. One lead from the power pack (on the right) is attached to the component and the other lead is attached to the plating tool (stylus), which is then dipped in the gold solution and brought into contact with the work, thus completing the circuit and plating the component. *Photograph courtesy of Selectron, Ltd.*

by some sculptors is brush plating. In this process, one lead from the plating rectifier or power pack is connected to the metal part; the other lead is attached to a stylus anode wrapped with a cotton swab; the swab is dipped into the plating solution and is swabbed on the metal part. Brush plating produces dense deposits that are equal, or superior to, bath-plating solutions. The distinct advantage in this system is that it is possible to do occasional plating without having to maintain large tanks of plating solutions; sculpture too large for plating tanks can be plated, and deposits can be made on irregular forms that would not take a uniform deposit in conventional bath-plating solutions. Nonmetallic surfaces can be coated with a conductive coating and then brush-plated. Cadmium, zinc, copper, nickel, gold, silver and

other metals can be deposited with this process. Commercial equipment and special solutions are available. (Figures 9-4 and 9-5)

Electroless plating. Deposits of cadmium, brass, copper, gold, lead, nickel, palladium, platinum, rhodium, silver, and tin can be formed on aluminum, zinc, copper alloys, iron, and steel by immersion in chemical solutions. These solutions consist of metallic sulfates, chlorides, oxides, and nitrates combined with other chemicals. Solution temperatures vary from room temperature to 255 degrees. Commercially prepared solutions are available.

Metallizing (flame-spraying). Metallizing with a flame spray is the process of spraying molten

Figure 9-6

Metallizing shop truck. Note cylinder of oxygen, acetylene, and control gauges, spool of wire and spray gun. *Photograph courtesy of Metco, Inc.*

would deteriorate rapidly because of the galvanic action between the metals. Zinc or aluminum coatings provide a corrosion-resistant surface on steel that has an exceptionally long life. Surface preparation for metallizing on metal surfaces consists of grit-blasting or sandblasting prior to application of the coating.

Many coatings not suitable on steel are potentially useful on wood, plastic, ceramic, plaster, and fabric. Low-melting-point alloys such as aluminum or zinc are the most practical on cloth. For higher-melting-point alloys such as copper or bronze, wood and plastic forms are first coated with a lower-melting-point alloy such as tin, zinc, lead, or aluminum. Plastic and wood surfaces must be clean and completely dry. Resinous woods such as yellow pine or cypress should not be used. Hard plasters such as hydrostone or hydro-cal should be sand-blasted slightly with a fine sand. Metal coatings on ceramics are applied to a hot surface, or the surface may be grit-blasted to provide a bond.

Metal coatings on plastics, such as fiberglass-reinforced plastic, are possible; however, the surface should be sandblasted prior to application of the coating. Fiberglass surfaces must be dense and completely free of air bubbles or pits will appear in the surface as a result of the sandblasting. Although flame-sprayed surfaces have a matt, sandblasted appearance, they can be buffed and polished to a bright surface finish. (Figures 9-6 and 9-7)

Figure 9-7

The metallizing gun.

metal on the surface of another material. The metals sprayed can be aluminum, bronze, brass, copper, lead, stainless steel, steel, zinc, cadmium, and nickel.

The process utilizes a spray gun attached to a supply of wire, air, and oxyacetylene. As the wire feeds through the gun, an oxyacetylene flame melts the wire. A jet of air blows the molten metal out of the gun and over the surface being sprayed. The spray gun and a proper-sized air compressor are quite expensive and would not ordinarily be purchased by a sculptor unless he intended to do extensive experimentation with the process. For occasional coating, metallizing shops that do individual work can be found in most major cities.

Zinc, cadmium, and aluminum are the only practical coatings for exterior steel work; coatings such as copper, brass, nickel and silver on steel

Vacuum metalizing. This process is used particularly on small plastic parts, which are primed with an undercoat and placed in a vacuum chamber. In the vacuum, it is possible to evaporate metal from an electrically heated tungsten-element coil without the metal oxidizing. The metal evaporates from the coils and gathers on the plastic object. The resulting finish is usually a bright aluminum surface which is rather fragile and can be protected with a clear topcoat.

CONVERSION COATINGS

These coatings are formed by chemically converting the surface of the material. This kind of conversion may result in a thin, inorganic film that suitably resists corrosion by itself, or that acts as a primer surface for subsequent coating applications.

Conversion processes consist of phosphate, chromate, anodic, and oxide coatings.

Phosphate coatings. Phosphate coatings consist of iron, zinc, and manganese formulations, which produce a corrosion-resistant film on steel. Paint adheres well to these coatings, which can also be used to produce more paintable surfaces on zinc and aluminum.

Industrially, these solutions are used extensively in dip or spray operations. Phosphate solutions are readily available on the market and can easily be applied by the sculptor with a hand brush or with a spray application. Although grease and oil should not be present on the metal, some solutions can be applied over rust; and they are designed to neutralize and destroy rust-producing agents, leaving a rust-inhibiting film, which also promotes better adhesion for subsequent coatings. For optimum results in coating steel a phosphate process should precede applications of the primer. Zinc and aluminum should also be surface-treated by phosphate or other processes if good adhesion of the coating is expected.

In addition to serving as a preparation surface for painting on iron, steel, and zinc-coated steel, the silvery, gray-to-black color is aesthetically rather pleasing, and is worthy of consideration as a final color. If used as a final finish, it should be sealed with a good-quality, clear-surface finish.

Chromate coatings. Chromate coatings are used for corrosion resistance or to render surfaces more paintable. In this process, chromium solutions are applied to cadmium, zinc, aluminum, copper, silver, or magnesium surfaces. Color can be achieved by immersion in dye solutions, following the chromate treatment.

Oxide finishes. Oxide finishes have been used by sculptors and industry for a considerable number of years. Although there is an infinite number of color variations possible, many of the processes require immersion and heating of the solution above room temperature. This is impractical, except for small work; and, consequently, the sculptor is limited to solutions that can be brushed, swabbed, or sprayed onto the metal surface.

The oxide finish is a result of oxides or salts formed on the metal surface because of reaction with the chemical solution. Solutions that are too concentrated may produce brittle films that lack surface adherence. Oxide surfaces are normally not permanent unless protected with a coating of wax, oil, or lacquer. Commercial paste waxes or clear lacquers can be used. Protective oil films can be deposited by rubbing the surface with linseed or lemon oil. The surface of exterior sculpture is sometimes not coated—particularly fountains, on which water would rapidly deteriorate any form of protective coating. The chemical oxide finish is simply used to start patination; natural chemicals in the air are allowed to continue the process.

In most applications, the surface must be clean in order to produce the desired effect. Typical solvent or detergent cleaning processes may be used. For some finishes, the cleaning is followed by sandblasting, abrasive finishing, wire-brushing, etc. For some surface finishes, buffing, wire brushing, rubbing with a water-based pumice paste, or buffing with greaseless compounds may follow the application of the oxide surface. This removes surface oxides and produces a translucent or transparent quality to the surface coating, allowing highlights of the metal to show through the oxide film.

Most swab, spray, or brush applications result in black, green, brown, or gray surfaces. Although, in the past, sculptors have formulated their own oxidizing solutions, I would recommend using commercial formulations when they are available. Birchwood Casey has excellent solutions for obtaining black on steel, aluminum, zinc, copper, and copper alloys. Jax Chemical Company, Inc. also has blackening, antique green, and rust coloring solutions.

Blacks and browns can be obtained on copper and copper alloys with four to eight ounces of ammonium sulphide or potassium sulphide to one gallon of water. This can be applied at room temperature, and may take more tham one application. Green on bronze and copper alloys can be obtained in several simple ways. Stippling or spraying the metal with a solution of two to four ounces of ammonium chloride per quart of water will produce a pale blue-to-green finish. Allow each coating to dry before applying the next coat; it may take four or more applications to achieve the desired results. Stippling or spraying the metal with repeated coats of five or six ounces of copper nitrate per quart of water will produce brownish tones that take on a blue-green tone. Applying a final coat of the ammonium chloride solution will turn the metal greener. Applying a final coating of the copper nitrate solution over the pale blue produced by the ammonium chloride solution will turn the pale-blue a greener tone. It is also possible to first darken the metal with the ammonium or potassium solution to give the metal a darker tone before applying the green. By heating the metal slightly with an oxyacetylene torch as the solution is applied, a pale green can be achieved very quickly with the copper nitrate solution. As the patination develops, the surface can be spattered occasionally with the ammonium sulphide solution, if additional dark spots are desired.

It is a good practice to experiment on sample strips of metal with variations of these solutions to become acquainted with the colors that are produced. The metal should be clean, although interesting results can be achieved by applying the solutions over welded copper, brass, or cast bronze without removing the existing oxides. The metal can be sandblasted or cleaned by swabbing with a solution of one part nitric acid to eight parts water, followed by a water rinse. Grease or oil should be cleaned off of the metal with a detergent prior to the application of the acid solution. Sandblasted surfaces react to the chemical solutions more quickly than surfaces cleaned by other means. When solutions are applied, different reactions and results may be produced. For example, copper alloys with a high percentage of zinc would react differently to a given formula than if the zinc content were very low.

Besides greens, blacks, and browns, other colors can be produced on metal with oxidizing solutions. A wide variety of formulas for these solutions can be found in books dealing with sculpture or metal finishing and metal coloring.

Anodic coatings. Anodizing of aluminum and magnesium, which is readily available at plating companies, involves both electrical and chemical processes: the piece of work becomes the anode and is submerged in a sulfuric or chromic acid and water solution. As the current passes, a rather soft oxide is formed. This film is hardened and sealed by subsequent immersion in boiling water or by exposure to steam. Prior to this final treatment, the soft film is rather absorptive and is easily treated with colored dyes. The final sealed surface is a hard, highly permanent, noncorrosive surface similar to the natural, protective surface oxide that forms.

Anodizing of sculpture is relatively practical: large anodizing tanks for anodizing architectural components are readily available and adaptable to sculptural needs. If aluminum sculpture is to be anodized, attention should be given to the alloy being used, since some alloys receive anodic surface and dye more readily. Alloys number 5005, 5050 and 6063 are excellent for this process, 6063 is often used for architectural components that are to be anodized.

In welded aluminum sculpture, care should be given in matching the weld alloy with the material alloy. Since the composition of the weld zone is inclined to be different from that of the base metal, difficulty can be encountered in achieving uniform color and texture.

STAINING

At times it may be desirable to alter the color of a material slightly, or considerably, and yet retain some of the color or characteristics of the original material. Staining with a transparent media containing colored pigments or dyes is a common procedure for achieving these results on many materials.

A stain usually consists of three basic ingredients: the pigment or dye, for coloring; the vehicle or media, which acts as a binder and holds the particles of pigment or dye together or in suspension; and a thinner, to reduce the stain to the desired consistency. The most common binder is linseed oil, but it can be any resinous material, such as shellac, varnish, gum arabic, acrylic, or other synthetic materials with suitable thinners, such as alcohol, turpentine, mineral spirits, lacquer thinner, acetone, methanol, or toluol. Japan drier, or other drying agents, are sometimes added to accelerate the drying. Wood, metal, fabric, plastic, concrete, stone, plaster, and paper are all susceptible to staining techniques.

Generally, a stain tends to be impermanent,

unless treated with a transparent sealer or finish coating. Permanency of the stain also depends on the degree of penetration into the material and on the amount and kind of binder present.

There are three basic techniques for staining sculpture. One: the stain is applied and allowed to penetrate and dry, or, if applied on a nonabsorbent material, dries on the surface. Two: the stain is applied and allowed to penetrate or dry partially, and the excess material is wiped off. And three: the staining pigment or dye is added to a sealer or clear finishing material and is applied as a finish coating.

Commercially-prepared stains are available for woods. Any paint supplier can provide a wide variety of stains, which are usually pigmented-oil, penetrating stains; pigmented-oil, wiping stains; and varnish stains, for one coat finishes. Available also are many synthetic stains utilizing synthetic aniline dyes, resins, and thinners. Although aniline dyes are not as permanent as most pigments, they do possess brilliance and staining qualities that frequently surpass pigmented stains. Water stains are available but tend to raise the grain when staining wood; specially-formulated non-grain-raising stains are available for wood finishing.

A simple way to test the degree of transparency of a stain is to make a pencil line on a scrap piece of material and brush a small amount of stain over the line. The extent to which you can see the pencil line through the stain indicates the density of the stain. It is also advisable to check the stain on a scrap piece of material, to judge its appearance. Experiment with the scrap material, and take note of the different results achieved by using the three methods of application mentioned earlier.

Many interesting stains are achieved by using two or more stains in order to obtain antique or variegated appearances. Stippling, wiping, spattering, dry brushing, wet in wet (brushing a stain into the wet surface of a previously applied stain), and sponging are common methods of application. Dark, transparent stains can be used as undercoats. Lighter, opaque highlights can be stippled or spattered on the dark undercoat with a brush, sponge, or crumpled paper. This produces depth of coloring and is the usual technique for assimilating bronze, antique green, and brown effects on plaster or other materials.

Most of the simple coating materials in the classroom or studio can be used for staining, if a suitable commercial stain cannot be found. Only a small amount of coloring material is needed, with binders or thinner, to produce the desired stain.

By coloring water with tempera paints, water colors, water-soluble aniline dyes, acrylic, or any water-based commercial paints, water stains can be produced that can be used on wood, paper, fabric, plaster, and concrete.

Universal colorants, commercial oil paints, lacquers thinned with an appropriate thinner, or tube oil colors thinned with linseed oil and turpentine can be used on wood, fabric, paper, plaster, and concrete. In many of these stains there is sufficient binder so that a sealer is unnecessary for interior use. If the color tends to rub off, it can be lightly waxed with a paste wax.

Finely-ground powdered pigments added to linseed oil, shellac, varnish, or lacquer thinned with appropriate thinner can be used in the same fashion as working with oil colors. The pigment should be mixed in a small amount of the media to form a thin paste before adding it to the thinned shellac, varnish, or lacquer.

Pigmenting paste wax is an excellent way to tint a surface with a dull finish. Liquid or paste shoe polish can also be used to finish and tint wood, plaster, concrete, and fiberglass. However, sometimes a final coat of clear wax is needed to prevent the finish from rubbing off.

Commercially-produced fabric dyes can be used as water stains although they tend to fade rather rapidly in sunlight. Acrylic plastic can be tinted by submergence in a boiling solution of water and fabric dye. Subtle stains have been produced on plaster and concrete castings with water tinted with natural, colored clays.

SPRAY PAINTING

If surfaces are properly prepared, professional results in spray painting with enamels, lacquers, and plastics are not difficult to achieve.

For small items and touch-up, pressurized, aerosol cans of paint are popular, and successful results can be achieved if manufacturers' recommendations are followed. Handling of the spray pattern is similar to working with a spray gun.

Proper distance from the work and speed (or rate of pass over material) need to be controlled to avoid sagging, running, and missing of areas.

For spray painting of large items, a spray gun, spray booth, and air supply are essential. Selection of one of the wide variety of spray outfits on the market depends on individual needs. If works are very large and spray needs are frequent, a high-capacity spray setup is recommended. (Figure 9-8) Occasional painting of large works can be done at a professional paint shop rather than investing in the proper equipment.

Performance of a spray gun depends upon its design and the capabilities of the air supply. Cubic feet per minute (c.f.m.) and pressure in terms of pounds per square inch (p.s.i.) determine the amount of spray a gun can deliver with the paint mixture at its proper consistency.

For example, a small, inexpensive spray out-fit might need 1.2 c.f.m. of air at 20 p.s.i., for its spray pattern to fan out five inches. A moderate-sized outfit would need 3.2 c.f.m. at 35 to 50 p.s.i., with its spray pattern fanning out seven inches. Larger-production spray setups require expensive air supplies capable of five to ten c.f.m. and 40 to 85 p.s.i. or larger, with spray areas fanning out from ten to 15 inches. If a large air supply is not available, the moderate-sized gun will be adequate; it is a reasonably priced and has a compactly-designed portable air supply. (Figure 9-9) For optimum results, the air supply should be equipped with an adequate pressure regulator and an air filter to

Figure 9-9
A small compact spray painting outfit.

Figure 9-8
A large capacity 10 hp air compressor used for operating spray painting, sandblasting, and metallizing equipment.

Figure 9-10
Dual air filter for controlling air and removing dust and moisture.

remove dust and moisture from the air. (Figure 9-10)

In the usual spray application, the gun is held six to ten inches from the surface and is moved horizontally, at a right angle to the surface. (Figure 9-11) Pointing the spray up or down produces uneven results. Irregular sculpture forms make it impossible to maintain ideal spray-gun position. Building up the surface with thin coatings of quick-drying lacquer, instead of slower-drying enamels, is the most practical solution to the problem.

Adjustment of the nozzle as to atomization or air-to-paint relationships is accomplished by the adjusting screws. (Figure 9-12) Too much air produces a misty spray or small particles, which, with lacquer, dry before hitting the surface. Large particles indicate insufficient amounts of air.

Manufacturers' recommendations concerning the consistency of the paint mixture and the thinner to be used should be followed. Paint should be strained through cheese cloth or some other suitable strainer to assure removal of any foreign particles. Running, sagging, and uneven application are often the result of the speed at which the spray gun is moved, the distance the spray gun is from the surface being sprayed, the viscosity of the paint,

Figure 9-12

Typical spray gun: (A) air control; and (B) fluid control.

Figure 9-11

The proper movements for the spray gun in spray painting.

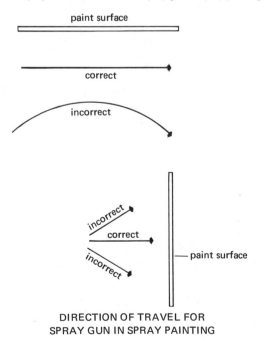

DIRECTION OF TRAVEL FOR
SPRAY GUN IN SPRAY PAINTING

excessive overlapping, spray-gun position, or mechanical problems with the equipment. The equipment should be cleaned thoroughly after each use; poorly cleaned equipment may result in spattering and uneven discharge of paint, or in air leaks due to improper seating of valves or the paint-tank seal.

Some form of air removal should be provided for all spray-painting operations, which should be confined to a specific area; for small and moderate-sized works, a spray booth can be fashioned in a corner of a room with a proper explosion-proof fan. If spray-painting is done on a regular basis, some method of controlling overspray and paint particles must be developed. Ideally, a commercial spray booth should be used. Essentially, there are three forms of spray booths: dry baffle, paint arrestor, and water wash. The dry baffle is least efficient in removing paint particles from the exhausted air. The paint arrestor uses a filter to trap some of the paint particles. Passing the exhausted air through a curtain of water is the most efficient method for cleaning exhausted air. The type of spray booth used and the location of the booth depends on the amount of contaminants that can be exhausted into the atmosphere. (Figures 9-13, 9-14, and 9-15)

Figure 9-13

Baffle type paint booth. *Photograph courtesy of Devilbiss Company*

Figure 9-14

Paint arrestor type paint booth. *Photograph courtesy of Devilbiss Company.*

Figure 9-15

Water wash type paint booth. *Photograph courtesy of Devilbiss Company.*

AIRLESS SPRAY-PAINTING

A more recent development in spray painting involves airless painting equipment. In conventional spray equipment the air atomizes the paint at the nozzle and propels the particles of paint out of the spray gun. In airless equipment, air pressure applied to the paint in the system provides sufficient force to atomize the paint. The air is dissipated in atomizing the paint and forcing it through the nozzle. In this system, the paint particle tends to fall by the action of gravity, resulting in less overspray than in the conventional spray-painting technique.

SURFACE PREPARATION OF MATERIAL FOR COATING AND FINISHING

Prior to putting on a coating, two conditions are essential: the surface must be clean and must possess the desired surface qualities in relation to the bonding characteristics of the coating and finish desired.

Cleaning which is usually done with soaps, solvents, detergents, chemicals, or abrasives, chemically or mechanically removes undesirable dirt, oil, rust, and scale. Hand application or mechanical processes, such as steam-cleaning, sand- or grit-blasting, dipping in chemical solutions, and power-sanding, buffing, and grinding, can be used. Sand-blasting, sanding, or grinding with abrasives are used when the surface needs a rough finish to assure bonding of a coating. When the surface needs a smooth finish, sanding with fine abrasives, polishing, and buffing may be used.

A wide variety of commercial cleaning compounds is available, designed specifically for cleaning metal or other materials. The cleaners are a combination of materials formulated to produce specific cleaning results. Degreasing cleaners for metal often consist of several alkaline compounds, such as sodium hydroxides, silicates, and carbonates, along with wetting and dispersing agents. Good cleaning compounds must be able to dissolve and disperse oil, grease, dirt, and soot; they must be such that after a water rinse they do not leave surface film or residue.

Paste cleaning-compounds, available as non-acid cleaners, should be particularly useful to sculptors; many are harmless to the skin and easy to use. They are brushed or wiped on the surface of the metal; after having time to react, they are washed off with water, leaving a clean surface. For heavy deposits of dirt or contaminants, two applications may be necessary.

A good test for cleanliness is to hold the material at a slight angle and pour some clean water on the surface: if the water readily covers a large surface, the material is clean; if it beads and separates, oil still remains.

Many tallow soaps or ordinary soaps are unfit for cleaning since they tend to leave oily or fatty residue. A local source for the right cleaning compound should be found. From moderately contaminated material, spots can be removed by hand scrubbing with a water-soluble cleaner. Abrasive cleaners such as BAB-O® or Ajax® are reasonably satisfactory.

Excessive films of oil, grease, and dirt on material usually need stronger abrasive or solvent action. Industrially, this is easily accomplished by soaking in proper solvents or solutions. Other means might be spraying, vapor degreasing, and electrolytic or electrosonic cleaning. Since these processes are usually not practical or feasible for the sculptor, he is often limited to hand operations. Excess oil, grease, etc. can usually be removed quickly with solvents such as mineral spirits, kerosene, acetone, methyl alcohol or a nonvolatile solvent (such as trichloroethylene) formulated for cleaning purposes. The solvent is usually applied to a rag and wiped onto the surface of the material; rags should be changed frequently as they become saturated with grease and oil. Solvent cleansing should be followed by further cleaning with a commercial alkaline cleaner, or detergent and a water rinse.

Automotive supply houses are a good source for small quantities of degreasing materials. Solvent emulsions, frequently available in pressurized cans, are easily sprayed on and rinsed off after having dissolved the grease and oil. Solvent wiping is fairly practical for cleaning small parts, material for fabrication, small areas for bonding, or sculpture with simple, flat surfaces; complex forms and textural surfaces require a dip, vapor or steam-cleaning process.

Special cleaners for cleaning and polishing plastics are available, many of which incorporate a de-staticizing material; such cleaners leave a

Figure 9-16
Steam cleaning a welded sculpture prior to painting.

thin, antistatic film of wax on the surface, which repels dust and lint. When plastics are being cleaned or surfaces are being coated, care must be exercised to be certain that the solvent does not dissolve the material.

Old paint and organic coatings can be removed quickly with nonflammable paint remover, which is brushed on, allowed to remain until the old coatings are dissolved, and then scraped off with a spatula.

Steam cleaning is one of the best ways of cleaning many materials. (Figure 9-16) In fact, if a large quantity of material needs to be cleaned and you do not own a steam cleaner, it is advisable to hire someone with a portable unit, or to haul the material to a steam-cleaning service. Steam-cleaning solutions have been formulated that will dissolve almost any oily or greasy film. Steam cleaning, which is also practically the only satisfactory way to remove flux remaining on metal as a result of brazing and bronze welding, is the simplest and most economical way to clean complex works of any size.

If surface deposits are insoluble solids (for instance, scale and heavy rust), more-radical methods, such as strong chemicals or abrasives, are needed for their removal. Metal-plating and finishing firms provide chemical removal of solid, insoluble surface deposits, which is usually impractical for studios and classrooms; oxidation, rust, and mill scale are chemically removed by pickling the material in sulfuric or hydrochloric solutions of ten to twenty percent acid to water; the solutions are often heated to accelerate the cleaning action. Light acid dips are also used to brighten and deoxidize materials such as copper, zinc, and aluminum.

Hand applications of mild acid solutions (one part acid to ten or fifteen parts water) with a cloth swab or bristle brush is practical. Small pieces can be handled in a sink; large pieces need to be treated over a floor drain or outdoors. The work can be rinsed with water from a garden hose, and should then be swabbed with a mild, neutralizing alkaline solution, such as one ounce of sodium hydroxide to one gallon water and then water rinsed again.

Figure 9-17
Small portable sandblaster being used to clean a bronze casting.

It is good practice to wear old clothing, rubber gloves, and protective goggles. Hand-applied solutions on irregular sculpture inevitably produce uncontrolled spatters that can damage the eyes, skin, and clothing.

If chemical cleaning is impractical or unavailable, abrasive cleaning may be the best way to remove mill scale and oxidation. Sandblasting, one of the most practical ways of rapidly removing heavy rust or scale, old paint, and dirt, leaves a good surface for receiving paint. (Figure 9-17) Hand sanding or steel-wooling is practical but tedious. Abrasive wheels, sanding discs, steel-wire wheels to fit electric drills, flexible shafts and portable grinders are commonly used, as well as belt and disc sanders. These tools are further discussed in Chapter 10.

An abrasive cleaning should be followed by further cleaning to remove dust or other contaminants. Superficial dust can be wiped or blown off with clean, compressed air, although it may be desirable to wash with a mild detergent or solvent.

Selecting the right method of cleaning ultimately depends on the availability of cleaning compounds and services, the material being cleaned, the kind of contamination present, as well as the final coating, finish, or bonding the material will receive, the performance desired, personal preference, and the manufacturers' recommendations. As previously mentioned, the student or sculptor is usually limited to simple manual-cleaning operations using water-based detergents, solvents, abrasives, or mild chemical solutions.

In a sense, each method has its advantages and disadvantages. Although the hand application of water-based detergent solutions is inexpensive and simple to handle, it is usually limited to non-porous materials and moderately-contaminated surfaces; drying time is prolonged and metallic surfaces are likely to corrode unless they can be force-air dried. Hand solvent-cleaning can remove greater deposits of grease and oil; rapid evaporation and drying is an advantage, although the toxicity and volatility of most solvent fumes necessitate some form of ventilation. In solvent wiping, there is also always some question as to whether minor oily deposits are still present.

Abrasive cleaning and abrading have the advantage of leaving a better bonding surface. On soft material, there is always the possibility of in-beading contaminants into the surface (particularly by sandblasting), and the rough surface is more difficult to further clean. Abrading, however, is advantageous for most opaque coating, and is usually an acceptable procedure for adhesive bonding.

Abrasive Finishing

TEN

Materials used as abrasives for sanding, grinding and cutting are, in the order of hardness, diamonds, silicon carbide, aluminum oxide, emery, garnet, and flint. Tripoli, pumice, rottenstone, and rouge are used for polishing.

Industrial diamonds are either natural or synthetic; silicon carbide and aluminum oxide are synthetically produced; the other abrasives are natural·materials.

Abrasives are used in varying grain or grit sizes, which are determined by the number of particles per lineal inch; particles are separated by screening and other methods. In other words, sixteen grit would mean that the particles are approximately 1/16 inch in length and width. Grit sizes are from number four to 800.

The cutting ability of the abrasive grit is determined by the shape of the particle, its position on the abrasive wheel or surface, toughness, hardness, and resistance to attrition. Hardness and attrition are related according to how readily the grain will wear down; toughness is concerned with how well the grain withstands fracturing. Particle shapes are oblong or polyhedral.

Devices for abrasive finishing are either in the form of grinding and cutting wheels, sanding or abrading sheets, belts, discs, and polishing wheels, and compounds applied to wheels, buffs, or pads.

GRINDING AND CUTOFF WHEELS

Grinding wheels are used primarily for rough grinding and finishing of metal, removal of metal stock, grinding down welding beads, grinding off rough spots on castings, and sharpening tools (Figure 10-1). Grinding wheels are manufactured by bonding together the abrasive particles into wheels of varying hardness and particle density. The wheel characteristics are identified by the kind of abrasive, the grit size, grain combination, grade, structure, and bond (Figure 10-2).

Aluminum oxide and silicone carbide are the only abrasives that are tough enough for grinding hard materials. Grit sizes run from 12 to 600. Grade refers to hardness of the wheel and is related to the bond. Bonds are: vitrified bonds consisting of various ceramic materials, resinous bonds utilizing

Figure 10-1

Typical grinding wheels.
Photograph courtesy of Products Division, Cincinnati Milacron, Inc.

Figure 10-2

Wheel markings. *Courtesy of Products Division, Cincinnati Milacron, Inc.*

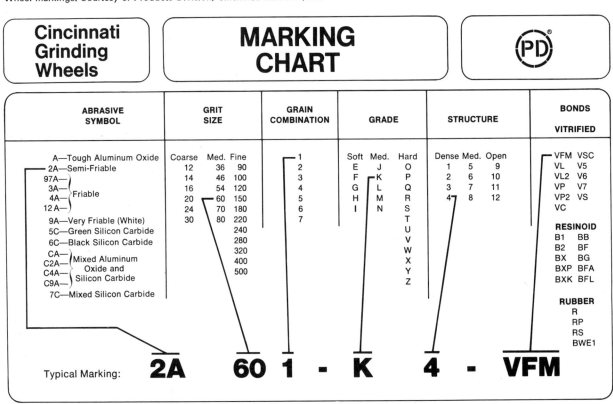

Cincinnati Grinding Wheels	MARKING CHART	(PD)®

ABRASIVE SYMBOL	GRIT SIZE			GRAIN COMBINATION	GRADE			STRUCTURE			BONDS VITRIFIED	
A—Tough Aluminum Oxide	Coarse	Med.	Fine	1	Soft	Med.	Hard	Dense	Med.	Open	VFM	VSC
2A—Semi-Friable	12	36	90	2	E	J	O	1	5	9	VL	V5
97A—	14	46	100	3	F	K	P	2	6	10	VL2	V6
3A— Friable	16	54	120	4	G	L	Q	3	7	11	VP	V7
4A—	20	60	150	5	H	M	R	4	8	12	VP2	VS
12 A—	24	70	180	6	I	N	S				VC	
9A—Very Friable (White)	30	80	220	7			T					
5C—Green Silicon Carbide			240				U				**RESINOID**	
6C—Black Silicon Carbide			280				V				B1	BB
CA— Mixed Aluminum			320				W				B2	BF
C2A— Oxide and			400				X				BX	BG
C4A— Silicon Carbide			500				Y				BXP	BFA
C9A—							Z				BXK	BFL
7C—Mixed Silicon Carbide											**RUBBER**	
											R	
											RP	
											RS	
											BWE1	

Typical Marking: **2A**   **60**   **1** - **K**   **4** - **VFM** phenol formaldehyde resins, and rubber bonds. Structure is a matter of the grit density or the spaces between the particles of the grit. Number one indicates the most dense and 12 indicates the most open structure.

The selection of a grinding wheel depends on the material being finished and on some personal experimentation. Vitrified bonds are usually used for grinding, whereas resinous bonds are used on cutoff wheels and high-speed grinding. Rubber bonds are often used for fine-finishing shapes, drums, and wheels. Aluminum oxide is used for grinding materials of high tensile strength, whereas silicon carbide is used on low-tensile-strength material.

Steel and hard materials are ground with fine-grit wheels with a soft bonding material that would break away, since the grit dulls rapidly. Soft materials, such as aluminum, copper and many copper alloys, are ground with a coarse-grit wheel with a hard bonding material, as the abrasive grit does not dull as rapidly. To prevent glazing of the abrasive surface, space between grit is essential. Thus, grinding soft materials requires more space between the grit than grinding hard material. Large grit with wide spacing produces coarse finishes; small grit with close spacing produces fine finishes. A 60-grit, four-to-seven-inch wheel is fairly satisfactory for general-purpose work. For rough grinding and fast removal of stock, grit as coarse as 16 might be used.

The speed of the wheel must also be considered. Vitrified-bonded wheels can be run at up to 6,500 surface-feet per minute. Resin-bonded wheels should be used for higher speeds. A seven-inch wheel on a bench grinder running at 3,450 revolutions per minute would have a surface speed for the wheel of approximately 6,500 feet per minute, which is adequate for most grinding and sharpening.

Flanges should always be used to hold the grinding wheels on the arbor or shaft. A disc of clean blotter paper, usually supplied with the wheel, should be between the flange and the wheel. The nut should be tightened enough to hold the wheel; if it is excessively tight, it may crack the wheel.

For high-speed grinding or cutoff with a portable grinder, resinoid or rubber-raised hub wheels should be used. These wheels are fiber-reinforced to withstand high speed and can be rigid or semiflexible. A typical seven-inch wheel would be one-eighth, 3/16, one-fourth or three-eighths inches thick, in a grit size from 16 to 120. Wheels are equipped with a discard mount, or a mounting kit is used to mount the wheel on the threaded shaft of the grinder. Five-eights inch is a typical shaft size. The resinoid wheel is used in sculpture for cutting and grinding off sprues in casting, surface grinding of castings, or grinding down beads and surfaces in welded sculpture. Wheels up to 16 inches in diameter are available for stationary cutoff equipment. Flat wheels can be used on table or radial-arm saws.

When wheels become worn, they require dressing to restore their original shapes. For bench- or pedestal-mounted grinders a hand-held dresser is held on the tool rest and is pressed against the wheel. For grinding wheels or portable tools, the wheel is held against the bench-mounted dresser. (Figure 10-3)

Grinding tools are either stationary and mounted or portable. Although stationary grinders are primarily used by industry, the sculptor can use good-quality stationary grinders for tool sharpening and occasional grinding of parts. Of greater use is portable equipment, such as an ordinary electric drill fitted with small grinding wheels, air or electric grinders, and flexible-shaft machines.

Figure 10-3

Wheel dresser for a bench-mounted grinding wheel.

Figure 10-4
Bench mounted grinder.

STATIONARY GRINDERS

The stationary grinder consists of a power source and a grinding wheel mounted on a shaft. Also necessary are proper protective guards, eye shields, and a guide on which to rest the material. Although stationary grinders are produced in a wide variety of designs for industry, the pedestal or bench model meets most of the sculptor's needs. (Figure 10-4) The typical pedestal or bench grinder accommodates a -six-, seven- or ten-inch wheel and is powered by one-third to one horsepower electric motor. It is a compact machine that will accommodate a wheel mounted on either side of the motor. The motor speeds are usually 1,725 or 3,450 r.p.m. If the sculptor's needs are primarily tool sharpening and occasional light grinding, the smaller model would probably be adequate. However, if heavy grinding is anticipated, the larger model should be used. The grinder is usually equipped with a coarse wheel (36 grit), for rough grinding on one shaft, and a medium (60 grit), for sharpening and fine grinding on the other.

PORTABLE GRINDERS

Portable tools including electric grinders, air grinders and electric flexible-shaft grinders, are available with arbors that are either horizontal or at a 90-degree angle to the machine. Horizontal grinders use flat wheels or cylindrical attachments while angle grinders are usually equipped with cup-shaped wheels. Grinding wheels on portable grinders should always be covered with adequate protective guards to protect the operator. The grinders are designed for specific-sized wheels. Particular attention should be given so as not to exceed the speed recommendations for wheels in relation to the grinder.

Electric grinders operate at speeds from 4,000 to 5,000 r.p.m., at about one-half to one horsepower. They use vitrified or resinoid wheels from four to seven inches.

Air grinders are often preferred when an adequate air supply is available. They can be operated with greater safety, particularly for wet grinding in areas with wet floors or with wet material present. They are also more compact and lighter than electric grinders. Small air grinders are available to accommodate small grinding attachments. These may operate at speeds as high as 25,000 r.p.m. Large grinders using four-, five-, six- or eight-inch wheels would operate at speeds from 3,000 to 6,000 r.p.m. Air grinders are often equipped with speed controls or governors to prevent them from exceeding their rated speed. (Figures 10-5, 10-6, 10-7, 10-8, 10-9, and 10-10)

Figure 10-5
Air angle grinder.

Figure 10-6
Air cone wheel grinder.

Figure 10-7
Horizontal air grinder.

Figure 10-8
Lightweight air grinder.

Figure 10-9
Surface air grinder. *5 through 9 photographs courtesy of Ingersoll-Rand.*

Figure 10-10
Electric grinder with a depressed center disc.

Figure 10-11
Flexible shaft machine.

The flexible-shaft machine which can be variable- or single-speed, consists of a mounted motor and flexible shaft. A typical variable-speed machine operates at speeds of 2,275, 3,000, 4,000, and 5,325 r.p.m., at one-third to three-fourth horsepower. The variable speed allows for the use of a greater variety of wheels and sizes. The flexible shaft has a threaded end. Wheels or chucks for small attachments are fastened to arbors that fit the threaded end of the shaft. An angle head can also be attached for cup wheels and discs. The flexible shaft is exceptionally useful for grinding in areas that would be inaccessible to larger air or electric grinders. (Figures 10-11, 10-12 and 10-13)

SANDING OR ABRADING

Sanding or abrading involves abrasives bonded to paper or cloth sheets, belts, discs, drums, and special shapes. In industry these are referred to as "coated abrasives." The abrasives may be flint, emery, garnet, aluminum oxide, and silicon carbide.

Figure 10-12
Small flexible shaft and motor being used to drill holes in a direct sand mold.

Figure 10-13
Chart on surface feet per minute.

R.P.M.	2"	4"	6"	8"	10"	Wheel Diameter
1,725	900	1,800	2,700	3,600	4,500	Surface-feet
3,400	1,800	3,600	5,400	7,200	9,000	per minute

Because of their tough wear-resistant qualities, aluminum oxide and silicon carbide are usually used for finishing operations. The backing for the abrasives is either paper, cloth, fiber or a combination of either paper and cloth or fiber and cloth. Paper backings are designated as "*A-, C-, D-*" and "*E*-weight" paper; "*C*" and "*D*" are intermediate-weight paper, and "*E*" is a heavy paper backing. Cloth is designated as "*J*" for lightweight and "*X*" for heavy, durable backing. The fiber is made from multiple layers of rag stock and is used to produce tough, relatively hard backing for discs and drums.

The adhesive used for bonding the abrasive grain to the paper consists of a bond coat applied to the backing and a size coat applied after the grain has been applied to the first coating. Adhesives are classified as "glue, glue and filler, resin over glue, resin over resin," and "waterproof." Resin coatings are the toughest and most heat-resistant. Papers with waterproof adhesives are used in wet sanding.

Abrasive grit, available in sizes from 12 to 600, is applied to the backing by a gravity or electrocoat process. In the gravity process, the grit is dropped or sprinkled on the adhesive-coated backing. Polyhedral-shaped grains are used. In the electrocoating process, the coated backing and grain pass through an electrostatic field. Oblong grains are used. As the grains are attracted to the backing, they adhere in such a manner that the maximum amount of cutting surface is exposed. This results in a coated abrasive with a cutting surface superior to the gravity-applied surfaces. Most abrasives today are electrostatically coated.

There are two distinct types of coatings: "closed coat" and "open coat." The terms refer to the density of the grain: in closed coat, the grains are as close as possible, whereas in open coat, spaces exist between the grains. In open coat, surface coverage may run from 50 to 70 percent. (Figure 10-14)

Coated abrasives are identified on the back side as to paper weight, cloth, type of bond, and size of grain. Garnet, aluminum oxide, and silicon carbide are identified numerically as to grain size, running from 16 to 600. Flint and emery are simply marked "Extra Coarse, Coarse, Medium, Fine" or "Extra Fine." (Figure 10-15)

Some experimentation is essential to determine individually preferred finishing methods. Fundamentally, finishing procedures are the same for all material: starting with a coarse grain and working progressively with a reduced grain size until the desired surface is achieved. The starting grain size depends on the condition of the material. (Figure 10-16)

Aluminum oxide can be used for most materials; silicon carbide is used on extremely hard surfaces, such as glass, ceramic, stone; in finish sanding; and on lacquered and enameled surfaces. It is also preferred sometimes for abrading plastics and nonferrous metals. Some woodworkers still prefer garnet instead of aluminum oxide for wood finishing. In fact, if a slower cutting action is desired in the final, fine, or extra-fine phases of finishing, it might be used. Emery is sometimes used for final

Figure 10-14

Closed coat and open coat abrasive paper.

Figure 10-15

Comparative grit size.

	Extra Coarse	Coarse	Medium	Fine	Extra Fine
Flint	36	50	80	120	220
Emery	30	40	60	120	
Garnet	16–36	40–50	60–100	120–180	220–280
Aluminum oxide					
	16–36	40–50	60–100	120–180	220–600
Silicon Carbide					

Material	Abrasive	Rough	Intermediate	Fine	Fine Extra
Wood	Aluminum oxide or Garnet	30–60	80–120	120–150	160–300
Plastic	Aluminum oxide or Silicon carbide	50–80	120–180	180–240	240–600
Aluminum	Aluminum oxide	40–60	80–100	100–150	160–240
Copper	Aluminum oxide	40–60	60–100	100–150	160–240
Bronze	Aluminum oxide or Silicon carbide	40–60	80–100	100–150	160–240
Steel	Aluminum oxide	20–50	60–80	80–120	120–240
Glass	Silicon carbide	50–60	80–120	120–200	220–320
Ceramic	Silicon carbide	50–60	80–120	120–200	220–320
Paint	Aluminum oxide or Silicon carbide		120–150	150–300	300–400

Figure 10-16

Grit selection for finishing.

phases of finishing and polishing metals. Open-coat abrasives should be used for finishing soft materials such as wood, plastic, or soft metals; close coat should be used on hard materials such as steel, ceramic, etc. Closed coat might be used for final finishing phases on some soft materials. For materials such as stone, glass, and ceramic, fine and extra-fine abrading should be a wet sanding process with silicon-carbide abrasive.

Extra-coarse and coarse grades, used when a considerable amount of material needs to be removed, are good for removing old finishes, rust and mill scale on metal, removing chisel marks, and final shaping for wood and soft-stone carvings, final shaping for casts and direct-modeled forms in plaster or synthetic materials, removing saw marks from wood and plastic, removing beads from welding, and working down rough spots in castings.

Medium and fine grades are used to remove scratches from the previous finishing process and to prepare the surface for the final finishing or the application of the lacquers, paints or varnishes. For the final fine finishing of coatings, porous materials are sealed; metals and nonporous materials are primed. In typical finishing, the dry sealed or primed surface would be dry-sanded with about 80 to 120 grit. In applying varnish, enamels, and lacquers, the next coating would be wet- or dry-sanded with 120 to 150 grit, until the gloss is removed and the surface is smooth. If additional intermediate coats are applied, they are wet-sanded with 150 to 300 grit. For fine varnish and lacquer surfaces, the final surface is wet sanded with 400 grit and then hand rubbed or buffed with a compound to restore the lustre. Final enamel coats are

not sanded. Each layer of a coating should be allowed ample time to dry prior to the sanding. Twenty-four hours is usually sufficient for primers and intermediate coats. Forty-eight hours should be allowed for the final coat. For fine finishes, a minimum of four or five coats is required. On wood surfaces, sanding is done in the direction of the grain.

SANDING AND ABRADING EQUIPMENT

As with grinding, sanding and abrading equipment is stationary or portable. Originally, this equipment was used primarily for the finishing of wood and soft materials. However, with the development of synthetic abrasives and improvements in bonding, abrasive finishing of metals and hard materials became possible. Sanding and abrading equipment is belt, drum, disc, or orbital. Portable machines have replaced virtually all of the tedious hand sanding and finishing of surfaces.

STATIONARY SANDERS

Bench- or floor-mounted sanders fall into three basic categories, depending on whether they accommodate flat, circular discs, continuous belts, or cylindrical tubes that mount on drums. The combination 12-inch disc and four- to six-inch wide

Figure 10-17
Stationary combination belt and disc sander.

horizontal belt machine is one of the most popular pieces of shop equipment. Its motor size should be three -fourths to one horsepower. (Figures 10-17 and 10-18)

Disc sanders range in size from eight to eighteen inches. As stated, the twelve-inch size is most often found in wood shops. The sanding disc is cemented to the metal surface of the machine. A layer of cement is applied to the machine backup disc by moving a stick of cement back and forth across the metal disc while the machine is running. Additional cement is smeared on the back of the sandpaper disc before it is applied on the backup disc. In recent years, adhesive-backed discs have become available. Slightly more expensive but are well worth the additional cost, they bond more satisfactorily to the backup disc and are far more convenient to use.

The disc sander is used primarily to sand edges and curves. A tilting table with a slotted top allows a miter gauge to be used to sand the ends on straight stock. The tilting table permits accurate sanding of angles.

The horizontal belt sander is used primarily for sanding flat surfaces. A backstop holds short stock on the machine; for sanding long stock, the backstock is removed. With the end guard removed, inside contours can be sanded on the idler drum. Vertical belt sanders with tilting tables are used for contour and edge sanding in a fashion similar to the disc sanding. In operating the belt sander, from time to time, the belt may need adjustment to remain in line with rollers and the platen or work surface. This is usually accomplished by turning the outside adjustment knobs on the idler wheel. Both

Figure 10-18
Stationary vertical belt sander.

adjustment knobs are turned for adjusting belt tension. It is important that the belt alignment be maintained. If the machine is operated with the edge of the belt rubbing against the belt guard or machine parts, damage can readily result. Belt sanders are equipped with three-fourth or one H.P. motors.

Figure 10-19
Drum sander on a drill press being used to sand an inside contour.

Figure 10-20
Portable machines for abrasive finishing. Top left: horizontal electric disc sander. Top right: small right angle sander mounted on an electric drill. Middle left: narrow belt air sander. Middle right: right angle air disc sander. Bottom left: 4-inch electric belt sander. Bottom right: orbital sander.

Narrow-belt vertical sanders are available for sanding difficult inside areas. On some machines, the belt is flexible and will follow curved contours.

Drum sanders are used for inside sanding of circles or convex contours. Drums range in sizes up to three inches in diameter and six inches in length. Larger diameters and lengths are used industrially.

The typical small drum sander is like the shaper, with the drum mounted vertically on a spindle. Rubber is used for the drum and the abrasive sleeve slides onto the drum. For most studio applications in which drum sanding is only occasionally necessary, drum sanding operations can be performed with sanding attachments on a drill press, shaper, lathe, or radial-arm saw. (Figure 10-19)

PORTABLE SANDERS

Portable sanders consist of orbital, belt, disc, and drum sanders. Air-operated sanders are available as well as the more common electric tools. Electric sanders are power-rated by amperage, with ratings such as 2.5 amps, 115 volts for orbital sanders, up to 8 amps for belt sanders, and up to 12 amps for heavy duty disc sanders. (Figure 10-20)

The orbital sander is used primarily for finish work. The sanding surface of the machine moves at a high speed in a circular fashion. The normal sanding-disc surface is designed to use one-third or one-half of a standard nine-by-11-inch sheet of sandpaper. The orbital sander is moved slowly back and forth across the surface of the board. The pressure should be moderate to light; excess pressure may overload the machine and cause the sandpaper to dig excessively into the wood. (Figure 10-21)

The belt sander is used either for coarse, moderate, or semifinish work. The belt moves in one continuous direction. Standard belt sizes are approximately three by 21, three by 24 and four by 24, depending on the saw manufacturer. In operat-

Figure 10-21
Orbital sander being used for finishing a flat surface.

ing the belt sander, it is important periodically to check the belt to be certain that it is tracking properly. If it is allowed to track against the sander housing, it can cut into the metal and ruin the machine. A screw adjustment on the side of the machine is turned slightly to bring the belt into alignment. Follow manufacturers' recommendations for changing and adjusting belts. As with the orbital sander, excess pressure should not be necessary. Special, narrow belt sanders are available for working in narrow spaces. (Figures 10-22 and 10-23)

Disc sanders are used primarily for rough sanding or for sanding in contours and areas inaccessible to the orbital or belt sander. The right-angle, air-operated disc sander with a low profile is particularly useful and is easy to handle. Standard disc sizes are six, seven, and nine inches. The disc sander must be handled carefully or the sanding disc will cut and gouge into the material being sanded. Power and performance of electric disc sanders are also rated by amperage or H.P. Satisfactory amperages would be 2.5 to 5 amps for light work, five to eight amps for general studio work and eight to 12 amps for heavy and continuous work. (Figures 10-24 and 10-25)

Sanding discs may be rigid or flexible; the flexible disc or mount is usually used. The sandpaper disc is held on the flexible rubber disc by means of a recessed tapered friction screw on the shaft of the sander. On rigid discs, the sandpaper is usually cemented or backed with adhesive. Torn

Figure 10-23

Narrow belt sander used to sand inside contours and hard-to-reach areas on a wood carving.

Figure 10-24

Disc sander with a flexible back being used to finish outside contours on a wood carving.

Figure 10-22

Belt sander finishing the edge of a wood laminate.

Figure 10-25

Disc sander on heavy duty operation finishing a casting. *Photograph courtesy of Ingersoll-Rand.*

or damaged sanding discs should be removed and replaced immediately.

Drum sanders, used as attachments to air- or electric-drill motors or motor-mounted flexible shafts, consist of circular sanding belts or bands mounted on a rubber drum. Sizes range from one-fourth to three inches in diameter and one-half to three inches in width. Cones and other special shapes are also available. (Figure 10-26) Small-diameter sanding drums can be made by gluing fine sandpaper on wood dowels. For finishing sculpture, special-shaped sanding devices are exceptionally useful on portable equipment. Strips of sandpaper mounted on drums called "flap wheels," slotted discs, squares and cross pads are used for sanding contours. The Sand-O-Flex® Wheel, manufactured by Merit Abrasive Products, Inc., is also excellent for this purpose; it is inexpensive and accommodates a variety of grit-sized rolls that are interchangeable, Small, rolled sandpaper cones and discs or abrasive rubber wheels are good for cavities and for hard-to-reach spaces. (Figure 10-27 and 10-28)

Figure 10-26

Special abrasive wheels and shapes. *Photograph courtesy of Merit Abrasive Products, Inc.*

Figure 10-27

Flap wheel on a flexible shaft. It is being used for rough finishing the inside of a cast bronze bowl.

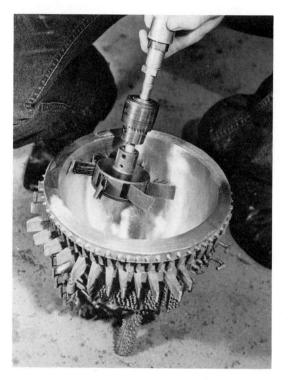

Figure 10-28

The Sand-O-Flex® wheel being used for intermediate finishing.

POLISHING AND BUFFING

Often, it is desirable to finish a material—particularly curved and irregular surfaces—with an abrasive less-rigidly backed than coated abrasives mounted on rigid or semirigid backing on abrasive machines. In this case, polishing and buffing devices coated with suitable abrasives are used. The appearance of the final surface depends on the kind of abrasive selected, the grit size, the kind of binder (grease or greaseless), and the kind of buff used. Although "polishing" and "buffing" are often thought of as interchangeable, "polishing" is used here to define the removal of material when lines or scratches may remain on the surface; "buffing" refers to the final removal of visible scratches to produce a satin or high, mirrorlike finish. Industrially, this is referred to as "coloring" or "color-buffing."

Polished surfaces tend to be satin, matt, or to possess a lustre, depending on the material and the abrasive used. Architectural metal work, hardware,

and metal furniture often appear to have a fine line-scratched surface still present in the finish. Polished finishes are produced with abrasive grit sizes from 80 to 220. Buffed surfaces require abrasives from 220 to 600, and special powdered compounds for mirrorlike finishes.

Abrasives used in finishing are aluminum oxide, silicon carbide, emery, and fine powders of white silica, unfused aluminum oxide, chromium oxide, and tripoli. These abrasives are available in bar or powder form. The bars are formed by adding a greaselike binder of fats, waxes, or greaseless water-soluble emulsions. Greaseless bars are often preferred today in manufacturing procedures. (Figure 10-29) For polishing, use a felt or sewed buff; for buffing, use a loose or ventilated buff. Hard materials, such as steel, can withstand higher buff speeds. Soft materials, such as plastic, require the lower speeds.

Buffs are produced in felt, sisal, sheepskin, or in a variety of fabrics, such as cotton, denim, flannel, and wool. The surface, density, and hardness of the cloth buff depends largely on the manner

Material	Polish	Surface Feet Per Minute	Buffing	Surface Feet Per Minute
Aluminum	80–220 Aluminum Oxide	4000–6000	Red Rouge, Tripoli Unfused Aluminum Oxide	6000–8000
Brass	80–220 Aluminum Oxide	5000–7000	Tripoli, Red Rouge, Silica Unfused Aluminum Oxide	5000–8000
Chrome	80–220 Silicon Carbide	4000–5000	Unfused Aluminum Oxide	5000–6000
Copper and Copper Alloys	80–220 Aluminum Oxide	5000–7000	Red Rouge, Tripoli, Silica Unfused Aluminum Oxide	5000–7000
Plastic	220–600 Silicon Carbide	3000–4000	Tripoli, Silica, Red or Green Rouge	3000–4000
Steel	80–220 Aluminum Oxide	6500–8500	Tripoli, Green Rouge Unfused Aluminum Oxide	7000–9000
Stainless	80–220 Silicon Carbide	6500–8500	Unfused Aluminum Oxide Pumice	7000–9000
Nickel	80–220 Aluminum Oxide	5000–7000	Green Rouge, Tripoli Unfused Aluminum Oxide	5000–7000

Figure 10-29
Buffing and polishing chart.

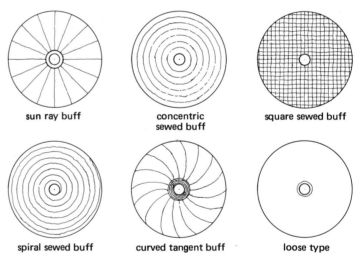

sun ray buff

concentric sewed buff

square sewed buff

spiral sewed buff

curved tangent buff

loose type full disc buff

Figure 10-30
Basic methods for sewing buffs.

Figure 10-31
Some common buffs. From top, left to right: sewed buff, loose buff, sewed buff, sheepskin buff for disc grinder, cone buff, nylon abrasive buff, round buff.

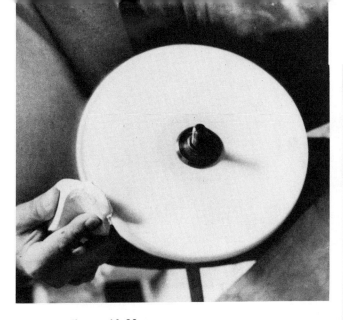

Figure 10-32
Compound being applied to a loose buff.
Courtesy of Roger Kotoske.

Figure 10-33
Cast plastic sculpture being buffed with a loose buff. *Courtesy of Roger Kotoske.*

Figure 10-34
Buffing plastic with a spiral sewn buff mounted on a drill press.

in which the buff is sewed: close stitching results in a harder buff; radial and square sewing results in more pockets in the buff to hold compounds. (Figures 10-30 and 10-31) The hard buff is used for polishing harder materials. Buffs with fewer stitches and lighter cloth are used on softer metals and on plastics. The loose buff, with sewing around the arbor hole only, is used for coloring or for producing the final mirrorlike finish. Sisal buffs can often be used without compounds to combine polishing and buffing operations. Ventilated or air-cooled cloth buffs are also excellent for final finishing. The most recent line of buffs on the market are synthetic fibered-nylon buffs that have aluminum oxide, silicon carbide, or flint bonded in the weblike material. These are used for coarse or fine satin finishes.

Buffing wheels, belts and pads can be used on most sanding or abrading equipment, lathes, drill presses; or small wheels can be used with electric drills. (Figures 10-32, 10-33, and 10-34)

BRUSHING

Besides polishing and buffing, another method is brushing. Brushes, which can be used for removing burrs, cleaning, surface finishing, and roughening, are available as wheels, cups, and special shapes for getting into confined areas. Brushes consist of steel, stainless steel, brass, bronze, beryllium copper, nickel silver, aluminum wire, and tampico or synthetic fibers. Brushes with a wire diameter of .008 to .035 are used for removing burrs, rust, dirt, scale, and flashings on steel. Brushes from .005 to .014 are used on aluminum, brass, bronze, and copper. Wire form is either crimped (wavy) or straight. Crimped wire provides a softer continuous action; straight wire is used when a more severe action is desired. For fine finishing and buffing, tampico or synthetic-fiber brushes would be used with appropriate abrasives or buffing compounds. This is a good approach for buffing a textural surface where other abrasives could not reach into surface cracks and crevices. Buffing speeds are relatively low, averaging around 1,700 to 3,600 surface feet per minute. Wire-brush finishes on metal resemble the line-scratch finishes produced by other abrasive methods. For final wire-brush finishing on non-ferrous metals, stainless steel or nonferrous brushes should be used for avoiding after-rust.

Brush speeds for finishing vary considerably. Surface-polishing speed is approximately 7,200 surface-feet per minute. Other speeds are: buffing, 7,200; dry cleaning, 3,600 to 5,400; wet cleaning, 3,600; rust, scale, burrs, and dirt-removal, 5,400 to 7,200. Some of these approximate speed ranges can be achieved by using different sized brushes for slower or faster surface-feet per minute or appropriate variable speed equipment should be used. A motor equipped with a flexible shaft is versatile, meeting many finishing needs. Brushes can be mounted on most of the other abrasive-finishing equipment. Brush speeds should be close to the maximum recommendation. The pressure of the

brush on the work should be fairly light; excess pressure reduces the cutting action of the brush, accelerates breakdown, and reduces the life of the brush. Periodic rotation of the brush resharpens the wire ends and maintains the efficiency of the brush.

In addition to wire brushing, steel wool is often used for hand finishing. It ranges in grades: "3, 2, 1, 0, 00, 000, 0000"; 3 is the coarse grade used for removing rust, old paint and scale; fine grades can be used for a line finish on metal; 0000 produces a satin finish on lacquer surfaces. (Figures 10-35 and 10-36)

Figure 10-36

Mounted wire cup brush being used in finishing. *Photograph courtesy of Ingersoll-Rand.*

SHARPENING OF TOOLS

Maintaining edges on cutting tools requires the use of abrasives, wheels, and stones. If a chisel, plane blade or knife has become nicked, damaged, or if it has lost the proper angle, it is necessary to grind the tool to restore the flat cutting edge or bevel.

An aluminum-oxide, 60-grit hard wheel can be used on a bench- or pedestal-grinder. The wheel surface should be flat. The tool rest is adjusted to a horizontal position; the flat chisel is pressed straight against the wheel and is moved back and forth to remove metal from the chisel until a flat edge is restored. The tool rest is next set at a 30-degree angle, and the chisel is brought down onto the wheel with the flat blade pointed against the direction of rotation. Chisels and plane blades are normally bevelled at a 30-degree angle. As the grinding progresses, the chisel may be dipped periodically in water to keep the metal cool and to avoid losing the temper. If a blue or black edge starts to appear on the edge, temper is being lost and the tool should be cooled more often. Chisels and plane blades normally are hollow-ground. In other words, the bevel surface is slightly concave as a result of being grounded on the curved edge of the wheel.

Wood-turning tools, most wood-carving tools, stone-carving chisels, axes, adzes, and plaster chisels are not hollow-ground. The bevel angles may also vary, depending on the particular tool. The simplest approach is to maintain the existing bevel angle. Flat chisels that are not hollow ground are ground on the side of the grinding wheel. Gouges are ground on the face surface of the wheel by holding the gouge at an angle to the wheel, with the gouge resting on the tool rest. The beveled angle is rolled back and forth against the revolving wheel. If the cutting edge is nicked on gouges or on other tools, it is first ground flat as with chisel and plane blades. Except for a few double-edged chisels, all chisels are bevelled from one side only. The other surface is kept perfectly flat. The grinding of the bevel continues until a burr forms on the chisel edge. At this point the chisel is ready to be honed on an appropriate oilstone.

As with other abrasive devices, abrasive stones consist either of natural or synthetic material such as aluminum oxide or silicon carbide. (Figure 10-37) The synthetic stones are fast-cutting and are used for developing a preliminary edge. For most sharpening purposes, combination stones, with a coarse surface on one side and a fine surface on the other, will be adequate. Stones are periodically lubricated with thin oil during sharpening. This increases the cutting action of the stone and prevents the stone from becoming clogged with metal particles.

For sharpening chisels without major nicks or faults, grinding is unnecessary. In sharpening a typical flat chisel, the chisel is held vertical to the coarse surface of the oilstone; it is moved back and forth a number of times to remove minor nicks. If

Figure 10-37

Sharpening stones. Left to right: combination stone, gouge slip stone, round-edge slip stone.

Figure 10-38

Sharpening a chisel on a combination stone.

Figure 10-39

Sharpening a gouge on a gouge slip stone.

the nonbevelled side of the blade has any burrs or nicks, the blade is placed flat on the stone and is moved in a circular fashion to remove them. Next, the bevelled side of the chisel is placed on the stone at an angle so that the back side of the bevel just clears the stone. The chisel is grasped with one hand, while the fingers of the other hand rest on the chisel to apply pressure. (Figure 10-38) With

Figure 10-40

Grinder attachment for sharpening drill bits.

the wrists rigid, the chisel is moved in a figure eight or oval pattern. The sharpening continues until a fine wire edge is developed. The fine wire edge can be broken off by rubbing the chisel back and forth several times across a hardwood block. If a chisel had been machine-ground to this point, the wire edge would be broken off in the same fashion. It might be honed slightly on the coarse side of the stone prior to the final honing. For the final honing, use the fine side of the stone and apply fairly light pressure. With the bevel edge resting on the stone in the same fashion as previously described, move the chisel in a figure eight or oval pattern. After light honing, turn the chisel over, with the non-bevelled side flat on the stone, and hone slightly. Keep repeating these two steps until the desired edge is achieved. The standard test for sharpness is to place the nonbevelled side against the thumb nail at a slight angle and push up; if the blade readily slides off the nail, it does not have a truly sharp edge; it should bite slightly into the nail.

Most other flat chisels are sharpened in the same fashion. Gouges are honed differently: a gouge slipstone, concave on one side and round on the other, is used; the bevelled edge is rocked back and forth on the concave side; the fine burr is cut off by placing the round edge of the narrow end of the stone, flat on the inside metal surface, and rocking it back and forth. (Figure 10-39) Axes, hatchets, and adzes are sharpened by holding the stone in the hand and stroking the edge. There is a wide variety of gouge slipstones and special shapes for sharpening auger bits, countersinks, knives, axes, shears, drill bits, and other tools. Special grinding wheels and grinder attachments are useful for drill bits. Although saws and blades can be hand sharpened or filed, it is advisable to have this done at a saw-filing shop. (Figure 10-40)

Adhesive Bonding

Although sculptors are generally skeptical of the adhesive bonding of metal to metal or metal to other material, adhesive bonds are often stronger and more suitable than other joining methods.

There are distinct advantages to using adhesives: there are no problems in bonding dissimilar materials; thin materials are easily joined; joints require less finishing; the load is bonded and distributed over a larger area; and the process is far simpler than welding or other joining methods.

In modern adhesive technology, if we consider the kind of performances required by adhesives in areas such as aircraft and aerospace industry, it is obvious that serviceable adhesives and bonding techniques are practical for the sculptor. Numerous adhesives are available with sheer strengths as high as 3,000 to 6,000 pounds per square inch; some even exceed these figures.

In the past ten years, the adhesive industry has developed at a tremendous rate, and good adhesives are available for most materials. In the area of epoxies, adhesives exist that can be used on almost any material with excellent results. Besides epoxy, silicones, polyurethanes, polyesters, acrylics, polysulfide rubber, cyanoacrylate, and neoprene phenolic are used in adhesive formulation.

Although special fabrication problems may occur in which the use of other adhesives would be necessary, epoxy formulations come close to meeting a wide range of adhesive needs: suitable for glass, brick, concrete, ceramic, wood, stone, plaster, and paper, they can be used for bonding metal to metal or for bonding metal or plastic to other materials. Plastics such as acrylic, polyethylene, or vinyl require special solvent-based cement when plastic is being bonded to plastic. (Figure 11-1) Rubber is usually bonded with flexible urethane or rubber-based adhesives. Special adhesives for fabric, leather, felt, cork, and paper are also produced.

Adhesives can be formulated as paste, liquid, tape, or powder. Physical properties may be hard or soft, brittle or flexible enough to withstand a wide range of expansion when dissimilar materials are bonded. In fact, it is possible to find an adhesive for any material, or combination of materials, on the market today.

Most hardware stores, department stores, etc. stock a reasonable line of epoxies and other adhesives in small quantities. If they are manufactured by major material formulators such as Devcon, Bostik or 3M, they are undoubtedly reliable. How-

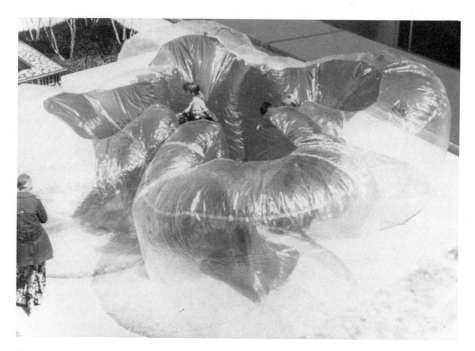

Figure 11-1

Inflatable sculpture, vinyl and air experience by Betty Voelker. (Seams were joined with a heavy-bodied solvent adhesive.)

ever, inexpensive substitutes should be avoided, since they may contain cheap ingredients and fillers.

If adhesives are regularly used, it is advisable to seek a good industrial supplier or manufacturer that can supply accurate data on the adhesive, its application, performance, and required material preparation.

A readily-available, room-temperature-cure epoxy should serve most of the sculptor's needs. Epoxy has good adhesion to a wide variety of materials, is resistant to moisture and solvents, and can withstand varied temperatures, depending on the formulation; some are capable of withstanding short-term temperatures up to 1,000 degrees Fahrenheit.

The epoxy adhesive is usually a two-component system. When the two materials are mixed, a chemical action called polymerization occurs. This can occur at room temperature or at elevated temperatures by oven-heating the article to be bonded. Curing time can be controlled in the formulations to meet both rapid and slow assembly problems.

Any failure of an adhesive can usually be attributed to some fault in selection of the adhe-

sive, preparation of the material being bonded, or the application of the adhesive.

A few basic concerns essential to satisfactory bonding are as follows:

1. Pay strict attention to manufacturer's instructions recommending usage of the adhesive and surface preparation of the material.

2. Recommended proportions of two-part systems should not be varied unless so recommended.

3. Temperature is critical in many systems, if polymerization of the adhesive is to take place. Temperatures above room temperature (70 to 75 degrees) are not a problem, and merely accelerate curing. However, temperatures below room temperature may retard or affect completion of polymerization. (Infra heat-lamps can be used to provide heat for curing when they are necessary.) Some adhesives are designed for applications below 70 degrees Fahrenheit, in which case the utilization of larger amounts of catalyst or hardener is involved.

4. The adhesive and material being bonded must also be at room temperature.

5. Use clean containers in all mixing operations; any contamination of the adhesive mixture may render it useless.

6. Observe safety procedures required for working with toxic materials. (*See* Chapter 15.)

7. For optimum results, surfaces being bonded must be cleaned. There are a few adhesives designed to stick to oily surfaces, but there is probably little reason for using them sculpturally.

8. The surface being bonded must be thoroughly dry. Solvents used in cleaning must be completely evaporated.

9. The adhesive must thoroughly wet the surface, penetrating into the most minute pores of the material; this is essential in achieving the intermolecular contact between the surface being bonded and the adhesive.

10. Adequate surface area must exist for the bond to be effective.

11. Temperature of the material in service must be considered. This would be a concern for sculptors producing outdoor sculpture, since sunlight can build up considerable temperatures on metal.

12. In industrial use of adhesives, the cleaning process of the material may become quite complex. The surface to be bonded should not be touched with the fingers after cleaning; oily fingerprints can seriously affect the performance of the bond.

The most typical cleaning processes involve a solvent or detergent cleaning, followed by some form of abrading, and then a final solvent or detergent cleaning. This seems to be adequate for many materials; however, in some cases, chemical etching and treatment are necessary to obtain optimum results. Final rinsing operations usually use distilled water since tap water contains some forms of contaminants.

Since complex cleaning procedures are often not possible in the classroom or studio, the sculptor or student has two alternatives. If he needs optimum performance in the bond, he may need to have the cleaning or both the cleaning and the bonding performed by an industrial firm. If optimum performance is not required, as is often the case, he can settle for a less complicated and practical approach. Reasonably good bonds can be obtained without chemical etching, which is often considered unnecessary for optimum results.

Solvent wiping or degreasing is essential in providing a grease- and oil-free surface for subsequent sandblasting or abrading. Abrading an oily surface would only result in the oil contaminants becoming more embedded in the surface of the material. In solvent wiping, clean, white cotton cloths should be used. The cloths should be changed frequently to assure maximum cleaning of the surface.

Sand- or grit-blasting should involve a clean, filtered air supply; oil or moisture in the air supply could contaminate the surface. Clean sand or grit should be used. In abrading surfaces, new sandpaper or emery paper should be used. The grit size of the paper is a matter of personal judgment in relation to the material being bonded. The purpose of sandblasting or abrading is to improve the adhesive grip; the ridges and depressions formed increase the surface area and provide optimum intermolecular contact between the adhesive and the surface.

Solvent wiping or degreasing of the surface following sandblasting or abrading is a matter of removing any remaining contaminants and loose material particles. If vapor degreasing with trichlorethylene is possible, this is perhaps desirable. If the material is solvent-wiped, I am inclined to believe that unless extreme care is used and cloths are changed an ample number of times, it is conceivable that the surface might become more contaminated.

Wood surfaces to be glued should be dry and clean. On used material, old paint or other films must be removed to expose the raw wood fiber. The surface should be slightly rough, sanded with fine sandpaper, or planed. To bond well-fitted joints, a white glue can be used, if the glue joint does not have to be waterproof. For waterproof gluing, resorcinal formaldehyde or epoxy glue can be used. In poorly-fitting joints, an adhesive that has the ability to fill cracks and voids should be used; an epoxy paste or putty would be suitable. For large surface-to-surface areas, contact cements are often used. A good surface-to-surface joint where there is adequate surface contact should be as strong as the wood, if it is properly cleaned, clamped, and allowed sufficient drying time.

Plaster and porous materials such as stone,

brick, and concrete can be bonded with epoxy adhesives. The material must be clean. Abrading with sandpaper, wire brushing, or sandblasting is acceptable. Dust should be blown off with an air hose. For coarse, highly porous materials a fairly heavy-bodied adhesive should be used.

Smooth, nonmetallic surfaces, such as glass or ceramic, should be degreased with a detergent or solvent, dried and sandblasted or abraded with emery or silicon carbide paper. All dust should be wiped or blown off of the surface. More complex processes, from which optimum results are desired, often use solvent wiping or degreasing after the sandblasting or abrading. For glass, the surface can be etched by dipping in a solution of one part chromium trioxide by weight to four parts distilled water. The glass is then washed with distilled water, dried, and heated at 210 degrees Fahrenheit for thirty minutes. The adhesive is applied while the glass is hot.

Rubber can be wiped with toluene or naphtha, or it can be etched by immersion in concentrated sulfuric acid for five or ten minutes. It should be thoroughly washed and dried. The material should be flexed prior to application of the adhesive. Epoxy, flexible polyurethane, rubber, or other proprietary adhesives can be used.

Metals with adequate surface area for bonding can be bonded with epoxy adhesives. Steel, zinc, tin, nickel, lead, cast iron, silver, copper, and copper alloys can be degreased or solvent-wiped, sandblasted, or abraded with emery paper; they can then be degreased or solvent-wiped again and bonded after being dried thoroughly. Vapor degreasing in trichloroethylene is preferred. However, if this process is not available, the material can be solvent-wiped with trichloroethylene, or acetone. For optimum results, copper and copper alloys are often immersed in a concentrated nitric acid (30 parts acid by weight) and water solution for a few seconds. The metal must be thoroughly rinsed and dried. Stainless steel or aluminum can be epoxy-bonded after having been sandblasted with a fine abrasive. Adhesive bonding of plastic is achieved by using heavy-bodied adhesives that bond the two material together, or solvents that dissolve the surface of the material causing it to bond. A wide variety of adhesives is available for specific plastics.

Surface preparation is always important. Plastic should be solvent-wiped, abraded, and again solvent-wiped, and then the adhesive can be applied. The solvent should be allowed to evaporate fully prior to adhesive application. Nylon, epoxy, reinforced plastics, melamine, formaldehyde, furane, formica, and phenolics plastics can be solvent-wiped with acetone and sanded with medium grit emery paper, followed by a final solvent wipe. Acrylic, polyethylene, tetraphthalate, polystyrene, polycarbonates, and cellulose plastics are solvent-wiped with methyl alcohol and abraded with fine emery paper, followed by a final wipe with solvent. Fluorocarbons, such as Teflon®, require special etching solutions.

For bonding plastic to wood, metal, or other surfaces, an epoxy adhesive can be used; or, in a few cases, adhesives related to the plastic to be bonded can provide better bond. Special heavy-bodied adhesives for vinyl or polyethylene and polystyrene foam are also available.

SOLVENT CEMENTING

Solvent cementing is a bonding process unique to solvent-sensitive materials such as plastics. In many cases, it is one of the most preferable fabricating techniques. The common methods of solvent cementing are joining by capillary action, dipping, soaking, and sponging or brushing the solvent onto the material. In this process, the solvent softens and dissolves the surface of the two areas to be joined, making it possible to cement them together. Good-fitting joints are needed for this process, particularly if the cementing is by capillary action. If joints are not well-fitted, there are viscous solvent cements consisting of a mixture of the material and the solvent. These are used if a slight fill is needed in the joint or where optimum strength is needed. Viscous solvent cements can be made by dissolving filings or scrapings of plastic into its solvent.

The toxic level of a solvent should be determined prior to its use, and appropriate working conditions should be arranged.

When joining parts by capillary action, the parts are placed in the desired position and a drop of solvent is deposited at the edge of both sides of the joint with a small brush or hypodermic syringe. The solvent flows into the seam by capil-

Figure 11-2
Solvent cementing acrylic by capillary action.

Figure 11-3
Dip or soaking plastic for cementing.

lary action. (Figure 11-2) Special cement-resisting tape can be used along the edges of the joint to prevent the solvent from bleeding out onto the finished surface. Capillary cementing is ideal for fast assembly. However, to achieve good, permanent joints on material such as clear plastic is often difficult: excess heat on cut edges during sawing can set up stresses that later produce crazing; excess humidity can produce cloudy effects; or, after prolonged exposure to weather, crystallization can occur if ethylene dichloride or methylene chloride is used as a solvent; special cements to minimize these problems can be obtained. Cementing at temperatures below 70 degrees can result in weak and ineffective bonds.

In dip or soak cementing, about one-eighth inch of solvent is placed in the bottom of a glass, stainless steel, aluminum, or galvanized metal tray. Place some lengths of 1/16-inch stainless steel or aluminum welding rod across the bottom of the tray to support the edge of the plastic and to keep it from touching the bottom of the tray. The piece of plastic can be held upright in the tray, using a wooden jig as in solvent cementing. (Figure 11-3) As soon as the edge is softened, it is lightly pressed and held in place. The soft edge will have a softening effect on the surface to which it is being bonded. Weights and jigs can be used to hold the piece in place until the joints have set. Soak cementing should be used if high strength is desired and the piece is to be placed out of doors.

When working with acrylic, strength and quality of a cemented joint can be improved by annealing, which should take place after the work has been completely assembled and finished. A circulating-air oven with temperature control is needed for annealing, although a kitchen oven can be used for small parts. The safest approach is to anneal at a low temperature for a long period of time. Materials up to one and a half inches thick can be annealed for 24 hours at 160 degrees Fahrenheit. Slightly higher temperatures, such as 175 to 180 degrees, will reduce annealing time to eight hours for thinner materials and to 12 hours for materials from one to one and a half inches thick. Although annealing can be accomplished at higher temperatures over a short period of time, deformation of the part may occur; sample runs are recommended before attempting high-temperature annealing. A simple annealing oven can be built out of insulation board or an old washer, dryer, or refrigerator case.

Solvents can also be applied to the edge of the material with a small brush; the solvent is

Figure 11-4

Holding plastic at an angle with metal strips and clamps.

Figure 11-5

Basic structural conditions in adhesive bonding.

repeatedly applied until the edge has softened and has a good wet appearance, at which point it is then set into place and supported until dry.

In any bonding operation, procedures must be developed for holding the material in place while the bond cures. For thick, stacked materials such as wood lamination, bar clamps are used. C-clamps and spring clamps can be used for clamping strips and edges. Flat pieces of material can be held in place with weights. To hold materials vertical, as in solvent-cementing plastics, special jigs or clamps often need to be developed. Flat pieces can be held upright using wooden jigs, as in Figure 11-2. When necessary, parts can be weighted down with cloth bags filled with metal washers, nuts, bolts, or steel shots. Flat pieces of sheet metal can be bent and held with spring clamps or cloth pins to hold pieces of material at an angle. (Figure 11-4).

Joint design is important when working with adhesives. Adequate surface area must be provided for the bond. Most joints are similar to wood joints or modified joints to produce maximum amounts of surface area. Joints that produce stresses at an angle should be avoided; they should be designed to put a uniform load on the bonded area. The load should be tensile or shear. Cleavage and peal stresses should be minimized or avoided. (Figures 11-5 and 11-6)

Figure 11-6

Common joint designs for metal.

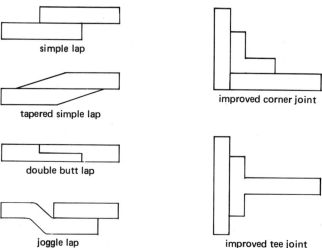

COMMON METAL JOINTS

Electrical and Mechanical Problems

TWELVE

As sculpture of the past few decades has been characterized by experimentation with new material, other technological influences have also been present. Electrical and mechanical devices normally associated with industry have, in recent years, found sculptural application. Energies produced by materials have also been investigated. Experimentation with air, water, light, magnetic forces, fire, explosives, smoke, soap suds, dissimilar liquids, heat, and solar energy have extended the sculptor's horizons to include any device or material with a potential to provide visual effects.

Consequently, the sculptor needs information and techniques not ordinarily associated with sculpture. The extent to which he becomes involved in these new areas is, of course, relative to the sculptural problems he is trying to solve. These may vary from simple problems involved in constructing light, mobile, or fountain sculpture, to complex problems requiring the services of mechanical or electrical engineers, chemists, physicists, mathematicians, or other specialists. In fact, the sculptor's concepts may be such that they cannot be realized without collaboration with other specialists. Organizations such as Experiments in Art

and Technology, Inc. (E.A.T.) in New York, and the Centre for Advanced Study of Science in Art in London, were formed to meet these needs. Today, many artists throughout the country are working with specialists in industry to solve their problems.

Primarily, this chapter presents basic electrical and mechanical information that should help the sculptor solve simple problems; simplified books on technology designed for the hobbyist and amateur provide further information that may help the sculptor communicate with specialists in technical areas.

A basic understanding of the principles of electricity is almost essential, since many light, water, or kinetic forms use electric power as their source of energy. In working with electrical energy, "volts, amperes, Ohms," and "watts" are the four terms most often encountered.

Voltage is the force of the energy being applied, like the pressure that is applied to water in order to force it through a pipe. Typical voltage in homes, shops, galleries, and buildings is usually 115–230 volt single phase alternating current (A.C.), 60 cycle, in which case, each wire alternates polarity, being positive 60 times per second and negative 60 times per second. In other words there would be current in the circuit 120 times per second. In alternating current (A.C.), three phase the circuit would have three cycles of 120. Higher voltage, such as 220 or 440, three-phase, might be used on large fountains, motors, or devices requiring large quantities of power. Lower voltage might be used for smaller systems using motors, pumps, and other electrical devices when higher voltage is not considered safe or desirable. Lower-voltage system are provided with batteries or transformers that reduce the 115-volt system to the desired voltage. Typical low-voltage systems might supply 6, 12, or 24 volts. In D.C. or direct current, one wire is always positive, and the other is always negative, with the current flowing in one direction. Batteries and battery-operated devices are D.C. In purchasing electrical motors or other components, it is essential that they be designed for the kind of current to be used.

Amperage, the measure of power or current being used, is like the amount of water flowing through a pipe when a given amount of pressure is applied. One ampere per second passing a given point is the current strength produced by one volt acting through a resistance of one Ohm. An Ohm, the unit of resistance produced as the current passes through the wire or conductor, is like the resistance in a water line due to friction and the diameter of the pipe.

In computing the total amount of amps, volts, or Ohms, if two factors are known, the third can be calculated: amps can be computed by dividing the voltage by the Ohms; voltage is determined by multiplying amps and Ohms; Ohms is determined by dividing amps into the voltage.

The total amount of electrical energy is normally described in watts, which are found by multiplying the volts times the amps. Or, if watts and voltage are known, amps can be determined by dividing volts into watts.

Some common concerns in working with electric power are:

1. the voltage of the system and whether the system is A.C. or D.C;
2. the total amperage or watts of the system and individual circuits;
3. utilizing proper wire size in relation to am-

perage and the distance that the wire must travel;
4. that switches and control devices are attached to the proper colored wires in the circuit;
5. proper color coding of the system.

Concern for the voltage of the system is a matter of efficiency and safety. Large motors and devices are more efficiently operated at higher voltages; lower voltage systems are often desirable in eliminating the hazard of electrical shock. Although alternating current is normally used, sometimes it is desirable to use direct current with a battery-operated system or a rectifier to convert A.C. to D.C. In this case, it is important that the motors or devices are designed for D.C. operation.

Computing the total amperage or watts of a system is important, since it is essential to providing electrical power for the system. In commissioned work with permanent installation, the electrical contractor must have this information in order to provide proper conduit, wire, switches, and fuses. The typical gallery or household circuit is 15- or 20-amp capacity. It would be pointless to design a light box or other electrical device with high amperage requirements if it were intended for general exhibition or sale where it would be plugged into a standard 15- or 20-amp circuit.

Wire size is important since it is concerned with the amount of current and the efficiency with which the current can travel along the wire. Excess amperage in relation to wire size results in inefficient flow of current and is hazardous. Although protective fuses are present in circuits, without proper fusing an overloaded wire can become hot enough to burn and start a fire. Motors cannot operate efficiently on undersized wire; they may overheat and burn out unless protected by a thermo-overload switch. Besides the size of the wire, the distance the wire has to travel is important; wire size should increase as distance becomes greater. Figure 12-1 shows some approximate wire sizes in relation to distance (Figure 12-2). In addition to selection of the right wire size, the color of the insulation of the wire must be considered: a white wire indicates the neutral ground; a black wire indicates the hot wire in the circuit (at times this may be another color such as red); a green wire, used for grounding the device to

Amperage	Distance in Feet						
	50	100	150	200	250	300	
10	14	10	8	6	6	4	Wire size
15	12	8	6	4	4	4	
20	10	8	6	4	2	2	
30	8	6	4	2	2	1/0	

Figure 12-1

Chart of wire sizes in relation to distance for 115 volts.

Wire Size	Ampacity
14	15
12	20
10	30
8	40
6	55
4	70
2	95
1/0	125
2/0	145
3/0	165

Figure 12-2

The ampacity for various wire sizes.

prevent electrical shock in the event that a short or malfunction occurs in the system, should always be used whenever an electrical circuit is near materials that can conduct electricity (such as lighting or motors on metal sculpture and submersible pumps or lights); the ground wire is connected to the metal housing of the object.

Single-pole switches or devices that break the circuit are fastened to the black or hot side of the circuit; double-pole switches are attached to both wires. Terminals on electrical switches and receptacles are often chrome or brass in color. White wires are attached to the chrome terminals, whereas the black or hot wires are attached to the brass.

In designing sculpture with complex circuits, some color-coding system should be devised. A diagram of the wiring should accompany the work so that an electrician could service the sculpture if necessary.

Standard electrical components that can often be used in sculpture are conductors, connectors, conduit for the wiring, switch and outlet boxes, plugs and receptacles, switches, lampholders, terminals, solderless connectors, sensors, transformers, programmers, and timers.

Conductors normally consist of insulated copper wire. Typical wire gauge runs from 18 to 0000; eighteen is the smallest diameter and has about a 3-amp capacity; the 0000 has about a 225-amp capacity. Much smaller gauges and wires, normally used in the electronic industry, are also available. Conductors may be solid or stranded for more flexibility. Insulation on the wire, which is usually rubber or plastic, can also be paper, asbestos, glass, cloth, or woven-glass cloth; often, combinations of these materials are used. The kind of insulation and wire used is a matter of the voltage and the application; for example, a standard wire with a rubber inner insulation and a fabric outer insulation might be used in close quarters in metal housings. Conductors with asbestos or other heat-resistant material would be used in heating devices. Conductors with an inner rubber insulation wrapped with jute and an outer rubber insulation would be used in damp places. Cables, or wire ordinarily used for wiring buildings, might be used where a lot of current will be used. The most commonly used wire is type T, which has a plastic insulation over a copper wire. Cables are nonmetallic-sheathed or armored. Nonmetallic-sheathed cables have three type-T wires, each individually wrapped with paper over the insulation, and all three enclosed in a moisture- and fire-resistant, braided fabric; spaces between the wrapped wires are filled with jute or cord.

Figure 12-3

Typical conductors: (A) three-wire motor cord with rubber insulation; (B) heat-resistant stranded wire, teflon coated, asbestos fire-resistant insulation; (C) flexible heater cord, stranded wire, rubber inner insulation, asbestos outer insulation with outer fabric cover; (D) lamp cord, stranded wire with plastic insulation; (E) small gauge solid wire, low voltage, plastic insulation; (F) armored cable, two Number 14 wires, plastic insulation with paper wrapping; (G) type N.M. 3 wire, two plastic insulated and one paper-wrapped ground wire with an outer layer of plastic; (H) lamp cord, fabric-wrapped stranded wire; and (I) 2-wire motor cord, stranded wire with rubber insulation, paper-wrapped with rubber outer insulation.

Armored cables consist of three insulated wires wrapped in paper inside a flexible spiral-steel covering. (Figure 12-3) Connectors are used for fastening heavy wires together and for fastening cables or conduit to switches and junction boxes.

Conduit, normally used when the wire or cable needs protection against possible damage, is classified as "rigid, thin-wall" or "flexible." The flexible conduit is similar to armored cable. Although conduit is ordinarily made of steel with a rust-resistant coating, available also are bronze conduit and fittings, which are used in moist or wet surroundings. Bronze sculpture or fountains with built-in lighting would use this material. Submersible, bronze light-fixture junction boxes and other fittings are used in pools. Steel conduit would be used in wood, steel, or concrete sculpture containing built-in lighting or other electrical features. Another form of metal covering is a raceway, which is a metal strip used to protect surface wiring. Special elbows, tees, switch boxes, and outlet boxes are designed to be used with raceway stripping.

Metal switch boxes, outlet boxes, box covers and fittings are used with conduits to produce a completely metal-enclosed electrical system. (Figure 12-4) These metal boxes have punch-out holes to accommodate conduit fittings or connec-

Figure 12-4

Metal fixtures for enclosed circuits. Left to right: box cover, conduit, elbow, outlet box, connector to fasten conduit to box, coupling to join two pieces of conduit.

tors. Bronze waterproof boxes have threaded holes to produce water tight fittings between the threaded pipe and the box.

Switches, used to open and close circuits, are either single-pole or double-pole. As stated earlier, single-pole switches are attached to the black or hot wire in the circuit; double-pole switches, to both wires. A switch is selected on

Figure 12-5

Switches. Top row, left to right: typical toggle switch, knife blade switch, rotary switch. Bottom, left to right: push button switch, feed through switch, toggle switch.

Figure 12-6

Plugs. Left to right: 2-prong straight blade plug, twist lock 3-prong 115-volt plug, 3-prong straight blade, 115-volt plug, 3-prong straight blade 230-volt plug.

the basis of the amperage load it is expected to carry, and is marked with its amp capacity. Other than the typical toggle switch we see on walls for control of lights, there are push-button, rotary, and feed-through switches; the pendant is another form of push button; knife switches, which have a hinged blade that clips between two contacts and are enclosed in a metal box, are ordinarily used to turn complete circuits off and on.

The relay switch is operated by an electro magnet controlled by a manually-operated switch. When the magnet is energized, the magnetic force closes the contact points on the relay. Relays can handle greater amperages and voltages than the typical manual switches. Locating a relay close to a device requiring high amperage or voltage allows the device to be turned off and on from a remote point. Since the amperage required to operate the relay is a fraction of the amperage required for the device, the wiring from the relay to the manual control switch can be much smaller. Relays are also used as overload-protection devices on motors. (Figure 12-5)

The standard plug for 110 volts consists of two or three prongs. The three-pronged plug, used when a ground is necessary, consists of two parallel flat prongs and a U-shaped prong. Prongs are positioned differently on plugs for a 220-volt circuit. In fact, there is a wide variety of different sizes of prongs and plug configurations, which eliminate the possibility of plugging an electrical device into an inappropriate circuit. Also available are twist-lock plugs that lock into the receptacle to prevent accidental removal of the plug. The plug receptacle is designed with holes to receive

Figure 12-7

Typical receptacles: 3-prong straight blade, 115-volt (left); 3-prong straight blade, 230-volt (right).

the appropriate plug. The configuration of the holes denotes the ampere capacity and the volts of the circuit. Multiple-pronged plugs and corresponding receptacles may be used in electrical components when disconnection of complex circuits is required. (Figure 12-6 and 12-7)

Light-bulb receptacles designed to receive screw, bipost, or bayonet-type bulbs are available in a variety of sizes corresponding to the sizes of bulb bases. Some may have switches as an integral part of the receptacle. A variety of porcelain and bakelite receptacles ordinarily used with incandescent or fluorescent bulbs are useful in building lighting devices. (Figure 12-8) Miniature light re-

Figure 12-8

Lamp holders. Fluorescent receptacle and bulb (top), miniature bulb and receptacle (center), small bayonet receptacle, small screw base receptacle, 2 standard surface cleat receptacle and outlet box receptacle (bottom, left to right).

ceptacles are available from electronic supply houses.

When wires are fastened to terminal screw points, it may be desirable to have a more positive contact than is achieved by simply fastening the wire to the terminal. In this case, a terminal connector would be used. These are small spade, ring, quick-connect or hook-shaped devices that are either soldered or crimped onto the wire. A special crimping tool is used for crimp-style connectors. Some terminal connectors employ a set screw that fastens the wire in the connector. (Figure 12-9)

Solderless, plastic connectors, used on spliced wire ends in place of tape insulation, have spiral-wire or threaded-metal inserts which are screwed onto the twisted wires; the connector must screw over the twisted wire to the extent that it also covers the insulation on the wires.

Resistors are used in circuits to control the flow of current. The variable resistor (rheostat) is typically used in light sculpture and in environments to increase or decrease levels of illumination. Motorized rheostats that can be set for different time sequences can produce automatic variable lighting.

Sensors, somewhat like switches, can control electrical or mechanical devices by reacting to phenomena such as temperature, humidity, light, sound, vibration, or air pressure: the thermostat that controls and maintains the temperature in a building is a form of sensor; kilns and furnaces use sensors to control temperature; the photoelectric cell senses a change in light intensity; wind control devices for fountains sense air pressure or wind velocity. Many of these devices can be adapted to kinetic and environmental sculpture. The color organ, which reacts to sound, has been used extensively in light sculpture and environments; in

Figure 12-9

Solderless connectors.

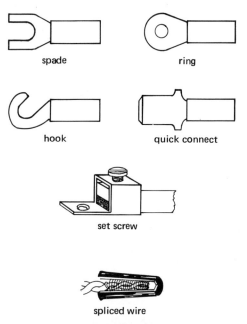

spade

ring

hook

quick connect

set screw

spliced wire

SOLDERLESS CONNECTIONS

typical application, different channels respond to different tone groups; each channel is attached to a series of colored lights; as music is played, the lights will turn off and on depending upon the musical tones. Color organs also respond to human voices or other sounds and may have up to eight channels. In working with color organs, the watt capacity of the channel must be observed.

Programmers and timers, concerned with controlling a circuit or circuits, might be simple, mechanical devices using clocks or motorized switches, or complex electronic instruments using capacitors, resistors, and triode tubes combined with relays. Clocks and motorized timers are readily available from industrial electrical suppliers. Complex electronic timers are custom-designed for specific needs. Timers or programmers, used in light sculpture to turn light circuits on and off at varying intervals, are also used in fountain design to vary illumination on the fountain or to energize solenoid valves for changing water patterns.

In wiring electrical devices, there are two forms of circuits: series and parallel, as well as a combination of the two If, in wiring a group of light bulbs for a light sculpture, we fasten the wires to the terminals of the receptacles so the current must pass through one bulb to get to the next, we have a series circuit; when one bulb burns out, the circuit is opened, and current can-

not pass on to the remaining bults. In a parallel circut, each bulb receives its current independently of the other bulbs. (Figure 12-10)

An electrical circuit normally consists of four parts: the electrical force or current, the conductor or wire to carry the current, a load such as a light bulb or motor, and a means of control such as switches, fuses, relays, or rheostats. Most simple wiring systems involving more than one load or device use parallel wiring. Series-parallel wiring is often used in more complex electronic circuits with groups of resistors and other devices. Control devices are wired in series with the device to be controlled.

LIGHTING

Lighting devices have served many purposes in contemporary sculpture. One of the simplest is to illuminate forms or materials. Light-transmitting materials, such as plastic or glass, combined with light have produced visually dynamic forms. Some sculptors have used light fixtures and devices in environmental settings creating environments of light and form; others have explored the shapes and luminous quality of light bulbs and fixtures in a more traditional sense, treating them as forms or parts of forms. Combined with mirrors, lenses and projection devices, light boxes with changing patterns and projected environments of colored images have been produced. *The Unique Lighting Handbook*, published by the Edmund Scientific Company of Barrington, New Jersey, is a good source for lighting-project ideas and devices. (Figure 12-11)

LIGHTING DEVICES

The light bulb, the fluorescent tube, and the neon tube or bulb are the three primary sources for illumination in light sculpture.

The light bulb is an incandescent lamp consisting of a tungsten filament in a glass bulb. When current passes through the filament, it becomes white hot, producing light. Air is removed with a vacuum pump from the bulb to prevent the filament from burning out. Nitrogen and argon

Figure 12-10

Basic electrical circuits.

BASIC CIRCUITS

Figure 12-11

Light sculpture by sculptor Harry Geffert. *Photograph courtesy of Atelier Chapman Kelly.*

gases are placed inside the bulb to extend its life further. Watt rating indicates the amount of light the bulb will produce; standard bulbs have from 15 to 1,500 watts; small appliance and indicator lamps have from 3 to 100 watts.

Miniature bulbs with lower watts and and voltage are often designed for direct current and can be operated from batteries. A typical one and a half-volt miniature bulb can be as small as 1/16 inch in diameter and one-eighth inch in length.

Normal bulb life is from 750 to 1,000 hours; extended-service lamps have a life up to 2,500 hours but produce less light; some miniature low-voltage lamps have a life expectancy of 15,000 hours. Using 130-volt, industrial bulbs on a 115 to 120 circuit will give longer bulb life.

Although we normally think of the ordinary pear-shaped household bulb, bulbs can be cone, globe, tubular, straight-sided, or other-shaped. Some of these are available in a limited range of color. (Figure 12-12)

Most bulb bases are bipost, screw, bayonet, prong, contact-ring, and wire-terminal. Wire terminals are usually limited to miniature bulbs. Screw bases turn into the receptacle, whereas bayonet types are held by an interlocking spring action between the base and the receptacle. Bipost and prong bulbs insert into the receptacle. (Figure 12-13)

The fluorescent lamp consists of a glass tube, starter, and ballast. As the filament in the tube heats, the starter breaks the flow of current. This

Figure 12-12

Some common bulb shapes.

pear shape   reflector   R.B. shape

parabolic aluminized reflector   tubular   globular   G.A. shape

arbitrary   cone shape   arbitrary   pear shape   straight side

217

screw

double contact
medium ring

bipost

bayonet

BULB BASES

Figure 12-13
Basic base types.

Using fluorescent coatings in the tube further extends the range of color possibilities.

Because of the high voltage of the transformers (2,000 to 15,000 volts), all electrical fittings on a neon tube must be well-insulated. All cable or wiring is coated with a high-resistance insulation capable of withstanding 15,000 volts or more. Porcelain or pyrex housings are used to enclose all terminals and connections.

Quality neon tube depends upon precise fabrication techniques. The interior of the tube must be free of all impurities. The kind and amount of gas, the amount of vacuum, the voltage, and the electrode material being used are all critically related factors. Neon is also used in the manufacture of miniature light bulbs. These bulbs have a considerably longer life than the incandescent bulb. A resistor that operates in relation to the bulb size is needed in the lamp circuit to protect the bulb from excess voltage.

Several other forms of light bulbs and devices exist that are not as commonly used as the incandescent, fluorescent, or neon. The quartz halogen and the mercury lamps are of long life and provide high levels of illumination. Mercury lamps require ballasting. Black-light mercury lamps can be used when the fluorescent tube proves to be too large. The electronic strobe light provides brilliant flashes of white light. The low-power laser beam with its wire-thin beam has been used to produce visual patterns and light environments. Black light would be used in dark environments with materials that fluoresce.

sudden break in the current causes a high-voltage kick from the ballast, which is essential to starting the current to flow between two filaments in the tube. As a current flows, argon gas in the tube reacts with mercury, producing ultraviolet light. The light strikes the phosphor coating inside the tube, causing it to glow and produce light. As with the incandescent bulb, air is removed and a vacuum is provided in the tube.

Fluorescent tubes are available in diameters of five-eighths inch to two and one-eighth inch and six to 96 inches in length. The six-inch bulb is four watts; a 96-inch bulb could be up to 200 watts. Fluorescent bulbs require less current to operate, produce more light, and have a longer life; typical bulb life is 7,500 hours. Bulbs are designed to produce cool, warm, or tinted light; yellow, red, green, pink, blue, and black light bulbs are also available.

The neon tube consists of a glass tube filled with neon or other forms of rare gas, such as argon, helium, xenon, or krypton. A high-voltage transformer is attached to an electrode on each end of the tube. As current from the transformer passes through the tube, the molecular activity of the electrically charged gas produces light.

Colors in neon are the result of the gases used and the filtering action of the colored glass.

ELECTRIC MOTORS

Use and understanding of electric motors applies to much of the equipment the sculptor works with daily as well as to kinetic art. An electric motor should be selected on the basis voltage, kind of current, the work load it is expected to perform (horsepower), motor type, and the speed at which the shaft turns (revolutions per minute).

Typical motors have 12, 24, 115, 230 and 460 volts. The 12-, 24-, and 115-volt motors are usually one horsepower or less. Single phase, alternating current, one-third-, one-half-, and one-horsepower motors, or larger, are often dual-voltage; in other words, they can be used on either 115 or 230 volts, by arranging the wires on the terminals inside the motor for the desired voltage. Motors over one horsepower are normally operated at the higher voltage. Three-phase motors are usually dual-voltage, 230-460. Some miniature motors operate on voltages from one and a half to 12 volts. A typical miniature motor would be about one and a half inches long and about one inch in diameter.

The kind of current would be either direct current, single-phase alternating current, or three-phase alternating current. Single-phase alternating-current motors would be used if the motor were plugged into existing current supplies in homes, shops, or buildings. Industrial areas of the city and large commercial buildings might also provide three-phase current. Direct-current motors would be battery-operated, or they can be plugged into an alternating-current system if a rectifier is used to change the alternating current to direct current. Universal motors can be operated on either A.C. or D.C. Fractional amounts of direct current, such as .2 to .5 volts, can be produced with miniature solar cells, which produce their energy by being exposed to sunlight or incandescent light. Silicon solar cells are more efficient when incandescent light is being used.

The work load of an electric motor is rated in terms of horsepower, which concerns foot-pounds of energy. One foot-pound is the amount of energy required to move one pound one foot in one second; moving 550 pounds one foot per second is one horsepower. Motors may possess from a small fraction of a horsepower up to 150 or more. Large motors are used in special industrial situations. Motors are rated at their idling speed. When required, a motor can deliver for a few seconds more power than its rated capacity without damaging the motor. This feature is especially useful when momentary overloads are needed during starting or while operating equipment. Overloading a motor for a long period of time is not advisable.

Some common types of motors are series (universal motors), induction, split phase capacitor, repulsion-induction, and synchronous-timing motors. Series motors can be used on either A.C. or D.C. Used in portable electric drills, sanders, polishers, and saws, this type of motor may also be used in some special shop applications, such as flame-cutting machines and electrical controls.

Induction motors, which operate only on single-phase A.C. and are by far the simplest in construction, can be used on fans, blowers, shop equipment, or on kinetic art forms when the starting load is light. These motors do not obtain full power until after starting. The split-phase motor is like the induction motor with a winding added for starting. In the capacitor motor, which is a variation of the split-phase induction motor, a capacitor is added to the starting winding of the motor; the electrical action of the capacitor gives the motor a greater torque for the starting load; used when heavy starting loads exist, it is also more efficient and uses less amperage during starting and in operation. Repulsion-induction motors are used for extremely heavy starting loads. Split-phase, capacitor, and repulsion-induction motors all operate on single phase A.C.

The synchronous motor, also an A.C. motor, is designed to run at a constant speed. Clocks, record players, tape recorders, and miniature gear motors use this kind of motor.

Three-phase motors, which operate more efficiently than single-phase motors, require a three-phase power source and are available in one-half horsepower or larger. It is advisable to use these motors when a power supply is available to accommodate them.

Motor speed should be selected in relation to the kind of equipment the motor is to operate. Single-phase and three-phase motors normally run at 1,725 or 3,450 revolutions per minute. Since their speed is fairly constant, they are used in most motorized equipment. Universal motors, on the other hand, run at inconstant speeds, which vary considerably under load or when the voltage is changed. Electric drills, grinders, etc., with universal motors, have two speed ratings; a typical three-eighths-inch drill, for example, might have a rated speed of 1,000 r.p.m. without a load and 600 r.p.m. under load. The speed of direct-current motors, which operate at around 1,800 r.p.m., is not as constant as that of A.C. motors. (Figure 12-14)

Motor controls can be added to motor circuits to produce variable speed. D.C. motors' speeds are readily varied by changing the applied voltage or current. Speed is not as easily varied with an A.C. motor; there are some variable-speed A.C. motors, but they are not in wide use and are not readily available. For variable-speed operating from A.C., variable-speed, direct-current motors with A.C.-to-D.C. rectifiers are often used. Since

Figure 12-14

Typical motors: Gear motor (upper left); 115-volt 1/3 hp appliance motor (upper right);
115-volt fractional hp motor (lower left); 115-volt, fractional hp gear motor, 1 rpm.

Figure 12-15

Floating sculpture by sculptor Alberto Collie; complex opposing magnetic fields are
used to float the form off the pedestal. *Photograph courtesy of Atelier Chapman Kelly.*

universal motors are both A.C. and D.C., their speeds can be varied easily. Portable hand tools can be readily converted with inexpensive speed controls, which are simply plugged into the A.C. power supply, and the tool is plugged into the control device.

Besides controlling speed electrically, one can reduce speed mechanically by using pulleys or gears. Speed reduction on saws, drill presses, etc. is achieved often by a simple pulley arrangement with a belt drive: a small pulley is placed on the motor shaft, and a larger one is placed on the drive shaft of the machine; this is adequate for reducing speeds when the reduction is not too great. For reductions down to just a few r.p.m., reduction gears are used; these gear boxes may be an integral part of a motor housing (called "gear motors"), or they may be mounted separately from the motor.

If there is danger that a motor will become overheated due to overloading, it should be equipped with overload protection; some motors have built-in thermal overload protection; otherwise, the protective device can be wired into the motor circuit. Motors normally run slightly hot or about 70 degrees above room temperature; if the hand can be placed momentarily on the motor housing, it is usually operating within a safe temperature range. Motors should be well-ventilated. They can overheat in pump pits or enclosures if proper ventilation is not provided.

ELECTROMAGNETS

Besides motors and lighting devices, electromagnets have been used to provide movement in some kinetic sculpture. When electrons move through a conductor, a magnetic field is produced. If the conductor is wound into a coil, the magnetic lines of force join together and reinforce each other. These forces can be used to attract or repel forms. The strength of the electromagnet depends on the number of turns in the coil and the amperage flowing through the conductor. Electromagnets such as solenoids can be combined with switches, relays, and timers to create and control movement. Permanent magnets or magnetized material can be attached to forms to make them adhere to metal surfaces. (Figure 12-15)

Fountains

Fountain design possesses some special visual and mechanical problems not ordinarily associated with sculpture. Although a sculptor may want to become involved with the design of water patterns only, he usually prefers fountains consisting of sculpture forms combined with water. The distinct advantage of this approach is that, in many architectural settings, year-round presence of a form in relation to the total plan is desired; in climates where fountains can be operated only during warm weather, the sculptured fountain serves in winter months as a piece of sculpture, maintaining interest and scale in the architectural setting.

Important considerations in fountain design include the piping system for water movement, the material being used, the kind of water pattern desired, orifice design, electrical installation of pump, filter systems, and supplementary problems such as water pattern control, lighting, and the relation of the fountain to the area in which it is installed. (Figure 13-1)

Movement of water to create the desired water effects in a fountain is accomplished with a centrifugal pump that recirculates the water in the pool; the pump receives the water on the suction end by means of an impeller turning at a high velocity and discharges the water into the piping system of the fountain. (Figure 13-2)

The amount of water that the pump delivers is measured in gallons per minute in relation to the height ("head") that the water is pumped. The head represents the amount of pressure the pump can produce. (Figure 13-3). Manufacturers can aid the fountain designer in determining his pump needs, which include the amount of water necessary to produce the given water effects and needs due to pressure losses resulting from friction and control devices in the piping system. There are two basic types of pumps and installations in fountain and pool design. Submersible pumps are used when it is not considered objectionable to have the pump and plumbing visible in the pool and in installations requiring small volumes of water. They usually do not exceed 1 H.P., delivering about 100 gallons of water per minute at a head of 10 feet. (Figure 13-4) Fractional-H.P. submersible pumps are 115 or 230 volts, single phase. Dry-type pumps are available in fractional to 15 H.P. or larger in 115 or 230 volt, single phase for small pumps and 208, 220 or 440 volt three-phase for larger equip-

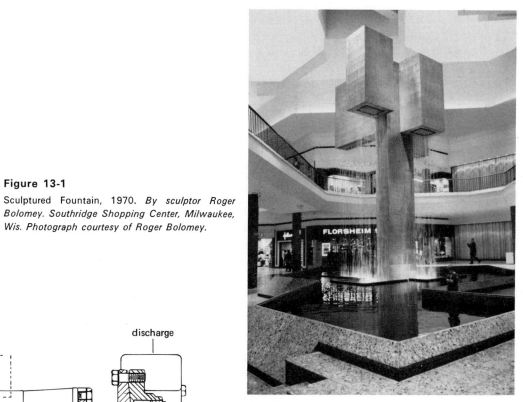

Figure 13-1

Sculptured Fountain, 1970. *By sculptor Roger Bolomey. Southridge Shopping Center, Milwaukee, Wis. Photograph courtesy of Roger Bolomey.*

discharge

suction

impeller

motor

Figure 13-2

Cross section of a centrifugal pump. *Courtesy of F.M.C. Corporation, Peerless Pump Division.*

Figure 13-3

Pump performance diagram. *Courtesy of F.M.C. Corporation, Peerless Pump Division.*

PE 33B (⅓ hp); PE 50B (½ hp)
PE 75C (¾ hp); PE 100C (1 hp); PE 150C (1½ hp)

ment. (Figure 13-5) A typical, large 10 H.P. 220 or 440 three-phase pump delivers approximately 750 gallons per minute at a head of 20 feet. In large installations, several pumps are often used in order to achieve the desired volume and for water control. Dry pit-type pumps are usually located below the water level of the pool for the most efficient operation. If the pump is located above the water level, a lift or check valve must be used on the discharge side of the pump to prevent the pump from losing its prime; this is necessary since water must always be present in the pump when the pump is started to effect pumping action from the impeller. A new installation of a pump above the water level requires that a priming tee be located on the discharge side of the pump so that water can be poured into the pump and piping.

The piping system for a fountain includes the pipes essential within the sculpture, piping from the pool to the pump, and from the pump to the sculpture. All piping and fittings should be copper, bronze, brass, copper alloys, or, in some cases, rubber or plastic. Copper tubing for a piping system should be Type K or Type L. Type K has a thicker wall than L and is used for underground service. Type L is less expensive and can be used in the fountain, pool, pumping pit, or building. Tubing is available in hard, straight lengths or in soft coils. Wherever straight runs of material are needed, hard tubing is used.

A variety of fittings are used in developing the piping system. Gate valves are used to control the volume of water from the discharge side of the pump and to control the water pressure on individual orifices. The gate valve differs from many other valves in that when it is in the full open position, it opens to the full diameter of the pipe to which it is attached; This is essential when maximum discharge from the pump or within the indi-

Figure 13-5
Dry type Peerless pump. Note gate valve on discharge side of pump to control volume of water.

vidual lines of the system is desired. Other valve designs may be used where a fully opened line is not anticipated.

In addition to gate valves, complex fountains with varying water patterns use electrically operated solenoid valves wired to a sequencing programmer to change the water patterns. Besides valves, other threaded or soldered fittings used in the system are in wrought copper or cast bronze; wrought fittings are preferred, to minimize friction loss. Typical fittings are long- or short-radius 90-degree elbows, in which the line changes direction 90 degrees; 45-degree elbows, for a 45-degree change in direction; tees, for 90-degree branches from a line; couplings, for joining two sections of pipe; and male or female adapters, to go from a soldered to a threaded fitting. Reducing couplings and flush-type fitting reducers are used to change from a larger- to a smaller-sized pipe. Unions are used between the pump and the piping system whenever it is anticipated that the system may need to be disassembled. Caps are used to close off the end of a pipe. (Figure 13-6)

Soldered joints are adequate in all piping systems except those in welded fountain forms; heat from the welding operation can damage the soldered joint. In this case, brazed bronze joints should be used.

The proper soldering of copper fittings requires clean metal. The copper tube and the inside of the fitting should be polished with 00 steel wool, fine sandpaper, or emery cloth. A thin coat of soldering flux should then be applied to the polished portion of the tube and fitting. The joint should be heated evenly by moving the torch back and forth; the joint should reach a temperature hot enough so that the solder will melt when touched to the metal. As the solder is applied to the joint area, it is drawn into the joint by capillary action. The heat should be removed whenever you are feeding the solder to the joint, and reapplied as needed. When the joint is completed, excess solder is brushed off to determine whether the joint is completely filled. Air-acetylene, oxygen-acetylene, or other types of torches can be used for applying the heat. The solder is either a 50-percent-lead, 50-percent-tin, or 60-percent-lead, 40-percent-tin alloy.

In the development of the pumping and piping system, it is important to minimize pressure losses to the system. Undersized tubing, obstructions, fittings, and excessive distances from the pump to the fountain can all cause pressure losses. As a rule, it is advisable to keep the tubing slightly oversized on the suction and discharge sides of the pump. Valves other than gate valves, or reduction of the size of the line, may represent an obstruction to the flow of water. In other words, a pump with a one and one-fourth-inch discharge might have one and a half-inch tubing, or larger, if the distance from the pump to the fountain is excessive.

The pump should be located as close to the pool and water level as possible. A pump placed on a basement floor in a building could mean an additional eight to 14 feet in head requirements. Elbows and tees cause friction losses due to the change in the direction of the water flow. In using

Figure 13-6

Some typical copper fittings: (A) 90° elbow with a reducing coupling; (B) straight coupling; (C) reducing coupling; (D) cap; E. 45° elbow; (F) hose clamp; (G) balancing valve for control of orifices; (H) gate valve; (I) manifold with crimped copper tube orifices; this type of orifice was used in the fountain in figure 13-9; (J) crimped copper tube orifice; (K) female adapter; (L) male adapter; and (M) tee.

elbows, long radius elbows are preferred. As stated earlier, wrought-copper fittings are also preferred, to minimize pressure loss. The piping system should follow as direct a route as possible from the pump to the fountain.

Every fountain plumbing system must include some form of filter to keep out debris. Although the filter normally, is included in the system that delivers water to the fountain, a separate filtering system might be used.

For most fountains a simple bronze screen or perforated brass-sheet filter on the suction end of the line is adequate. It is a good practice to oversize the filter in terms of surface area recommended by the manufacturer. Allow at least one square inch of surface area per gallon of water pumped, using a preforated brass or bronze screen with 1/16-inch holes on one-eighth-inch staggered centers; this would be about eighty holes per square inch. Prefabricated filters can be purchased, or they can be fabricated easily out of perforated metal fastened to a welded-brass angle frame. Submersible pumps are often designed with the filter as a integral part of the pump (as in Figure 13-4).

The filter should be located in the vicinity of the fountain rather than at the pool's edge, since the splashing water tends to conceal the filter and to drive leaves and debris away from the filter; a filter located in the corner or at the edge of a pool tends to gather a maxium amount of debris. If the presence of the filter in the pool is considered visually unacceptable, custom-fabricated, perforated-metal filters can often be concealed in the base of the sculptured fountain. Another approach is to have the filter recessed in the bottom of the pool; this usually requires the addition of an antivortex plate over the filter; the vortex plate establishes a water action that keeps leaves and debris away from the suction intake. A removable screen filter underneath the plate removes fine particles of debris. It is also possible to create, remote from the pool, a sump area, into which water flows, and which can be designed to catch large debris; the filter mounted in the sump filters out small particles. Fountains requiring extremely large volumes of water use this system, which can be designed by mechanical engineers.

An inline filter, consisting of a brass screen filter within a container, is located in the suction line; the water passes through the screen prior to entering the pump. The inline filter can be used with an antivortex plate, and may be used as a secondary filter, along with the larger perforated brass metal filter. Secondary filtering would be desirable if the fountain orifices were of such small diameter that it were necessary to filter out particles that could pass through a 1/16-inch hole.

Using an inline filter as a primary filter is seldom a good practice, since the surface area of the filter is not large enough to accommodate large volumes of debris; this results in excessive maintenance requirements or inefficient operation of the fountain.

In pools that require exceptionally clean water a diatomaceous earth filter is used. (Figure 13-7) This can be a separate system or part of the fountain system itself. Here, water flows over fabric discs covered with a film of diatomaceous earth. An inline filter is used to remove coarse debris prior to passing through the diatomaceous earth filter. A series of valves allow the water flow to be reversed for cleaning the filter. Such a filter is commonly used in swimming pools.

The pump and plumbing from the pump to the fountain are usually installed by electrical and plumbing contractors. One exception is the small fountain with a self-contained pump that can be plugged into an available electrical outlet; units of

Figure 13-7

Permanent media filter for cleaning water. Note additional in-line filter on pump suction to remove coarse debris. *Photograph courtesy of Kim Lighting, Inc.*

BRONZE 2" ANGLE FRAME
TO HOLD TERRAZZO SLABS

ORIFICES

←1½" COPPER TUBING
TYPE L

2'8"

CONTROL VALVE

115 VOLT SUBMERSIBLE
PUMP, 1 H.P. 90 G.P.M.

UNDERWATER JUNCTION BOX

2'0"

6" 1'0" 6"

7'0"

6" 1'0" 6" 1'0" 6" 1'0" 6"

WATER PATTERN

FABRICATED COPPER & BRONZE
METAL WORK BY SCULPTOR
RUSTIC TERRAZZO BY OTHERS

2'0"

6" 1'0" 6"

7'0"

3'0"

SCALE 3/8" = 1'

PROPOSED FOUNTAIN © VERHELST STUDIO

Figure 13-8

Typical drawing of a fountain installation using a submersible pump and exposed piping.

227

Figure 13-9

Completed fountain from drawing
Figure 13-8, by author, 1971. *First
National Bank, Arlington, Texas.*

filter
screen
in base

waterproof
fitting
around cord

Figure 13-10

Diagram of small self-contained
fountain installation using a submersible pump.

filter
attached
to pump

Figure 13-11
Typical dry pit installation.

this kind should always be properly grounded with a third wire. Another exception is the fountain that uses a submersible pump, with the tubing from the pump to the fountain exposed in the pool. (Figure 13-8, 13-9, 13-10, and 13-11) Although it is possible for the sculptor to do his own plumbing and to supply the pump, an electrician would be hired to hook up the pump, whereas an electrical contractor would install a waterproof junction box and the wiring to the pool; in the case of dry installations, the plumbing contractor installs the pump, filter, and the piping to the pool. The sculptor need only concern himself with the problems of connecting his sculptured fountain to the discharge line and to specifying the location at which the discharge line enters the pool. He must also define his water needs in gallons per minute at a specific head. The sculptor's specifications, combined with the plumbing contractor's (or mechanical engineer's) estimates of pressure losses in delivering the water to the system, determine the pump size that is needed. It is a good idea to oversize the pump slightly, since it is not necessary for a centrifugal pump to operate at full capacity.

Having discussed the basic methods of providing a water system for a fountain, we can now concern ourselves with the design of the fountain. Since water is being used, material must be noncorrosive; traditionally, bronze or copper alloys have been used most extensively; in recent years, however, aluminum, stainless steel, natural or arti-

ficial stone, fiberglass, plastic, and other forms of material have been used as well. With the use of water, surface changes in the material must be expected: copper alloys ultimately turn dark colors, ranging from antique black to green; aluminum tends to form a white oxide on its surface; stainless steel may turn gray. To compound the problem, minerals in the water tend to collect on the surface of the materials to further alter their appearance. Normally, most of these conditions are acceptable in metal fountains; in fact, metal fountains often receive some form of patination prior to installation. It is important to anticipate changes in material, however, since the effect on other material may be less desirable. White or light-colored cast stones tend to show discolorations from yellow ochre to reddish iron oxide colors along with grays and blacks due to minerals in the water or to decomposed material being left in the pool. In these cases, it may be advisable to select colored materials that are compatible with the existing conditions. Water flowing through clear plastic forms may be a striking concept, but in a short time, unwanted mineral deposits destroy the visual effect. Reinforced fiberglass proves to be a reasonably satisfactory material; a wide range of colors can be achieved, and the surface can be cleaned easily.

In building metal fountains, metal materials should never be mixed, since two dissimilar metals in the presence of moisture may produce a galvanic corrosion due to electrolytic action; this can result in the rapid deterioration of the least noble of the metals. Any of the copper alloys can be mixed readily; however, in a mixture such as aluminum and copper, the aluminum would deteriorate quickly wherever it came into contact with the copper.

The development of a water pattern in relation to the structure of a fountain is undoubtedly one of the most challenging problems of fountain design. This might consist of water flowing over forms, jets, sprays, or a combination of all these. In some cases, the water may be used as a form of energy to move parts of the fountain, or jets and sprays may be located in parts of the pool independent of the sculptured fountain.

In the design of fountains, it is a simple matter to run copper tubing to the desired locations, with control valves on the tubing to control the quantity of water. These control valves are located underneath the fountain or close to the orifice, with removable access panels to allow adjustment. Piping sizes should be as large as possible, with reductions in size taking place at the valve. In other words, in a fountain with a one and a half-inch tubing running from the discharge of the pump, it would be desirable to maintain the one and a half-inch tubing to the fountain. If a large number of smaller tubes are to branch out to various locations, a good practice is to run the one and a half-inch tubing into a manifold, to maintain water volume and pressure. The manifold can be

constructed of a length of four- or six-inch copper tubing. (Figure 13-12) Holes can be drilled into the manifold, with couplings welded to the manifold to receive the pieces of tubing.

If the water is to flow over the forms, the open pipe ends simply discharge the water into the desired locations. If jets or sprays are needed, a male or female adapter should be soldered or welded to the tube at the jet location. Orifices for jets or sprays can be purchased from commercial suppliers or fashioned out of copper tubing or other material by the sculptor. If high, straight streams are desired, commercial orifices with adjustable flanges may be used. (Figure 13-13) Adjustable flanges can be purchased separately and used with orifice designs where adjustment of the water stream is critical. In some cases, the commercially manufactured orifice does not meet the sculptor's needs, since he may be concerned with creating unusual and nonsymmetrical patterns. Experimentation with orifices made from short pieces of one-half-inch, or larger, copper tubing can result in a variety of water patterns. In fashioning these orifices, the copper tube is heated to a dull red to soften the material. Working with hammers and pliers it is possible to bend the copper tube into figure eights, flat, or star shapes to produce different water patterns; cutting slits in the sides of the tube end will produce other results. The short length of copper tubing is soldered to

Figure 13-12

A fountain manifold and piping system being fabricated by author.

Figure 13-13

Commercially manufactured orifices: (A) aerating nozzle; (B) geyser nozzle; (C) adjustable smooth bore nozzle; and (D) jet pod. *Photographs courtesy of Kim Lighting, Inc.*

Figure 13-14

Fountain by author using deflecting jets to create parts of the water pattern. *First Methodist Church, Alexandria, Louisiana, 1969*

a male adapter. The male adapter can be turned into the threaded female adapter or flange at the jet or stream location.

Irregular, fan-shaped water patterns can be created by directing a jet against a flat or spoon-shaped piece of metal or a surface area on the fountain. (Figure 13-14 illustrates this technique.) A simple way to experiment with simple orifice designs is to fasten a one-half inch female adapter to a garden hose with a suitable fitting. Short lengths of copper tubing bent to varied shapes can be slipped into the tubing end of the adapter and held in place with a piece of masking tape. Hold the hose in a vertical position and increase the water pressure until the desired water pattern is achieved. To determine the approximate gallons

Figure 13-15
Sequencing programmer. *Photograph courtesy of Kim Lighting, Inc.*

per minute, allow the water to flow from the orifice into a five-gallon pail, and note the amount of time required to fill the pail. The approximate head will be determined by the height of the water pattern.

Experimenting with orifices attached to a small, approximately one-third-H.P. pump from which gallons per minute are known is a good way of determining quantities of water required to produce various effects. Water requirements for commercially designed orifices are furnished by the manufacturer. On large-scale, complex fountains a mechanical engineer should be consulted.

If variations are desirable in the height of the water patterns or if the volume of water is to be decreased or shut off, timing devices are used. These sequence program control units operate electrically controlled valves to control the water. Timers are also used to turn on lights at varied intervals. (Figure 13-15)

Other components that might be included in fountain design are underwater lighting, wind control units to reduce the height of the water pattern at predetermined wind velocity, and water-level control units.

Underwater lighting fixtures are available in 12- or 115-volt systems. In some locations, low voltage would be required as a safety factor. Good-quality underwater fixtures of all-bronze construction can be submerged or built into the walls of the pool. (Figure 13-16)

Wind-control devices operate on the basis of a sensory device sensitive to wind velocity; they,

in turn, trigger a control panel that operates a valve that reduces the water flow and pattern.

Water-level control devices, either mechanical or electronic, are located in a recessed niche in the pool wall. Mechanical controls operate on the basis of a float that turns on the water when the pool level drops. The electronic controls consist of a low-voltage system with a set of probes to sense the water level. When the water level drops, a solenoid valve on the water line is energized, allowing the pool to fill to the proper height.

One last consideration, often overlooked in fountain design, is the suitability of the fountain to the site in regard to water patterns. High patterns are often impractical in small pool areas even with wind-control devices. (Figures 13-17, 13-18, 13-19, 13-20, and 13-21) The splashing of water on the fountain's surface may result in wet surfaces outside the pool area which may be slippery or hazardous and may interfere with normal access to buildings. Sculptured fountains usually have water configurations with relatively low profiles and pose a less serious problem than fountains consisting entirely of water patterns.

There is no fixed rule for the control of these conditions. Common sense in designing should result in a regard for the size of the fountain in relation to the pool and the trajectory created by jets and splash patterns. The need for controlled conditions many times requires unique solutions in the

Figure 13-16
Underwater lights: (A) underwater fountain light; and (B) underwater reflecting pool light. *Photographs courtesy of Kim Lighting, Inc.*

A

B

Figure 13-17

Large fabricated fountain by author. 35-feet high. Exchange Park, Dallas, Texas. The fountain was designed for relatively a small pool area. Flowing water was confined primarily to surfaces and inner areas and dropped from one level to the next to control the water.

Figure 13-18

Strips of 1/8-inch silicon bronze used in the fabrication of the fountain shown in Figure 13-17.

Figure 13-19
Internal piping system for the fountain.

Figure 13-20
Sections of fabricated metal strips being assembled around the internal piping system.

234

design of the water pattern. The design of the fountain can be such that it controls splash patterns; or water may be directed to flow through interior areas a suitable distance from the pool's edge The sound of falling water must be considered as well. In an inside environment, a trickling sound may be objectionable, whereas a stronger, splashing sound may be acceptable. All of these matters should be discussed with clients and architects when planning construction of a fountain.

Figure 13-21
Fountain nearing completion prior to moving to site.

Studio Organization

FOURTEEN

Thus far we have discussed material, techniques, and the problems involved in developing skills and knowledge as a sculptor or designer. In most cases, this training takes place in the private art school or university art department. The atmosphere and conditions in the classroom are often quite unlike those encountered in the studio. The school takes on the responsibility of providing tools, equipment, many materials, the space to work, the maintenance of space, and care of the equipment. At some point, these responsibilities must be assumed by the sculptor himself. This transition from classroom to private studio is, in fact, less difficult if the student assumes a responsible attitude. Caring for tools, putting them back in the proper place, not abusing equipment or wasting material, and cleaning work areas should become part of the work routine.

In a sense, operating a sculpture studio is like the operation of any other small business: some form of records must be kept on income and expenditures; items such as taxes, insurance, contracts, sales records, location of works, and business transactions must be attended to; the equipment and physical space for working must also be maintained.

Organizational problems and details are, of course, bothersome to most sculptors; however, they are necessary and can make the difference in the success or failure of a studio. Studio space requirements vary considerably in terms of the scale and media in which the sculptor works. Seldom does a sculptor have as much space or the kind of space he genuinely needs. Usually he is confronted not only with the problem of necessary space but also the amount of space he can afford. Studio spaces have been created in buildings as varied as chicken coops, garages, abandoned stores, and factories. Some sculptors find a small space adequate, whereas others, working on a large scale, need not only large amounts of space but overhead hoists and heavy industrial equipment for moving and handling massive weights.

Personalities also play a varying role in terms of the space sculptors desire and the degree to which they organize their space and equipment. When the space is small and must be used to its utmost advantage, there is a strong argument for a clean, well-organized studio. At some point, a poorly organized space will jeopardize the efficiency of the worker, or it may result in dangerous or hazardous conditions for the sculptor, his assistants, clients, or visitors. (An important factor to be discussed later is that the sculptor is responsible for the safety of his helpers, clients, and visitors in his studio.)

Work areas for various media or operations should be defined and isolated. This is essential when more than one individual is working in the studio and multioperations are a daily occurrence. The romantic notion of a large, single-room studio with works, tools, and equipment interspersed throughout may be picturesque but is seldom functional. Operations such as patternmaking, moldmaking, welding, metal casting, plastic or wood fabrication, and all forms of finishing need to be isolated from one and another. In a small, one-man studio space can serve many purposes when necessary, but additional attention should be given to cleaning areas and to keeping flammable materials away from welding or casting operations. Portable walls or fireproof screens can be used to isolate these activities further.

When the climate permits, roofed work areas out of doors are highly desirable for welding, metal casting, dust-producing finishing operations, and working with toxic fumes and materials.

As mentioned in Chapter 15, the removal of dust, dirt, and fumes must be considered, particularly in small spaces where toxic or irritating levels of contamination are quickly reached. Often a clean area is needed to paint and coat. Adequate fire extinguishers should be available; flammable and explosive materials should be stored in areas isolated from sparks or fire hazards.

Trash should be stored in metal containers with metal covers. Paper, cloth, or material saturated with flammable liquids or resins should not be packed tightly in a trash container; preferably, they should be stored outside or incinerated daily if possible.

Floors and work areas should be kept clean. Spilled liquids should be cleaned up immediately. Trash should not be allowed to accumulate on the floor.

Adequately-marked tool boards, racks, and storage cabinets will facilitate clean-up and work efficiency. Closed storage cabinets are preferable. Open-shelf storage should be kept to a minimum, especially in a small, multipurpose studio where irritating or toxic dust from finishing, welding, casting or molding operations should not be allowed to accumulate.

Equipment should be kept clean and maintained according to manufacturer's instructions; proper maintenance of equipment can mean considerable savings in the life of the machinery.

Good-quality, used equipment can often be purchased at considerable savings. Avoid low-priced, inferior equipment. The accumulation of necessary equipment from year to year should be considered an essential part of yearly expenses.

BUSINESS PROCEDURES

As mentioned earlier, operating a studio is like running a small business; in most states, in fact, a studio that produces sculpture is regarded as a small manufacturer; if works are sold out of the studio, it is also considered a retail business. City, state, and federal policies and requirements concerning small retail businesses apply to sculpture studios as well; these policies and requirements cannot be avoided; fines and penalties can be assessed for failure to comply.

Establishing a studio as a small business may seem unnecessary and bothersome; however, there are advantages. As a small businessman, you are operating in a recognizable form that allows all the reasonable costs for producing sculpture and for maintaining a studio to be deducted against income from sales of work and other sources. As a manufacturer or retail business, your studio can often purchase materials and supplies wholesale, effecting considerable savings.

As a small business, the studio must keep some form of permanent records relating to expenditures and income. For most studios, an accurately kept check book listing income, deposits, and expenditures on the check stubs are sufficient. The nature of the expenditure should be recorded, that is, whether it was for rent, materials, utilities, etc. The source of income should also be recorded when deposits are made. Receipts for all purchases should be retained. Receipts for cash purchases can be recorded in a separate ledger. If a large number of transactions is involved, a monthly summary of expenditures and income should be made. If the volume of work and income is sufficient, it might be advisable to hire an accountant or bookkeeping firm to keep these records and to prepare monthly and yearly statements, particularly if the studio hires individuals and is involved in more complex records, such as payroll, quarterly tax reports, etc.

If transactions are few, as is the case with most studios, a yearly summary, breaking down forms of income and expense, is sufficient. (Figure 14-1) This type of summary can be used by an accountant to prepare the necessary yearly income-tax forms; retaining a capable accountant to prepare income-tax forms is inexpensive, and ability to translate your records into proper tax-return form is indispensable.

A brief analysis of some of the items listed in Figure 14-1 examplifies a studio operated independently of the sculptor's residence. If the studio were operated at home, figures such as rent, utilities, and phone would be a reasonable portion of the total expenditures in relation to the scope of activity and the amount of the space devoted to the business. If one vehicle is used for both personal use and business, studio transportation cost must also be calculated on the basis of the amount it is used.

For the sculptor involved in large commissioned works material costs are usually the major expenditure. Cost of labor and service may follow; services usually involve another business doing work for the sculptor, which might be as simple as sandblasting, steam cleaning, or painting a work; or as complex as fabricating a total work for the sculptor.

Telephone expenses may often be more than anticipated; business transactions with out-of-town galleries or clients often require long-distance calls.

Utilities are the cost of gas, electricity, and water. To reflect more accurately the cost of producing work, a separate breakdown of these figures may be desirable if much electricity or gas is used in welding or metal casting, for example.

Transportation involves the operation of a motor vehicle as an expense to the business, and includes gas, oil, maintenance, and depreciation of the vehicle. Travel expenses, including the cost of airlines and lodging, are usually incurred during gallery or commission contacts, installation of works or attendance at trade or professional conventions related to the sculptor's activities.

Small tools and equipment are hand tools and small mechanical equipment that would be considered expendable in the course of a single year.

Major permanent sculpture equipment normally depreciates over a period of several years. Records of the date of purchase and itemized lists of major equipment should be kept for the accountant so that he can determine the rate of depreciation.

Office supplies are often neglected in recording expenditures. Items such as postage stamps, stationery, pencils, and miscellaneous materials are often purchased on a cash basis and are overlooked in keeping records of cash transactions.

Entertainment expenditures are also often neglected, particularly small expenditures such as paying for a client's lunch or serving him a few drinks at the studio, which can be business expenses if a reasonable record is kept of these occasions; the cost of serving refreshments or food at a studio open house or exhibition is also legitimate expenditure if the occasion is the exhibition or promotion of the sculptor's work. Promotion and advertising expenses are incurred in the printing and mailing of brochures announcing exhibition openings or promotional-type material to architects, builders, collectors, etc. Expenses for advertising space in newspapers or art magazines may also be incurred in the process of promoting an exhibition or other studio activity.

The cost of books or publications that supply information pertinent to the operation of the studio are legitimate expenses, as are memberships in professional organizations. Taxes and insurance are discussed later in this chapter.

Another important function in the keeping of income and expense records is that it allows the studio to evaluate its operations from year to year. For the sculptor, it is one yardstick he can use to determine whether he is receiving adequate prices for his work in relation to other costs. It also allows an evaluation of expenditures to determine cost for each work, waste, methods of effecting savings, or better distribution of earnings invested in the development of the studio. The cost of each work is not only a matter of the material used but must reflect the other expenditures involved. For example, if a piece of sculpture requires two months

```
                        (Summary of income and
                        expenditures)
                        1970
                        John Jones Studio, 3727
                        Penn. St.
```

Income
    Commissions $13,200.00
    Sales through dealers   3,075.00
    Sales of work in studio   1,650.00
    Private classes & lectures   4,200.00

                                    $22,125.00 $22,125.00

Expenditures
    Rent $ 1,500.00
    Utilities   400.00
    Maintenance   109.00
    Labor   3,120.00
    Hauling & Shipping   175.00
    Services   412.00
    Promotion & Advertising   255.00
    Entertainment   120.00
    Organizational membership   45.00
    Telephone   178.00
    Expendable small tools & Equipment   374.00
    Postage   86.00
    Office supplies   46.00
    Office equipment   64.00
    Travel expense   310.00
    Car expense   275.00
    State sales tax   78.00
    City sales tax   35.00
    Federal excise tax   17.00
    Withholding tax & Social security   410.00
    Insurance   268.00
    Checking account charges   34.00
    Tax return preparation   25.00
    Materials   2,600.00

Depreciation schedule
Equipment 10 year life
       1964—$600.00, 10%   60.00
       1968—$350.00, 10%   35.00
       1970—$940.00, 10%   94.00
       5 year life
       1969—$750.00, 20%   150.00

                                  $11,275.00

                                           $11,275.00
                                  Net Profit $10,850.00

Figure 14-1

A typical yearly financial statement for a studio.

to build, two months of rent, utilities, insurance, etc. must be considered a part of the cost of the work. Remember that the cost of experimentation on, or production of, works that do not sell must also be considered in the price of the work that ultimately sells.

If a sculptor is about to start a studio, one of his first problems is the location of a suitable space or building. If it is located in a city, zoning would affect its location in relation to the scope of activity. If a large amount of metal casting or welding were to be done, it might require an industrial location. For smaller amounts of work, or for work with other materials, a manufacturing or light manufacturing zone might be appropriate. In some cases, it might be acceptable to locate in a retail area or to operate out of a residence. These matters should be checked with appropriate city-zoning departments prior to renting or leasing a building. Local fire codes and restrictions may also determine the areas in which it would be permissible to operate.

If works are sold out of the studio located in a city and state where sales taxes are collected, the studio is responsible for collecting these taxes. A retail sales license and store license, normally a matter of a few dollars, are usually required. Taxes are normally paid on a quarterly basis; the tax forms are quite short, simple, and require little time to prepare. If jewelry is produced or sold by the sculptor, federal excise tax must be collected. License and tax forms can be obtained from the state or federal tax office. If works are sold purely through galleries or other agents, a sales license is not necessary. If the studio is large enough to employ workers, as is the case when executing sculptural commissions, the keeping of records becomes complex. Payroll records must be kept. Withholding taxes and social security must be withheld from wages and paid on a quarterly basis. When workers are employed, workman's compensation and payment may be required as well. The number of workers and conditions for these may vary according to the state.

Insurance requirements may vary according to the scope of activity and the risks the studio owner is willing to assume personally. Generally, insurance is a bargain in relation to the protection it provides to the business and its owner. In the one-man studio producing only studio works, fire protection for the contents of the building, the

building (if it is owned by the sculptor), theft of equipment or works, car insurance, and liability insurance (in the event that a client or visitor suffers injury while on the premises) are usual insurances.

In commission works, and when employees are involved, insurance requirements may become more complex. The architect and client may want the assurance that proper insurance is carried to protect the work while it is being produced or during delivery. The sculptor, as an independent contractor, assumes his responsibilities and liabilities during his presence on the construction or building site, and this requires insurance as well.

The work being produced in the studio needs to be protected against loss due to fire or other causes. It may need protection against damage or loss during shipment, transportation to the site, and erection or installation. If the sculptor is doing the installation, liability insurance is necessary in the event that the owner's building or property is damaged in the course of installation and the sculptor is responsible. Manufacturer's product insurance may be advisable, since the sculptor is responsible for the performance of his work. For example, if a piece of metal breaks off a wall relief, falls, and injures someone, the sculptor could be held responsible for defective workmanship. The total cost of insurance, which would be calculated in relation to the volume of business and activity, is a small percentage of total operating expenses and should be included in the expenses for a professionally-run studio. A reliable insurance agent can provide insurance and advice to the studio owner.

Besides records of expenses and income, records should be maintained on the works produced, as to cost, date of completion, location when at an exhibition or gallery, and location, and ownership when sold to a collection or client. Routine files on correspondence, exhibition, commission, contracts, insurance material, supplies, etc. should be kept also.

In addition to the problem of maintaining a studio and producing works, one of the sculptor's principal concerns is marketing his work. Although market conditions are undoubtedly, improving for the sculptor, some sculpture is more marketable than others. The kind of market the sculptor needs depends on the style and quality of his work. To sell a work or to produce something for sale is simple; if marketable works are the sculptor's objective, he need only cater to the popular tastes —whatever people like and are familiar with. For the serious sculptor, however, the first concern is not selling an object but producing a form he feels a need to create, in which case, his market becomes smaller and more difficult to find or develop.

To produce sufficient income solely from the sale of studio-produced work is extremely difficult. Except for a fortunate few, sculptors are seldom successful solely as a result of studio income; usually, they keep their studios operating with income from more than one source, such as:

1. sales through galleries or other retail outlets;
2. sales of studio-produced sculpture, directly through the studio;
3. commissioned work;
4. income produced through private classes, lectures, and demonstrations;
5. income produced through design activities related to sculpture;
6. exhibition prizes.

In developing markets, the sculptor must be resourceful and aggressive. If he is interested in making a living from his studio, he must forget snob appeal—although it is a sales approach in some cases—and be concerned with any market that will sell his work; he must seek out gallery, architect, or client. This is not difficult: appointments can be arranged by phoning or, in the case of out-of-city contacts, by writing the party he wishes to contact.

One of the first requirements in making a sales contact is the need for a portfolio illustrating his sculpture to present to the gallery, architect, or client. A select group of mounted, black and white or colored photographs in an attractive leather carrying case is perhaps one of the most convenient forms of portfolios; this can be easily handled, placed on a desk or table, or passed around if there are several people present for the viewing. When mailing examples, colored slides are equally effective. It is also a good idea to invest in business cards and in a printed, professional-looking brochure that lists educational background, exhibitions, prizes, and shows a few examples of work; these can be left with the gallery, architect, or client as material they may wish to file for

future reference. If the gallery, architect, or client are interested, they may want to visit your studio, have a small example of your work brought to their place of business or, in the case of architectural works, see the models for the project.

Ideally, it is desirable to leave the whole problem of marketing to a gallery or agent. However, few galleries are successful enough to guarantee the artist (except for a few nationally known artists) a reliable income from the sale of his works.

In seeking a gallery, it is important to be familiar with the gallery that is willing to handle your work. When possible, select a gallary that has been established for some time and has had time to develop a clientele. The business of selling art is often far more complex than simply hanging works on a wall or placing them on a pedestal and waiting for a buyer. If possible, in order to appraise the gallery clientele and the fashion in which the gallery handles sales, attend several public openings that the gallery might have for artists it represents; evaluate the kind of invitations, brochures, newspaper publicity, and promotion the gallery uses. Also, be concerned with the quality of the work the gallery handles and whether the sales philosophy of the gallery is compatible with, and conducive to, the sale of your work. Ask some of the artists represented by the gallery how successful they feel the gallery has been in handling their work.

One of the most essential items in the relationship between the gallery and the artist is the written contract. This is the only concrete assurance that either party has that conditions concerning sales and the handling of the artist's work will be met. The gallery and artist should draw up a contract that they mutually agree on. It may be advisable to have the contract checked by an attorney. A contract should state the percentage of the retail sale to go the gallery (usually 33-1/3 to 50 percent), payment schedules to the artist upon the sale of work, and the insurance provided by the gallery. All other services paid for by the gallery should also be defined, including the cost of mailing brochures, refreshments at openings, packing and shipping costs, and other promotional expenses. If the sculptor is responsible for any of these items, it should be clearly stated in the contract. The length of time the contract is to be effective and required notice for cancellation should also be stated. If the contract is for exclusive representation, it should state the geographic area that it represents. Unless a gallery operates nationally, exclusive representation should apply only to the city and area in which the gallery does business. The exclusive contract should also state whether it includes commissions. If it includes commissions, the gallery usually takes a smaller percentage (usually ten to 15 percent) than on the sales of works. Unless the gallery is exceptionally active in obtaining commissions for the sculptor, the sculptor should hesitate to give the gallery full contract rights in this area. Preferably, the contract can state that the gallery will receive its commission only when it directly provides a commission for the sculptor. Obtaining commissions, particularly of architectural sculpture, involves sales approaches that the gallery does not always pursue. Moreover, the sculptor may have developed his own clientel in this area; if he is willing, he can as readily, perhaps more effectively, obtain commissions by himself.

One last point is that when a contract is agreed upon with a gallery, as with other contracts, the sculptor should live up to the terms of the agreement. The gallery is in business and is working for the artist. A capable gallery fully earns and deserves the commission it charges for selling a work. To remain in business, it relies upon the artist to deliver works on time and to meet the terms of the contract.

Besides galleries, there is a variety of sales outlets. The extent to which a sculptor participates in some of these depends upon his professional standing and his personal objectives. Belonging to groups that organize sales exhibitions in shopping centers and public buildings, or participation in other forms of sales exhibitions, are two ways of selling moderately priced work. Showing in quality interior design shops, where works are seen in relation to home or office may not have the prestige but often yields better sales results than exhibiting with galleries. This is particularly true if the shop has a staff of professional designers who do a lot of residential and commercial interior-design contract work. If the designers like to include sculpture in their overall plans, works are readily sold under these conditions.

The extent to which a sculptor might want to undertake retail selling out of his own studio or shop again depends on the ability, temperament,

and personality of the individual. There are some sculptors with the ability to handle their own sales with as much or more success than a gallery might. This usually calls for some form of exhibition space or gallery in conjunction with the studio; it also assumes that he has been in an area long enough to have some form of clientele, or that he is prepared to do the necessary work and has sufficient capital to survive while developing a clientele.

Three of the most prevalent approaches to personally handling sales are to show works by appointment only, to do occasional exhibitions, or to have the exhibition space or gallery open daily, as if it were a commercial art gallery. The last approach is perhaps the least desirable, unless income from sales merits the hiring of an individual to attend to the gallery and its operation. A combination of the first two approaches usually works more satisfactorily. One or two exhibitions a year serve to acquaint the public and art patrons with the sculptor. The appointment-arrangement makes his work accessible the remainder of the year.

Regardless of the approaches used, the sculptor must be prepared to do the necessary kind of promotion that selling his own work entails. If he is new to an area, one of his first tasks is the development of a clientele. A mailing list of individuals in a community who would be interested in art can be helpful in this situation. Belonging to groups having access to lists of potential patrons, museum and art-organization memberships, and careful reading of local art publications or newspapers with articles concerned with persons who collect art, can also yield results. Attending other gallery openings and exhibitions is also helpful. Often, if a sculptor is opening a studio in the same area in which he attended school, he has some contact with clientele through school exhibitions or galleries with which he may have been associated. It is also a good procedure to ask guests attending the sculptor's exhibition to sign a guest book, which can act as a mailing list.

Newspaper publicity also attracts new individuals to exhibitions or gallery openings. To have notices of exhibition openings listed in local art columns is not difficult. A simple, typewritten news release sent to the writer of the art column will usually yield some results; or you can phone the writer or newspaper and ask for the form in which they prefer to have such information presented.

The news release should include information such as dates of exhibition, number of works, media, and personal background such as education, commissions, exhibitions, or collections. Several eight by ten black and white photographs should also accompany the release. News releases and periodic new information on major commissions received, prizes won, or exhibitions participated in should also be sent to art columnists.

Obtaining commissions and working with architects, interior designers, and their clients requires an approach somewhat unlike dealing with galleries and collectors. These people are often less concerned with education, exhibition, and award records and more concerned with the sculptor's ability to execute, and install, and complete the work on time. A sculptor interested in commissions must be aggressive in contacting the people who can provide them. Reading real estate sections of the daily newspaper and trade journals dealing with building, or noticing buildings being constructed in your area can supply leads on prospects for commissions.

It is possible to approach the architect, landscape designer, interior designer, and building owner in the same manner as other businesses use to sell their products. Essentially, there are two approaches that are useful in contacting these individuals; both should be used in an effective sales program: direct mailing of information is important; an attractive brochure, mailed once or twice a year, serves to acquaint them with your work and indicates your interest in working with them; direct contact by calling the individual's office and making an appointment to show a portfolio of work is also effective, and is exceptionally useful in the case where the sculptor knows of a building, interior, or land development that might require sculpture. In many instances, the architect or interior designer may have plans in the formative stage; by calling on him at that point, the sculptor may persuade him to include sculpture in his plans.

Getting the first commission and developing a portfolio to present may often be a problem. The architect needs to be assured that the sculptor is capable of doing large-scale works. Unless a portfolio contains several photographs of large works, he might hesitate to recommend the sculptor for the commission. As a beginning, it is often necessary to do several large works experimentally and

photograph them in architectural setting in order to develop an effective portfolio.

Assuming that an architect requests some sketches or ideas for a possible commission, the next problem is to convince the architect and client that the sculpture will add to the total architectural environment. A professional-looking presentation is of utmost importance; if the presentation is poorly executed, the client may very well think that the finished work will be handled in the same fashion. The client and architect will want a convincing presentation of what the finished product will look like. Normally, this should be a colored rendering of the proposed work and a blueprint of the building elevation showing the work in relation to the architectural setting. The blueprint, perhaps including construction and installation details, is printed from a drawing on tracing paper, which allows copies to be made of the drawing so that the sculptor can keep the original. Figure 13-8 in Chapter 13 is a typical example of a drawing for a fountain. This drawing was accompanied by a colored, larger-scale drawing of the fountain. The blueprint of the drawing and the colored sketch were mounted and presented in a folder made of attractively-colored illustration board. If a commission is an exceptionally large, complex work, a scale model might be built after approval of the drawings has been secured.

Although sculptors should be paid for their sketches and models, clients are often skeptical and unwilling to pay to see the initial ideas. Whether or not to do drawings on speculation is a matter of personal choice. I have often done preliminary drawings and presentations on that basis, and have found it worth the gamble. In a way, these sketches are not produced free of charge, since speculation should be considered as part of the cost of operating a studio and should be allowed for in the price charged for commissions and sales that are realized.

Designing work beyond the preliminary presentation, such as further clarification of the plan with models and detailed drawings, should be paid for by the client. It may also be necessary to supply material samples.

If a client and architect accept a proposal, it then becomes necessary to draw up some form of written contract. Figure 14-2 is a simple form of contract I have found acceptable when doing com-

PROPOSED FOUNTAIN
(name of building, city
and state)

Form	—Approximating drawings and model submitted, minor modifications to improve aesthetic or structural elements at the discretion of the sculptor.
Size	—Per scale of drawings submitted, approximately____ ft. long,____ ft. high and____ft. wide.
Material	—(State material)
Finish	—Per sample submitted
Insurance	—(State Insurance)
Cost	—(State cost) including all material and labor, delivery to site, installation and sales tax.
Payment Schedule	—35% initial retainer, payable prior to beginning the project. 35% payable at 50 per cent completion 15% payable at completion in studio 15% payable at completion of installation
Guarantee	—One year on material and workmanship with any repair and labor furnished without cost to owner.
Contract Limitations	—All conditions of proposal subject to change if not accepted within 30 days from date of proposal.
Delivery	—(State date)

Sculptor agrees to furnish sclupture in general accordance with the stated conditions. Sculptor ___(Signature)___ Date _____

Address _____

Owner or agent authorizes sculptor to proceed with sculpture in accordance with above terms and conditions. Owner _____

Figure 14-2

A simple contract form for commission work.

missions. Items can be added or deleted, depending on the type of work being produced. In the first item, it is necessary to state the form of the sculpture and the right of the sculptor to make necessary changes in the full-scale development of the work. The size of the work can be defined in terms of refering to the drawings, model, or stated in terms of length, width and height. The kind of material should be specified; material thickness and method of fabrication might also be included in this category. A sample of the finished material can be provided, or the finish can be described as approximating the colors of the submitted sketch or drawing. List the insurance protections provided. Sometimes the client may require written verification from the insurance company or agent providing the insurance. Cost is all inclusive; it must allow for all emergencies and errors; the client cannot be expected to assume these risks. The payment schedule is designed to give the sculptor operating money as the work develops. The scheduled percentages of payment may vary according to anticipated costs in producing the work. The initial retainer normally needs to be a high percentage of the total in order to allow for large outlays for purchases of material and for starting the project. Never order material or start a project until the first payment is received. The second and third payments may be distributed more evenly if cost factors permit. At the completion of the project at the studio or at a fabricator, the sculptor should have received about 85 to 90 percent of the total charge. In the event that installation is delayed, the sculptor would have received the bulk of his fee for services performed. The guarantee assures the purchaser that the work will be executed in a sound and workmanshiplike manner. Contract limitations are merely a routine matter and allow for renegotiation of the contract in the event that the project is delayed and labor, material, or other costs have increased. Every effort should be made to meet the delivery date agreed upon; this is important to the owner and architect, since the official opening of a building depends on all contracts being completed. If a sculptor becomes known as being unreliable in terms of delivery, he may soon discover that he no longer has clients.

Reproduction rights and copyrights are often overlooked by the artist until someone infringes upon his work, at which point, it is often impossible to do anything about the infringement. There are a few simple things that can be done to protect the sculptor from infringements: all works assigned to a gallery should be listed on a consignment form that clearly states that reproduction rights are reserved by the artist; the sale of each work should be documented with a bill of sale stating the reservation of reproduction rights; it should be signed by the artist or his agent and by the purchasers of the work. A simple form of copyright is to place a "C" with a circle around it in front of the signature and date on the work. Sculpture, models, and drawings are protected in this fashion. If these simple procedures are followed and the work is infringed upon, an attorney would have some basis on which to act in enforcing the artist's rights.

Safety

FIFTEEN

A cautious attitude toward all materials and equipment in sculpturing is one of the best ways to avoid health hazards and injury. Good working habits involve proper protective and safety procedures, not only for the individual in the studio but for fellow workers and possible visitors entering the work area. Contaminants and potential health hazards are present in many sculptural materials used today, and the possibility of injury when working with tools and equipment is always present. These conditions are not a cause for alarm but should be a matter of continuous concern in developing good work habits.

When working with materials, the sculptor should always think of them in terms of their basic properties and possible hazards. Although reading the labels on packages and containers is an essential discipline that should be practiced, labels are often incomplete, or material may be purchased in bulk or in such a way that it is not labelled or not required to be labelled. Material manufacturers, however, often provide safety and toxicity information along with their products. Otherwise, a good reference, such as *Accident Prevention Manual, for Industrial Operations* by the National Safety Council (Chicago, 1964) should be consulted. The material and all of its constituents should be considered when toxicity is being evaluated.

Four basic hazards exist when toxic or dangerous materials are being used: the material, its vapors, fumes, or dust may come into contact with the skin; vapor or dust may be inhaled; the material may be flammable, explosive, or reactive with other material; or it may be ingested accidentally.

Skin contact with toxic or hazardous material involves risks of surface-skin irritation, dermatitis, burns, and systemic poisoning through absorption of some material. The skin, however, is a highly effective protective barrier against surface penetration of most foreign materials. Absorption into the system through the skin is often more likely to take place through unattended open scratches, cuts, and abrasions. Protective measures against skin contact when toxic materials are being handled are relatively easy to incorporate in the work schedule: rubber gloves can be worn to protect the hands; long-sleeved shirts, shop or laboratory coats, and other proper clothing protect the arms and body. A face shield should be worn to protect eyes and face during pouring, mixing, or brushing, or when danger of splashing or spattering exists. Skin irritation due to fumes or vapors is usually controlled by removal of the fumes from the atmosphere with a proper exhaust system, or protective hoods and clothing. In handling hot materials, the sculptor should use proper tongs or devices. Protective, heat-resistant asbestos, leather gloves, aprons, or other clothing should be worn when necessary; if gloves develop leaks or become worn, or if clothing becomes spattered or contaminated, they should be replaced. Skin contamination should be attended to immediately.

Inhalation of dust, vapors, or fumes poses the greatest hazard in working with toxic or hazardous materials. Inhaled substances may readily enter the blood stream through the lung tissue. Inert dust may accumulate and ultimately produce respiratory complications. Nontoxic dusts, although not injurious, can be irritating. Accumulation of dust or fumes in the atmosphere can also be flammable or explosive. Safe working procedures require removal of the contaminating material from the atmosphere or the use of suitable protective masks.

The removal of contaminants from the atmosphere is one of the most desirable solutions to controlling toxic fumes or dusts. The simple, rule-of-thumb approach, such as changing the air every three minutes, may be workable in some circumstances while inadequate or excessive in others. Ideally, the rate of air contamination and tolerance levels for a particular material should be determined, and the rate of removal should be based on those factors. The size of the working space, ceiling height, number of other workers in the room, and the kind of ventilating system are all matters to be considered.

Considering the variety of materials the sculptor works with today, every studio or classroom should be equipped with some form of air removal. A good ventilating system involves two principal components: a means of removing air and a means of replacing the air removed. Replaced air often needs to be heated in the winter to maintain comfortable working conditions. Hoods or fume collectors to remove air from selected work areas are the most efficient and economical. It is about the only workable system for work areas involving more than one worker. Exhausting air alone is insufficient.

Ideally, a system should exhaust the contaminated air while fresh air is being driven past the worker, driving the contaminated air into the hood or removal system. In a one-man studio, a simple approach is to have an exhaust fan mounted in a wall with the work area placed next to the fan. The other end of the work area should have a smaller fan to blow air past the worker in the direction of the exhaust fan. (A fan with a volume of air greater than the exhaust fan would cause the fumes to be recirculated in the room before they could be exhausted.) A window or door should be open on the opposite end of the room to supply make-up air. In the winter, a heated air supply should be used for make-up air. An economical way of solving this problem is to localize the make-up air. A flexible duct on the air supply that can be positioned to blow the make-up air past the worker, driving the fumes into the hood or exhaust, is a practical approach. In this case, the volume of air need not be as great as in the case of trying to supply air to the whole room.

Fans and motors should be explosionproof and fireproof, for exhausting flammable dusts and fumes. When large volumes of exhausted, contaminated air are handled, city or state antipollution codes may require the air to be filtered or washed prior to its discharge into the atmosphere. The design of a ventilating system can become complex. The volume of air desired, the kind of fan used, the type of filter, ductwork or means of placing the air where desired, air velocity or feet per minute of air in the ducts and at the work station, and the kinds of hoods or fume collectors used are all factors be be considered. As just stated, for the one-man studio, these problems can usually be solved in a rather simple fashion. However, if a space involves several or more workers and large volumes of contaminants are used, good safety engineering advice is essential.

Another common practice for sculptors working with toxic materials is to work outdoors when climate permits. This approach is not foolproof; on a day when there is little wind or moving air, the fumes may not be adequately cleared or dissipated. A fan should be used in these circumstances to blow across the work area.

In many circumstances, air removed alone is not sufficient, particularly if the sculpture being worked or is large and it is necessary to move around it a great deal. Under these conditions, the sculptor often finds himself in the path of the fumes being removed. The same problem exists

Figure 15-1

Respiratory masks. Right to left: dual filter mask with chemical cartridge type filters for the removal of toxic fumes and dust, inexpensive dustmask, single filter mask with mechanical filter for the removal of non-toxic dusts.

when working over a piece of work. In this situation, the only solution is to use a suitable respiratory device. Respiratory devices for working in fumes, vapors, or dust-contaminated atmospheres are of several types. (Figure 15-1) The face mask with a mechanical filter for removing dust or particles is the simplest form. It is adequate for sawdust, stone or silica dust, and dust from abrasive grinding or finishing. Toxic dusts require special filters. For fumes and vapors, masks with chemical filters that remove the toxic material should be used. These must be purchased with specific filters for particular contaminants or classes of contaminants. The filter should have the approval of the U.S. Bureau of Mines. Twin-filter masks provide greater filtering surface and less resistance to breathing. Less breathing discomfort is experienced when this type mask is used. If an air supply is available, an air mask is the most ideal and convenient means of protection, Since it eliminates the problem of resistance and breathing discomfort associated with the filter mask. The air supply can be provided by an air compressor or low-pressure blower. The air must be supplied from a source other than the work area. Air compressors must have proper filters, pressure gauges, and protective devices. Air supplied by low-pressure blowers is more desirable; airfrom a poorly maintained air compressor can contain dangerous carbon monoxide produced by decomposing oil lubricants in the compressor.

Protective masks should be of good quality, with adequate straps and adjustments to assure a good fit and absence of air leakage. Filters should be replaced as required. Masks should be checked daily for faulty valves or defects. Inexpensive paper, cloth, or fiber masks should be avoided. They rarely fit adequately and serve only to remove small portions of dust or other material.

Dust is usually removed by using dust collectors rather than exhausting it. Dust collectors may be built into the shop with a central collecting and air exhausting system, or an individual dust collector can be attached to each individual machine. In a small, one-man shop, simple attachments, which can be purchased or easily fashioned for most equipment, will equip a shop vacuum for low-volume, nontoxic, nonflammable dust removal. An idividual dust collector can also be used and moved to the machine being used. When dust is not removed from the atmosphere, suitable masks provide adequate protection for nontoxic dusts. Toxic dusts require the use of masks with chemical filters, protective face shields, hoods, and clothing.

Vapor, fumes, and dust may often be flammable or, at concentrated levels, explosive. All dust-collecting and ventilating equipment should be flame and explosion proof, which is usually accomplished by use of enclosed motors or motors remote from the exhaust system. The fans are rigid and are so designed that the possibility of metal parts striking and causing sparks is eliminated. Fans and other metal parts may also be made of or coated with nonmetallic materials. Any finishing or fabricating room using flammable materials must also practice other precautions: smoking should not be allowed; heating systems should be remote from the work area or they should be explosionproof; appliances with open flames, such as water heaters or heating devices, should not be present in the room; electric hand tools should not be used if fumes are at a concentrated level, since sparks from the motor brushes can start fires; air tools should be used in these circumstances.

Caution should be exercised in the mixing of chemicals, catalysts, plastics, resins, and other materials. Improper mixtures may be flammable, explosive, or highly reactive. Indiscriminate mixing of chemicals may result in the formation of toxic fumes and gases. Heating materials can also be hazardous in causing changes in, or acceleration of, the reaction between materials. The most essential precaution in these circumstances is not to deviate from manufacturer's recommendations or recommended formulas unless the chemistry of the material is understood.

Ingestion of toxic materials is the least frequent of accidents, yet it is possible. The most obvious and usual means of ingesting toxics is due to contamination of the hands and subsequent handling of foods or cigarettes. Smoking while handling some toxics can be particularly hazardous; fumes or small quantities of material transferred to a cigarette can be extremely dangerous when they combine with burning tobacco and inhaled smoke; a no-smoking policy while working should be enforced. Removal of gloves and proper cleanup should precede the handling of food.

Most hazards involving equipment can be minimized or eliminated with proper work procedures and the use of safety equipment. All electrical equipment should be properly grounded to avoid the possibility of electric shock in the event the equipment should short out or malfunction. Mechanical equipment should have proper guards over exposed wheels, gears, grinding, and cutting devices. Stationary equipment should be properly fastened or mounted on the floor or work bench. Equipment should be properly maintained. Loose bolts, pulleys, and other malfunctioning parts should be repaired immediately. The equipment should be kept clean. Electrical equipment should be disconnected during repair or major maintenance. When equipment is being operated, it is important to become aware of the normal working sound of the machine. A change in the usual sound is usually an early indication that something is not functioning properly and is in need of repair or adjustment; odors may indicate overheating. Adequate work space should be allowed around each piece of equipment. In classrooms, it is often helpful to paint lines defining work space around each machine and restrict the area to the operator of the machine. Maintaining a clean, well-organized studio or shop can contribute immeasurably to safety. Debris and obstacles in a work area can inhibit material handling and hinder the feeding of material through a machine. It is easy to slip on small scraps of dowelling, welding rod, or spilled liquids. Accumulated trash can also pose a fire hazard. Abrasive, nonslip strips can be attached to the floor around machinery to avoid slipping. Shop floors should never be waxed or maintained with an excessively smooth finish. Good lighting is important for good craftsmanship as well as for contributing to the safe operation of equipment.

Loose clothing can be hazardous around moving parts. Proper protective goggles, masks, gloves, and clothing should be worn while welding, metal casting, sandblasting, woodworking, and metalworking, or when working with hazardous machinery. Construction-type clothing, such as hard hats, safety shoes, and other garments, may be necessary when large sculpture is being built or installed.

Since the sculptor has become involved in the use of a wide variety of mechanical equipment, noise can become a hazard. Prolonged exposure to excessive noise can result in temporary or permanent impairment or loss of hearing. Ear plugs or ear muffs can be worn to reduce noise levels. These must be well-fitted; small leaks can reduce considerably the effectiveness of the protection.

Perhaps the most essential aspect of safety involves the attitude of the individual. If the individual does not take the problem seriously, well-designed protective devices for equipment and in work areas, clothing, goggles, masks, signs, color codes as reminders, etc. are ineffective. It is imperative that the individual enter a work area with concern for his safety. He must be willing to take the time to provide himself with necessary protection. An attitude of awareness toward hazards must be uppermost in his mind at all times. This is the only way to insure the adherence to safety practices.

WOODWORKING

Woodworking accidents are avoided by keeping equipment in proper condition and by use of proper jigs and protective devices. The worker should be aware of the proper techniques for using equipment. While blades are being changed or while woodworking equipment is being worked on, the equipment should be unplugged from the electrical outlet, or a suitable cutoff switch should be provided. Safety goggles should be worn in all woodworking operations. (Figure 15-2) Sawblades and cutters can throw wood splinters and chips at a velocity great enough to embed them in the eye. Loose clothing should not be worn. Free-hanging

Figure 15-2

Protective face shield and goggles for eye protection.

shirttails, loose, unbuttoned jackets, unbuttoned long sleeves, neckties, or any loose-hanging accessory around the neck are especially hazardous. Long-haired shop workers should tie back their hair. Sawdust and woodchips should be cleaned away from blades and cutters with a brush or stick, with the machine off.

Accidents on the circle table-saw are usually the result of allowing the hands to slip off the material when they are very close to the saw blade. Another common accident occurs when the material kicks back during ripping operations. Hands can be kept away from the blade by use of a proper push stick. Kickback can be prevented by use of a spreader on the outfeed side of the sawblade or by the use of antikickback devices. Feathered boards clamped to the fence and table for ripping operations hold the material in place and are adequate to prevent kickback in a small studio.

Improper alignment of the rip fence can also be hazardous. The front and rear of the fence must always be locked securely and must be in line with the saw blade. In crosscutting operations, stock should be held or clamped against the miter-gauge guide; it should never be cut freehand. Attempting to remove small scraps and cutoffs next to the sawblade with the blade in motion can also result in accidents. In all sawing operations, the worker should stand out of line with possible kickback material.

Saw blades should be kept sharp and clean, and they should be inspected periodically for defects. Dull or gummed-up blades can bind on the

material and cause kickback or unsafe cutting action. Saw blades should not be used improperly; for example, ripping with crosscut blades or crosscutting with rip blades should be avoided. For safe operation, blades should not project more than about one-fourth inch above the material being cut.

The safety recommendations for the table saw also apply generally to the radial-arm or the cutoff saw. If stock is held firmly against the fence and hands are kept a proper distance from the blade, there is little cause for accidents in crosscutting. Reaching across the path of the blade frequently causes accidents. Ripping should be done from the proper side of the blade, and the antikickback device should be used. A saw should not be operated without its guard when ripping or cutting is being done. The saw should be mounted with its arm slightly higher on the end away from the column, preventing the saw from creeping out or forward while it is in an idling position.

When the saw is positioned for cutting angles or special details, extra precaution should be exercised, particularly when the operation calls for running the saw without a guard or when using shapers and routers.

Band saws and jig saws are normally not considered very hazardous. Most accidents occur at the completion of a cut, particularly in cutting curves, in which case, the stock is inclined to jump forward as the pressure of the blade is released upon completion of the cut. Easing pressure on the stock, keeping fingers clear of the path of travel, and a slower feeding for completion of the cut minimize this danger. Cutting with dull blades that require greater feed pressure contributes to this hazard. The band saw upper guard and guide should be set just above the material. The jigsaw hold-down foot should rest on the material. Blades should be adjusted to proper tension; excessive tension can cause blade breakage. Good lighting and a jet of air or a blower to keep the dust away from the markings on the stock contribute to safer operations as well.

Jointers are as dangerous as circle saws. When short stock is being surfaced, fingers are inclined to get too close to the cutting head. When surfacing the wide side of a board is being done, the heel of the hand is in danger of touching the cutting blades. Using a push stick in these circumstances can minimize the hazard. A proper guard should be in place at all times. The standard leg-of-mutton guard on most machines keeps the blade covered except for the width of the material being fed through the machine. The depth of cut should never exceed more than 1/16 inch. Excessively deep cuts contribute to the possibility of kickback; the worker should stand to the side of the machine while feeding in the stock.

Accidents on the shaper, as on the jointer, usually involve the fingers or hand coming into contact with the cutting edges as stock is being cut. A proper jig should be used in these circumstances to keep the fingers an adequate distance from the cutters. Standard guards can be used, or guards can be fashioned for special detailing operations. Cutters should be covered except for the cutting edges that need sufficient exposure to cut the stock. Knives breaking or working loose from the cutter head is another cause of accidents. Ring guards for the shaper cutter-head provide some protection. Using solid cutter heads also reduces this hazard. Deep cuts should be avoided; it is safer to make several passes to achieve the desired cut. Be particularly aware of the machine sound, as vibration and unusual sound may mean that the blades are loose or defective or that cutters are out of balance. The fence or guide pin should always be used to support and guide the material past the cutters.

In operating planers, keep fingers away from the feed rollers and stand to the side as the stock feeds through the machine. A board thinner than the machine setting would not make proper contact with the feed rollers and could be kicked back. Stop the machine completely to remove chips or to make adjustments. Keep other workers or spectators an adequate distance from the discharge side of the machine.

Although accidents on sanders are seldom as serious as those occurring during sawing, jointing, or planing, painful bruises and abrasions do occur. Minor abrasions are usually the result of the fingers touching the sanding belt or disc. Serious cuts and abrasions that can result in the loss of fingertips occur when the fingers touch the abrasive surface and are pulled into the space between the belt or disc and the sander table or backstop.

Miter guides, backstops, and jigs should be used to hold or guide the material when possible. Belts should be kept in line. Worn or frayed belts should be replaced.

The principal hazard in working with wood-turning lathes is flying wood chips, fingers getting caught between the revolving stock and the tool rest, or loose clothing catching on the machine. Wearing proper goggles and clothing and keeping the tool rest properly adjusted are the normal precautions to observe in preventing these accidents.

Good stock without loose knots should be used; tools should be kept sharp and held in the proper position. On a variable-speed lathe, always bring the machine back down to the lowest speed or to a stop before turning it off to discontinue operations. Proper lathe speeds should be observed. Before starting the lathe, revolve the material by hand to be certain that it clears the tool rest. Check to be certain the machine is set at its lowest speed before putting in stock for the rough cutting. Be certain that the tailstock is locked in place and that the work is properly centered.

Although hand woodworking tools do not present the hazards normally associated with power tools, injuries can occur if tools are defective or improperly used, or if the hands and fingers are in a position where they can come into undesirable contact with the tool. Saw cuts on the fingers occur when guiding the blade to start a cut, or during, or upon completion of, a cut. Hands and fingers in the path of chisels, punches, and drills, or fingers too close to nails being driven, also result in injury.

Operating power hand tools involves a number of risks peculiar to this form of equipment. Loose clothing can get caught in revolving drill chucks, saw blades, or belt-sanding mechanisms. A drill can be driven through material and into the hand when material is hand-held. Hand-holding stock while cutting with a saber saw or a portable circle saw also causes this dangers. Always place stock on saw horses, low worktables, or workbenches. Hold it down firmly with clamps, jigs, the free hand, or with the knee resting on the material. Be certain the cord is clear of the operating parts of the tool and not in the path of travel for the tool. Tools should have proper guards and guides. Keep them clean and inspect periodically for defects in the cord and the tool.

Wood dusts from woodworking operations are usually a nuisance that can be controlled with dust-removal equipment or mechanical-filter dust masks. Concentrated levels of wood dust can be explosive; some wood dust may cause dermatitis or allergies; East Indian Satinwood and South American boxwood are toxic; allergies may be developed to woods such as pine, birch, dogwood, and mahogony. Power tools and equipment should be periodically cleaned by blowing the dust out of motors and mechanisms with low-pressure air.

WELDING

The principal hazards in welding are in handling hot materials, spattering of metal, radiant energy from the welding flame or arc, toxic fumes, and gases, the combustible nature of acetylene or other gases, and the danger of electrical shock in arc welding.

Eyes can be protected by using suitable goggles in acetylene welding and a helmet to protect the eyes and face in arc welding. The darkness or shading of the lens in the goggles or helmet depends on the size tip being used in oxyacetylene welding or the amperage in electric welding. Ordinary dark glasses are not suitable protection; special optical glass is used for welding glasses. In oxyacetylene welding, lens shades may be from 3 to 4 for light work and from 5 to 8 for medium to heavy welding or cutting. In arc welding, a number 10 or 11 is usually adequate for amperages up to 200 amps; if the amperage is lower than 50 amps, a lighter lens should be used; for amperages between 200 and 400, a number 12 or 13 should be used; amperages in excess of 400 require a number 14. (Figure 15-3)

Burns can be avoided by wearing adequate protective clothing. Leather or asbestos gauntlet-type gloves, aprons, jackets, leggings, and hats provide the most desirable protection. Fabric flame-resistant and ultraviolet-resistant garments can be worn and are often satisfactory for light and medium work. Wool fabric is preferred since it is less flammable and less susceptible to ultraviolet deterioration than cotton. Fabric should be dark in color to be less reflective. Pockets, the belt line, cuffs, and low shoe tops readily catch sparks and hot particles of slag: pants should be cuffless; the jacket or apron should have no pockets and hang over the beltline of the pants; high, leather boots are advisable, with the pants legs hanging over the boots. In electric welding it is essential that all skin

Figure 15-3

Basic protective devices for welding. Right to left: fire resistant jacket, leather gloves, arc welding helmet (top), oxyacetylene welding goggles (bottom).

Figure 15-4

Fume collector with exhaust fan. Note great range of hood for use in varied working positions. *Photograph courtesy of Ruemelin Manufacturing Company.*

areas be covered. Ordinary cotton clothing is not adequate protection since the ultraviolet rays can penetrate the material. Hot metals should be picked up with pliers or tongs. Always use a friction lighter when lighting the oxyacetylene torch; never use matches. Welding should be conducted in an isolated area, or protective screens should be used to protect other workers or visitors. In electric welding, screening should be sufficient to completely isolate the ultraviolet rays. Rays bouncing off white, metallic, or reflective surfaces can cause burns. Welding-booth walls should be dark-colored and nonreflective. Screens should be placed so that they do not shut off cross ventilation. Warning signs should be posted outside shop or work-area doors, advising personnel or visitors of welding operations in progress; warning signs should be placed next to hot materials if they are left unattended.

Toxic fumes from welding should be removed from the atmosphere or protective masks should be worn; in some cases, both precautions may be necessary. Fumes are removed by localized means: working with the object under a hood, with a fume collector placed next to the weld zone; or by general ventilation. (Figure 15-4) Under most circumstances, it would be reasonable to assume that the majority of studios and sculpture classrooms are not large enough and do not have sufficient ceiling height to permit any amount of welding without some form of ventilation. Ventilation is even required for welding or cutting uncoated, ferrous metals such as steel, unless the space is large enough to prevent an undesirable level of fume concentration. For one worker, any space smaller than 20 by 35 feet, with a ceiling height less than 16 feet, would be considered inadequate for any form of sustained welding operation, unless ventilation were supplied.

Fumes in welding are usually the result of melting or burning metal or welding rods during cutting or welding, fluxes or coatings on the rods, and coatings or contaminants on the metal, which are usually additives or alloys. Metals, welding rods, or fluxes containing lead, zinc, copper, cadmium, mercury, fluorine, beryllium, and manganese can produce toxic fumes; paints and coatings on new or used materials may contain some of these materials. Excess exposure to fumes will often result in metal-fume fever. The fever may occur during or a few hours after welding with the material. Symptoms are usually chills, fever, nausea, headaches, or a weak and ill feeling. In some cases, immunity may be acquired with daily exposure to some of the less toxic agents. However, concentrated exposure to toxic materials such as cadmium fumes can cause death. Some of the common materials and welding operations involving toxic fumes are welding or cutting galvanized metal, bronze, copper, or brass, silver soldering, lead soldering, and welding or cutting metals that have been painted or primed with lead- or zinc-filled coatings.

In arc welding, dangerous oxides of nitrogen are produced in the high-temperature area of the arc. Ozone is also formed by the ultraviolet radiation acting on the air. The latter is more prevalent in the gas-shielded arc-welding operations. Usually, the gases dissipate and combine with the atmosphere a few feet from the arc and do not reach toxic levels. However, in high-volume welding and in confined spaces, ventilation should be provided.

Fire hazards are caused by welding near combustible material, misuse of welding equipment, or defective equipment. Work areas should be kept clean and free of combustibles; oil and flammable contaminants should be cleaned off metal before welding the material. When welding in areas next to combustible materials such as wood, metal or abbestos-board shields should be used to confine the sparks to the welding area. Check the area thoroughly upon completion of the job to be certain sparks have not ignited any material. A thirty-minute fire watch with another spot check thirty minutes later is recommended if there is any possibility of sparks having dropped into concealed places. Welding should not be carried out close to any containers of highly flammable liquids. Oily

and greasy clothing is also a fire hazard. In sculpture classrooms or work areas, be certain your make-up supply of air is not coming from a room containing large quantities of flammable liquids or where work with flammable materials is being done.

In handling oxyacetylene equipment, always keep tanks chained or fastened to a wall or support so that they cannot be tipped over. Work at proper recommended pressures; never exceed 15 pounds of pressure on the acetylene. Oxygen is not flammable but supports and accelerates combustion. Oil should not be used on any oxygen fittings and oxygen should not be released around oily metal or material; both of these situations are potentially highly explosive and flammable. Oxygen valves and equipment should not be handled with oily hands or while wearing oily gloves; keep oil off gloves used to handle the welding torch; if oily metal must be handled, use separate gloves for handling the material and change into clean gloves for the oxyacetylene welding or cutting of materials.

Check the oxyacetylene equipment periodically for defects and for leaks; leaks can be checked by brushing soap suds on the fittings and watching for soap bubbles to form.

Never weld or flame-cut containers that have contained inflammable materials without first cleaning the container; filling the container with water about up to the weld zone and properly venting the remaining space are recommended for further precaution. Never weld enclosed forms without providing a vent hole so that pressure and gases built up by heat can escape. Forced venting can be achieved by directing compressed air into the container; a vacuum cleaner can also be used as an air supply. Keep cylinders a sufficient distance from the work area. Be certain that the lighted torch is never turned so that it might accidentally direct heat on the cylinder.

Accidental electric shock can be avoided in arc welding if the equipment is properly grounded and the operator of the equipment is properly insulated to handle the equipment. If gloves and clothing are dry and equipment is in good repair, there is very little hazard involved. Clothing and gloves frequently become moist from perspiration in warm weather; although it is impractical to change clothing, changing gloves periodically is possible and is a good practice. Welding cables and electrode holders should be checked for breaks in the insulation and for defects. Cables should be placed so that they do not become damaged by flying sparks, slag, falling hot scraps of metal; and so that they do not come into contact with the hot work. Hanging the cables overhead is a good practice. The electrode holder should be well-insulated. Electrodes should never be changed with bare hands or while wearing moist gloves. Never work on moist floors. Working on metal ladders can also be hazardous.

CARVING

Sawdust and contact with wood in wood carving pose hazards similar to those discussed for woodworking. Cuts and bruises are perhaps the most common problems. Dull tools and tools loosely mounted in their handles contribute to accidents in wood carving. In finishing work, when the chisel is pushed with one hand, accidents often occur if the chisel slips and the hand is in the path of the chisel. In roughing-out with an axe, injury can occur if the axe is being swung improperly; the blade may glance off the log and strike the leg or a foot. It is also important to be certain obstacles or bystanders are not in the path of the axe when it is being swung. When an adze or hatchet is being swung, it is also necessary to be cautious that a wrong or glancing blow does not strike any part of the body. Loose heads on axes, adzes, and hatchets can fly from the handle, striking other workers in the area.

When pneumatic chisels are being operated in both wood and stone carving, noise levels may be objectionable or harmful, necessitating the use of ear plugs or muffs. Exposure to the continuous vibration of the tool, the exhausted air, and hand strain in holding the tool can result in a condition known as "dead hand" or "white finger." Although this damage to the circulatory system of the hand is usually temporary, prolonged and continuous exposure has in some cases produced permanent injury. Exhausted air from pneumatic tools also causes greater quantities of dust to become airborne, increasing dust hazards. Directing the air away from the hands and using a comfortable tool size for the hands can reduce the possibility of dead hand.

Hazardous dusts in stone carving are primarily the dusts containing crystalline free silica. Inhalation of large quantities of these dusts over a long period of time may result in silicosis. Quartz, sandstone, and granite contain high percentages of crystalline free silica, which is also present in varying amounts in some marbles, travetine, soapstone, and some limestone. Since most dusts may be irritating, it is probably advisable to use a suitable dust mask or dust-removal ventilating system in any carving operation when dust-particle levels are high. Suitable protection from the crystalline free silica dusts is imperative.

Stone-carving chisels have a tendency to mushroom on the ends because of the striking force of the mallet; chisel ends should be kept trimmed, with a slight bevel, to prevent serious cuts from mushroomed ends.

ABRASIVE GRINDING

Hazardous materials in abrasive grinding are often present in the material being ground as well as the dusts from abrasive wheels. Being struck by pieces of wheels that break at high speed is another danger. Wearing proper protective garments and using adequate dust-collecting systems minimize these dangers. Protective goggles or face shields should be worn at all times. In operating abrasive wire brushes, a full-face shield is essential; a leather apron and arm guards should also be used as protection against possible loose wires being propelled into space from the revolving wheel.

If dust collectors are not used, proper dust masks should be worn. Dust from most metals can be hazardous and irritating. Accumulations of magnesium dust are exceptionally explosive and flammable. Magnesium dust requires special wet-dust collecting systems.

Standard abrasive wheels should be mounted on the shaft of the grinder with protective flanges. The flange diameter should be approximately one-third of the diameter of the wheel. Larger-diameter safety flanges are used for wheels when they are operated without protective guards, which should be used whenever possible. Wheels should not be operated in excess of the recommended speeds, should be inspected for cracks and defects; and should be dresses when they become worn, to restore the working surface and balance to the wheel. A proper work rest should be used to support and guide the work. Grinding should be confined to the work surface of the wheel; the flat side of the wheel should not be used except when necessary in the sharpening of some types of chisels and tools.

METAL CASTING

Hazards in foundry work exist primarily in dust and fumes and in the handling of molten metal during casting. Dust conditions are usually produced when mold-making materials such as talc, flint, silica flour, silica sand, plaster, portland cement, and asbestos are being used. Dust and fumes from lead, chromium, iron, phosphorous, tin, zinc, magnesium and copper-based alloys that contain beryllium produce conditions that are hazard-

ous or irritating. Aluminum and magnesium dust pose fire and explosion hazards in dust-collecting systems.

Fumes from resins used as binders that contain phenol-formaldehyde, urea-formaldehyde, furfural alcohol, phosphoric acids, or others are also toxic. Binders and additives or catalysts, which should always be added to sand according to manufacturers' recommendations, should never be mixed together in the liquid form; severe chemical reaction can occur. Fumes from solvents may also be toxic. Silicone in mold-release materials may be irritating to the skin and can be hazardous if inhaled. During melting operations, toxic metallic fumes are present in the dross and disintegrating, oxidizing, low-melting point alloys in the metal. Proper use of fluxes, temperature control, and minimizing the holding period for the molten metal reduces these hazards. Fumes from burning polyurethane or polystyrene foam in displaced-foam casting can also contain toxic fumes. Prolonged skin contact with sand and chemical additives in mold construction may cause dermatitis. Adequate ventilation or protective masks should be used when exposure to dusts and fumes is a possibility.

Figure 15-5
Protective clothing for metal casting. Left to right: leather jacket, leather apron (top), asbestos leggings (bottom), asbestos gloves (top), face shield (bottom)

Melting and handling molten metal are particularly hazardous and require precaution. Proper care of crucibles is essential; metal should not be wedged or forced into the crucible; crucibles must be dry, and the metal that is added to molten metal in a crucible must be dry—moisture coming into contact with molten metal can produce severe reactions. Proper lighting procedures for furnaces and ovens should be adhered to strictly.

Safety goggles or face shields should be used at all times. Long sleeves, shirts buttoned around the wrists, and cuffless pants over high-topped shoes provide protection in the average sculpture studio. Asbestos or leather gloves that fit snugly around the wrist, with the shirt sleeve or jacket sleeve over the glove, provide the best protection. Asbestos or leather protective hoods, jackets, aprons, leggings or spats, skull caps, and gloves should be worn in handling large quantities of molten metal. (Figure 15-5)

Pouring areas should be kept well-organized. Particular attention should be given to keeping obstacles out of the way of the workers handling crucibles of molten metal. Crucibles or ladles of metal being transported on overhead tracks should never be allowed to pass over other workers. Ladles should be equipped with manual or automatic safety locks to prevent accidental overturns. When large castings or heavy molds are being handled, proper lifting devices should be used, and care should be exercised when they are being hand-lifted. Wearing hard-toed shoes is a good practice. Injury to the fingers or toes is commonplace in the handling of heavy materials.

PLASTICS

Although plastic materials are generally inert and nontoxic in their finished forms, the raw materials used to produce finished products are often toxic: skin contact with adhesives, fumes from coatings, resins, solvents, and from heating or welding plastic, and dusts from fillers and from sanding and milling coatings produce hazardous working conditions. Reasonable precautions, with adequate ventilation, dust-collecting equipment or protective gloves, face masks, and clothing are necessary and should be considered mandatory.

Polyester, epoxy, and urethane resins, coatings, their solvents and catalysts are being used today in considerable quantities in studios and classrooms. Working with these materials under unsatisfactory conditions has produced skin irritation, dermatitis, eye irritation, temperary illness, and permanent internal injury.

Styrene monomer, cobalt or aniline accelerators and methyl ethyl ketone or benzoyl peroxide catalysts are toxic materials used in the formulation of, or when working with, polyester resins. Normally, the accelerators, present in the resin, are not handled in quantities sufficient to cause a problem. Accelerators and catalysts highly reactive and flammable, should never be mixed together. The dispersion of each one individually into the resin reduces their reactions to safe working limits. Although acetone, used in cleaning brushes and equipment, is not highly toxic, it can be irritating to the eyes, nose, throat, and skin; excess inhalation of the fumes may result in headaches, temporary illnesses, and depression. Excess exposure can cause internal injury.

Although epoxy resins are normally considered safe and nontoxic, the amine curing agents added to the epoxies to effect polymerization are extremely irritating to the skin; concentrated vapors or fumes from the liquid curing agents, or those formed during the curing of the resin, can cause nose and throat irritation; continuous exposure can cause internal injury. Alkanol amines and anhydride curing agents are more often used today and are less toxic.

Today, urethane resins have been compounded that are fairly safe; the toxicity of the fumes has been reduced considerably over earlier foam systems. It is the isocyanate or diiocyanate used in foam formulas that produces the toxic fumes. First symptoms in excessive exposure are bronchial irritation and asthmalike attacks; prolonged contact and inhalation may result in internal injuries to the lungs, liver, and kidneys. Skin contact with the resins should also be avoided.

Skin contact and fumes from methyl methacrylate (acrylic resin), urea-formaldehyde and melamine-formaldehyde resins, phenolic, and polystyrene resins may have varying degrees of toxicity.

Burning of most plastics will cause toxic fumes due to chemical decomposition (pyrolysis).

Dust from most polymerized plastics is inert and harmless if the material is completely polymerized or cured. In machining, sawing, or sanding plastics that have not been completely cured, it is not the dust but the release of fumes that are still internally present in the material that is irritating and toxic. A typical example would be sawing or sanding freshly cast polyurethane blocks or castings. Vapors would not have completely dissipated, the remainder being trapped in the closed cells of the material. When reinforced fiberglass or cast blocks of plastics are sanded, dust from fillers—typically, glass fiber, metal fillers, asbestos, and silica—added to the resin may be a hazard.

Normal precautions should be exercised in handling any of the flammable solvents or resins. Particular care should be exercised in disposing of polymerizing plastic scraps, solvent-soaked cloth, or cleaning materials; when packed in a waste container these materials can readily produce spontaneous combustion; they should be collected in small containers and emptied periodically into large open metal containers out of doors. The materials should be loosely packed in the containers so that vapor and heat can dissipate, minimizing combustion hazards. Even small quantities of scrap should not be allowed to remain in the studio or unattended for a long period of time.

Dyes and pigments added to resins are sometimes hazardous or toxic. Pigment dust should not be inhaled. Skin contact with these should be avoided; skin contact with aniline dyes is particularly dangerous, since aniline is readily absorbed through the skin and is extremely toxic.

COATINGS AND SURFACE PREPARATION OF MATERIAL

In recent years, the coating industry has developed some coatings that are extremely safe and convenient to use. On the other hand, this new technology has also produced coatings that need to be handled with considerable care. The typical oil- or water-based paints purchased in the neighborhood paint store are relatively free from toxic materials. Epoxy and urethane coatings need to be handled with care. Many industrial coatings containing plastic materials that are extremely durable require special precautions in handling and applying. Primers containing lead or zinc should be handled carefully; solvents, vehicles, and additives to paints may be toxic and flammable. Paint thinner, turpentine, lacquer thinner, acetone, and solvents for plastics should be used with caution. Hardeners or curing agents for resins are often toxic. Labels on all coating or solvent containers should be read for handling precautions.

Utmost attention should be given to working conditions when coating is being applied. Good ventilation should be provided, particularly during spray painting. Paint application with brush, spray, or roller should not take place near open flames from space heaters, hot water heaters, stoves, welding operations, or other sources when paints are used that contain flammable resins or solvents. When spraying is being done, it is a good idea to use a face mask to filter out paint particles; if fumes are toxic, a cartridge-type face mask with suitable filters should be used. It is good practice to cover up surrounding areas that could be damaged by overspray; a suitable spray booth should be used when possible. If there are other workers in the area, they should be advised that toxic material is being used.

Most of the acids or chemicals used in metal plating, cleaning, or oxide-application operations are toxic to some extent. Nitric and sulfuric acid can produce severe burns. Fumes must be removed from the atmosphere. Alkaline cleaning compounds are somewhat less hazardous to handle. Suitable rubber gloves, protective masks, and clothing should be worn. Eyes should be protected from spattering by goggles or a face shield. When mixtures containing acids such as nitric or sulfuric are being used, they should be added to the water when the solution is being made; the reverse procedure can produce strong and hazardous reactions. In mixing chemicals for oxide finishes, materials should never be mixed unless familiarity has already been established with the possible results: some chemicals may be highly reactive with other materials, producing deadly-toxic fumes.

In surface preparation of material for painting or adhesive bonding, good ventilation should be provided when cleaning is being done with solvents such as acetone, mineral spirits, methyl alcohol, or other flammable materials that may also contain toxic fumes. Trichloroethylene and perchloroethylene are good nonvolatile substitutes for many of these solvents; however, the fumes are toxic. Precautions should also be exercised in swab or dip applications of acid or alkaline solutions. In steam-cleaning operations, rubber gloves, apron, and boots should be worn. Instructions for the operation of the steam cleaner should be carefully followed. It is good to be certain that all safety devices are functioning and to be on the alert for excess pressure in the system. For sandblasting, a protective hood and face shield should be worn as well as a protective dust mask.

Bibliography

BROWN, NELSON COURTLANDT, AND BETHEL, JAMES SAMUEL. *Lumber*. New York: John Wiley & Sons, Inc., 1958.

BURNS, ROBERT MARTIN, AND BRADLEY, W. W. *Protective Coating For Metal*. New York: Reinhold Publishing Corp., 1967.

CAGLE, CHARLES V. *Adhesive Bonding*. New York: McGraw-Hill Book Company, 1952.

COLEMAN, DONALD G. *Woodworking Fact Book*. New York: Robert Speller & Sons, 1966.

COLEMAN, RONALD L. *Sculpture*. Dubuque, Iowa: Wm. C. Brown Company, 1968.

COLLINGWOOD, G. H., AND BRUSH, WARREN D. *Knowing Your Trees*. Washington, D.C.: American Forestry Association, 1955.

DOYLE, LAURENCE E. *Manufacturing Processes and Materials*. Englewood Cliffs, N.J.: Prentice-Hall, Inc., 1961.

EDLIN, HERBERT T. *What Wood is That?* New York: Viking Press, 1969.

GUTTMANN, WERNER H. *Concise Guide to Structural Adhesives*. New York: Reinhold Publishing Corp., 1961.

HAMMOND, DONNELLY, HARROD, AND RAYNER. *Wood Technology*. Bloomington, Ill.: McKnight & McKnight Publishing Co., 1966.

HAYWARD, CHARLES H. *Complete Book of Woodworking*. Philadelphia, Pa. and New York: J. B. Lippincott Co., 1955.

HOWARD, E. D. *Modern Foundry Practice*. New York: Philosophical Library Inc., 1959.

LINDBERG, ROY A. *Processes and Materials of Manufacturing*. Boston, Mass.: Allyn & Bacon, Inc., 1965.

LISTER, RAYMOND. *The Craftsman in Metal*. Cranbury, N.J.: A. S. Barnes and Co. Inc., 1968.

MILLER, SAMUEL C. *Neon Signs and Cold Cathode Lighting*. New York: McGraw-Hill Book Company, 1952.

MILLER, WILLIAM G. *Using and Understanding Miniature Neon Lamps*. Indianapolis, Ind.: The Bobbs-Merrill Company, Inc., Howard W. Sam & Co., Inc., 1969.

MORRIS, JOE L. *Metal Casting*. Englewood Cliffs, N.J.: Prentice-Hall, Inc., 1957.

NELSON, GLENN C. *Ceramics*. New York: Holt, Rinehart and Winston Inc., 1960.

NEWMAN, THELMA R. *Plastics as an Art Form*. Philadelphia, Pa.: Chilton Company, 1964.

PATTON, W. J. *The Science and Practice of Welding*. Englewood Cliffs, N.J.: Prentice-Hall Inc., 1967.

PATTOU, ALBERT B. *Practical Furniture and Wood*

Finishing. Chicago: Frederick J. Drake & Co., 1956.

RICH, JACK C. *The Materials and Methods of Sculpture.* New York: Oxford University Press, 1947.

RICHTER, H. P. *Wiring Simplified.* Minneapolis, Minn.: Park Publishing, Inc., 1965.

RHODES, DANIEL. *Kilns: design, construction and operation.* Philadelphia. Pa.: Chilton Book Co., 1968.

ROUKES, N. *Sculpture in Plastic.* New York: Watson Guptill Publications, 1968.

SAMS, HOWARD W. *Basic Electricity and an Introduction to Electronics.* Howard W. Sams & Co., Inc., Indianapolis, Ind.: The Bobbs-Merrill Company, Inc., 1967.

SCHMITT, BUBAN P. *Understanding Electricity and Electronics.* New York: McGraw-Hill Book Company, 1962.

SIMONDS AND BREGMAN. *Finishing Metal Products.* New York: McGraw-Hill Book Company, 1946.

SLOANE, T. O'CONNOR. *Henley's Twentieth Century Book of Ten Thousand Formulas, Processes and Trade Secrets.* New York: Books Inc., 1970.

SODERBERG, GEORGE A. *Finishing Materials and Methods.* Bloomington, Ill.: McKnight & McKnight Publishing Co., 1959.

WALKER, JOHN R. *Modern Metal Work.* Homewood, Ill.: Goodheart Willcox Co. Inc., 1965.

Accident Prevention Manual for Industrial Operations. Chicago, Ill.: National Safety Council, 1964.

Encyclopedia of Science and Technology. New York: McGraw-Hill Book Company, 1966.

Metal Finishing Guidebook and Directory. Westwood, N.J.: Metals and Plastics Publications Inc., 1970, 1971.

Modern Plastics Encyclopedia. New York: McGraw-Hill Book Company, 1970–71, 1971–72.

Plastics Engineering Handbook. New York: Reinhold Publishing Corp., 1960.

Proceedings of the National Sculpture Conference. University of Kansas, Lawrence, Kansas: National Sculpture Center Publications, 1960, 1962, 1964, 1966, 1968, 1970.

The Oxy-Acetylene Handbook. Linde Air Products Company, A Division of Union Carbide Corp., New York, 1957.

Unique Lighting Handbook. Barrington, N.J.: Edmund Scientific Co., 1969.

INDUSTRIAL BOOKLETS AND TECHNICAL PUBLICATIONS

Acrylic Fabrication Manual. Publication NO. C.S. 101460M 267. Wakefield, Mass.: American Cyanamid Co., Building Products Division, 1967.

Adhesive Bonding Copper and Copper Alloys to other Building Materials. Technical report 406/6. New York: Copper Development Assoc. Inc., 1966.

Adhesive Applying (Methods and Equipment). Adhesive Reference Series. Middleton, Mass.: USM Corporation, Chemical Division, 1970.

Brass and Bronze Casting Alloys. Bulletin NO. V-1. New York: American Smelting and Refining Co., Federated Metals Division, 1967.

Brushing Tools for Industry. FORM MC1-764-1. Worcester, Mass.: Anderson Corporation.

Cement Masons Manual. publication NO. EBO15.01T. Skokie, Ill.: Portland Cement Association, 1960.

Cincinnati Grinding Wheels. Publication no. PG-320-1. Cincinnati, Ohio; Cincinnati Milacron Inc., Products Division, 1965.

Cor-Ten Steel. AIA. file NO. 13-A. Pittsburg, Pa.: United States Steel Corp., 1966.

Design and Control of Concrete Mixtures. Publication NO. EBOO1-11T. Skokie, Ill.: Portland Cement Association, 1968.

Fabrication of Plexiglass. Publication NO. 383d. Philadelphia, Pa.: Rohm and Hass Co.,1959.

Fabrication of Stainless Steel. Publication NO. ADVCO-03092-62. Pittsburg, Pa.: United States Steel Corp.

Flame Spray Handbook. H. S. Ingham and A. P. Shepard. Westbury, Long Island, N.Y.; Metco Inc., 1964.

Getting the Most Out of Your; Circle Saw and Jointer, 1953; Shaper, 1954; Bandsaw and Scroll Saw, 1954; Abrasive Tools, 1955 Drill Press, 1954; Radial Saw, 1956; Lathe, 1954 (separate publications on each item). Pittsburg, Pa.: Rockwell Manufacturing Company, Delta Power Tool Division.

Guide to Plastic Welding, Equipment and Techniques. Norwood, Mass.: Kamweld Products Co. Inc.

Guide to Plywood Properties and Grades. A.I.A. File No. 19-F 1966. Tacoma, Wash.: American Plywood Association.

How to Apply Surface Colors. Technical report 121/8. New York, N.Y.: Copper Development Association, 1968.

How to do Manual Metal Inert Gas Welding. Publication NO. F-51-110-A, Union Carbide Corp. Linde Division, N.Y.C., N.Y.

How to do TIG (Heliarc) Welding. Publication NO. F-1607-D. New York: Union Carbide Corp., Linde Division.

How to Sand. Publication NO. A2002. Nigara Falls, N.Y.: The Carborundum Company, Bonded Abrasive Division.

How to Sharpen. Publication NO. 2127-50. Worcester, Mass.: Norton Company.

How to Sharpen Knives and Tools. Publication NO. A21140. Nigara Falls, N.Y.: The Carborundum Company.

Investment Casting With Nalcoag® Colloidal Silica and Nalcast® Fused Silica, Chicago, Ill.: Nalco Chemical Co., Metal Industries Division.

MIG *Welding Aluminum.* Publication NO. ADV. NO. 802-20-7. Richmond, Virginia: Reynolds Aluminum Co., 1966.

Polyesters, General Methods of Application. Kansas City, Mo.: Cook Paint and Varnish Company.

Rough Grinding. Worcester, Mass.: Norton Company, 1969.

Selection and Use: Hack Saws and Band Saws. Hartford, Conn.: The Capewell Mfg. Co., 1960.

Self Cure No-Bake Binder. Bulletin NO. 5. Detroit, Michigan: Aristo International.

Structural Adhesives. Publication NO. ZSWBR(7710) P.I. St. Paul, Minn.: 3M Company, Adhesives, Coatings and Sealers Division.

Surface Preparation, Methods and Equipment. Middleton, Mass.: USM Corporation, Chemical Division, 1968.

Syton® 200-1C, Colloidal Silica. Bulletin NO. 1-199. St. Louis, Mo.: Monsanto, Inorganic Chemical Division.

Directions for Using Manganesed Phospholene #7, Bulletin 15-A Cleveland, Ohio: Western Reserve Laboratories, Inc.

The Hydroperm® Process. Bulletin NO. 1GL 151. Chicago, Ill.: United States Gypsum, 1966.

Tips on Air Tools. Publication NO. A-IS-3815. Bryan, Ohio: The Aro Corp.

Uvex® Plastic Sheet for Vacuum Forming. Publication NO. PS-I (8-68). Kingsport, Tenn.: Eastman Chemical Products, Inc.

Welding, Soldering, Brazing Aluminum. FORM 802-21-9 (61-15-0D). Richmond, Virginia: Reynolds Metal Co., 1958.

Guide
to
Materials
and
Suppliers

The materials listed here can often be purchased locally. The yellow-page section of the telephone book usually lists local sources for material or representatives of major companies.

Explore local sources before contacting major manufacturing companies. When it is necessary to contact a major company, ask for the nearest source for their product.

For additional information on materials and manufacturers not listed in this guide, consult *Thomas Register of American Manufacturers* at most university or public libraries. Most products and their manufacturers can be located in this manner.

Abrasives, belts, discs, wheels, etc. 34, 38, 89, 100, 125, 137, 145 157
Abrasive compounds, 34, 137
Accelerators, 116
Acrylic resins, 50, 123
Acrylic sheet, rod, etc., 12, 32, 50
Adhesives, 32, 47, 116, 145, 150
Air arc torch, 19
Air compressors, 24, 43, 44, 48, 76
Air tools, 20, 43, 67, 76
Alcohol, Isopropyl, 116
Aluminum, 9, 14, 36, 121, 130

Arcair torch, 19
Arc welders, 93, 97, 147
Armatures, 126, 128
Asbestos fiber, 109, 138
Asbestos gloves, aprons, etc., 85

Binders, 61, 62, 78, 115, 156
Black light, 52
Blowers, 44, 80
Bolts, 23
Bronze for casting, 14, 130
Bronze sheet, angle, etc., 36
Brush plating, 129

Buffs, 11, 42, 59, 88, 137
Buffing compounds, 18, 42, 59, 69 88, 125, 137
Bulbs, 52, 63
Burners, 80
Burning bar, 31
Burnout furnace, 3, 85, 7, 45

Cab-O-Sil®, 32, 109, 116
Carving tools, 42, 67, 99, 126, 128
Casting resins, 1, 32, 40, 109, 116, 119, 120
Casting compounds, 1, 126, 136

Numbers following guide entries correspond to the numbered list of suppliers and manufacturers starting on page 267.

List
of
Suppliers
and
Manufacturers

1. ADHESIVE PRODUCTS CORP.
   1660 Boone Ave.
   Bronx, N. Y. 10460

   Casting compounds, epoxy and polyester resins for casting, rubber-mold materials, coloring agents for resins, resins for rigid and flexible polyurethane foam.

2. ADJUSTABLE CLAMP CO.
   417 North Ashland Ave.
   Chicago, Ill. 60622

   Spring and hinged clamps.

3. A. D. ALPINE, INC.
   353 Coral Circle
   El Segundo, Calif. 90245

   Gas-fired ceramic and burnout kilns.

4. ALABAMA METAL
   INDUSTRIES, INC.
   Box 3928
   Birmingham, Ala. 35208

   Steel- and aluminum-expanded metals for decorative use.

5. ALCAN METAL POWDERS
   DIVISION OF ALCAN
   ALUMINUM CORP.
   Box 290
   Elizabeth, N. J. 07207

   Manufacturers of metal powders.

6. A.L.C. CO., INC.
   Box 506
   Medina, Ohio 44256

   Good low-cost sandblasting gun and tank.

7. ALEXANDER SAUNDERS AND Co.
   Box 265
   Cold Spring, N. Y. 10516

   Investment materials, furnaces, and casting equipment; colloidal silica and materials for ceramic-shell molds; waxes for patterns.

8. ALL-STATE WELDING ALLOYS Co.
   840 North Michigan Ave.
   Chicago, Ill. 60611

   Manufacturers of a wide variety of welding rods.

9. ALUMINUM Co. OF AMERICA (ALCOA)
   1501 Alcoa Bdg.
   Pittsburg, Pa. 15219

   Producers of aluminum sheet, casting alloys, and many other aluminum materials.

10. AMERACE ESNA CORP.
    CHEMICAL SPECIALITIES DIVISION
    74 Hudson Ave.
    Tenafly, N. J. 07670

    Paint strippers, dip and brush-on materials in industrial quantities.

11. AMERICAN BUFF INTERNATIONAL, INC.
    624 West Adams St.
    Chicago, Ill. 60606

    Nylon-web buffing wheels.

12. AMERICAN CYANAMID COMPANY
    PLASTICS DIVISION
    Wayne, N. J. 07470

    Manufacturers of acrylic sheet and alkyd, melamine, polyester, and urea molding compounds; polyester resins and other materials.

13. AMERICAN INDUSTRIAL SAFETY EQUIPMENT Co.
    3500-T Lakeside Ave.
    Cleveland, Ohio 44114

    Manufacturers of safety goggles, glasses, face shields, helmets, respirators, welder's plates, replacement lens, etc.

14. AMERICAN SMELTING AND REFINING Co.
    FEDERATED METALS DIVISION
    120 Broadway
    New York, N. Y. 10005

    Aluminum, bronze, brass and low-melting-point alloys for casting.

15. ANACONDA AMERICAN BRASS Co.
    Waterbury
    Connecticut 06720

    Manufacturers of a wide variety of brass and copper-alloy sheet, tube bar, angles, and other shapes; silicon-bronze conduit and electrical fittings.

16. ANDERSON CORPORATION
    1029 Southbridge St.
    Worcester, Mass. 01610

    Manufacturers of wire and fiber brushes.

17. A. P. GREEN FIRE BRICK CO.
Mexico
Missouri 65265

Firebricks and castable refractories.

18. ATLANTIC COMPOUND CO.
2 Charles St.
Chelsea, Mass. 02150

Manufacturer of greaseless buffing compounds.

19. ARCAIR COMPANY
Box 406
Lancaster, Ohio 43130

Manufacturer of Arcair cutting torch.

20. THE ARO CORPORATION
INDUSTRIAL DIVISION
Bryan
Ohio 43506

Manufacturer of a wide variety of air tools.

21. BABCOCK AND WILCOX CO.
REFRACTORIES DIVISION
Old Savannah Road
Augusta, Georgia 30930

Refractory materials; ceramic refractory material called "Kaowool®," available in blanket, paper, strip, block and mesh-covered forms; also available in castable and tamping mixtures; will stand temperatures up to 2,300 degrees F.

22. BARRE GRANITE CO.
Barre
Vermont 05641

Granite.

23. BETHLEHEM STEEL CORPORATION
Bethlehem
Pennsylvania 18016

Producers of a wide variety of steel materials and products, such as I beams, nails, bolts, wire, etc.

24. BINKS MANUFACTURING CO.
Box 66090
A.M.F. O'Hare
Chicago, Ill. 60666

Spray-painting equipment, spray guns, booths, air compressors, pressure tanks, hose, and all accessories.

25. BIRCHWOOD CASEY
DIVISION OF FULLER LAB, INC.
Eden Prairie
Minnesota 55343

Swab-on solutions for black finishes on metal; BST 4 for iron and steel; M 24 for brass, bronze, copper, and zinc; A 14 for aluminum; available in quarts and larger.

26. BLACK AND DECKER MANUFACTURING CO.
Townson
Maryland 21204

Portable power tools, air and electric traveling saws.

27. BRADFORD PARK CORP.
7 Tamarack Lane
Elnora, N. Y. 12065

B–P metal cleaners for ferrous and non-ferrous metals; harmless to normal skin and materials, gives off no toxic fumes; available in paste or liquid, one gallon or larger.

28. **Brevel Products Corp.**
Broad Ave. & 16th St.
Carlstadt, N. J. 07072

Manufacture of slow-speed electric motors, fractional horsepower; one to 120 r.p.m.

29. **Bristol Saybrook Co.**
500 Coulter Ave.
Old Saybrook, Conn. 06475

Manufacture of slow-speed, fractional-horsepower miniature motors, speeds above and below one r.p.m.

30. **Buck Brothers, Inc.**
Millbury
Massachusetts 01527

Fine wood-carving tools.

31. **Burning Bar Sales Co.**
6010 Yolanda Ave.
Tarzana, Calif. 91356

Burning bar for cutting slag, metal, concrete, etc.

32. **Cadillac Plastic & Chemical Co.**
Box 810
Detroit, Mich. 48232

Good variety of plastic sheet, rod, tube, film, and other shapes; polyester and epoxy resins; adhesives for all forms of plastics and other material; good source for almost any plastic needs.

33. **The Capwell Mfg. Co.**
61 Governor St.
Hartford, Conn. 06102

Manufacturer of hack-saw and band-saw blades.

34. **The Carborundum Company**
Bonded Abrasives Division
Box 337
Niagara Falls, N. Y. 14302

Manufacturer of coated and bonded abrasives and other abrasive products.

35. **Cerro Sales Corporation**
300 Park Ave.
New York, N. Y. 10022

Low-melting-point alloys.

36. **Chase Brass & Copper Co.**
Waterbury
Connecticut 06720

Manufacturer of copper, copper-alloy sheet, angle, bar, strip, plumbing copper fittings and valves; also aluminum and stainless steel materials.

37. **Cincinnati Foam Products Inc.**
1641 Blue Rock St.
Cincinnati, Ohio 45223

Foam beads, molded boards, and slabs of polystyrene.

38. **Cincinnati Milacron, Inc.**
Products Division
Box 9013
Cincinnati, Ohio 45209

Manufacturers of a wide variety of bonded abrasive wheels.

39. **Clementina Ltd.**
2277 Jerrold Ave.
San Francisco, Calif. 94124

Sandblasting equipment.

40. COOK PAINT AND
VARNISH CO.
Box 389
Kansas City, Mo. 64141

Polyester laminating resins, clear cast and casting resins to be used with fillers; urethane-foam resins; good range of colored gel coats and pigment concentrates; alkyd, epoxy, chlorinated rubber, coal-tar epoxy, polyester, vinyl, acrylic latex, vinyl urethane and zinc-rich primer industrial coatings; also good source for many other coating supplies.

41. CPR DIVISION
THE UPJOHN COMPANY
Box 2978, Annex
555 Alaska Ave.
Torrance, Calif. 90503

Urethane blocks for carving.

42. THE CRAFTOOL COMPANY
1 Industrial Road
Woodridge, N. J. 07075

Sculpture plaster and clay tools, ceramic supplies, buffing compounds and wheels, stone- and wood-carving tools, small flexible-shaft machines, metal craft hammers, small portable spray-paint equipment, sharpening tools, and other supplies.

43. DAWSON MACDONALD CO.,
INC.
141 Pearl St.
Boston, Mass. 02110

Sandblasting equipment, air compressors, pneumatic tools for stone carving, polishing machines, stone saws, protective clothing, air and electric grinders, hoists, and marble-finishing supplies.

44. DAYTON ELECTRIC MFG.
CO.
5959 W. Howard St.
Chicago, Ill. 60648

A large variety of ventilating fans, motors, pumps, air compressors, and hand and electric tools.

45. DENVER FIRE CLAY
2401 E. 40th Ave.
Denver, Colo. 80217

Kilns, burnout furnaces, chemicals for glazes, clays and refractories.

46. THE DESMOND-STEPHAN
MFG. CO.
317 S. Walnut St.
Urbana, Ohio 43078

Manufacturer of grinding wheel dressers.

47. DEVCON CORPORATION
59 Endicott St.
Danver, Mass. 01923

Adhesives, epoxy coatings, zinc-rich coatings and primers; epoxy putty with bronze, aluminum, lead, steel carbide or stainless steel fillers; Devcon rubber for caulking, repair, sealing, etc.; Devcon two-Ton epoxy adhesive readily available at most hardware stores, etc.

48. THE DEVILBISS CO.
Box 913
Toledo, Ohio 43601

Manufacturer of conventional, airless and hot spray-painting equipment. Air compressors, hoses and fittings, spray booths, air-replacement equipment.

49. Dow Chemical Co.
Midland Road
Midland, Mich. 48640

Producers of polystyrene foam, plastic film, sheets, resins, powders, and pellets; wide variety of chemicals and other products; available in industrial quantities or through appropriate distributor.

50. E. I. Du Pont de Nemours & Co.
1007 Market St.
Wilmington, Del. 19898

Manufacturer of nylon, acetal, acrylic, fluorocarbon resins; industrial quantities; good source for acrylic beads; also mold-release agent called "VYDAX®" that does not interfere with postfinishing.

51. Eastman Chemical Products Inc.
Box 431
Kingsport, Tenn. 37662

Acetal, propionate, butyrate, polyethylene, polypropylene, resins, pellets and powders; cellulose acetate butyrate sheet material (trade name "UVEX®"), excellent for vacuum forming; good descriptive technical bulletins available on all of their products.

52. Edmund Scientific Co.
700 Edscorp Bldg.
Barrington, N. J. 08007

A wide variety of useful devices, projectors, lenses, miniature light bulbs, motors, lasers, black light, etc. Write and ask for catalog.

53. Ellen Products Co.
125 South Liberty Dr.
Stoney Point, N. J. 10980

Zinc stearate, paintable silicone, and polymer release agents in aerosol cans. Available in small quantities.

54. Engelhard Industries, Inc.
Hanovia Liquid Gold Division
1 W. Central Ave.
East Newark, N. J. 07029

Metallic-luster glaze materials.

55. Erdle Perforating Co., Inc.
100 Pixley Industrial Parkway
Box 1568 T
Rochester, N. Y. 14603

Perforated metal, square, round, hexagonal patterns. Aluminum, bronze, steel, monel, and other metals as stock items.

56. Erico Products, Inc.
Plastic Equipment Division
34600 Solon Road
Cleveland, Ohio 44139

Clamps.

57. Eutectic Corp.
40-40 172nd St.
Flushing, N. Y. 11358

Manufacturer of special-purpose welding rods for oxyacetylene and arc welding; also cutting rods.

58. FOREDOM ELECTRIC CO.
BLACKSTON INDUSTRIES, INC.
Route 6, Stoney Hill
Bethel, Conn. 06801

Manufacturer of a variety of electric flexible shaft machines for grinding and buffing.

59. FORMAX MFG. C.
3171 Bellevue Ave.
Detroit, Mich. 48207

Grease and greaseless buffing compounds for metal and plastic; case quantities; cloth and sisal buffs primarily for large industrial machines.

60. FORREST MFG. CO.
231 Route 17
Rutherford, N. J. 07070

40-, 60-, 80-, and 100-tooth saws for cutting plastics; also carbide-tipped blades.

61. FREEMAN SUPPLY CO.
4125 W. Fullerton Ave.
Chicago, Ill. 60639

Foundry supplies; source for almost any metal-casting needs; equipment of all kinds.

62. FOUNDARY SERVICE &
SUPPLY CO.
1505 Greenwood Road
Baltimore, Maryland 21208

A source for almost any foundry-room equipment and supplies.

63. GENERAL ELECTRIC CO.
Nela Park
Cleveland, Ohio 44112

Manufacturer of incandescent and fluorescent lamps, mercury lamps; large and miniature; special-purpose lamps, such as heat lamps, black light, and others; most lamps ordinarily available in local markets.

64. GEORGIA MARBLE CO.
11 Prizor St. S. W.
Atlanta, Georgia 30303

Marble and limestone blocks.

65. GILMAN BROTHERS CO.
100 Main St.
Gilman, Conn. 06336

Polystyrene, polyethylene, acrylonitrile, butadiene and styrene rigid sheet and film in colors; also with velour surfaces; available in industrial quantities, 500 pounds or more.

66. GLAS-CRAFT OF CALIFORNIA
9145 Glenoak Blvd.
Sun Valley, Calif. 91352

Spray equipment for fiberglass and urethane foam.

67. GRANITE CITY TOOL CO.
St. Cloud
Minnesota 56301

Wood- and stone-carving tools for pneumatic equipment; hand stone-carving tools, pneumatic tools, air grinders, sanders, sandblasting and fume-collecting equipment.

68. GLIDDEN-DURKEE DIVISION
OF S.C.M. CORPORATION
900 Union Commerce Bldg.
Cleveland, Ohio 44115

Manufacturer of Glidden paints; a wide variety of excellent coating materials for interior and exterior use.

69. HANSON-VAN WINKLE
    DIVISION M & T CHEMICAL
    INC
    Rahway
    New Jersey 07065

    Buffing and polishing compounds.

70. HI-ALLOY WELD
    SPECIALTIES, INC.
    DIVISION OF VAN DRESER &
    HAWKINS, INC.
    Box 916
    Pearland, Tx. 77581

    Manufacturer of welding rods for oxyacety-lene and arc welding.

71. HOTPACK CORP.
    5083-A Cottman Ave.
    Philadelphia, Pa. 19135

    Industrial ovens.

72. HOSSFELD MFG. CO.
    IRON BENDER DIVISION
    Winona
    Minnesota 55987

    Universal iron bender.

73. H. V. HARDMAN CO., INC.
    600 Cortlandt St.
    Belleville, N. J. 07109

    Relatively inexpensive flexible-mold material; ask about compound 336 or 7153.

74. HYDREL MFG. CO., INC.
    9415 Telfair Ave.
    Sun Valley, Calif. 91352

    Fountain supplies; submersible and dry pit pumps, filters, underwater lighting fixtures, and other fountain controls and components.

75. HYPRESSURE JENNY DIVISION
    HOMESTEAD VALVE
    MFG. CO.
    11 Johnson St.
    Coraopolis, Pa. 15108

    Steam-cleaning equipment.

76. INGERSOLL-RAND CO.
    11 Broadway
    New York, N. Y. 10004

    Manufacturer of wide variety of air compressors, vacuum pumps; and air tools.

77. INSTA-FOAM PRODUCTS, INC.
    880 S. Fiene Dr.
    Addison, Ill. 60101

    Insta-Foam urethane-foam spray containers.

78. INTERNATIONAL MINERAL &
    CHEMICAL CORP.
    5401 Old Orchard Road
    Skokie, Ill. 60076

    Manufacturer of Aristo no-bake binder.

79. JAX CHEMICAL CO., INC.
    78-11 267th St.
    Floral Park, N. Y. 11004

    Metal cleaners, metal coloring solutions, bronze, brass and copper blackener, silver and copper plate, antique-green brush solutions for copper and brass; available in five-gallon quantity.

80. JOHNSON GAS APPLIANCE CO.
1940 O'Donnell
Cedar Rapids, Iowa 52400

Gas equipment: crucible furnaces, forge furnaces, safety and temperature controls, atmospheric and forced-air burners, pyrometers, crucible tongs, and shanks.

81. KAMWELD PRODUCTS CO., INC.
90 Access Road
Box 91
Norwood, Mass. 02062

Plastic-welding equipment and supplies.

82. KELLER DIVISION
SALES SERVICE MFG. CO.
2363 University Ave.
St. Paul, Minn. 55114

Manufacturer of power hacksaws.

83. KIM LIGHTING AND MFG. CO.
Box 1275
City of Industry, Calif. 91747

Excellent source for submersible and dry pit pumps, underwater lighting fixtures, filters, orifices, and other fountain components and controls.

84. LITEWEIGHT PRODUCTS
707 Funston Road
Kansas City, Ks. 66115

Source for Perlite.

85. L & R SPECIALTIES
Sherwood Road
Route 8, Box 349B
Springfield, Mo. 65840

Melting furnaces, precast furnace linings and lids, crucibles, asbestos gloves, aprons and leggings, pyrometers, clay tools and other foundry and sculpture supplies.

86. LUTRON ELECTRONIC CO., INC.
Coopersburg
Pennsylvania 18036

Manufacturer of Speed Dial; a variable speed adapter for drills, sanders and tools with universal motors; available in varying capacity.

87. MASTER APPLIANCE CORP.
Box 545
1745 Flett Ave.
Racine, Wis. 53403

Manufacturer of heat guns, air heater blowers and flameless heat torches for heating, drying and welding of plastic.

88. MATCHLESS METAL POLISHING CO.
840 W. 49th Pl.
Chicago, Ill. 60609

Buffs and buffing compounds.

89. MERRIT ABRASIVE PRODUCTS, INC.
201 W. Manville
Compton, Calif. 90224

Sand-O-Flex® wheel, all kinds of unusual shaped sanding drums, discs, and devices for abrasive finishing of contours and hard-to-reach areas.

90. MERIX CHEMICAL CO.
2234 E. 75th St.
Chicago, Ill. 60649

Anti-static and cleaning solutions; "ANTI-STATIC NO. 79," for destaticizing all types of plastic.

91. METCO, INC.
    1101 Prospect Ave.
    Westbury, N. Y. 11590

    Metallizing equipment and supplies.

92. MIDWEST SCULPTURE
    PRODUCTS
    Box 301
    Portage, Mich. 49081

    Wide variety of carving woods.

93. MILLER ELECTRIC MFG. CO.
    781 Bounds St.
    Appleton, Wis. 54911

    Good quality A.-C. and D.-C. electric arc welders.

94. MILLERS FALLS CO.
    Greenfield
    Massachusetts 01301

    Good-quality portable electric hand tools, grinders, drill motors, etc.

95. MIXING EQUIPMENT
    CO., INC.
    138 Mt. Read Blvd.
    Rochester, N. Y. 14603

    Manufacturer of heavy-duty portable mixers for mixing materials such as ceramic shell slurry.

96. MONSANTO COMPANY
    INORGANIC CHEMICAL
    DIVISION
    800 N. Lindberg Blvd.
    St. Louis, Mo. 63166

    Manufacturer of plastic resins and compounds in industrial quantities; also colloidal silica for ceramic shell molds; ask for bulletin 1-199 on colloidal silica; Product called "Syton® 200-1C."

97. MUREX
    METAL & THERMIT CORP.
    Box 5342, Church St.
    Station
    New York, N. Y. 10008

    Manufacturer of arc-welding machines, rods, and accessories.

98. NALCO CHEMICAL CO.
    METAL INDUSTRIES DIVISION
    9165 South Harbor Ave.
    Chicago, Ill. 60617

    Nalcoag® colloidal silica and Nalcast® fused silica for ceramic-shell molds; booklet available on the process; colloidal silica available in five-gallon containers; fused-silica in 100-1b. bags.

99. NATIONAL SCULPTURE
    SERVICE
    9 East 19th St.
    New York, N. Y. 10003

    Clay and plaster tools, rasps, stone- and wood-carving tools, sculpture stands, and other supplies.

100. NORTON COATED ABRASIVE
     DIVISION
     NORTON COMPANY
     50 New Bond St.
     Worcester, Mass. 01606

     Manufacturer of belts, discs, flap wheels, abrasive cut-off wheels, and special shapes.

101. PACKAGING INDUSTRY SALES
     CORP.
     Airport Road
     Hyannis, Mass. 02601

     Ultrasonic welding equipment for welding plastics.

102. PECK, STOW & WILCOX CO.
Mill St.
Southington, Conn. 06489

Manufacturer of foot-squaring shears, bending brakes, roll-forming machines, steel stakes and other sheet-metalworking equipment.

103. FMC CORPORATION
PEERLESS PUMP DIVISION
Box 88114
Indianapolis, Ind. 46208

Manufacturer of dry pit pumps for fountains.

104. PERMACEL
U. S. Highway No. 1
New Brunswick, N. J. 08903

Manufacturer of pressure-sensitive tapes.

105. PERMA-FLEX MOLD
COMPANY
1919 Livingston St.
Columbus, Ohio 43209

Good source for flexible materials; Koroseal® reusable P.V.C. polysulfide mold materials called "Blak-Tufy®," "Blak-Stretchy®," "Gra-Tufy®," and others; polyurethane flexible-mold materials; water- and oil-based clays; fibers for reinforcing plaster molds and release agents; excellent technical bulletins on their products.

106. PETROLITE CORP.
BARECO DIVISION
Drawer K
6910 E. 14th St.
Tulsa, Okla. 74115

Ceraweld brown wax. Micro crystalline wax available in 50-lb. cartons.

107. PITTSBURGH CORNING CORP.
One Gateway Center
Pittsburg, Pa. 15222

Manufacturer of glass nodules that can be used as a lightweight filler material.

108. PLASTI-VAC, INC.
Box 5543
214 Dalton Ave.
Charlotte, N. C. 28206

Commercial vacuum-forming machines.

109. POLYPRODUCTS CORPORATION
13810 Nelson Ave.
Detroit, Mich. 48227

A good source for student quantities of resins, additives, fiberglass, pigments, fillers, metal powders, and mold materials; write for *Polyproducts General Material Information* and *Polyproducts Project Guide* (cost: $2.00).

110. POTTER BROS., INC.
Box 14
Carlstadt, N. J. 07072

Manufacturer of glass spheres that can be used as a filler material.

111. THE POLYMER CORPORATION
P. O. Box 422
Reading, Pa. 19603

Manufacturer of plastic mill shapes, rods, tubes, etc. in nylon, acetal, fluorocarbon, polycarbonate, and acrylic; powder coating materials and custom powder coating service. Facility for coating parts up to ten feet long and three feet in diameter, weighing up to 2,000 pounds.

112. POWERMATIC DIVISION
HOUDAILLE INDUSTRIES,
INC.
Highway 55
McMinnville, Tenn. 37110

Manufacturer of excellent-quality wood-working and metalworking machines; drill presses, scroll saws, jointers, table saws, bandsaws, shapers, lathes, and planers.

113. P.S.H. INDUSTRIES, INC.
3713 Grand Blvd.
Brookfield, Ill. 60513

R2 plaster and plastic spray gun, flocking gun, mixing containers, mixers, hand cleaners, mixing blades, and other plaster and plastic supplies.

114. PULMOSAN SAFETY
EQUIPMENT CORP.
30-46 Linden Place
Flushing, N. Y. 11354

Manufacturer of goggles, face shields, respirators, asbestos gloves and clothing, welding helmets, and other safety equipment.

115. QUAKER OATS COMPANY
CHEMICAL DIVISION
Merchandise Mart
Chicago, Ill. 60654

Producers of industrial chemicals; Furan no-bake binders.

116. RAM CHEMICALS
DIVISION WHITTAKER
CHEMICAL CORP.
210 E. Alondra Blvd.
Gardena, Calif. 90247

Suppliers of accelerators, adhesives, fiberglass materials, fillers, gel coatings, mold-making products, polyester resins, release agents, solvents and thinners, clear resin colors for casting, pigment dispersions, coatings, and wide variety of other products.

117. RAMCO HEMP FIBER
COMPANY
6272 W. North Avenue
Chicago, Ill. 60639

Hemp fiber for plaster casting.

118. RANSBURG
ELECTRO-COATING CORP.
Box 88220
Indianapolis, Ind. 46208

Manufacturer of electrostatic spray guns and necessary components.

119. REICHOLD CHEMICALS, INC.
525 N. Broadway
White Plains, N. Y. 10602

Epoxy, urethane, and polyester resins, clear-cast resins; industrial quantities.

120. RESIN COATING
CORPORATION
3593 N.W. 74th St.
Miami, Fla. 33147

Epoxy and polyester resins, fillers, fiberglass, flexible resins, dyes and pigments, polyurethane resins, metallic powders, catalysts, and other materials packaged in small units.

121. REYNOLDS ALUMINUM
SUPPLY CO.
325 West Touhy Ave.
Park Ridge, Ill. 60068

Manufacturers of aluminum sheet, building panels, expanded metals, and mill shapes.

122. ROCKWELL MANUFACTURING CO. POWER TOOL DIVISION *662 North Lexington Ave. Pittsburg, Penn. 15208*

Manufacturer of portable and stationary wood- and metalworking tools.

123. ROHM AND HASS *Independence Mall West Philadelphia, Pa. 19105*

Producers of acrylic, alkyds, melamine, phenolic, polyester, and urea resins and compounds in industrial quantities.

124. RUEMLIN MFG. CO. *3860 N. Palmer St. Milwaukee, Wis. 53212*

Fume-removal and sandblasting equipment.

125. SCHAFFER MFG. CO., INC. *21 Schaffer Center Pittsburg, Pa. 15202*

Buffing compounds and coated abrasives.

126. SCULPTURE HOUSE *38 East 30th St. New York, N. Y. 10016*

Clay and plaster tools, wood- and stone-carving tools, domestic and imported woods, kilns, clays, casting compounds, rasps, rifflers, sculpture stands, and other supplies.

127. SCULPTURE IN WOOD *127 East Branch St. Arroyo Grande, Calif. 93420*

Logs in walnut, magnolia, japonica and others.

128. SCULPTURE SERVICE, INC. *9 East 19th St. New York, N. Y. 10003*

Clay and plaster tools, rasps, carving tools, sculpture stands, and other supplies.

129. SELECTRONS LTD. *116 East 16th St. New York, N. Y. 10003*

Brush-plating equipment, solutions, and supplies.

130. S. G. METAL INDUSTRIES, INC. *2nd and Riverview Kansas City, Kas. 66118*

Aluminum and copper alloys in small or large quantities for casting.

131. THE SHERWIN WILLIAMS CO. *101 Prospect Ave. Cleveland, Ohio 44101*

Manufacturer of acrylic enamels and other coatings and materials.

132. SIMOND SAW AND STEEL DIVISION WALLACE MURRAY CORP. *Intervale Road Fitchburg, Mass. 01420*

Manufacturer of steel- and carbide-tipped saw blades for wood, plastic, and metal.

133. SKIL CORPORATION *5043 Elston Ave. Chicago, Ill. 60630*

Manufacturer of portable power tools for wood and metal.

134. SMITH GRANITE CO.
     Westerly
     Rhode Island 02891

     Granite.

135. SMITH WELDING
     EQUIPMENT DIV.
     TESCOM CORPORATION
     2633 4th St.
     Minneapolis, Minn. 55414

     Manufacturer of excellent-quality oxyacetylene welding equipment.

136. SMOOTH-ON, INC.
     1000 Valley Road
     Gillette, N. J. 07933

     P.V.A. and other release agents, flexible urethane-mold material and epoxy casting compounds.

137. SOUTHWEST SMELTING &
     REFINING CO.
     1708 Jackson St.
     Box 2010
     Dallas, Tx. 75221

     Good assortment of buffs, buffing compounds, plaster-investment material, wax sprue and vent material, Foredom flexible-shaft machines, small grinding burrs and wheels, metalworking tools and stakes, and many other tools and materials.

138. SPECIAL ASBESTOS CO.
     3628 W. Pierce St.
     Milwaukee, Wisc. 53215

     Asbestos fibers one-eighth to one-fourth-inch long.

139. SPRAY PLATING SYSTEMS,
     INC.
     Box 6468
     Greensboro, N. C. 27405

     Equipment for spray application of silver or copper plating.

140. STANDARD CERAMIC
     SUPPLY CO.
     Box 4435
     Pittsburg, Pa. 15205

     Clays, glaze chemicals, prepared glazes, plasters, modelling tools and other items.

141. STANLEY POWER TOOLS
     DIVISION OF THE
     STANLEY WORKS
     77 Lake St.
     New Britain, Conn. 06050

     Manufacturer of hand and power tools for woodworking.

142. THE L. S. STARRET CO.
     Athol
     Massachusetts 01331

     Manufacturer of quality measuring tools, vises, precision instruments, band- and hack-saw blades and other items.

143. SUREFIRE PRODUCTS CORP.
     6445 Bandini Blvd.
     Los Angeles, Calif. 90022

     Plastic cleaner and destaticizer for plastic; scratch remover, hand cleaner, and spray-on degreasers.

144. THERMATRON
     DIVISION OF WILLCOX &
     GIBBS, INC.
     60 Spence St.
     Bayshore, N. Y. 11708

     Industrial heat-sealing equipment.

145. 3M COMPANY
3M Center
St. Paul, Minn. 55101

Manufacturer of a wide variety of industrial adhesives, coatings, tapes, abrasives belts, discs and special abrasive shapes, nylon-web abrasive wheels, flap wheels, and many other materials.

146. TOMPKINS KIEL
35-08 Vernon Blvd.
Long Island City, N.Y. 11106

Imported marble.

147. UNION CARBIDE CORP.
LINDE DIVISION
270 Park Ave.
New York, N. Y. 10017

Manufacturer of oxyacetylene and arc-welding equipment of all kinds; also thermal torch for stone cutting.

148. U. S. BRONZE POWDER, INC.
Route 202
Flemington, N. J. 08822

Manufacturer of metallic powders.

149. U. S. GYPSUM COMPANY
101 S. Walker Dr.
Chicago, Ill. 60606

Manufacturer of molding plasters, hydro-stone® and hydrocal®, plaster investment materials; excellent technical bulletins available on all their materials.

150. USM CORPORATION
140 Federal St.
Boston, Mass. 02107

Manufacturer of full line of adhesives under trade name "Bostick;" screws and other fasteners; wall- and sheet-metal anchors; pop rivets and pop-rivet tool; construction anchors and industrial brushes.

151. UNITED STATES STEEL
CORP.
525 William Penn Place
Pittsburg, Pa. 15230

Manufacturer of steel materials, hot- and cold-rolled steel, many alloys for special applications, stainless steel, copper alloyed steel called "Cor-Ten®"; materials in many forms, such as sheet, bar, strap, tube, I beams, angles, etc.

152. VERMONT MARBLE CO.
Proctor
Vermont 05765

Marble.

153. WESTERN RESERVE
LABORATORIES, INC.
1438 St. Clair Ave.
Cleveland, Ohio 44114

Producers of Manganesed Phospholene No. 7, a room-temperature, water-based liquid that can be brushed or sprayed onto steel, aluminum or zinc for a phosphatized primer surface; also serves as a temporary corrosion inhibitor; ask for technical manual on its uses.

154. EDWIN L. WIEGAND
DIVISION
EMERSON ELECTRIC CO.
7500 Thomas Blvd.
Pittsburg, Pa. 15208

Chromolox electric heating elements, a wide variety of strip heaters, immersion and wrap-around; hot plates, melting pots, infrared units for ovens, thermostatic controls for electric ovens.

155. WILSON PRODUCTS DIVISION
ESB INCORPORATED
Box 622
Reading. Pa. 19603

Manufacturer of safety equipment, goggles, welding helmets, respirators, sandblasting hoods and sound-barrier ear muffs.

156. WOLVERINE FOUNDRY
SUPPLY CO.
14325 Wyoming Ave.
Detroit, Mich. 48238

Aristo no-bake binder called "W-10" and additive; silica sand for molds, mold and core wash, and other foundry supplies.

157. WOOD CARVERS SUPPLY CO.
3112 W. 28th St.
Minneapolis, Minn. 55416

Wood-carving tools, mallets, sharpening stones, hand saws, vises, Sand-O-Flex® wheels, flap wheels, other supplies.

158. THE WYCO TOOL CO.
223 N. California Ave.
Chicago, Ill. 60612

Flexible-shaft machines.

Index